COMPUTER ORGANIZATION
AND PROGRAMMING

McGRAW-HILL COMPUTER SCIENCE SERIES

RICHARD W. HAMMING
Bell Telephone Laboratories

EDWARD A. FEIGENBAUM
Stanford University

Gear *Computer Organization and Programming*
Hellerman *Digital Computer System Principles*
Liu *Introduction to Combinatorial Mathematics*
Rosen *Programming Systems and Languages*
Salton *Automatic Information Organization and Retrieval*
Wegner *Programming Languages, Information Structures, and Machine Organization*

COMPUTER ORGANIZATION
AND PROGRAMMING

Professor C. William Gear
Department of Computer Science
University of Illinois

McGraw-Hill Book Company

New York   St. Louis   San Francisco   London
Sydney   Toronto   Mexico   Panama

**COMPUTER ORGANIZATION
AND PROGRAMMING**

Library of Congress Catalog Card Number 69-13220

23075

1 2 3 4 5 6 7 8 9 0   **M A M M**   7 6 5 4 3 2 1 0 6 9

To Susie

preface

This text is intended for a second course in programming. Students are presumed to have completed a basic course in a procedure oriented language such as Fortran, Algol, or PL/I and consequently to have been introduced to the fundamental concepts of digital computers and programs. The book discusses machine language and the design of computers as it affects the language. It then continues with an examination of software systems, programming philosophy, input/output systems, interpreters, macro assemblers, and compilers. Because table lookup techniques are important in assemblers and compilers, a chapter is devoted to searching and sorting. The detailed simulation of one computer on another is discussed in order to explain the way in which instructions are executed by the hardware.

The book does not deal with a specific machine: it draws examples from a number of them. The IBM 360, however, receives more attention than any other machine because it embodies many of the newer concepts in hardware and software.

The notes for this book have been used for a course at the University of Illinois since 1965. It is a 44-hour lecture course which is essentially identical to ACM course number B2 in its proposal for a computer science curriculum. This course has used three different machines on different occasions. In all cases, the Principles of Operation and Assembly Language manuals were also used as texts. As material from the book was covered, examples from the machine being used were discussed in class.

Chapter 9, on compilers, was not covered in depth in this course, since it is the start of a more advanced course in system programming. It has been included here because many students wanted additional material to read, particularly on compilers.

It has been found important to give programming assignments sufficiently complex that the students may use some of the more advanced features of the available operating system. Since the background of incoming students has been varied both in depth and type of experience, it has been helpful to assign an assembly language problem at the start of the semester. This has consisted of a working, well-documented but simple program which the students first have to keypunch and get running and then modify in a simple manner with the aid of the machine manuals. By the time they have completed this, they have used the operating-system control cards, some machine language, and some simple input/output from machine language. By this time enough of Chapter 2 has been covered in class that a more difficult assignment can be given. Usually this has been the body of a subroutine that will be used in later assignments.

Considerable emphasis has been placed on Chapter 5 by assigning the simulator as a programming task. On different occasions students have been required to write the whole thing, debug a partially working version, and complete and add other features to a working portion of the simulator. The latter approach has been more successful because it provides the weak students with something to build on slowly while giving ample opportunity for the bright students to experiment. In fact, one problem has been the amount of machine time that some of the better students use in fairly sophisticated extensions of the basic machine.

Most of the questions at the end of the chapters are taken from exams used in the course. The students are usually told that some of these questions (with minor changes in numerical values, etc.) will be used on their exams to encourage them to work the problems.

The emphasis throughout the book is that there is no best way of either designing a machine or programming a given problem of any size. Rather, the point is made that there are many methods, any one of which may be the best in a particular situation, but that a general solution is a compromise between many goals. Different machine designs and different programming techniques are introduced in an historical order in most cases because this usually represents the buildup from the simple to the complex and provides a better perspective of the situations in which given techniques are valuable.

C. William Gear

contents

1

introduction

The digital computer arose in answer to man's need for quicker and more efficient ways of completing large numerical computations. Such computations arise in practical situations, as in the solution of engineering design problems, as well as in the course of theoretical endeavors, such as the attempt to locate prime numbers. Tasks such as these *could* be done without the help of computer technology, but in many instances their value would be negated by their cost in man-hours and human endurance.

However, some fairly large computations had to be done even before the development of automatic digital computers, and these were handled in the following way: they were split up into many sections—each relatively independent of the others—which were then computed separately. Each section was broken down into a set of instructions and the data to which they were to be applied. The various sections were then handed on to a number of assistants, who would perform the indicated computations using desk calculating devices. Today, the instructions and data are given to the digital computer, which has replaced these assistants.

After the initial use of computers in numerical problems, workers began to explore other areas of application. It was noted that any finite class of objects could be related to the sets of numbers that the computer would handle, and could be manipulated in the same way. *Nonnumeric* data processing became important. (Even before the automatic digital computer, nonnumeric data processing had become available for some business applications through the use of punched-card machines.)

Nonnumeric processing is basically similar to numeric processing in that various logical processes, or *algorithms*, which manipulate finite sets of objects (either numbers or other data) can be prepared for the same computer. As an example, the letters of the alphabet can be assigned numeric values 1 through 26 and a space represented by 0. (Space, or *blank* as it is usually

1

called in computer usage, is one of the possible characters that a computer must be able to "print" on a page.) A machine capable of manipulating 12-digit decimal numbers can be used to manipulate six-letter words or less by replacing each letter by its equivalent number and adding spaces, or 0s, if there are less than six letters. Thus, MOTHER is "represented" as 13 15 20 08 05 18 and MAT as 13 01 20 00 00 00. Words can be arranged alphabetically by arranging their representations in numerical order. MAT precedes MOTHER because 130120000000 is less than 131520080518.

By such techniques business data processing, usually involving the manipulation of large amounts of data (called *files*), both numeric and alphabetic, has been automated for computers. Nonnumeric processing has been extended to applications involving the manipulation of abstract mathematical quantities, such as groups; to the problems of natural language translation, such as Russian to English; to graphical or pictorial data processing, such as the matching of fingerprints; and to the control of complex processes such as those involved in the running of oil refineries.

As computer applications grow in number and variety, increasingly automatic operation is required. Such automatic operation makes the computer available to people with decreasingly detailed knowledge of the inner structure of the computer. A given computer is capable of a basic set of operations, and various combinations of these can be used to perform different tasks. The user is unconcerned with the details of these basic operations; his only concern is that the job to be done be specified in as direct a manner as possible. The computer operator, in turn, is unconcerned with the details of each job. He simply wants to get the work load processed as quickly as possible with a minimum of delay between jobs. Therefore, to the basic computer *hardware* (that is, the component parts of the computer) is added the *software* of *system programs*, which translate the language of the user and operator into that of the computer, and vice versa. The hardware and the system programs together constitute the *computer system*. The hardware provides the ability to do basic operations, the software the ability to specify the job in a convenient notation and to move from one job to another without delay.

This book discusses computer organization by describing the various ways in which the basic components of the computer are logically connected, the reasons for the different organizations, and the advantages of each. This material is then used as background for a discussion of the basic principles of system programming, which consists of (1) the translation of programs written in a language applicable to a job, called a *source language*, into an equivalent program expressed in a language obeyed by the computer, called a *machine language;* (2) the supervision of these user programs by other programs, usually referred to as *monitor* and *supervisor* programs; and (3) the assistance of the program in execution by *system subroutines* which are typically concerned with input/output and related functions. There is an almost unlimited amount of material that could be included in a study of system programming. We will have to be content with an introduction to the concepts common to most systems.

A computer system should provide a tool for solving problems quickly—in terms of the computer's time as well as that of the user. The hardware should be designed to operate as fast as possible within a given cost. The software should be designed to minimize the amount of computer time wasted and yet provide as flexible a means of controlling the operation as possible. Computer functions that can be expected to be fixed throughout the life of the machine should be provided by hardware where possible. Functions that will change— by increase of capabilities without negation of earlier properties—should be controlled by the software. A computer has no value of itself; it can only be justified on economic grounds. The objective of system design must be one of minimum cost for the whole job, including the cost of programming the problem and of running it.

Throughout this book, we shall refer to the *programmer* and the *user* with the following specific meanings: a system programmer is any person who writes programs for a computer system—that is programs that help other programmers to use the computer; whereas a user will mean a person who writes application programs that perform useful computations and produce answers to problems (for example, the complete analysis of a psychology experiment). The user is not, in general, allowed access to facilities available in the hardware that could interfere with other users.

1.1 THE BASIC CAPABILITIES OF COMPUTERS

A digital computer is capable of basic operations on finite sets of numbers. These include the usual arithmetic operations add, subtract, multiply, and divide. In addition, a computer has the important ability to compare two numbers or nonnumeric quantities in order to take one action if the comparison is successful or another if it fails. These comparisons usually include tests for GREATER THAN OR EQUAL TO, EQUAL, LESS THAN, etc. As well as operating on information, the computer must be able to input the initial data from the user, retain it for additional computations, and output the answers to the user. Therefore, in addition to the operational power, it has facilities for *memorizing* numbers, and for inputting and outputting them in a form intelligible to a human. The next few sections will trace briefly the historical development of these facilities and the importance of each new feature.

1.1.1 The desk calculator

The desk calculator was one of the first computing tools. With its ability to perform the arithmetic operations add and subtract (and multiply and divide by repetitive addition and subtraction), it replaced a lot of tedious human calculation. However, human intervention was still needed, both to control the steps in the calculation and to memorize intermediate results (by *storing* them on scratch paper). In order to use a desk calculator effectively, the steps of a problem must be carefully organized. In other words, the operator must first program *himself*.

More recent desk calculators provide a number of *storage registers* which eliminate the need to copy intermediate results. However, the efficiency of a desk calculator is still limited by the speed with which a human operator can issue instructions by punching a keyboard.

1.1.2 The stored program computer

The step to *stored program* computers, which bypassed the speed limitation imposed by human control, occurred in two stages. The first stage was marked by the introduction of sequence-controlled calculators. A fixed cycle of steps was *programmed* by preparing a punched tape or a plugboard. The calculator could get its sequence of operations from this storage device and repeat the cycle of steps indefinitely. The capabilities provided by such mechanisms were equivalent to those of a computer in which programs consisting of only one or two Fortran statements could be executed repetitively.

These techniques could be used for repetitive operations such as summing numbers punched in cards. With the addition of auxiliary cycles of steps that could be activated under certain conditions (and with a lot of ingenuity), quite sophisticated jobs were tackled. The sequence-controlled calculator was limited by its inability to change its cycle of steps except within narrow confines.

This limitation was overcome by the introduction of the stored program computer, in which the sequence of steps was stored in the same memory as the data. Because operations could be performed on the contents of the memory, this computer could modify its own programs during execution. This feature made it possible to vary the program according to need. It was first thought that this would be an important step towards operating efficiency, but subsequent developments (indexing, to be discussed in Chapter 2) have made it possible to avoid program modification, a characteristic now thought to be very desirable.

1.1.3 Operating systems and translators

After the introduction of stored program computers, complex tasks could be tackled. However, many errors could be made during the preparation of a program. In the early days, the programmer sat at the console of the machine to run his program. The computer would often stop on errors, and the programmer would then have to examine the contents of registers and other devices to locate the errors. As machines increased in speed, this correction process became uneconomic. A program that would execute for 1 second could take 5 minutes of human intervention. Therefore, the *operating system* was introduced. This took the form of a program that regained control of the machine when an error was committed by the user program. It attempted to provide the user with diagnostic information he would have received before, but at computer rather than human speeds.

Because the operating system allows for no human intervention, the user has to be able to tell it what is wanted. This is done by *commands*. These are similar to the instructions issued to control the machine operation, but they control the operation of the software. Commands can be used to cause standard system programs to be loaded from special storage devices and to control the machine devices (hardware) available to the user program.

With increase in speed it also became necessary to simplify the drudgery of rote programming. Large volumes of code had to be produced, much of it repetitious and similar—if not identical—to code previously written. Conventions for writing standard codes and ways for using these codes were adopted for each machine so that any user had access to a *library* of codes generated by the users' groups. To simplify the programming of a piece of code that could not be obtained from other services, *higher-level languages* were designed. Each machine executes code in its own machine language which is needlessly detailed for a human statement and understanding of the underlying problem being programmed. These higher-level languages were oriented toward solving the problem rather than detailing the work of the machine. System programs were developed to translate from these user oriented languages to machine oriented languages. These programs are examples of the nonnumeric processing that occurs every day in the most scientifically oriented computer department. In fact, many computers spend up to 50 percent of their time in translations and analogous system activities. It is therefore very important that efficient techniques be integrated into system programs.

1.1.4 Time sharing and remote consoles

Operating systems, and the desire of management to own the most efficient computer organization in terms of actual versus possible running time, took the programmer out of the computer rooms so that he could no longer interact with his program during execution. Although this certainly eliminated much nonsense, it did slow down the maximum rate at which a program could be developed. Long *turnaround times* (the period between handing a job in for processing and receiving the output) and the inevitable occurrence of unexpected conditions left the programmer sitting idle, waiting to correct minor faults. It also led to many inefficiencies not immediately apparent to management. Because the programmer could not predict the types of errors that would be encountered, he found it necessary to have enough data printed that all probable contingencies were covered. During test runs of programs, a lot of the time saved by the efficient operating system was lost by excessive printing.

In order to allow the user to interact with his program while it was being executed and also to request only the output that he thought significant on the basis of the completed run, many consoles were attached to a single computer. Programs for each programmer were stored in various different parts of the computer memory, and the processing section of the computer switched from one program to another while it switched from one console to another. While one program was being executed for a brief period, the other programmers could be examining their results so far and preparing further input. These consoles are often typewriter-like devices.

1.2 PREPARATION OF PROGRAMS

The preparation of programs for computers has been described as follows:

> "I program,
> you code,
> she keypunches."

The first stage, called programming, consists of analyzing the task and reducing it to a set of logically well-defined steps. The second stage involves the coding of these steps into a language acceptable to the computer system. The third and last stage consists of transcribing the language onto a medium, such as punched cards, which can be read by the computer.

In order to examine these steps in more detail, we shall follow an example through the various stages of its preparation and execution. Suppose that the task is to find the shortest distance from city I to city J. This distance is to be determined on the basis of a table showing the lengths of roads between pairs of directly connected cities. (It is assumed that the only road junctions are at cities, or, alternatively, that every junction is called a city. See Figure 1.1.)

The first stage is to find a method, or *algorithm*, to solve the problem, and to plan its implementation on the computer. An algorithm is a rote method—involving no intuition or value judgment—that will yield the answer when applied to the data. It must terminate, after a finite number of steps, at the correct answer. The steps themselves must be basic operations of the device for which the algorithm is specified. An algorithm is a method that could be used by anybody who will blindly follow instructions, and so it is precisely what is needed for a computer.

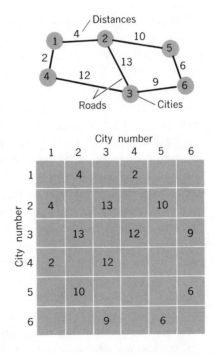

		City number				
		1	2	3	4	5	6
	1		4		2		
City number	2	4		13		10	
	3		13		12		9
	4	2		12			
	5		10				6
	6			9		6	

FIGURE 1.1 Road map and corresponding distance table.

FIGURE 1.2 Input for distance problem.

The problem posed above can easily be solved by first constructing a table showing the shortest distance from any one city to any other city and then looking up the answer in this table. The table can be constructed in a commonsense way by first entering the known distances along direct connections, and then, for every pair of cities I and J, asking if a route via any other city will lead to a shorter distance. A "yes" answer should cause the table to be updated for that I and J. If a complete scan of all pairs of cities yields no shorter distances than are already known, then the table is complete.

Before continuing, it is necessary to do one important thing with a proposed algorithm, and that is to show that it really is one—that it will always work. There is little point in writing a program for a method only to find that it doesn't work for all cases. In our case, it is necessary to justify the last statement of the last paragraph—that the table is complete when no changes can be made—and also that this state is produced in a finite number of steps. Obviously, methods which take an infinite amount of time cannot be used as algorithms. A proof for this algorithm can be constructed as follows: Consider the number of cities on the shortest path between each pair of cities. Initially, we know all shortest paths with no intermediate cities. After one complete scan, all shortest paths with no more than one intermediate city are known; after two scans, those with three cities; after three scans, those with seven cities, etc. Since no more than N-2 intermediate cities can be between any two cities if there are N cities on the map altogether, the method will know about all shortest paths after a finite number of steps. When all shortest paths have been determined, there can be no further reduction in the table entries.

Having found an algorithm, we must now plan its implementation on a computer. This frequently leads to a *flowchart*, which is a two-dimensional representation of the problem-solving procedure. Suppose that N cities are involved and that N is known to be less than, say, 21. Let us also suppose that the first stage will be to input a series of cards giving the names of a pair of cities and the direct distance between them. The end of this sequence of cards could be indicated by a negatively punched distance (assumed to be physically impossible, otherwise the algorithm will not work). Subsequent cards are assumed to contain the names of pairs of cities. The program is to print these together with the shortest distance. See Figure 1.2 for an example of the input data. The last card has a 0 city number.

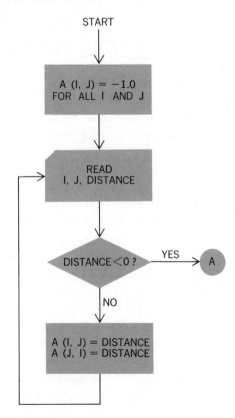

FIGURE 1.3   Read-in section for distance problem.

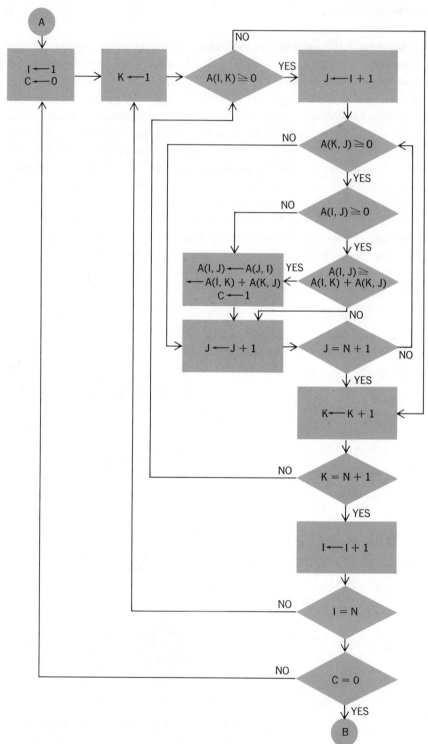

FIGURE 1.4 Calculation section of distance problem.
10

To simplify the program, let us assume that the names of cities are positive integers between 1 and N, so that arithmetic operations can be used. Let us represent the table of distances in the computer as an N by N square array, $A(I,J)$, where the value of $A(I,J)$ is the shortest known distance between I and J. Note that $A(I,J) = A(J,I)$. This is called *symmetry*. Since we also know that $A(I,I) = 0$ for all I, it is not necessary to bother with values of J less than or equal to I. Initially there are positions in the table corresponding to routes not yet known. To indicate this, start by putting -1.0 in such positions.

The flowchart of the program is shown in Figures 1.3, 1.4, and 1.5. It has been broken into three parts which are well separated: 1.3 inputs the initial data—the known distances between cities; 1.4 calculates the minimum-distance table; and 1.5 uses it to answer the questions contained on the input cards. Figure 1.4 is the only chart of any complexity. Each combination of I, J, and K is examined to see if the distance from I to J is shorter if a route via K is taken. Values of J are always taken larger than I because of symmetry, but for ease of programming, the full array is stored.

Note that certain conventions are used in the flowcharts. Rectangular boxes are used for calculation, diamonds for test, circles for connections to

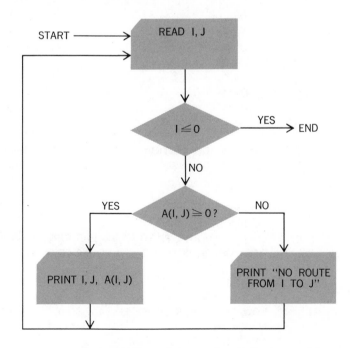

FIGURE 1.5 Print section of distance problem.

other pages (or other parts on the same page in complicated charts), and card-shaped boxes for input and output. There is no standard set of conventions: these represent this writer's tastes. The student is urged to adopt a convention and stick with it. (Parenthetically, it should be noted that this program is not a fast way to solve this problem. Very large tables of cities with complex interconnections could take a long time.) These flowcharts provide a fairly concise description of the method, but it is not yet in a form suitable for most computers. It has been programmed: it must now be coded into a computer language.

In this example any of the algebraic languages such as Fortran, Algol, Mad, etc., can be used with ease. A version of the program coded in Fortran is given below. Note that it is commented and broken into sections corresponding to the three flowcharts.

```
C***   READ IN SECTION.  D IS THE DISTANCE BETWEEN I AND J.
C***   IF D IS NEGATIVE, THE SECTION IS TERMINATED.
       DIMENSION A(20,20)
       READ  (INPUT,1000) N
1000   FORMAT(I10)
C***   SET ALL DISTANCES TO −1.0, MEANING UNKNOWN.
       DO 1 I=1,N
       DO 1 J=1,N
1      A(I,J)=−1.0
2      READ  (INPUT,1001) I,J,D
1001   FORMAT(2I10,E10.0)
       IF(D) 4,3,3
3      A(I,J) = D
       A(J,I) = D
       GO TO 2
C*****************************************************************
C***   CALCULATION SECTION.  C IS A MARK WHICH INDICATES
C***   WHEN NO CHANGES HAVE BEEN MADE IN A SCAN.
4      C=0.
       I1=N−1
       DO 10 I=1,I1
       DO 10 K=1,N
C***   CHECK IF ROUTE FROM I TO J IS SHORTER VIA CITY K.
C***   FIRST CHECK IF THERE IS A ROUTE FROM I TO K.
       IF(A(I,K)) 10,5,5
5      J1= I+1
       DO 9 J=J1,N
C***   NOW CHECK FOR ROUTE FROM K TO J,
       IF (A(K,J)) 9,6,6
C***   AND FROM I TO J.
6      IF (A(I ,J)) 8,7,7
```

```
C*** IS DISTANCE SHORTER
7         IF (A(I,J) —A(I,K) —A(K,J)) 9,9,8
C*** SET NEW DISTANCE, AND SET C=1 AS MARK OF CHANGE.
8         A(I,J) = A(I,K) + A (K,J)
          A(J,I) = A(I,J)
          C=1.
9         CONTINUE
10        CONTINUE
C*** REPEAT SCAN IF ANY CHANGES.
          IF(C) 11,11,4
C*************************************************************
C*** PRINT SECTION.
11        READ (INPUT,1002) I,J
1002      FORMAT(2I10)
          IF(I) 15,15,12
12        IF(A(I,J)) 14,13,13
13        WRITE (IOUTPT,1003) I,J,A(I,J)
1003      FORMAT(15H DISTANCE FROM ,I2,4H TO ,I2,4H IS , E20.5)
          GO TO 11
14        WRITE (IOUTPT,1004) I,J
1004      FORMAT(15H NO ROUTE FROM ,I2,4H TO ,I2)
          GO TO 11
15        CONTINUE
          END
```

This can now be keypunched and processed. The steps in this processing will involve translating, by system programs, from Fortran into machine language, loading the machine language into memory, and executing it.

1.2.1 Machine and assembly languages

The programmer usually has a choice of languages at his disposal. These range from assembly language at the lowest level to sophisticated compilers at higher levels. Machine language refers to the sequences of instructions that are used to control the sequences of steps of the machine when performing a task. Machine language is usually a long and unnecessarily detailed statement of the problem, but in some situations it is necessary that the programmer control precisely each step of the operation. These situations can arise when efficiency of the running program is paramount or when the system is trying to clean up after malfunctions.

In order to avoid some of the tedium of machine language, such code is usually written in *assembly language*. This language is translated by a program called an *assembler* into machine language in a straightforward fashion. Historically, assembly language was the first language used to communicate with computers. It allows a precise specification of the details of the computer code while retaining some *symbolic* and *mnemonic* information. *Symbolic* information refers to names used by the programmer to refer to numbers and other data. Since these names can be chosen arbitrarily, they can be used to indicate their operational significance to the human. A *mnemonic* is a means to aid memorization. In this context it refers to the use of symbolic codes for machine operations which indicate what they do. For example, internal to the machine (in machine language), 112 may be the code for a subtract order. In assembly language this may be replaced by SUB. The assembler replaces each occurrence of SUB by 112. The macrofeature in an assembly-language translator provides an additional symbolic facility that allows the user to define operations consisting of sections of assembly-language code. This enables the input form of the program to be abbreviated and clarified further.

Assembly language is used mainly by system programmers who have to be concerned with the details of what the computer does. The form of assembly language and the construction of assemblers will be taken up in a later chapter.

1.2.2 Procedure oriented languages

Just as machine language, with its excessive detail, obscures the form of the code, so assembly language, with its detail of each basic machine operation, obscures the nature of the method used to solve the problem. To combat this, languages were developed which are intended to reflect clearly the procedure used for solution. This clarity allows the original problem to be coded more quickly, errors to be more easily removed, and changes to be more readily added—by the original programmer or by another. These languages are called *procedure oriented languages*. They include Fortran (FORmula TRANslation), Algol (ALGOrithmic Language), Cobol (COmmon Business Oriented Language), Mad (Michigan Algorithm Decoder), PL/I (Programming Language One), and others. These languages provide a means of expressing the flowchart of the task in a precise way, a way which the computer has been conditioned to accept in lieu of machine language. Translator programs, usually called *compilers*, are used to convert from the procedure oriented language to machine or assembly languages.

1.2.3 Problem oriented languages

Once a program has been written, it may be desirable to save it for future reuse in order to avoid reprogramming. To implement this, a library of programs is accumulated at a computer installation. Programs with a limited or moderate amount of flexibility are usually used in conjunction with other programs in order to fit them to a particular need. However, it is possible for programs to be written with such flexible input options that they can be used without any additional programming. Suppose, for example, that a number of programs have been written to solve polynomial equations under various conditions. Some may work for real coefficients, others, for complex coefficients, etc. They could be collected together in a package so that the user would see a single program into which he fed his coefficients and some control information requesting action, in this case, to solve the equations.

When this happens, the user does not have to have any knowledge of programming nor need he know any details of the computer hardware and software. A description of the routine will tell him how to prepare his input and how to interpret the output. From the point of view of such a user, the communication with the system is the language accepted as input by the program. This language is normally sufficient to specify what the problem is, but it does not completely specify how to solve it. (The user may be allowed to request one of a number of methods for solution.) It is called a *problem oriented language*. For each different class of problems, a new program must be written by the computer professional to enable the nonprofessional user to talk to the computer in a suitable problem oriented language. The procedure for solution is specified within the program, not by the user.

A problem oriented language is only a program that accepts a flexible data input. It is therefore difficult to distinguish between any program with data input and problem oriented language. However, the boundary can reasonably be drawn by asking what the program does with incorrect data input, or, in other words, what happens if there are errors in the input language. A language translator will give numerous diagnostic messages to aid the user in understanding what is wrong. The typical library program will either give wrong answers or just quit with little comment. (Unfortunately, this is a measure under which many procedural language compilers fare badly.)

Some well-known examples of problem oriented languages include Cogo (COordinate GeOmetry), which can be used in surveying tasks, and Stress (STRuctural Equation System Solver), which accepts a description of a frame or truss of beams, joints, and supports and calculates the deflections and stresses under various loading conditions. To illustrate the principle we shall develop the distance program above into a very simple problem oriented language translator.

The language must allow us to specify the direct distances between various cities and to ask questions about the distance between two cities. In addition, let us also require that it tell us how to get to a given city (by listing the intermediate cities), as well as the names of its nearest and farthest neighbors. Since we must be able to restart with another problem, add cities at any time, and mix up the questions, we shall use *control cards* or statements in the problem oriented language. The first 6 characters of the card will contain a word which specifies the action to be taken.

The language is:

card column 1-6	10-19	20-29	30-49	action
CLEAR				Start another problem.
ROAD	I	J	D	Enters indication that a road exists from I to J distance D.
LENGTH	I	J		Prints distance from I to J.
ROUTE	I	J		Prints distance from I to J and route through intermediate cities.
NEAR	I			Prints nearest city to I.
FAR	I			Prints furthest city from I.

The flow of the program is straightforward. A decoder section reads the next card, tests the first 6 columns, and branches to an appropriate section for execution. If there have been any new roads specified since the last use, it is necessary to recalculate the distance-and-route table. The questions can be answered by direct reference to the table

The name "problem oriented language" is used very loosely for all sorts of trivial processors such as the one described above. It would be better to reserve the term "language" for larger systems with some structure in the input and to continue calling these simple packages *library programs*.

1.3 EXECUTING THE PROGRAM

The task has been described in a language acceptable to the system. From the user's viewpoint, this language is the language obeyed by the machine. In fact, the input usually consists of two or more levels of language—the commands which control the system programs and the statements which will be translated into machine language. If this translation is from assembly language, it is usually called *assembly;* if it is from a procedure oriented language, it is called *compilation*. In either case, the input statements are first processed by a system program to produce machine language. We say that the *source language* is the input to the translator and the *object language* is the output or object of the translator. The object code for each of the translated sections of programs is combined with any required library programs and *loaded* into the computer memory. The loading process links together all of the elements of the job and assigns them space in the computer memory.

The next step is the execution phase, during which the user's program is in control of the machine.

Contrast this with the use of a problem oriented language as described above. In this case, the processor for the language is in direct control of the machine. Statements are not translated, rather they cause an action immediately.

From another viewpoint, we can call this *interpretation*. An *interpreter* is a program which executes statements in a language by decoding each statement and immediately executing it, that is, causing the appropriate action. Interpreters can be written to process procedure oriented languages directly. The source language is read into memory and stored there. The combination of the interpreter program and the machine resembles a machine which executes the source language directly.

The distinction between translation and execution on the one hand and interpretation on the other is not clear cut. We can draw a simile from the translation of natural languages. The translator is a professional language expert who accepts input in one language, say French, and produces output in another, say English. If he is working in a technical field like mathematics, for example, the translator does not have to understand his text. That can be checked for sense afterward, by an English-speaking mathematician. Interpretation, on the other hand, is similar to the work done by a mathematician fluent in both English and French. As he reads each statement in the source language, he immediately understands (executes) it.

In practice, both translation and interpretation are involved in reading a foreign-language book. So, in computers, is a mixture of translation and interpretation used to get the best balance of speed and flexibility.

Subsequent chapters will consider the characteristics of various hardware devices. They will also deal with the design and implementation of translators, interpreters, and system programs in relation to these characteristics.

PROBLEMS

1. How could the program which finds the minimum distance between two cities be reorganized so that it will also print out the shortest route between those two cities? Consider only methods which do not require more than $2N^2$ storage locations. Can a method be found that does not require any more data storage than used in the distance problem described in the book?

2. If a new road is added to the map after a minimum-distance matrix has been found, and if the original input data is no longer available, how would the matrix be updated? Prove that the proposed algorithm works.

3. Prepare, in Fortran or similar procedure oriented language, a problem oriented language processor for the distance problem.

4. Add to the following statement whatever is needed to make it into an algorithm: "To find the square root of a positive number A, set $X_0 = 1$, and calculate $X_{n+1} = (X_n + A/X_n)/2$ for $n = 0,1,2, \ldots$. The square root of A is the limit of X_n as n goes to infinity."

2

hardware organization:
the main machine

The hardware components of a computer system are classified into four
groups:

1. Memory
2. Central Processing Unit (CPU for short)
3. Input/Output (I/O for short)
4. Control

These units are shown connected together in Figure 2.1. The input/output
units are for communication between the internal representation of information by electrical signals used in the computer and the external representation
needed by the human, such as printed paper, punched cards, and other *hard
copy* media. The CPU is the equivalent of a desk calculator. It contains hardware for performing addition, subtraction, multiplication, and division. The
memory is used to store both intermediate results and a copy of the program
being executed. The information is read by I/O devices and placed directly
into memory in most computers, although in some smaller machines the
information passes through the CPU on the way to the memory. This will
be discussed in more detail in Chapter 6, which deals mainly with input/
output. Some units, such as magnetic tape units, can be used either as
memory devices or as input/output units. This chapter will deal only with
the *main* memory (usually called the *core storage*), the CPU, and their relevant
control units. Other memory devices, called as a group *auxiliary storage units*
or *backup storage units*, will be discussed in Chapter 6.

The CPU, the main memory, and their controls contain the hardware
necessary to perform the arithmetic and logical operations on numeric and
nonnumeric data. There are many different methods for performing these

FIGURE 2.1   Computer organization.

operations, but there are many similarities between different machines. In order to clarify the common problems of software system design, this chapter will discuss the different types of operations in common use. The reader should study the machine (assembly) language of a computer which is accessible to him in order to compare and contrast that machine with the different structures discussed below.

For any given machine, there are a number of programming tricks that can be used to provide shortcuts. Some of these are deliberately built into the computer by the designer, others are "discovered" at a later date by programmers. The fast and effective programming of any given computer in any specified language requires a knowledge of these tricks so that the programmer immediately knows the "best" way to do a given set of operations. However, these tricks are beyond the scope of this book since they depend on the particular machine. They are best learned by direct experience. Rather, the theme of this chapter is that no one machine manual constitutes the "gospel" of machine design. Each machine represents the idiosyncrasies and beliefs of one design team, with the result that some machine features may become drawbacks because of changing needs. (An example of this is the negative indexing on the IBM 7090 series. This will be discussed in Section 2.4.1.) In the polytheistic programming universe, it may be necessary to make temporary obeisance to a particular machine design; but it is better to understand the way of machine design in general before becoming a disciple of one specific model.

We shall discuss the various functional elements that make up a computer in order to trace the way in which instructions are executed by the hardware. However, this is not a text on machine design.†

2.1 THE MAIN MEMORY AND REPRESENTATION OF INFORMATION

The main computer processes information which can be obtained from the main memory and the results are returned to the main memory. There is usually a minimum amount of information that can be processed in any one operation and moved to or from memory. This is called a *word*. A word may represent a number to be used in numerical calculations or one or more characters of nonnumeric information. The length of the word—that is, the number of *bits* it has or the amount of information it holds—differs from machine to machine. On most machines, however, a word consists of a number of *bits*, the most common lengths being between 6 and 64 bits.

Bit is the name for the amount of information that is contained in a number which can only take the value 0 or 1. The word "bit" is a contraction of "binary digit," meaning a digit that can take one of the two values 0 or 1, just as a decimal digit can take one of the ten values 0, 1, 2, . . . , or 9. Although human beings commonly use decimal digits to represent numbers, machines commonly use binary digits because most physical devices used in machines can retain one of two states most reliably. (For example, *on* or *off*, *positive* or *negative*, *north* or *south* magnetization, etc.)

A word, consisting of a number of bits, may be used to represent anything that the user cares to represent. Each bit of an N bit word can be a 0 or a 1 independently, so that a word can assume any one of 2^N different states. With one word, the user can represent one out of not more than 2^N different objects. These could be different numbers, different letters, different species of trees, etc.

2.1.1 Sign/absolute-value representation of a number

The most common use of a word is for number and alphabetic character representation. Much of today's computer terminology reflects the fact that, at the outset, computers handled mainly numbers. If a word consists of N bits, we usually draw it as in Figure 2.2. The bits have been numbered arbitrarily

† If the student is particularly interested in this topic, he may refer forward to Chap. 5 and to texts such as T. C. Bartree, I. L. Lebow, and I. S. Reed, "Theory and Design of Digital Machines," McGraw-Hill Book Company, New York, 1962.

FIGURE 2.2   A computer word.

from 0 to $N - 1$. Bit 0 is often referred to as the *left-hand bit* or *most significant bit* and bit $N - 1$ as the *right-hand bit* or *least significant bit*. The word is referred to as being N bits *long*. In many computers, one bit is referred to as the sign bit, since it is used as a sign when the word represents a number. Thus if a word contains 6 bits and bit 0 is the sign bit, a 0 representing positive numbers and a 1 representing negative numbers, then integers between -31 and $+31$ can be stored by representing the absolute value of the number in the remaining 5 bits. This is called the *sign/absolute-value* or *sign-magnitude* system

number	binary word
−31	111 111
−30	111 110
−29	111 101
. . .	. . .
−1	100 001
−0	100 000
+0	000 000
+1	000 001
. . .	. . .
+29	011 101
+30	011 110
+31	011 111

because the sign and absolute value of the numbers are represented separately. Notice that there are two representations for 0, one positive and one negative. If the bits of the word are $b_0, b_1, \ldots$, and b_5 where b_0 is the sign bit, then the number is given by $(1 - 2b_0)(b_1 \cdot 2^4 + b_2 \cdot 2^3 + b_3 \cdot 2^2 + b_4 \cdot 2^1 + b_5 \cdot 2^0)$.

2.1.2 Fractions

If the user needs to represent fractions rather than integers, then the *binary point* can be thought of as being between b_0 and b_1. This corresponds to moving the point five places to the left or dividing by $2^5 = 32$. Now the numbers represented are:

number		representation
$-31\!/\!32 = -.96875$		111 111
$-30\!/\!32 = -.9375$		111 110
. . .		. . .
$-1\!/\!32 = -.03125$		100 001
$-0 = -0$		100 000
$+0 = +0$		000 000
$+1\!/\!32 = +.03125$		000 001
. . .		. . .
$+31\!/\!32 = +.96875$		011 111

The value of the number is now given by

$$(1 - 2b_0)(b_1 \cdot 2^{-1} + b_2 \cdot 2^{-2} + b_3 \cdot 2^{-3} + b_4 \cdot 2^{-4} + b_5 \cdot 2^{-5})$$

2.1.3 Rounding and range

If the word contained N bits rather than 6, then the sign/absolute-value representation of a fraction would end in $b_{N-1} \cdot 2^{-N+1}$, while the *range* of an integer would be from $-2^{N-1} + 1$ to $2^{N-1} - 1$. The range of the representation of a number is the set of values that can be represented. This is necessarily a finite set. Thus when numbers between $-31\!/\!32$ and $+31\!/\!32$ are represented in a 6-bit word, only 63 discrete values can be represented. This is shown in Figure 2.3. If a number which is not one of these discrete values is to be represented, then only an approximation can be made. For example, if $2\!/\!3$ is to be represented in a 3-bit machine, then either $1\!/\!2$ or $3\!/\!4$ must be used instead (see Figure 2.4). As a binary fraction, $2\!/\!3$ is 0.101010 . . . ad infinitum. This can be reduced to two bits by chopping off, or *truncating*, all bits after the second, so that $2\!/\!3$ is approximately 0.10. However, it is generally better to choose the closest available value, in this case $3\!/\!4$ or 0.11, since the error is then $-1\!/\!12$ rather than $1\!/\!6$. Taking the closest value is called

Numbers between $-31/32$ and $31/32$

Each point can be represented exactly in a 6-bit word.

FIGURE 2.4

rounding. The error introduced is called *roundoff error* in either case. By round-ing rather than truncating, the roundoff error can be kept to not more than half the distance between two adjacent representable numbers, or 2^{-N}. It is important to remember that integer arithmetic is exact as long as the range is not exceeded, whereas fractional arithmetic is only exact in those unusual cases where the numbers represented are exact. Generally, fractions will be in error by a small amount. For example, $\frac{1}{10}$ cannot be represented exactly in a binary machine.

Because representable numbers have only a finite range, arithmetic oper-ations will give incorrect answers if the result is not in range. The error can be one of two types. If the answer is larger than the largest representable number, then the answer supplied by the machine will be grossly in error and we say that *overflow* has occurred. In the other case, the answer may be in between two representable numbers, so that the machine can choose one or the other as its answer. This is another example of roundoff error. Multipli-cation of two fractions, for example, may lead to roundoff error if the answer is to be represented in a single word.

2.1.4 Floating point

It is not always convenient to restrict the representable numbers to either integers or fractions. In many problems, numbers which vary in size from 10^{10} to 10^{-10} must be used. For this reason, floating-point arithmetic was added to machines. We frequently use decimal floating-point arithmetic to write down numbers. For example, we may write

	1052000	as	$.1052 \times 10^7$
or	.0000531	as	$.531 \times 10^{-4}$

The first part of the floating-point representation of 1052000, namely .1052, is called the *fraction* or *mantissa*. The second part, 7, is called the *exponent*, in this case the base-10 exponent. In a binary machine we usually use an expo-nent base which is a power of 2, such as 2, 4, 8, and 16, rather than 10. Part of the word may be used to represent the mantissa as a binary fraction and part to represent the exponent as a binary integer. Figure 2.5 shows the representation used in the CDC 3600. The exponent is a base-2 exponent E between -1023 and $+1023$. The mantissa is a sign-plus-36-bit fraction F between $-1 + 2^{-36}$ and $1 - 2^{-36}$. The value of the number represented is $F \times 2^E$. Note that in floating-point arithmetic, roundoff error in representing a number depends on the exponent. Thus in the CDC 3600, the error in the fraction can be limited to 2^{-37} (half of the spacing). However, the actual error is limited by $2^{-37}2^E$. Hence it is desirable to make E as small as possible so as to make the error as small as possible. For each unit that E is reduced, the fraction F is doubled. However, the absolute value of F must be less than 1, so it can only be doubled until it is greater than or equal to $\frac{1}{2}$ (unless it is 0). A floating-point number which is represented in the form with a minimum exponent is called *normalized*. The number .001730 can be represented as

.000173 × 10¹
.001730 × 10⁰
.017300 × 10⁻¹
.173000 × 10⁻²

In a six-digit decimal machine, only the last form is normalized.

Arithmetic operations on floating-point numbers can cause overflow if the resulting exponent is too large. The exponent may also be less than the most negative representable number, in which case the answer is very small. This is called *underflow*. Some computers will replace the result with a formal 0 consisting of a 0 fractional part and the smallest exponent allowed.

Even if the result of a floating-point operation is not 0, it is important to note that errors which are large relative to the size of the answer can occur. In fixed-point addition, the number of bits and their position relative to the binary point do not change, so the error is in a known bit position. When two floating-point numbers with opposite signs are added, the result may contain very few significant bits. The user may, however, be fooled by printing the answer to high precision. For example, if the two decimal floating-point

FIGURE 2.5   Floating-point word in the CDC 3600.

numbers $.65284 \times 10^{-3}$ and $-.65252 \times 10^{-3}$ are added, the result, after normalization, is $.32000 \times 10^{-6}$. However, it is no longer accurate to 5 digits. If the original numbers had errors as large as 1 in the least significant digit, the result has an error as large as 2 in the second digit. The problems of floating numerical errors are complex and not a subject for this text or this level: they belong in a study of numerical analysis.

2.1.5 Twos complement representation of numbers

The sign/absolute-value system of negative number representation is familiar in everyday life. A number of computers use this system, but there are two other systems that are important. The first is the *twos complement* system. It arises in the following manner: consider a 6-bit machine in which bit 0 is reserved for a sign bit yet to be discussed and the other 5 bits represent a fraction in the usual way. Suppose two numbers are subtracted, such as $\frac{5}{32}$ from $\frac{11}{32}$:

$$
\begin{array}{cc}
0.01011 & \frac{11}{32} \\
-0.00101 & -\frac{5}{32} \\
\hline
0.00110 & \frac{6}{32}
\end{array}
$$

When everything is positive we can consider the sign bit just as any other bit in the arithmetic process. However, if the number being subtracted is larger, we usually perform the subtraction in the other direction. Thus, if you are asked to subtract 43 from 25, you say that the answer is minus $(43 - 25)$ and subtract 25 from 43. A computer is not equipped with the foresight to reverse the operation, so a computer which could only perform two-decimal-digit arithmetic would perform as follows:

$$
\begin{array}{r}
25 \\
-43 \\
\hline
82
\end{array}
$$

The answer of 82 is not correct because a borrow from the next position to the left was ignored. But in two-digit arithmetic, 82 will act like the true answer of -18. Thus, if we add 34 to 82 in two-digit arithmetic, we perform the operation

$$
\begin{array}{r}
82 \\
+34 \\
\hline
16
\end{array}
$$

The carry into the hundreds position is ignored because only two-digit arithmetic is allowed. This is the correct answer of 34 − 18. Note that 82 is in fact 100 − 18. The hundred arose because of the neglected borrow from the hundreds position. Suppose that $11\frac{1}{32}$ is subtracted from $\frac{5}{32}$ as though the sign bit in a binary representation were a regular bit in the number

$$
\begin{array}{ll}
0.00101 & \frac{5}{32} \\
-0.01011 & -11\frac{1}{32} \\
\hline
1.11010 & -\frac{6}{32}
\end{array}
$$

In some sense, the answer, 1.11010, represents $-\frac{6}{32}$. Note that the borrow from the top bit of the answer was ignored. Since the first bit of the answer arose by subtracting 1 from 0, it is really a −1, that is, it has a negative *weight*. The word 0.00101 represents $\frac{1}{8} + \frac{1}{32}$ and the number .01011 represents $\frac{1}{4} + \frac{1}{16} + \frac{1}{32}$. The answer 1.11010 represents

$$-1 + \frac{1}{2} + \frac{1}{4} + \frac{1}{16} = -\frac{6}{32}$$

since the weight of the first bit is negative. Now let us add $-\frac{6}{32}$ to $11\frac{1}{32}$ in this representation:

$$
\begin{array}{ll}
0.01011 & 11\frac{1}{32} \\
+1.11010 & +-\frac{6}{32} \\
\hline
0.00101 & \frac{5}{32}
\end{array}
$$

since the weights of the fraction bits are positive, they are added. The arithmetic in the sign position for this example is "0 + −1+ a carry of 1 is 0." Notice that this is the same as saying "0 + 1+ a carry of 1 is 0, carry 1—forget the carry because there is no place to put it."

The name "twos complement" is derived from the fact that the negative form of the number can be obtained by subtracting it from 2. Two is too large for the representation, but if we ignore this, we can find $-\frac{6}{32}$ by the following arithmetic:

$$
\begin{array}{ll}
2 & 10.00000 \\
-\frac{6}{32} & -0.00110 \\
\hline
 & 1.11010
\end{array}
$$

The result is indeed the twos complement form of $-\frac{6}{32}$. This relation will hold for fractions of any length. It is true because the statement that "the weight of the sign position is negative" is the same as the statement that "2 was added to a -1 in the sign position to get a $+1$."

SUBTRACTION IN TWOS COMPLEMENT

The reason for the use of the twos complement representation in the machine is that the addition can be done directly. It is not necessary for the machine to examine the signs of the numbers to decide whether to add or subtract, or, in the case of subtraction, to decide which number to subtract from which. Rules for subtraction in a twos complement representation can readily be formulated. Alternatively, it can be done by addition of the negative of the number; that is, $A - B = A + (-B)$. Given B, we need a rule for forming $-B$. The value of a twos complement number $b_0 \cdot b_1 b_2 \cdots + b_{N-1}$ is

$$-b_0 + b_1 \cdot 2^{-1} + \cdots + b_{N-1} \cdot 2^{-N+1}$$

Hence minus this number is

$$b_0 - b_1 \cdot 2^{-1} - \cdots - b_{N-1} \cdot 2^{-N+1}$$

Note that

$$1 = 2^{-1} + 2^{-2} + 2^{-3} + \cdots + 2^{-N+1} + 2^{-N+1}$$

Therefore, by adding and subtracting 1 from $-B$ we get

$$
\begin{aligned}
-B &= b_0 - 1 - b_1 \cdot 2^{-1} + 2^{-1} - b_2 \cdot 2^{-2} + 2^{-2} - \cdots \\
&\qquad\qquad - b_{N-1} \cdot 2^{-N+1} + 2^{-N+1} + 2^{-N+1} \\
&= -(1 - b_0) + (1 - b_1) \cdot 2^{-1} + \cdots \\
&\qquad\qquad + (1 - b_{N-1}) \cdot 2^{-N+1} + 2^{-N+1}
\end{aligned}
$$

This number is a 1 in the least significant position plus the value of a twos complement number which is the *digit-wise complement*, or simply *complement*, of the original number. The digit-wise complement of a number is formed by writing a 0 for each 1 and a 1 for each 0. Thus $-\frac{6}{32}$ can be obtained from $\frac{6}{32}$ by the following steps:

$\frac{6}{32}$	0.00110
complement	1.11001
add 1	$+\qquad 1$
$-\frac{6}{32}$	1.11010

Table 2.1 Transformations from decimal to twos complement

Decimal	Decimal $+32$	Binary integer (characteristic form)	Twos complement form
-32	0	000000	100000
-31	1	000001	100001
-30	2	000010	100010
-1	31	011111	111111
0	32	100000	000000
$+1$	33	100001	000001
$+2$	34	100010	000010
$+30$	62	111110	011110
$+31$	63	111111	011111

Hence subtraction can be done by the adder hardware in a twos complement machine equipped with a complementing mechanism which is usually trivial.

Example of Subtraction

$$
\begin{aligned}
1\tfrac{1}{32} \quad &- \quad \tfrac{6}{32} && \text{decimal form} \\
=0.01011 \quad &- \quad 0.00110 && \text{binary form} \\
=0.01011 \quad &+ \quad 1.11001 + 0.00001 && \text{complement subtrahend} \\
=0.01011 \\
+1.11001 \\
+0.00001 \\
\hline
=0.00101 \\
=\tfrac{5}{32}
\end{aligned}
$$

Yet another way of viewing twos complement is as follows. We wish, say, to represent integers between -32 and $+31$ in a 6-bit word. (There are exactly $2^6 = 64$ such integers.) Add 32 to the integer I that we wish to represent in order to get a positive integer in the range 0 to 63. Represent this as a 6-bit binary integer. This form is frequently used for exponents (for example, in the IBM 7094) and is then called a *characteristic*. Because 0 is now represented by 100000 rather than 000000, the sign bit of every number is complemented. The sequence of transformations is shown in Table 2.1.

2.1.6 Ones complement

The other method of representing negative numbers is the *ones complement* system. This is derived by requiring that the negative of a number be the digit-wise complement of that number. Thus the negative of $6/32$, which is 1.11010 in twos complement, is 1.11001 in ones complement. The least significant 1 is not added in after the complementation. Because of this, the weight of the sign position is $-(1 - 2^{-5})$ rather than -1, so that the value of the number with the ones complement representation $b_0 \cdot b_1 b_2 b_3 b_4 b_5$ is

$$-(1 - 2^{-5})b_0 + b_1 \cdot 2^{-1} + b_2 \cdot 2^{-2} + b_3 \cdot 2^{-3} + b_4 \cdot 2^{-4} + b_5 \cdot 2^{-5}$$

The addition rules for ones complement are the same as for twos complement except that the carry from the sign position must be added to the least significant position. This is called *end-around carry*. It arises when a carry into the sign position which has a value of $+1$ is added to a 1 already there which has a value $-1 + 2^{-N+1}$. The result is 2^{-N+1} which is a 1 in the least significant position. Thus if $11/32$ is added to $-6/32$ in ones complement

```
    0.01011    11/32
   +1.11001   +-6/32
  =(1)0.00100

  +  └────→1  end-around carry
  =   0.00101  =  5/32
```

This can be written out as

$$0 + 0/2 + 1/4 + 0/8 + 1/16 + 1/32 \quad (001011)$$
$$+(-1 + 1/32) + 1/2 + 1/4 + 0/8 + 0/16 + 1/32 \quad (111001)$$

Add to get

$$1/32 + 0/2 + 0/4 + 1/8 + 0/16 + 0/32$$

Carry the $1/32$ around to get

$$0 + 0/2 + 0/4 + 1/8 + 0/16 + 1/32 \quad (000101)$$

EXTENDING THE PRECISION OF A ONES COMPLEMENT NUMBER

One confusing facet of ones complement representation arises when the precision of a number is increased, that is, when the number of bits is increased. When the decimal representation of $1/5$ is increased from one digit to two digits, 0s are added to the representation to go from .2 to .20. Similarly in twos complement, $-3/4$ represented in 3 bits is 1.01, and the same quantity represented in 4 bits is 1.010. However, in ones complement form $-3/4$

is 1.00 in 3-bit accuracy, but 1.001 in 4-bit accuracy. The bits added must agree with the sign bit, because the weight of the sign bit is $-1 + 2^{-N+1}$ and hence is determined by the number of bits of accuracy.

2.1.7 Nonnumeric data

In addition to representing numbers, words are often used to represent non-numeric data such as alphabetic characters. In program translation, business data processing, and work such as the differentiation of algebraic expressions or word-frequency studies, it is often necessary to represent natural language text such as English or American. To do this, each character (letter, digit, punctuation mark, etc.) is represented by a different bit pattern. The number of bits needed to represent a character is determined by the number of different characters. N bits can represent up to 2^N characters.

N	maximum number of characters
6	64
7	128
8	256

A very common representation of the upper-case letters, the ten digits 0 to 9, and the special characters $+ - * / , . ( ) \$ = '$ and space (48 characters altogether) uses 6 bits. It is commonly known as the BCD code (binary coded decimal). With a few variations, it is standard over many computers and can be found in most machine manuals. It is shown in Table 2.2. More recently a need has arisen to represent more than 64 characters. (Other special characters and the lower-case letters, for example.) Because 7 turns out to be an awkward number of bits, 8 bits are used. One such code is known as ASCII (American Standard Code for Information Interchange). Not unusually, the largest computer manufacturer has its own standard, known as EBCDIC (Extended BCD Interchange Code).

Both of these codes are shown in Table 2.2 for the 48-character set common to all three representations (BCD, EBCDIC, and ASCII). Only one version of the EBCDIC code exists because it has only been used on a few different machines. However, there are several versions of both BCD and ASCII in use because they have been implemented on many different machines by different manufacturers. The BCD code shown is the form that is used internally on the IBM 7094. It is not, for example, the same as used on IBM magnetic tapes commonly attached to the 7094, and neither is identical to that used in the IBM 1401. The ASCII code shown is the standard for use in an 8-bit environment. Some equipment will produce a different code by

TABLE 2.2   BDC and EBCDIC codes and card punches and corresponding ASCII codes

Character	BCD code	EBCDIC code	ASCII code	BCD cards	EBCDIC cards
blank	110 000	0100 0000	0100 0000	no punch	no punch
.	011 011	0100 1011	0100 1110	12,8,3	12,8,3
(	111 100	0100 1101	0100 1000	0,8,4	12,8,5
+	010 000	0100 1110	0100 1011	12	12,8,6
$	101 011	0101 1011	0100 0100	11,8,3	11,8,3
*	101 100	0101 1100	0100 1010	11,8,4	11,8,4
)	011 100	0101 1101	0100 1001	12,8,4	11,8,5
—	100 000	0110 0000	0100 1101	11	11
/	110 001	0110 0001	0100 1111	0,1	0,1
,	111 011	0110 1011	0100 1111	0,8,3	0,8,3
'	001 100	0111 1101	0100 0111	4,8	8,5
=	001 011	0111 1110	0101 1101	3,8	8,6
A	010 001	1100 0001	1010 0001	12,1	12,1
B	010 010	1100 0010	1010 0010	12,2	12,2
C	010 011	1100 0011	1010 0011	12,3	12,3
D	010 100	1100 0100	1010 0100	12,4	12,4
E	010 101	1100 0101	1010 0101	12,5	12,5
F	010 110	1100 0110	1010 0110	12,6	12,6
G	010 111	1100 0111	1010 0111	12,7	12,7
H	011 000	1100 1000	1010 1000	12,8	12,8
I	011 001	1100 1001	1010 1001	12,9	12,9
J	100 001	1101 0001	1010 1010	11,1	11,1
K	100 010	1101 0010	1010 1011	11,2	11,2
L	100 011	1101 0011	1010 1100	11,3	11,3
M	100 100	1101 0100	1010 1101	11,4	11,4
N	100 101	1101 0101	1010 1110	11,5	11,5
O	100 110	1101 0110	1010 1111	11,6	11,6
P	100 111	1101 0111	1011 0000	11,7	11,7
Q	101 000	1101 1000	1011 0001	11,8	11,8
R	101 001	1101 1001	1011 0010	11,9	11,9
S	110 010	1110 0010	1011 0011	0,2	0,2
T	110 011	1110 0011	1011 0100	0,3	0,3
U	110 100	1110 0100	1011 0101	0,4	0,4
V	110 101	1110 0101	1011 0110	0,5	0,5
W	110 110	1110 0110	1011 0111	0,6	0,6
X	110 111	1110 0111	1011 1000	0,7	0,7
Y	111 000	1110 1000	1011 1001	0,8	0,8
Z	111 001	1110 1001	1011 1010	0,9	0,9
0	000 000	1111 0000	0101 0000	0	0
1	000 001	1111 0001	0101 0001	1	1
2	000 010	1111 0010	0101 0010	2	2
3	000 011	1111 0011	0101 0011	3	3
4	000 100	1111 0100	0101 0100	4	4
5	000 101	1111 0101	0101 0101	5	5
6	000 110	1111 0110	0101 0110	6	6
7	000 111	1111 0111	0101 0111	7	7
8	001 000	1111 1000	0101 1000	8	8
9	001 001	1111 1001	0101 1001	9	9

changing the bit in position two, so that the number of bits equal to 1 is even in all characters. This is called *parity* and is discussed in Section 2.5.

EBCDIC has one advantage over the other two codes. The binary codes are in *collating sequence;* that is, if a character is alphabetically after another character, its code, considered as a binary integer, is larger. Table 2.2 is arranged in collating sequence for EBCDIC. Alphabetizing of data can be done by a numerical sort in EBCDIC. In the other cases, special hardware is needed or a code conversion must be done by software.

2.1.8 Packing data into words

If the word size of the computer is considerably larger than 6 or 8 bits, it is obviously wasteful to have a single character in each word. Therefore several characters are packed into a word (which is typically a multiple of the length of a character). Figure 2.6 shows the character packing in three machines. Some machines, such as the IBM 1401, have single-character words. Since the IBM 360 can manipulate a single character, it could be said to be an 8-bit-word machine, but it should be viewed as a 32-bit-word machine for most purposes.

However long the word of a computer, the occasion may arise to represent a set of items that is too large for one word. This frequently happens when more numerical accuracy is required in a calculation. In this case, several words may be coupled together to form a multiword item. Some computers have hardware to deal with such items directly, on others it must be programmed.

The key point to remember is that the meaning assigned to the bit patterns

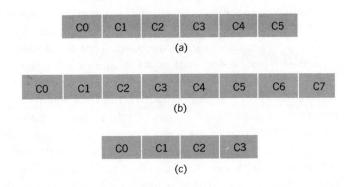

FIGURE 2.6 (*a*) IBM 7090, six 6-bit characters/word; (*b*) CDC 3600, eight 6-bit characters/word; (*c*) IBM 360, four 8-bit characters/word.

in a word is assigned by the programmer—although the machine has hardware which gives preference to some representations over others. If the machine has an ADD order that assumes that numbers are sign/absolute-value fractions, the programmer is a fool to use a twos complement representation, although it could be programmed. However, he may use the same word at one time as a sign/absolute-value number and another time as a set of BCD characters; the machine will not know the difference. Indeed, it may be useful to perform arithmetic on alphabetic data in nonnumeric jobs (such as alphabetizing).

2.1.9 Addressing memory

The uses of a single word have been discussed above. A typical job will have to deal with many thousands of words, be they numbers or strings of characters. Therefore the main memory must store many words and have some way of getting at them when they are needed. The memory can be likened to the boxes at a post office. Each box-holder has a box with a unique number which is his *address*. This address serves to identify his box. Each box or *location* in a memory has a unique number, called its *address*, associated with it. This serves to identify it for storage and retrieval. Usually, addresses are integers between 0 and $M-1$, where M is the number of locations in memory. Each location can store one word of N bits, where N is normally the same for all locations. Thus the memory may be asked to store the bit pattern 1011- - -0 in location 1027. Later on, if it is asked what is in location 1027, it is expected to reply "1011- - -0." Here the analogy with the post office box breaks down. If the post office customer fetches the contents from box 342, then box 342 is empty. A computer location cannot be empty. It consists of hardware capable of being in one of 2^N states or bit patterns, and it is always in one of them. Hence, if the contents are fetched from a location in memory, the memory retains a copy of the word. That is, its state does not change.

Section 2.1 defined a word as the minimum amount of information that could be transmitted between the memory and its environment at one time. Some of the more complex computers, the IBM 360 in particular, allow the user to refer to varying amounts of information in an instruction. It then becomes difficult to define a word precisely. Physically, the memory may have a certain width, and this could be said to be the word size. However, the physical width may have no effect on the instructions available to the user. Indeed, the IBM 360 is available in various models with different memory widths, but the models are identical from the programmer's point of view. A second definition that could be adopted is to equate the word size to the minimum amount of information that is addressable. The 360, for example, allows the user to address any 8-bit character (called a *byte*) in memory. On most machines, one can find at least one instruction that allows a single bit to be specified, so this definition could lead to a 1-bit-word characterization. As usual with computers, we must compromise and say that the word size is that number of bits used in the majority of instructions and therefore probably the most efficient to use in a calculation. With this definition, the 360 can be said to be a 32-bit-word machine, although we shall see in Section 2.6 that it can address 8-, 16-, 32-, or 64-bit quantities for fixed-length operations, and that it can manipulate strings of n 8-bit bytes for any n from 1 to 256.

Addressing memory with a number is the most common method, and all machines generally available use it. However, there does exist an important concept of *content addressing* which will be discussed in more detail in Chapters 7 and 8. In content addressing, a word is specified by stating the value of part of its contents. For example, the first 10 bits could be specified. The memory may have to return no value or several values.

2.1.10 Symbolic addressing

The information to be processed is stored in the memory and brought to the CPU for processing. For example, it may be necessary to add two numbers together and to save the result for later processing. These two numbers are in two locations in memory and the result is to be put back into memory. In Fortran and other high-level languages, this operation might be written as

$$X = Y + Z$$

We think of X as a variable which is assigned the result of adding the values of two variables Y and Z.

Corresponding to each of these variables is a memory location. Perhaps location 10571 corresponds to X, location 10732 to Y, and location 27501 to Z. The contents of locations 10732 and 27501 are to be added together and the result stored in location 10571. We shall use the notation C (10732) to mean the contents of location 10732.

The Fortran statement

$$X = Y + Z$$

is equivalent to the operation

$$C (10732) + C (27501) \text{ to be stored as } C (10571)$$

It is not always convenient to use numerical addresses when talking and writing about the computer because the action of an operation is not dependent on the particular locations used. In the above example, the important information (to the user) is that X, Y, and Z are the variables involved. Therefore we shall write

C (Y) + C (Z) to be stored as C (X)

instead.

This is a confusion of variable names and location names which is in common use, so the student should endeavor to become clear on the different uses of X, Y, Z above. In the Fortran statement X = Y + Z, we must think of X, Y, and Z as the *names* of variables, not as the variables themselves. The values of variables named Y and Z are to be added and the result is to be stored as the value of the variable named Z. In machine language, X, Y, and Z are the names of locations which contain the variables. Therefore, there are two pieces of information associated with the name Z: first, the contents of the location; and second, the actual address of the location. To avoid pedantry, we usually refer simply to Z, the context makes it clear whether the contents or the address of the location is intended. Because a name, such as Z, has an associated address, it is often called a *symbolic address*.

2.1.11 Physical organization of memory

The machine-language programmer is usually only aware of the memory as a device with M cells, such that a word of information corresponds to each of the integer addresses between 0 and $M-1$. Even at the machine-language level, he usually works through an assembly program which allows the use of symbolic addresses, so that he is unaware of actual addresses. However, at this stage it is a good idea to examine the way the hardware is organized in the physical machine.

As shown in Figure 2.7, there are two *registers*. These are devices which can store sets of bits. The *memory data register* (MDR) can store one word, while the *memory address register* (MAR) can store enough bits to represent any integer in the range 0 to $M-1$. When the CPU wishes to store a word into memory, it sends the word down the memory data *bus*. (A *bus* is a collection of wires which carry information signals or power.) It is stored in the MDR. At the same time it sends the address to the MAR along the memory address bus. It then sends a signal on the wire marked *write request*. This signal causes the memory to *decode* the address in the MAR and to use this

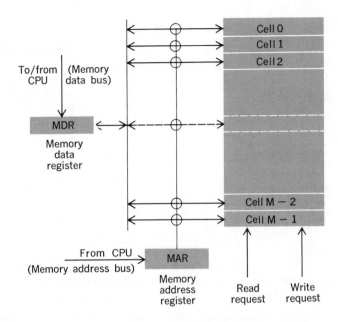

FIGURE 2.7 Memory unit.

information to select the appropriate cell. The information in the MDR is copied into the selected cell. When the CPU wishes to read a number from memory, it sends its address to the MAR and then sends a signal along the *read request* line. The memory selects the appropriate cell, copies it into the MDR, and then sends the contents of the MDR along the memory data bus to the CPU.

2.2 THE CENTRAL PROCESSING UNIT (CPU)

The CPU is capable of a number of elementary operations such as addition, subtraction, multiplication, and division. Section 2.1 discussed ways in which fixed and floating-point numbers can be represented in memory. The CPU is capable of performing arithmetic in one or more of these representations. Most large machines will perform some form of floating-point arithmetic and some form of integer arithmetic. The majority of arithmetic operations require two *operands*, that is, two numbers on which to operate. In addition, the result has to be placed somewhere. In the familiar desk calculator, there is usually a *register* or *accumulator*. An operation such as addition adds the number entered in the keyboard to the number in the accumulator, leaving

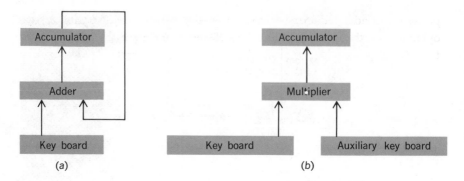

FIGURE 2.8 (*a*) Addition on a desk calculator; (*b*) multiplication on a desk calculator.

the result in the accumulator. Multiplication, however, usually multiplies the number entered in the keyboard by a number entered into an auxiliary keyboard (see Figure 2.8). Addition gets its operands from the keyboard and the accumulator, while multiplication gets its operands from two keyboards. The CPU of a digital computer may have one or more accumulators similar to the desk calculator. These will initially contain operands. The analogy of a keyboard is the memory. CPUs can be classified according to their use of accumulators in instructions. This will be done in the next four sections.

2.2.1 Three-address machines

It is not necessary to have any accumulators available to the user in the CPU if an operation of the form "C (X) + C (Y) to be stored as C (Z)" is to be performed. The CPU could be told that an ADD operation is to be obeyed, and it could be given the three addresses X, Y, and Z. Such an operation is called a *three-address instruction*. If the CPU predominantly executes three-address instructions as its basic operations, it is called a *three-address machine*. (We shall see that almost all computers will execute mixtures of instruction types, so this definition is necessarily loose.)

In order to be able to evaluate arithmetic expressions involving addition, subtraction, multiplication, and division, three-address instructions for each of these operations can be provided. The operations

Add	(ADD)	X, Y, Z
Subtract	(SUB)	X, Y, Z
Multiply	(MPY)	X, Y, Z
Divide	(DIV)	X, Y, Z

perform the indicated *binary* or *diadic* operation (that is, an operation on two operands) on the contents of locations X and Y and store the result in location Z. Thus

    DIV P, Q, R

is equivalent to

    C (P)/C (Q) to be stored as C (R)

The Fortran assignment statement

    A = B * (C + D * E − F / G)

is equivalent to

    MPY D, E, T1
    ADD C, T1, T1
    DIV F, G, T2
    SUB T1, T2, T1
    MPY B, T1, A

T1 and T2 are the addresses of two *temporary storage* locations, that is, locations which are used for scratch working storage in evaluating the expression. Note that there are five operations indicated in the expression B * (C + D * E − F/G), and that it takes exactly the same number of three-address instructions. This will be true for all expressions using only the binary operations provided by the computer, regardless of parenthesization.

2.2.2 Two-address machines

The three-address structure is not used in many machines for cost reasons. If A = B + C + D + E + F + G is to be programmed, the three-address code is

    ADD B, C, A
    ADD A, D, A
    ADD A, E, A
    ADD A, F, A
    ADD A, G, A

All but the first instruction needed only two different addresses, but the programmer had to provide three. This is recognized in the two-address machine by providing *two-address instructions*. A two-address instruction has the form

    ADD   A, B

which means

    C (A) + C (B) to be stored as C (A)

A *two-address machine* is one which uses predominantly two-address instructions. The four basic arithmetic instructions ADD, SUB, MPY, and DIV are usually provided in the form

    ADD   A, B
    SUB   A, B
    MPY   A, B
    DIV   A, B

meaning

    C (A) + C (B)
    C (A) − C (B)
    C (A) * C (B)
    C (A) / C (B)

to be stored as C (A). Note that the result is stored in the first address. The second address could have been used equally well in addition and multiplication because they are theoretically *commutative* operations; that is, C (A) + C (B) = C (B) + C (A) and C (A) * C (B) = C (B) * C (A). However, subtraction and division are not commutative; that is, C (A) − C (B) is not C (B) − C (A) and C (A) / C (B) is not C (B) / C (A). Because of this, we shall see that it is useful, although not necessary, to have *inverse* subtraction and division operations available.

An inverse operation, as the name implies, produces the "other-way-around" of the result. A two-address subtraction, SUB A,B, forms C (A) − C (B). A two-address inverse subtraction would form C(B) − C (A) and store it as C (A). A two-address inverse division would form C (B) / C (A) and store it as C (A).

The equivalent of the three-address operation MPY A, B, C can be performed by the two-address instructions as

    SUB   C, C
    ADD   C, A
    MPY   C, B

The effect of the first two instructions is to move the contents of location A to location C by first *clearing* it, that is, setting it to 0, and then adding C (A). Since this is a very common operation, it is usual to have a single two-address instruction MOVE A, B which puts C (B) into location A.

$$A = B + C + D + E + F + G$$

is equivalent to

```
MOVE   A, B
ADD    A, C
ADD    A, D
ADD    A, E
ADD    A, F
ADD    A, G
```

Note that this sequence contains one more instruction than operations in the expression. In general the equivalent two-address code will contain at least one additional instruction in order to move one of the operands into position. Let us consider the assignment statement $A = B * (C + D * E - F / G)$. This can be performed by the two-address code

```
MPY    D, E
DIV    F, G
SUB    D, F
ADD    D, C
MOVE   A, B
MPY    A, D
```

Notice, however, that this destroys the contents of locations D and F. In fact, F now contains F/G and D contains $C + D * E - F / G$. In general, this is not permissible, because the variables stored in these locations may be needed in the evaluation of other expressions. Therefore, additional move orders must be used, resulting in the code:

```
MOVE   A, D
MPY    A, E
MOVE   T1, F
DIV    T1, G
SUB    A, T1
ADD    A, C
MPY    A, B
```

This is the shortest code which will evaluate this expression without changing any of the variables on the right-hand side; that is, assuming that all of the symbolic addresses A, B, C, D, E, F, and G represent different locations. If there is a possibility that A could represent the same location as one of B, C, . . . , F, then A must be replaced by a temporary location, say T2, in the above code and the additional instruction MOVE A, T2 must be appended.

In many calculations a *unary minus* is used. This is a subtraction operation with only one operand. It is called a unary or *monadic* operation. Thus the subtraction in A = −B is unary. Some two-address machines will provide for this with either a MOVE-NEGATIVE two-address instruction or a SET-NEGATIVE, which only requires one address (the other would not be used).

2.2.3 One-address machines

In addition to saving the programmer work by requiring him to specify only two addresses rather than three, the two-address machine can also result in a lower overall cost, since less information has to be used to represent each instruction. If the cost can be reduced by decreasing the number of addresses, we naturally look for ways to reduce the number more. The conventional desk calculator uses an accumulator for one of its operands. In a similar manner, the CPU of a computer can be provided with an accumulator that will always contain one operand of a binary operation. The four basic arithmetic operations are now provided in this form

```
ADD   A
SUB   A
MPY   A
DIV   A
```

SUB A means C (AC) − C (A) stored as C (AC) where AC is the name of the accumulator. Because of the noncommutivity of the subtraction and division operations, it is convenient to have the inverse operations available also. Whereas DIV A means C (AC) / C (A) stored as C (AC), INVERSE-DIV A means C (A) / C (AC) stored as C (AC).

The accumulator of the one-address machine can be used as a scratch working register to evaluate expressions. The equivalent of the two-address MOVE operation is needed to place the contents of a memory location into the accumulator. This is often called LOAD. LOAD A means C (A) stored as C (AC). B + C + D + E can be calculated in the accumulator by

```
LOAD   B
ADD    C
ADD    D
ADD    E
```

If the result is to be stored back in memory, a MOVE from the accumulator to the memory is needed. This is called STORE A, and means C (AC) to be stored as C (A). The assignment statement $A = B * (C + D * E - F/G)$ can be calculated by

```
LOAD   F
DIV    G
STORE  T1
LOAD   D
MPY    E
ADD    C
SUB    T1
MPY    B
STORE  A
```

Note that this took two LOAD and two STORE instructions, just as the two-address machine took two MOVE instructions (plus an additional one if A could be the same as one of the right-hand-side operands). The equality of the number of LOAD, STORE, and MOVE instructions can be shown to be true for all assignment statements where only binary operations provided in the machine are used, all operands on the right-hand side are different, and it is stipulated that these operands cannot be changed.

Corresponding to the two-address machine's MOVE-NEGATIVE and SET-NEGATIVE instructions are the one address machine's LOAD-NEGA-TIVE and SET-NEGATIVE instructions. The latter requires no address since it operates on the accumulator. Because the names of these instructions are unduly long, they are abbreviated in use to a form determined by the system. On many systems, LOAD will be replaced by a name such as CLEAR AND ADD, abbreviated CLA or CAD. This refers to the way the LOAD instruction operates by first clearing the accumulator to 0 and then adding the operand to it. On other machines, such as the IBM 360, it is abbreviated to L, in order to save the programmer writing. We shall use LOAD in this book.

2.2.4 Stack or zero-address machines

If a saving is effected by reducing the number of addresses in instructions, it is natural to examine *zero-address instructions*. Since a binary operation requires two operands and both of these must be specified registers prior to the execution of the instruction, the CPU must have at least two accumulators. Machines with several accumulators which can be used in various ways have been designed. Often it becomes necessary to indicate which accumulators are to be used, which means that accumulator addresses—although they are not memory addresses in the strictest sense—have to be provided. We will discuss one such design, the IBM 360, in Section 2.6. However, there is one type of CPU design in which arithmetic orders do not require any addresses. It uses the *stack* principle, also known as the *push-down list*, the *cellar*, or the *last-in-first-out* (LIFO) *queue*.

The accumulators in a stack machine can be thought of as a stack of registers, one on top of another. We refer to the top register as the *top level*, the next one down as the *second level*, and so on. Each of these registers holds a word of information. A binary operation operates on the top of two registers, puts the result in the second level and discards the top level, leaving the result as the new top level. The operation of discarding the top level is called a POP because it can be thought of as the result of moving each word up one register so that the top one *pops* out. The inverse operation, placing a word on top of the stack as a new top level, is called a PUSH because it can be thought of as the result of pushing a new word on top, causing all of the others to move down one register. A simple analogy to keep in mind is a stack of cards. A new word is pushed into the stack by writing it on a new blank card and placing it on top of the stack. A word is popped out by removing the top card from the stack. In this analogy, ᵗhe four basic binary operations are equivalent to removing the top two cards, performing the operation on the words written on the cards, writing the result on a new blank card, and putting the new card on top of the stack. The two cards removed are thrown away. The action is shown in Figure 2.9.

A machine that uses this organization for its CPU is called a *zero-address machine*. It is obvious that if a word is to be fetched from memory or stored into memory an address must be provided, so a zero-address machine will have some instructions with addresses. Two essential instructions are LOAD and STORE. LOAD A fetches a word from memory location A and pushes

FIGURE 2.9   Zero-address addition.

it into the stack. STORE A pops a word from the stack and puts it into location A. The six basic operations for a zero-address machine are therefore:

```
LOAD    A            PUSH  C(A) STORED AS C(TL)
STORE   A                  C(TL)  STORED AS C(A).        POP
ADD           C(SL) + C(TL)  STORED AS C(SL).        POP
SUB           C(SL) − C(TL)  STORED AS C(SL).        POP
MPY           C(SL) * C(TL)  STORED AS C(SL).        POP
DIV           C(SL) / C(TL)  STORED AS C(SL).        POP
```

SL and TL stand for second level and top level respectively. As with two- and one-address machines, an inverse subtract and an inverse divide are useful instructions, although not necessary.

An assignment statement can be performed by code in many ways for any type of machine. There is always a way of coding a simple statement for a zero-address machine such that only one STORE instruction is used. (That one is needed to complete the assignment.) For example, the statement $A = B * (C + D * E - F / G)$ is equivalent to the zero-address code

```
LOAD   B
LOAD   C
LOAD   D
LOAD   E
MPY
ADD
LOAD   F
LOAD   G
DIV
SUB
MPY
STORE  A
```

This form is obtained by writing LOAD VAR in turn for each variable VAR that appears in the expression and by inserting the arithmetic instructions into the code at the first opportunity; that is, when the top two levels of the stack contain the appropriate operands.

There must be a zero-address instruction for each operation in the original expression, a one-address LOAD instruction for each operand on the right and a one-address STORE instruction for the assignment. Since there is one more operand than binary operation in the expression, an N-operation assignment statement will use N zero-address instructions and $N+2$ one-address instructions.

2.3 THE CONTROL UNIT

The CPU is required to execute a sequence of instructions. In order to make use of the high speed of a typical processing unit (10^3 to 10^6 instructions per second), it is necessary to feed instructions to the CPU at a commensurate speed. This means that they must be stored in a high-speed memory. Some early proposals for computers suggested that this memory should be separate from the data memory. However, the one-memory crowd won the day (although we shall discover that there is now a tendency to separate data and instruction storage for other reasons), so that in addition to representing numbers or alphabetic characters, a word may also represent an instruction.

The way in which the instructions are represented varies from machine to machine, so this section will only discuss the general features. We have seen that there can be zero-, one-, two-, or three-address instructions. Since memory is usually addressed by a positive integer between 0 and $M-1$, A bits, where 2^A is at least M, are needed to represent each address. In addition, some bits are needed to distinguish between the various instructions. The word may be divided into a number of *fields*, each field representing an address or the instruction. For example, if M is $65,636 = 2^{16}$ and the word length is 40 bits, the "instruction format" for a two-address machine might be as in Figure 2.10. Eight bits of instruction code allow for $2^8 = 256$ different instructions. In practice, a machine may have both one- and two-address instructions, so that more than one format must be used. For example, the IBM 7090 uses one- and two-address instructions with some special zero-address instructions.

A rule must be set up to determine which location in memory is used to provide the next instruction. In some early machines, the address of this location is provided with each order. If the accumulator structure of the machine is two-address, say, this would be referred to as a two-plus-one-address machine. The most widely known machine that provides the instruction sequence in this way is the IBM 650, with a one-plus-one address structure. This technique is used because the main memory of the 650 is a non-

8	16	16
Instruction code	Address 1	Address 2

FIGURE 2.10 Instruction format.

random access storage drum. The access time for the next instruction depends on the length of the current instruction and the locations of both. In order to keep this time low, the next instruction has to be in one of a set of optimum locations. Machines with a random access storage do not need to use such a technique.

(Advertising usage of computer manufacturers has given the description "random access" to nonrandom access devices, such as drums and disks. The description "immediate access" then has to be used for the truly random access devices such as core stores. Nonrandom access will be discussed in a subsequent chapter.)

If the address of the next instruction is not provided in the current instruction, then there must be a simple rule for calculating it. The most obvious rule is to use the next-higher location in store, and this is what the majority of computers use. A *control counter*, which is a register in the control unit containing an address-length number, contains the address of the next instruction to be obeyed. Each time that an instruction is fetched from memory, the control counter is incremented by one. The action of sending the address contained in the control counter to memory, incrementing it, and reading the instruction addressed is called the *fetch cycle*.

If instructions are always stored in successive memory locations, the memory space will be exhausted long before an appreciable amount of computation has been performed. A computer derives a lot of its power from its ability to repeat a sequence of instructions many times. This means that the sequence of successive locations must be broken and control transferred back to an earlier section of the program. A TRANSFER instruction is usually provided for this purpose. (It may also be called a BRANCH or a JUMP instruction.) It is a one-address instruction. TRA X means execute the next instruction from location X by putting X into the control counter.

The TRA instruction allows a section of code to be repeated indefinitely, but it provides no means for stopping the section of code and starting another. Therefore, *conditional transfer* instructions are provided. These can be constructed to test any internal machine condition or even external conditions such as switches. In a one-address machine the accumulator can be tested by these instructions. A typical instruction is TPL (Transfer if Plus). TPL X causes *branch address* X to be placed in the control counter if the accumulator is positive or 0. Similar orders include *transfer if minus but not zero, transfer if zero,* and *transfer if non-zero.* If the condition is met, the next instruction is taken from the branch address. If not, it is taken from the next location in sequence.

Two-address machines usually provide two-address instructions to test one location and branch to another if the test is successful. Zero-address machines usually test the top level of the stack and branch in a one-address instruction.

Conditional transfer orders can be used to construct program loops. If, for example, it is required to execute a sequence of instructions a given number of times, say N, a counter can be set to N initially and decreased by 1 after each execution of the loop. It will be 0 after the Nth pass through the loop. Thus if N is greater than 0, 2^N can be constructed by the following code for a zero-address machine:

```
      LOAD    NN        NN is the address of a location containing N.
      LOAD    TWO       TWO is the address of a location containing 2.
      TRA     B
A     LOAD    RESULT
      LOAD    TWO
      MPY               Multiply result by 2 and store back in result.
B     STORE   RESULT
      LOAD    ONE       ONE is the address of a location containing 1.
      SUB               Decrease counter in stack by 1.
      TNZ     A         Transfer control if non-zero.
      - - -
```

The TNZ (Transfer if Non-Zero) instruction is assumed to transfer if the top of the stack is non-zero, but not to pop the stack. The location to which control is transferred is indicated symbolically by writing a symbolic address in the transfer and on the left of the instruction which is the *object* of the transfer. It is evident that this symbolic address may only appear on the left of one instruction.

In some problems it is necessary to execute a sequence of instructions until a given condition is met. For example, the square root of a positive number A is the limit of the sequence X_n, $n = 1, 2, \ldots$

where $X_1 = (A + 1)/2$
$$X_n = (A/X_{n-1} + X_{n-1})/2$$

It can be shown that if X_n is calculated to infinite precision, it decreases to $\sqrt{A}$ as n increases. Therefore $X_{n+1} - X_n$ is theoretically less than 0. With finite-precision arithmetic $X_{n+1} - X_n = (A/X_n - X_n)/2$ will eventually become 0 or positive, so this fact can be used to end the *iteration*. The code for a square-root program on a one-address machine is

```
      LOAD   A
      ADD    ONE
      MPY    HALF   Initial approximation X₁.
      TRA    L1
   L2 ADD    X
   L1 STORE  X      New approximation Xₙ.
      LOAD   A
      DIV    X
      SUB    X
      MPY    HALF   Xₙ₊₁ − Xₙ = (A/Xₙ − Xₙ) * 0.5.
      TMI    L2     Stop when no further decrease (Transfer if Minus).
      - - - - - -
```

The program lines above contain the following equation:

$$X_{n+1} - X_n = (A/X_n - X_n) * 0.5.$$

(Result is in X.)
HALF is the address of a location containing $\frac{1}{2}$. A multiply by $\frac{1}{2}$ was used instead of a divide by 2, since multiplication is faster than division by a factor of 2 or 3 on most machines.

2.3.1 Instruction representation

The word length of a computer is decided by the needs of the data to be processed. The typical instruction may not require as many bits as the word provides, although in some cases it may require more. If all instructions are to occupy the same number of bits, then the maximum must be chosen. This maximum may not be the same as the length of the word. If it is smaller but close to the length of the word, then the word may as well be used as the basic instruction. Historically, this has been the most common choice. If, however, the number of bits required for an instruction is considerably less than a word, then several instructions can be *packed* into a word. The control counter must, in effect, address a part word so that it can *point* to the next instruction.

If the difference between the shortest and the longest instruction (that is, in the number of bits required) is considerable, then it is more efficient to use *variable-length instructions*. Each instruction occupies a certain number of bits, usually a multiple of some divisor of the word length such as 6 or 8, and instructions are packed into memory as tightly as possible. An example of this, the IBM system 360, will be discussed in Section 2.6 when other desirable machine features have been examined.

2.4 INSTRUCTIONS FOR INCREASING THE EFFICIENCY OF THE MACHINE

A task can be coded using only the simplest of instructions, such as those discussed above. Indeed, neither addition, multiplication, nor division are necessary, but without them an arithmetic task would take longer to program and longer to execute. Since the purpose of a digital computer is to perform a given task for the minimum cost, the job of a machine designer is to provide instructions which reduce the cost of programming and execution. This section will examine some classes of instructions and related hardware that help in this direction.

2.4.1 Index registers

It is frequently necessary to process arrays of data in a sequential fashion. For example, it may be necessary to execute the equivalent of

$$A(I) = B(I) + C(I)$$

for values of I from 1 to 1000. Let us assume that the variables $A(1)$, $A(2)$, . . . , $A(1000)$ are in locations A, A+1, . . . , A+999 in memory, where A+1 is the address one larger than the address represented by A, and similarly for the arrays B and C. The task can be executed for $I = 1$ by the one-address program

```
LOAD   B
ADD    C
STORE  A
```

but it is certainly not desirable to repeat this a further 999 times. Assuming that the machine contains one instruction per word, that the address in an instruction is on the right-hand side of the word, and that integer arithmetic in twos complement is being used, then the instruction set previously discussed can be employed to *modify* the instructions by making use of the fact that the instructions and data are in the same memory.

```
X  LOAD   B
Y  ADD    C
Z  STORE  A
   LOAD   X
   ADD    = 1
   STORE  X
```

```
      LOAD   Y
      ADD    = 1
      STORE  Y
      LOAD   Z
      ADD    = 1
   T  STORE  Z
```

= 1 is a notation for the address of a location containing fixed point 1. The instruction sequence LOAD X, ADD = 1, STORE X puts a copy of LOAD B into the accumulator, adds 1 to it, which adds a 1 to the address B (which is on the right-hand end) and stores it back where the LOAD B instruction was stored. After the sequence from X to T has been executed, the first three instructions have been modified to

```
   X  LOAD   B+1
   Y  ADD    C+1
   Z  STORE  A+1
```

If a counter to loop the required 1,000 times is added, the loop is complete. However, beware . . . at the end of execution, the first three locations have been changed to LOAD B+1,000, etc. If the loop is to be used again, it must be reset. A number of programming tricks can be used to reduce the execution time of a loop such as this. About the best that can be done is

```
      LOAD   = LOAD B              Load initial value of location X
      TRA    W
   X  LOAD   B
   Y  ADD    C
   Z  STORE  A                     A(I) = B(I) + C(I)
      LOAD   X
      ADD    = 1                   Add 1 to address
   W  STORE  X                     Update location X
      ADD    =(ADD C − LOAD B)
      STORE  Y                     Update location Y
      ADD    =(STORE A − ADD B)
      STORE  Z                     Update location Z
      SUB    = STORE A+1000
      TMI    X                     Repeat loop 1,000 times
```

Many of the small machines now on the market provide simple instructions that can be used to reduce the length of this program. Two examples are the instructions ADD TO MEMORY, which performs an addition leaving the result in the addressed memory location rather than the accumulator, and INCREMENT MEMORY BY ONE which adds 1 to a specified memory cell.

The code above has twelve instructions inside the loop, an additional two outside of the loop, and requires five additional storage locations—although $=1$ is undoubtedly used by other sections of code. Only three of the twelve instructions contribute directly to the arithmetic being performed, so, in a sense, the loop is only 25 percent efficient.

Recognizing that what is needed is an efficient scheme to modify addresses of orders in a sequential fashion, the machine designer provides one or more *index registers*. An index register is functionally similar to an accumulator in that it is a mechanism for storing a number. This number only need represent a positive integer in the range 0 to $M-1$ where the memory contains M locations, so an index register is typically shorter than a regular word. For example, if $M = 65,536 = 2^{16}$, an index register need only be 16 bits long. Each index register is usually assigned an address which must be distinguished from a memory address. It is a small integer, since there are usually only a small number of index registers. For example, if there are 15 index registers, they could be addressed by the integers between 1 and 15. The function of an index register is to provide a displacement to the address of an instruction. Each memory address in the instruction format has an associated index address. The *effective address* for the instruction is the sum of the actual address and the contents of the indicated index register. Figure 2.11 shows a typical instruction format for a 32-bit-wide, 65,536-word memory machine with 15 index registers. If the index address is 0, then the effective address is Y, otherwise the effective address is Y + C(XI) where C(XI) means the contents of index register I. We can indicate this in our program writing by using Y to mean the unindexed address Y (that is, the index bits are 0) and by using Y,I to mean the address Y indexed by index register I. Other notations are used in place of this. The 360, which separates multiple-address fields with commas, uses the parenthesized notation Y(I) to mean address Y plus the contents of register I. Other systems have used $Y + X_i$, where i is an

12	4	16
Operation code F	Index address I	Address Y

FIGURE 2.11   Instruction format with indexing.

integer. If we use the code

```
X   LOAD    B,1
    ADD     C,1
    STORE   A,1
```

for the statement $A(I) = B(I) + C(I)$, $I = 1, 2, \ldots , 1,000$, it is only necessary to arrange that I is stepped from 0 to 999 in steps of 1. Many schemes can be devised to do this efficiently; each such scheme involves the specification of instructions which act on index registers. We shall examine one design below.

Note that there are four items of information to be specified—the start of the loop in memory (X), the initial value of the index (0), the increment (1), and the end condition on the index (999). Each of these items of information is an address-length quantity. In a one-address machine, therefore, either four instructions will be needed or the value of some of the items must be assumed to be fixed by the machine. The latter approach will yield designs which are efficient for a limited class of problems, but the design should allow for the most general case. Therefore, instructions should be provided which will allow an arbitrary number to be loaded into an index register, to be added to an index register, or to be compared with an index register.

Since the contents of an index register are an address-length quantity, the number used as data in such instructions should also be address length. This means that either the value of the address contained in the instruction could be used directly as data, or the contents of the cell addressed could be used. The advantage of the former is that it is faster, requiring one less memory reference. The advantage of the latter is that it is not necessary to change the program when the data changes. For our present discussion we shall assume that the index instructions LOAD INDEX and ADD TO INDEX refer to the data in another memory location addressed by the instruction.

The end test must compare the contents of an index register with an arbitrary number. In addition to the data, a branch address is needed. This dictates either a two-address instruction in an accumulator machine or a combination of two instructions. The IBM 7094 uses some two-address instructions in these situations, whereas the 360 uses two instructions. They make use of a *condition register*.

The 360 will be discussed later. A condition register contains 1 or more bits that can be set as the result of test instructions. Conditional branch instructions test the condition register which has previously been set by comparison instructions. A one-address machine could contain a COMPARE INDEX instruction which would set a condition register, and then use the conditional branch instructions TRANSFER HIGH, TRANSFER EQUAL, or TRANSFER LOW, which might transfer if the comparison had shown the index to have the specified relationship.

A third possible organization uses the idea of a SKIP instruction. This instruction increases the control counter by an additional amount, typically 1 or 2, so that the next 1 or 2 instructions are not executed. A COMPARE instruction could conditionally skip on the basis of the result. The IBM 7094, for example, has a COMPARE ACCUMULATOR WITH MEMORY instruction which skips one location if the contents are equal or two locations if the accumulator is larger.

If a condition-register organization is used, the loop for $A(I) = B(I) + C(I)$ can be written as

	LOAD INDEX	= 0,1	Put 0 in index 1.
X	LOAD	B,1	
	ADD	C,1	
	STORE	A,1	
	ADD TO INDEX	= 1,1	Increment index 1 by 1.
	COMPARE INDEX	= 1000,1	Compare index 1 with 1,000.
	TRANSFER LOW	X,1	Jump if the index was low.

The loop now contains six instructions, three of which contain the arithmetic. There are four additional instructions, each of which provides an address-length item for the basic loop structure.

Index registers are also called *modifiers*, *tags*, *B-lines*, or *B-boxes*. On some machines, such as the IBM 7090, their contents are subtracted from the actual address to obtain the effective address. This was done to allow the indexing in a loop to be done by one additional instruction (the TIX instruction). However, it is so specialized that programs produced automatically by compilers do not usually use it. Other machines allow for multiple indexing of an address; that is, the contents of more than one index register can be added to an address. The IBM 360 is in this class.

2.4.2 Indirect addressing and immediate operands

A facility related to indexing is called *indirect addressing*. A bit in the instruction format is allocated to indicate an indirect address. If this bit is a 1, then the actual address plus the contents of an index register is used to fetch a word from memory. This is not used as the operand, but itself provides the

FIGURE 2.12   Indirect addressing.

address of the operand (see Figure 2.12). This is called *single-level indirect addressing*. Since the word fetched from memory may have bits in addition to the address bits, it could contain another indirect address bit. This could lead to *multiple-level indirect addressing*. The *effective address* is the address finally obtained for use by the instruction. Thus for a LOAD, it is the address of the data loaded into the accumulator. Indirect addressing can be used to supplement the number of index registers. If several instructions use the same element of an indexed array, say A(I), the address of A(I) can be kept in a fixed memory location and all references to it made indirect via this address. A second important application is the parameter transfer in subroutines. This will be discussed in Chapter 4. For example, suppose that a program has to square A(I) and return the result to memory for I from 1 to 1,000. Suppose further that no index register is available for I. In this case the following code could be used (an * after the instruction indicates indirect addressing):

```
X   LOAD*                   AI
    MPY*                    AI
    STORE*                  AI
    LOAD                    AI
    ADD                     = 1
    STORE                   AI
    SUB                     = 1000   Test for end of array of 1,000 elements.
    TRANSFER-IF-NEGATIVE   X
```

AI is a location initially containing the address A. It is incremented by 1 on each pass through the loop. This is similar to the instruction modification schemes above, but only one address has to be modified rather than three.

If the word fetched from memory contains enough bits to allow for flags in addition to the indirect address, then additional levels of index modification can be performed. Figure 2.12 showed the indexing being performed before the address was sent to memory. There are situations in which it is preferable to index after the indirect addressing has been done. (Such situations can occur in some of the small machines which permit the address in an instruction to reference only a small part of memory in order to minimize the number of bits used in the instruction. Indirect addressing usually allows a longer address to be fetched for accessing the remainder of memory. Since this is used as a device to get a regular address, the long address after the indirect operation should be indexed. In this case, the index bits in the original instruction should be used for the index specification.) Parameter transfer, discussed in Chapter 4, is a case where indexing is needed before the indirect addressing. Some machines give the programmer the choice. The IBM 7094 allows one level of indirect addressing with indexing beforehand, while the 360 does not allow indirect addressing.

The concept of an immediate operand is, in a sense, the inverse of indirect addressing. Many orders will call for the use of simple integer operands such as 0, 1, 2, 10, etc. If the integer is no larger than the maximum address, then the value of the address, rather than the contents of the addressed location, could be used as the operand. A number of instructions therefore will have an *immediate* option. An ADD-IMMEDIATE N instruction, for example, would add the number N to the accumulator of a one-address machine. Care must be exercised in the use of immediate operands since, if they ever have to be changed, it is necessary to modify the program rather than a data location in memory.

2.4.3 Logical operations and shifting

When nonnumeric data, such as alphabetic data, are being processed, it is often necessary to examine parts of a word. For example, in the IBM 7090, 6 BCD characters are packed into a word, each occupying 6 bits. In order to examine an individual character, it is necessary to extract a single group of 6 bits and possibly move it to a standard position in a word. The logical and shifting orders can be used for this. They are generally useful for manipulating any bit or bit string in memory.

The logical orders are bit-wise operations; that is, they treat each bit separately and identically. The three basic logical operations are AND, OR, and NOT. If a binary 1 is thought of as corresponding to *true* and binary 0 to *false*, then the result of A AND B is true if both A and B are true individually. A OR B is true if either A or B is true individually, while NOT A is true if A is false. Thus we have the *truth tables*

```
0 AND 0 = 0
0 AND 1 = 0
1 AND 0 = 0
1 AND 1 = 1

0 OR  0 = 0
0 OR  1 = 1
1 OR  0 = 1
1 OR  1 = 1

  NOT 0 = 1
  NOT 1 = 0
```

In addition, the EOR (Exclusive OR) is usually made available. It has the truth table

```
0 EOR 0 = 0
0 EOR 1 = 1
1 EOR 0 = 1
1 EOR 1 = 0
```

A one-address machine will usually provide instructions AND Y and OR Y, which perform a logical AND or OR between the contents of the accumulator and the contents of location Y in each bit position and leave the result in the accumulator. Suppose that a 36-bit accumulator contains six 6-bit BCD characters and it is necessary to extract the second from the left. Then an AND Y where Y contains

```
000000  111111  000000  000000  000000  000000
```

will set all but the second character to 0. The contents of Y are usually called a *mask* in such a use. Instead, an OR Z where Z contains

```
111111  000000  111111  111111  111111  111111
```

will set all other characters to binary 1s. Once the character has been extracted by an AND or an OR, it can be moved into a standard position by a *shift* instruction. In one-address machines, shift instructions change the accumulator by moving the bit pattern to the right or left a specified number of places. The designer will specify what happens to the bits that "fall off the end" in the shifting process and what is put into the positions vacated. If the 12-bit word 101110011110 is shifted right 4 places, the result is XXXX10111001. The 4 bits 1110 were moved off the right end of the word, and 4 bits XXXX must be specified by the designer. Possible choices include forcing the X to be 0, duplicating the left-hand end bit (in this example, 1), or using the bits that fall off the right-hand end. The latter is called a *circular shift*. The result of a 4-place circular right shift of 101110011110 is 111010111001.

Note that a single shift right or left of a positive binary number corresponds to a halving or doubling respectively, provided only 0 bits "fall off the end." Thus 011010 considered as a binary integer is 26. 110100 is 52, and 001101 is 13. The rules for negative numbers are more complex. Sign/absolute-value numbers can be doubled or halved by shifting the non-sign part of the number. Zeros should be inserted, and no non-zeros should fall off the end. Twos complement numbers can be doubled by left shifting, including the sign bit in the shift, and inserting 0s on the right-hand end provided that the sign bit doesn't change during any stage of the operation. They can be halved by right shifting, including the sign bit, and shifting in copies of the sign bit on the left-hand end. No non-zero bits may be shifted off the right-hand end. Ones complement numbers may be doubled or halved by circular shifting left or right respectively. The sign bit must not change during the operation. It is always possible to halve a number and get an approximation without overflow. Many machines make a distinction between arithmetic shifts, which are based on the number representation used and will detect overflow, and logical shifts, which will usually insert 0s or be circular. If more than one register is available in the accumulator area, then double-length shifts are usually available. These shift two or more registers which can be considered as one longer register for the shift instruction. These are useful for stripping off groups of bits from a word.

2.5 INTERRUPTS

A number of unusual conditions can arise from time to time. For example, the result of an arithmetic operation can exceed the range of the representation (this is called *overflow*), or, because of either machine or human error, the bit pattern in the next word used as an instruction may not represent any of the allowed instructions. (This is called an *illegal* instruction.) In the former case, it is possible to design instructions to test for the overflow condition (TOV—Transfer if OVerflow), although it is not desirable to have to follow every arithmetic instruction with a test. In the latter case, it is not possible to test for the condition since some action must be taken immediately. Early machines would stop on such conditions, but this only pushes the problem down one level to the operator on duty. With high-speed machines, it is desirable to take action immediately to avoid wasting time. The action required is presumably to gather some statistics about the error or unusual condition and continue with that job, if possible, or else to move on to another job. A modern computer system will use a monitor program to perform these tasks, so it is first necessary to initiate the required program.

When the control unit recognizes an error or unusual condition, it will stop executing whatever it was trying to do and branch to another location. This location is assumed to contain the start of a program to take care of the condition. Some machines will branch to a different location for each condition, others will branch to one location and store information which specifies the condition in another location or register. In either case the net result is the same, a new program has been initiated and it knows what conditions caused the initiation. This feature is called an *interrupt*.

An interrupt caused by the user's program, whether it be by illegal instructions, overflow, or similar conditions, can be likened to a transfer of control to enable the user to handle the programming more easily. This should be contrasted with an interrupt—due to a condition external to the user's program—which is a signal to the machine to initiate or terminate some other process. The latter will happen in input/output processing, to be discussed in Chapter 6, and in time sharing, which is beyond the scope of this book.

After the interrupt program has taken care of the condition causing the interrupt, it may be necessary to return to the user's program and continue execution. Because some interrupt conditions can arise from conditions external to the user's program, it should not be aware of the interrupt. Since the status of all registers and memory locations available to the user's program must not be changed, the interrupt program must save the contents of any index registers, condition registers, indicators, or accumulators that it uses and restore them to their original state after the interrupt. In order to return to the user's program, it is necessary to know the location at which execution should resume. The interrupt hardware will usually save the address contained in the control counter at the time of the interrupt and put it in some convenient register or location.

A typical interrupt mechanism will branch to a fixed location in memory, perhaps location 1, and simultaneously store the contents of the control counter into another fixed location, say 0. The program which starts in location 1 will first save any registers that it plans to use in memory, then take the necessary actions, and finally reload the registers from memory cells before executing an indirect transfer to location 0.

It is possible that other interrupt conditions could arise during the execution of the program initiated by the first interrupt. This could cause problems, because the contents of location 0 would be overwritten and lost. Therefore, during the period in which one interrupt is being serviced, others must be disabled. This is handled by a 1-bit register which contains the interrupt status. If the bit is a 0, interrupts are allowed, but the occurrence of an interrupt sets the bit to a 1, which disables further interrupts. An instruction, often called *return from interrupt*, must be added to the repertoire. This instruction transfers control (back to the interrupted program) and resets the interrupt-status register to 0, thus enabling future interrupts.

During the period in which interrupts are disabled, conditions due to other than the user's program can occur (input/output conditions, for example). Since these must eventually be serviced, they must be saved until interrupts are re-enabled. This is done by means of an interrupt-condition register. This is a register which contains a bit for each interrupt condition that can occur. The corresponding bit is set to a 1 whenever an interrupt condition arises. This register controls the interrupting mechanism and saves the condition until it can cause an interrupt. On some machines, the bits must be reset by program instructions which are included in the repertoire for that purpose. Other machines will automatically reset the interrupt bit when the condition is recognized.

The early interrupt schemes allowed the programmer to read the contents of the interrupt-condition register so that he could determine the cause of the interrupt. This provided for program flexibility at the expense of speed. In particular, it allowed the programmer to assign a priority to one interrupt over another, so that when several occurred nearly simultaneously, one could be given precedence over another. This may be necessary if some of the interrupts have to be serviced within a given period. In some applications, an interrupt can arise from an external source in *real time*. Such an interrupt must be serviced within a given time, typically within a few tens of microseconds up to a few milliseconds. Such interrupts can also occur from mechanical input/output, such as card readers. They must be given high priority, because after a given time it is no longer possible to service them.

Unfortunately, some of the programs that process interrupts may take so long to execute that other conditions are lost. In this case, it is necessary to enable interrupt during interrupt processing. This can be done by saving the return address (in location 0) elsewhere, and enabling interrupts by executing a return from interrupt. This solution, while possible, is tedious and leads to very complicated programs. Instead, it is common to build the priority into the hardware. In a *priority interrupt* scheme, the interrupts are assigned to groups and each group is assigned a priority level. We can take this priority level to be an integer between 0 and $N-1$ if there are N groups. If an interrupt condition occurs in group J, then it causes an interrupt provided that no other interrupt condition from the same or higher numbered group is in progress. In order to keep several nearly simultaneous interrupts from overwriting each others' storage, the hardware makes a different transfer for each group. Thus, in a typical design, group I may transfer to location $2I + 1$ after storing the control counter in location $2I$. This reduces the amount of work needed to determine which condition caused the interrupt.

In a large computer installation, many interrupt conditions can occur. For example, there could be as many as 20 different interrupt conditions from input/output units. At any given time, the programmer may wish to disregard some of them. To allow for this, the hardware may include a *mask register*. This is a register which contains one bit for each bit in the interrupt-condition register. The hardware looks at the interrupt-condition register "through" the mask register, that is, the condition bit and the mask bit are ANDed together, and an interrupt only occurs if the result is a 1. This is shown in the logical diagram of a 5-bit interrupt group in Figure 2.13. In this diagram we can distinguish two ways in which interrupts might be ignored. If the status is such that interrupts in this group are disabled, then the condition is saved in the interrupt register. If the mask is set to ignore a given condition, then it will not cause an interrupt regardless of the interrupt status. This is sometimes called disarming the interrupt. The mask register can also be connected in such a way that bits cannot be set into the condition register when the mask is off, or so that setting a mask bit to a 1 to reenable an interrupt condition clears the condition bit. This can prevent certain conditions from causing interrupts—conditions that arose far in the past and that are of no interest to the programmer.

The program which handles the interrupt must be in the machine with the user's program, and at least a part of it must be in the main memory. Obviously its purpose will have been defeated if the user's program is allowed to change it, whether by error or by malicious intent. To prevent this from happening, the monitor program is kept in an area of the main memory that

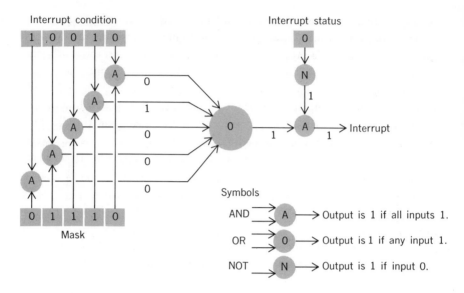

FIGURE 2.13   Interrupt logic.

is *protected*. When the user's program is in execution, it is not allowed to access the protected area of memory. (This protection is done by hardware devices.) An attempt to access protected memory is itself an error condition that will cause interrupt. Because the contents of the interrupt registers (condition, mask, status) are critical to the operation of the system, the user's program is not allowed to change them. Therefore, all instructions that change them are protected instructions that can only be executed when the interrupt-status register is 1.

The basic types of interrupt that can occur are discussed in more detail below.

2.5.1 Arithmetic conditions

These interrupts are due to unusual arithmetic conditions such as overflow. Although the user could handle them with test instructions, it is preferable to have the hardware continuously monitor the arithmetic register for the occurrence of such conditions. This procedure is more efficient in terms of execution time because it means that no additional orders need be executed until the condition occurs.

The user may wish to specify what action is to be taken after any particular condition. He may, for example, wish some conditions to be ignored and others to ultimately cause a branch to a location in his area of main memory where he has a program to handle the condition. The monitor must accept requests from the user's program to cause these actions when the conditions occur.

In addition to overflow, other conditions in this category include *divide check* (caused by attempted division by 0) and *underflow*. Underflow occurs when floating-point arithmetic gives an answer smaller than the absolute range allowed. This must be represented by 0, but it can give rise to severe inaccuracies in numerical programs. It may therefore be necessary to warn the user.

2.5.2 Illegal conditions

The various illegal conditions that can arise include attempted execution of illegal instructions and attempted access of protected memory. Just as part of the memory is protected from access by the user, so is some of the input/output equipment. Therefore, some of the input/output instructions are protected, so that attempted execution of them by the user program will cause an interrupt. When an interrupt on illegal condition occurs, the job in execution is usually terminated because it can be assumed to be due to a programmer error. Information concerning the error and the state of the user's program is output for printing and another task is initiated. An instruction may be illegal because it is protected or because it is undefined. It is not usually necessary for the system to distinguish them for the user because either is incorrect, however the hardware may distinguish them at the time of the interrupt.

2.5.3 Timer interrupts

It is desirable to time the program in execution for several reasons. Three of these are:

1. To charge the program for the amount of computer time used.
2. To detect infinite loops such as

   X TRA X

   which would never stop.
3. To allocate certain quanta of time to each of several programs in turn in a time-sharing environment.

The latter two reasons require that an interrupt be caused after a certain length of time has elapsed. There are two types of clock commonly available, the real-time clock and the interval timer. The latter is a device that can be set to a given number of seconds (or fractions of seconds) and is then counted down to 0. The end of the count provides an interrupt condition. (Some systems allow the interval timer to be reset to 0 and to cause an interrupt when the upward count reaches a quantity stored in another register.) The real-time clock is a counter which is continuously incremented so that—in principle—it provides the time of day. If it is properly initialized, it can be read later to provide the time. Some systems allow an interrupt to occur when the counter reaches a value stored in another register, others allow interrupts whenever a specified position in the clock changes. In a sense, it is identical to an upward interval timer, but it is usually in a form that provides immediate readout in an hours–minutes–seconds–fractions-of-seconds form.

2.5.4 Machine errors

Some errors are automatically detected by hardware in the machine. The design philosophy should be to provide such error detection that the probability of an undetected error will be small enough that, for each basic operation, the expected time between one such error and another will be many hours. Usually all memory devices have some error detection equipment, typically a *parity bit*.

A parity bit is an additional bit appended to a word of N bits. It is always set so that the total number of bits equal to 1 is even (odd). This is called an even (odd) parity scheme. This provides for single-error detection. If a single error occurs in a word, say a bit is changed from a 0 to a 1, then the number of 1 bits is changed from even to odd. Therefore no single error in a word can escape detection, although a double error can. If the probability of a bit error in a word is independent of all other bit errors, and is, say, 1 chance in 10^9 for each memory fetch, then the probability of 2-bit errors simultaneously is 1 chance in 10^{18}. If the memory cycle is 1 microsecond (10^{-6} seconds), then the expected time between undetected memory errors has been increased from 10^3 second to 10^{12} seconds or about 3×10^4 years.

If the probability of errors is too large, then it may be necessary to use automatic error correcting schemes.† A simple example will illustrate the point.

Suppose the 5-by-5 array of bits in Figure 2.14 is to be stored. By storing an additional row and column of bits such that the column and row parities

† A discussion of this much-studied problem can be found in W. W. Peterson, "Error Correcting Codes," M.I.T. Press, Cambridge, Mass., 1961.

1	0	0	1	1	1
0	1	1	0	0	0
1	1	0	1	0	1
1	0	(1)	1	1	1
0	1	1	0	1	1
1	1	0	1	1	0

FIGURE 2.14

are all even, a single-error correcting code is formed. In the example, the circled bit has been changed from a 0 to a 1 so that the parities of the 3d column and the 4th row are incorrect. This indicates that the circled bit is incorrect. A double error will always be detected because there will be parity errors in two rows or columns. A triple error could be mistaken as a single error. For example, if the 3 bits in square boxes in Figure 2.14 are wrong, this would be indistinguishable from a single error in the circled bit.

Whatever scheme of error detection is used, the monitor program will have to deal with the problems caused by detected but uncorrected errors. An attempt can be made to repeat the operation that caused the error, but if this attempt fails, the task involved may have to be abandoned or repeated from the beginning.

2.5.5 Input/output conditions

These will be discussed in greater detail in the chapter on input/output. We shall see in that chapter that I/0 operations can be performed simultaneously with computation. In order to bring the two parallel processes into step when necessary, the input/output events can interrupt the CPU execution sequence.

In a time-sharing environment, interrupts from input/output equipment may not be related to the program currently in execution. It must therefore be possible to save the conditions until the appropriate program *has* been put into execution.

2.6 THE IBM SYSTEM 360 MACHINES

This section will discuss the organization of the memory and CPU of the System 360. In this way a particular example of machine organization—from the point of view of our earlier general discussion—will be provided. The student should be able to examine the manner in which the 360 achieves its various goals and to realize why certain features are present. The 360 system is a series of computers ranging from the model 30 to the model 75. (Two other models, the 20 and the 91, are left out of this discussion because they do not fit fully into the range; that is, they are partly incompatible with others.) The five basic computers in the range (models 30, 40, 50, 65, and 75) are of increasing speeds (but not in proportion to their numbers), and they differ in their electrical construction. However, they are identical as far as the programmer is concerned.

An enterprise—be it industrial or academic—that uses a computer expends a lot of effort and money in the preparation of programs for its machine. In fact, it is generally believed that the expenditures on programming are now considerably greater than the expenditures on hardware. When it becomes necessary for an organization to increase the amount of its computing power, the cost of rewriting these programs can be prohibitive. The obvious solution is to avoid rewriting them, but the problem is, "how?"

The use of procedure oriented languages is supposed to ease the problem. Ideally, only the compiler need be rewritten, and then all other programs can be retranslated. Life, unfortunately, falls far short of this utopian goal. In order to achieve efficiencies, many programs will not restrict themselves to the *machine independent* part of the language but will use features of the particular translator that will not be available on other machines. In spite of standards being set, there is no consistency between translators for the "same" language among different manufacturers, or even among different machines from the same manufacturer.

A second solution is for the purchaser not to buy a different machine, but to purchase additional versions of the machine that he already owns. The drawback to this solution is that the computing power of a system tends to increase faster than its cost. In fact, a "square law" has been observed to be a close approximation to the relationship. That is, the computing power is roughly proportional to the square of the cost, so that if the system cost is doubled, it is about four times as powerful. (In other words, two machines will have double the computing power of one; but a *larger* machine, at twice the price of the small one, may have *four times* the power.) Therefore, if a computer owner needs to increase his computing capacity, it would be more economical for him to purchase or rent a larger system than to duplicate the system he already has; provided, of course, that the costs of reprogramming are not excessive.

A third solution, the one chosen by **IBM** in its System 360 and by other companies in similar series of machines, is to manufacture a range of machines identical in their machine language. A customer may then change from one member of the range to a faster member if he needs additional processing power.

Each of the models in the System 360 has many optional attachments. The configuration of I/0 equipment (discussed in Chapter 6) is at the discretion of the buyer. Also, the amount of main memory and the sets of different instructions provided are optional. The instructions are divided into three groups. The first group is basic and is provided on all processors. It consists mainly of fixed-point binary arithmetic instructions. We shall see later that they could be called zero-, one-, or two-address instructions, depending on the viewpoint taken. For purposes of classification, we shall say that they are basically zero- and one-address instructions for a machine with more than one accumulator. The other two groups of instructions are optional on the slower machines but are provided as standard on the model 75. The first is referred to as the "commercial set," consisting mainly of two-address variable-length-decimal arithmetic instructions. The second, called the "scientific set," consists mainly of one-address floating-point binary arithmetic instructions. (In fact, floating-point is hexadecimal base-16 arithmetic, but the distinction will be seen to be relatively unimportant except for consideration of numerical errors.)

In the following sections we shall discuss the machine features in more detail. However, this discussion is intended to be no more than a survey.†

2.6.1 The memory

The main memory of the 360 is more flexible than the organizations discussed earlier. This was done to allow for commercial and nonnumeric working,

† The student who is going to program the 360 in assembly (machine) language should refer to the "Principles of Operation" manual, document number A22-6821, available from IBM.

in which the basic unit of information is usually a character, and for numeric working, in which the basic unit of information is a word. One of the problems facing machine designers is the length of word to choose. If it is too short, then the range of numbers that can be represented is inadequate for most uses; if it is too long, then there are more bits than most jobs require, making the machine unnecessarily expensive. The 360 is a 32-bit-word machine, but it is arranged so that any multiple of 8-bit *bytes*, from 1 to 256, can be handled as a unit. Variable-length operations—typically from the commercial set—can operate on the strings of bytes, while fixed-length operations are available to operate on 16-bit groups (halfwords or half precision), 32-bit groups (single or full words), and 64-bit groups (doublewords). The types of data groups allowed are shown in Figure 2.15. Figure 2.15*a* shows a 32-bit group which can be used in the logical operations (AND and OR, etc.). Figure 2.15*b* shows a 16-bit halfword with a sign bit on the left, while Figure 2.15*c* shows a 32-bit fullword also with sign. The two latter forms can be used in the fixed-point arithmetic operations, which use twos complement arithmetic. Figure 2.15*d* and *e* shows fullword and doubleword floating-point numbers. They both start with a sign bit, are followed by a 7-bit characteristic which contains 64 plus the exponent of the number as a

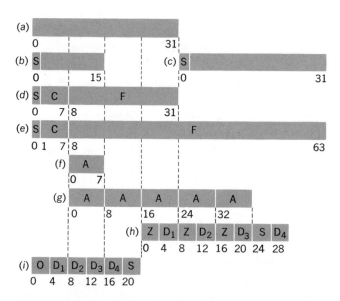

FIGURE 2.15 Data formats in IBM 360.

binary integer (sometimes called the *excess 64* representation). The exponent is to the base 16 rather than the base 2, which means that the 24- or 56-bit binary fraction that follows is normalized by shifts of 4 bits at a time so that it is in the range $\frac{1}{16} \leq$ fraction < 1. The fraction times the power of 16 specified by the characteristic gives the absolute value of the number, so we can say that floating-point representation is by sign/absolute-value for the fraction, and by characteristic, or excess 64, for the exponent. Figure 2.15*f* shows a single 8-bit byte which can be used either as a logical quantity, or as a special case of a string of bytes shown in Figure 2.15*g*. Operations are available which move strings of bytes and combine them with other strings. Figure 2.15*h* and *i* shows the two forms in which decimal data can appear. In the former, the zoned decimal, each digit is represented in 8 bits, the same form that is used for character representation. In this representation (EBCDIC, Extended BCD code for Information Interchange), the left 4 bits are 1s and the right 4 bits represent the binary value of the number. The left 4 bits are called the *zone*. The zone of the last byte contains the sign of the number. If it is 1011 or 1101, then the number is negative, while if it is 1010, 1100, 1110, or 1111, the number is positive. Zoned decimal is used by some I/0 devices. Arithmetic is always done in the packed decimal form (as shown in Figure 2.15*i*) so as to conserve memory space and hence processing time, which is often proportional to the number of memory references required for the instruction and its data. In packed decimal, two binary-coded decimal digits, each in 4 bits, are packed in each 8-bit byte. The last byte of the string may only contain one digit on the left, and a 4-bit sign group on the right. Instructions are available to convert from packed to zoned form and back.

ADDRESSING

The program must be able to refer to each of the various types of data allowed. It is necessary, therefore, to specify the type of data and where it is in memory. This is done in the instruction by indicating its memory address, its length, and its type. Instructions that handle binary and logical data in half-, full-, or double-length words are called fixed-length operations. Those that handle strings of characters or decimal digits are called variable-length operations. They include a specification of the length of the operands involved. In order to refer to any 8-bit byte in memory, each byte is assigned a unique address which is a number between 0 and $N-1$, where N is the number of bytes of storage available. The main memory of a 360 machine can contain between 8,192 and 1,048,576 (2^{13} and 2^{20}) bytes. Slower storage can be added to increase this to 8,388,608 (2^{23}) bytes. We say that the 360 has byte addressing, because it is possible to specify any byte individually. Variable-length operations that use strings of bytes specify the address of the leftmost (lowest address) and the number of bytes involved. Such strings of bytes can start anywhere in memory. Fixed-length operations involving 2-, 4-, or 8-byte quantities only need specify the leftmost byte address. The instruction indicates whether it is a half-, full-, or doubleword operation. However, there is an addressing restriction that must be followed in these fixed-length operations. The address must be divisible by the length of the data. That is, halfword data must start on even byte addresses (called a halfword boundary), fullword data must start on addresses divisible by 4 (called fullword boundaries), and double-length data must start on double-word boundaries or addresses divisible by 8. This restriction makes it easier for the machine designer to build a fast machine.

2.6.2 The central processing unit of the 360

The one-address organization is the most common for scientific computers, while the two-address organization is perhaps more common for commercial machines. We have seen that some of the drawbacks of these organizations are that the two-address machine uses too many bits of memory for specifying addresses, and the one-address machine uses twice as many "extra" instructions in order to load and store the accumulator. The calculation A * B + C * D uses a store after the first multiply in order to free the accumulator for the second. We studied one multiple-register organization, the zero-address machine, which avoided this.

In the early stages of the 360 design, many organizations were investigated with a view to determining the best way in which the registers could be used in the CPU. Since they are faster than main memories, there is an advantage to using them for temporary storage of intermediate results that occur in calculations such as A * B + C * D. Since there are typically fewer of them than there are locations in the main memory, it is possible to address them with fewer bits, so that the amount of memory used for storing instructions could be less. They could be treated as a stack in a zero-address organization, a small additional fast memory, or (as is done in the 360) a set of accumulators in a basically one-address organization.

Figure 2.16 shows two groups of registers, four 64-bit floating-point registers and sixteen 32-bit fixed-point or general-purpose registers. Each of these registers can be treated as an accumulator (with certain exceptions in the multiply and divide instructions discussed later). Because there are 16 different fixed-point accumulators, each of the fixed-point instructions must

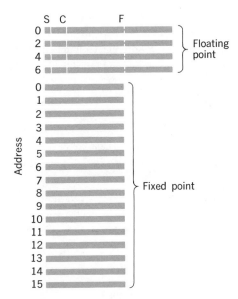

FIGURE 2.16   CPU registers in IBM 360.

not only specify the memory address but also the accumulator involved. Therefore, the fixed-point instructions take the form

L	3,A	Load accumulator 3 from location A.
ST	5,B	Store accumulator 5 into location B.
A	4,C	Add location C to accumulator 4.
S	15,D	Subtract location D from accumulator 15.
M	4,E	Multiply (discussed later).
D	6,F	Divide (discussed later).

These operate with twos complement numbers. They are, strictly, two-address instructions, but the address of the accumulator only requires 4 bits; it is therefore shorter than a normal memory address. Each of these instructions fetches or stores a 32-bit unit of data into the memory. A 16-bit halfword may also be used in the instructions LH (Load Halfword), AH (Add Halfword), SH (Subtract Halfword), STH (STore Halfword), and MH (Multiply Halfword). There is no divide halfword.

In order to allow for the contents of one register to be used as an operand, there is a form of most instructions in which the data address is a register address. These are called RR (Register-to-Register) instructions. They take the form:

LR   3,6   Copy contents of register or accumulator 6 into register 3.
AR   5,0   Add register 0 to register 5.
SR   2,7   Subtract register 7 from register 2.
MR   4,9   Multiply (discussed later).
DR   10,1 Divide (discussed later).

The STR (STore Register) instruction is not provided since it is, of course, identical to the LR (Load Register) instruction.

Floating-point arithmetic is handled similarly, except that the floating-point registers are used. These only have addresses 0, 2, 4, and 6, and are all double length. However, single-length arithmetic may be performed on them, in which case the low order 32 bits can be ignored, in general. The floating-point instructions follow the same pattern as the fixed-point instructions, and are:

LE   2,A   Load the 32-bit floating-point number from location A to floating register 2.
STE 4,B   Store floating register 4 in B to 32 bits.
AE   0,C   Add C to register 0.
SE   4,D   Subtract D from register 4.
ME   4,E   Multiply register 4 by E.
DE   6,F   Divide register 6 by F.

Double-length operands from memory are used in the instructions LD, STD, AD, SD, MD, and DD. Each of these instructions, except for STE and STD, has a register-to-register form of LER, AER, SER, MER, DER, LDR, ADR, SDR, MDR, and DDR. Thus

SDR 2,6

means subtract the double-length number in floating-point accumulator 6 from accumulator 2, also considered as a double-precision number.

Single-precision floating-point multiplication results in a double-precision answer in the register because the number of digits in a product is the sum of the number of digits in each operand. However, single-precision floating-point division uses only the first 32 bits of the addressed accumulator(s). This differs from fixed-point division, discussed next.

Fixed-point multiply and divide operations produce or start with double-precision numbers respectively. A fixed-point multiplication of a single-precision number in a register (the multiplicand) by a single-precision number from a register or from memory (the multiplier) produces a 64-bit result in a pair of registers. The multiplicand and the multiplier are 32-bit twos complement integers, the result is a 64-bit twos complement integer; its sign is at the left of the first register, and the integer consists of the remaining 31 bits of that register followed by the 32 bits of the second register. These registers must always be an even-odd pair; that is, the most significant part of the result is in an even-numbered register, while the least significant part is in the next-higher-numbered (odd) register. The multiplicand *must be in the odd-numbered register*, but the multiply instruction *must specify the even number*, or the instruction is illegal. The contents of the even-numbered register before the instruction do not affect the result (unless it supplies the multiplier). Thus, to form I * J + K * L in location N, assuming that the result is a single-precision integer, we can write

```
L    5,I
M    4,J
L    7,K
M    6,L
AR   5,7
ST   5,N
```

regardless of signs of the numbers, because the double-precision version of a twos complement integer has its sign bit duplicated to the left. Consequently, the leftmost bit of the odd-numbered register will contain a copy of the sign in the even-numbered register if the result is within the range of a single-precision register. The action of the multiply operation is shown in Figure 2.17.

Division is also shown in that figure. It starts with a double-precision number similar to that produced by the multiply operation and leaves a quotient in the odd-numbered register and a remainder in the even-numbered register. The divide instruction must also refer to the even-numbered register or an error will result.

In all arithmetic instructions, it should be noted that overflow can occur if the result is too large to be represented. In the 360, this can cause an interruption, or it can set a bit in the condition register (to be discussed in Section 2.6.4).

In some cases, it is desirable that overflow not be detected. "Logical" instructions are provided for that purpose. AL (Add Logical), ALR, SL (Subtract Logical), and SLR perform additions and subtractions in twos complement without checking overflow, otherwise they are identical to the regular add and subtract operations. Floating-point instructions normally

Operand from memory or register

MULTIPLICATION: Multiplier M
DIVISION: Divisor D

FIGURE 2.17   Fixed-point multiply/divide register usage.

produce a normalized result; that is, one in which the fraction is as large as possible. There are also instructions to produce unnormalized results in floating point. These results are not normalized after the operation has been completed for reasons of error control which will not be studied here.

There are many other instructions which involve the fixed-point registers. It is not the purpose of these notes to provide an exhaustive listing. That can be found in the IBM manual. There are the usual range of logical instructions, such as AND, OR, shifting, and complementing. The shift instructions can affect a single register, such as

    SRL 3,5

which shifts register 3 right logically five places, inserting 0s in the top five places of the result. The shift can also affect double registers, such as

    SLDL 4,7

which shifts registers 4 and 5 as a double-precision word left logically seven places. Seven 0s are inserted at the right-hand end of register 5, the top 7 bits of register 5 are placed in the bottom 7 of register 4, and the top 7 bits of 4 are discarded. Shift instructions are also available for doubling and halving single- and double-precision fixed-point numbers in the registers. These duplicate the sign bit on right shifts and can set the overflow indicator on left shifts.

The variable-length operations are true two-address instructions, specifying two memory addresses (and the length of the operands). They include instructions for moving data from one memory location to another, for comparing two strings of characters, and for decimal arithmetic. The variable-length compare instruction and the variable-length move instruction have a single-length specification of 8 bits. This means that from 1 to 256 bytes can be moved from one contiguous set of byte locations to another by a single instruction. The arithmetic instructions, on the other hand, include length specifications for both operands. Each is 4 bits, so the operands can be from 1 to 16 bytes long. Since decimal arithmetic operates on the packed format, there can be from 1 to 31 decimal digits plus a sign group in a number. The instruction

    AP   A,B

adds the packed decimal number in location B to the number in location A. We shall see in the next chapter that the length of the operands may not have to be directly specified by the programmer. If they do, however, and B was the first address of a 5-byte number while A corresponded to a 7-byte number, we could write it as

    AP   A(7),B(5)

In multiplication and division, there are additional restrictions placed on the lengths of the operands in order to guarantee that the results will fit into the available space in the first address. These can be found in the "Principles of Operation" manual. †

The 360 also provides special instructions for converting from one representation to another. The conversion from packed to zoned decimal and back has already been mentioned. Binary integers can be converted to and from decimal integers by single instructions, and there are translation and editing instructions which can be used to convert from one binary representation of characters to another. They can also perform operations such as replacing all of the 0s on the left of an integer decimal number by blanks, so that the

† IBM document number A22-6821.

number 000345.67 would be printed as bbb345.67, where b stands for the blank character.

2.6.3 Indexing

One of the advantages of the 360 organization with multiple accumulators is that these accumulators can and do serve as the index registers. An index register is represented in a 4-bit address in an instruction, so that all 16 registers could be used. However, it is necessary to allow for no indexing, so that accumulator 0 is not allowed as an index register. If the index address is between 1 and 15, the contents of that accumulator is added to the address of the instruction, but if it is 0 it is not. The maximum-size address that is allowed is 24 bits, so after the arithmetic, the top 8 bits of the address are discarded. The remaining 24 bits must specify an address that is within the storage capacity of the machine in use. Many instructions, typically those we have termed one-address instructions, allow double indexing; that is, the address can be modified by two index registers. In the next section we shall see that there is a special purpose for the second indexing, so that it should not be normally used by the programmer. If he does wish to use it, then it can be specified by writing

```
L   4,23(6,9)
```

which says that register 4 should be loaded from the (byte) location "23 plus the contents of registers 6 and 9." This must result in an address which is a multiple of 4, because of the requirements of the load instruction.

Because the index registers and the fixed-point accumulators are one and the same, no additional instructions are needed for arithmetic on the index registers. The test instructions for arithmetic results can also be used for the index test. They are discussed in the next section. Indirect addressing is not provided on the 360. The effect of using a location to provide the address of another location is achieved by the load instruction. Thus the sequence

```
L   4,A
L   4,0(4)
```

first loads the contents of location A into register 4, and then loads the contents of location "0 + contents of register 4" into register 4. In other words, A contains the address of the data loaded into register 4. If only single indexing is required, the second index need not be specified, although, of course, one could write for the second instruction above:

```
    L  4,0(4,0)
or  L  4,0(0,4)
```

2.6.4 Control

Instructions in the 360 are fetched from memory in order. The fetching is controlled by a control counter which is 24 bits long. We shall see that instructions can be multiples of 2 bytes in length and must start on halfword boundaries. Therefore, the control counter must always contain an even number. The control counter forms a part of what is known as the "program status word." It is shown in Figure 2.18. It also includes bits of information that indicate the status of the program in execution. The majority of bits in the status word are of no interest to most programmers. The second 32 bits contain the control counter in the last 24 bits; and they contain the instruction-length code, condition code, and program mask in the first 8 bits. The instruction-length code indicates the number of 16-bit halfwords in the current instruction (1, 2, or 3), the condition code is discussed below, while the program mask concerns the interrupt status of the program.

A branch instruction causes the last 24 bits of the PSW to be changed. Thus

```
    B  T
```

causes an unconditional branch to location T. Conditional branching is performed by means of the condition code in the program status word. This code is set as the result of a number of instructions. In particular, the add and subtract instructions set the code to be 0, 1, 2, or 3 as the result is 0, less than 0, greater than 0, or overflowed, respectively. The BC (Branch on Condition)

FIGURE 2.18 360 program status word.

instruction is used to test the condition code. The BC instruction contains a 4-bit group (in place of the usual accumulator address) which specifies the condition to be tested. If the bits in this group are numbered 0 through 3, then a branch occurs if the bit corresponding to the condition code is a 1. For example, the instruction

```
BC   10,T
```

will cause a transfer to location T if condition 0 or 2 is true, since 10 decimal is 1010 binary. Thus it is a branch on ≥ 0 after an add or subtract. To add accumulators 3 and 5 together and to branch to location S if the result is less than or equal to 0, we can write

```
AR   3,5
BC   12,S
```

The AR (Aid from Register) instruction sets the condition code to be 0 if the result is 0 or 1 if negative. The BC (Branch on Condition) 12 branches if code 0 or 1 is set, since 12 decimal is 1100 binary. In order to test a number already in a register, there is an instruction LTR (Load and Test from Register), which loads one register from another as an LR does, but also sets the condition code as for the add instruction. Thus to branch if register 3 is strictly positive, we can write

```
LTR   3,3
BC    2,T
```

The LTR instruction does not change register 3, but it does set the condition code to 2 if it is strictly positive. Since 2 is binary 0010, the BC 2 branches in this case.

It was stated that the instructions occupy 1, 2, or 3 halfwords. The designer of a machine must choose the most efficient way in which to pack instructions into words. The fewer bits per instruction, the less memory space and time required for instruction fetching. Some instructions in the 360 require two memory addresses, and such instructions will require more than 32 bits. If all instructions are made the same length, then many will waste bits of memory. To overcome this, the designers of the 360 chose to use variable-length instructions. They could have used multiples of 8-bit bytes to get even more flexibility, but they simplified the situation somewhat by restricting the freedom to three different sizes. Five different formats of instructions are

Ri — Register containing operand i, i = 1, 2, 3.

Xi, Bi — Register containing two index quantities for operand i.

D — Adders to be added to index register for operand i address.

FIGURE 2.19   Instruction formats.

shown in Figure 2.19. It is not necessary that the programmer know every detail of instruction representation, but there are some key points that must be understood before the 360 can be used. After that, the programmer can use the reference manual to determine the format of an instruction when it is needed.

We see from the figure that only 12 bits are allowed for the address labeled D. Since 24 bits of address are needed, there seems to be a problem. In the 360 terminology, these addresses are called *displacements*. They should not be thought of as the principal memory address, but rather as the distance from the address in one of the index registers to the required address. This means that an instruction will always require at least one index register unless its address is in the first 4096 ($=2^{12}$) bytes. Conventionally, the second index is used for this, and it is called a *base register*. It is labeled B in Figure 2.19 to distinguish it from the index-register address labeled X. The purpose of using short addresses is simply to save memory space. It normally takes 16 bits in the 360 (12 displacement bits and 4 base-address bits) instead of the 24 of the actual address. At first sight, the 360 appears to be very difficult to program if one always has to worry that there is an appropriate address in a base register to use in each instruction. This is true to a limited extent, but fortunately the assembler will take care of many of the problems, as will be seen in the next chapter. Note that in the instruction formats in Figure 2.19 a displacement always appears with a base-address register. Only one format, the RX format, has a second index register which is also added to the effective address. R always refers to a register address, I is an 8-bit "immediate" quantity used in some instructions, while L_1 and L_2 are the lengths -1 of the two operands in the SS format (as used in decimal add, for example).

In order to place addresses in the registers used for base addresses, the load instructions can be used. There is also one important branch instruction that can be used to place the contents of the control counter into a register. This enables the programmer to use it as a base for future branch instructions. The instruction is the BAL (Branch And Link).

        BAL   15,T

places the second half of the PSW into register 15 and changes the control counter to contain the address T. Since the control counter always contains the address of the next instruction to be obeyed, register 15 now contains the address of the instruction following the BAL, and the next instruction executed is from location T.

The BAL instruction is also very important for subroutine linkages, discussed in Chapter 4. It is used with another form of the branch instruction, the BR (Branch to Register), in which the branch address is taken from the register. Thus the code

        ---
        BAL   3,S
    B   AR   2,4

    S   BR   3

causes location address B to be placed in register 3, a branch to location S, followed by a branch to the contents of register 3, which takes control back to the AR instruction. The register form of this instruction is BALR R1,R2, which places the control counter into R1 and branches to the address given in register R2 provided that R2 is not register 0. If register 0 is specified, then no branch takes place, so that BALR R,0 can be used to place the control counter into register R. Thus

        BALR 2,0
        B   6(2)
        xxxx   Halfword (16 bits) of data.
        LH   3,4(2)

would set register 2 to the address of the branch instruction and branch 6 bytes beyond the branch. Since the branch instruction is 4 bytes long, this would transfer control to the LH instruction, which would load the halfword of 16 bits preceding it into register 3. Register 2 could be used as a base register for the next 4,095 bytes of program.

SAMPLE 360 PROGRAM

This program prints a table of N, 1/N, N^2 and SQRT(N) for N = 1 to 100. 1/N is printed to four digits after the point, while the integer part of SQRT(N) is calculated. The arithmetic is done in binary fixed point, and the results are converted to decimal and then to character strings using the special 360 instructions for that purpose. SQRT(N) is calculated using the Newton iteration

$$x_0 = (1 + N)/2$$
$$d_j = (N/x_j - x_j)/2 \qquad j = 0,1,2, \ldots$$
$$x_{j+1} = x_j + d_j$$

Since the x_j theoretically converge downward to the square root, the finite-precision integer part of d_j will eventually be 0 or positive, at which time the iteration can stop.

All arithmetic is done with integers. Since 1/N is a fraction, 10,000/N is calculated in order to get the four digits of the fractional part. Note that this means that the result for 1/N is truncated rather than rounded.

This program is intended to be read in conjunction with the 360 Principles of Operation manual.

	OPEN	(OUTPTDCB,(OUTPUT))	This will be discussed briefly in Chapter 6. It tells the system that the name OUTPTDCB is associated with a set of output information.
	LA	2,1	Load address uses the address (1) and loads it directly into register 2. It will be used for incrementing the count in the BXLE instruction later.
	LA	3,100	100 is the end test for the loop.
	LA	4,1	Register 4 holds the value of N, initially 1.
LOOP	CVD	4,N	Convert to decimal changes the contents of the register (4) into packed decimal format in 8 bytes starting at location N, which must be on a double-word boundary.

MVC	LINE+10(3),ED1	Move characters moves 3 characters from the field starting at ED1 into the field starting at LINE+10. These characters are defined at the end of the program.
ED	LINE+10(3),N+6	N+6 addresses the last 2 bytes of the packed decimal number N. These contain three decimal digits and the sign of N. They are edited into a form with leading 0s suppressed by the ED instruction.
L	7,=F'10000'	This loads register 7 from a location which will contain fixed point 10000. The LA instruction could not be used because its address would be greater than 4095.
SR	6,6	This clears register 6. It is necessary because the division to follow divides the double-length number in registers 6 and 7.
DR	6,4	Divide register 6 by register 4. The quotient is in 7 and the remainder in 6. The quotient is the integer part of 10000/N.
CVD	7,N	Convert the quotient to packed decimal.
MVC	LINE+20(6),ED2	Move characters for editing.
ED	LINE+20(6),N+5	This time, 5 characters from the packed decimal number are edited, and a period is added from the edit field for a decimal point.
LR	7,4	Move binary form of N to register 7 and multiply it by N.
MR	6,4	
CVD	6,N	Convert it to decimal
MVC	LINE+30(5),ED1	and edit it also.
ED	LINE+30(5),N+5	This puts square of N into LINE+30.
LA	5,1	1 to register 5.
AR	5,4	Add N to register 5.
SRA	5,1	Shift right arithmetic. Halves N+1.
LOOP1 LR	7,4	N to register 7.
SR	6,6	Clear register 6.
DR	6,5	N/x
SR	7,5	N/x − x
SRA	7,1	(N/x − x)/2
BC	10,LOOP2	Branch if positive or 0 condition.

	AR	5,9	New value of iterant x.
	B	LOOP1	Repeat square-root iteration.
LOOP2	CVD	5,N	Convert square root to decimal.
	MVC	LINE+40(3),ED1	Get edit field
	ED	LINE+40(3),N+6	and edit square root for printing.
	PUT	OUTPTDCB,LINE	This tells the system to print the 133 characters starting in LINE.
	BXLE	4,2,LOOP	Register 2 is added to register 4 to increment N by 1. If the result is less than or equal to register 5 (the odd register equal to or greater than 4 by 1), then a branch occurs. Thus the loop is repeated while N is less than 101.
	CLOSE	(OUTPTDCB)	Informs the system that output printing is over for this program.
	ABEND	16,DUMP	Will cause a dump of core for debugging purposes.
OUTPTDCB	DCB	DSORG=PS,MACRF=PM,DDNAME=SYSPRINT, LRECL=133,BLKSIZE=133,RECFM=FA	Tells the system about the output.
LINE	DC	CL133' '	Reserves 133 spaces for the output line.
N	DS	D	Reserves one double-precision word for N.
ED1	DC	X'2020202020'	A hexadecimal string for editing.
ED2	DC	X'214B20202020'	Ditto.

PROBLEMS

1. Add the following four signed binary numbers together

    ```
      1.00110
    + 0.01101
    + 0.10101
    + 1.11101
    ```

    as if all four are in the (a) sign/absolute-value, (b) twos complement, or (c) ones complement number representations.
2. What is the result of multiplying 1.0010 by 1.0101 as numbers in each of the representations?
3. Divide 0.01010111 by 0.1001 to get a sign, a 4-bit quotient, and a positive remainder in each of the three representations.

4. How many different representations of 0 are there in an N-bit ones complement number?

5. What is the range of an N-bit ones complement fraction?

6. How many bits are required to represent all numbers between -1 and $+1$, with an error of not more than 0.0001 decimal, in the sign/absolute-value representation?

7. What are the answers to questions 4, 5, and 6 for twos complement numbers and sign/absolute-value numbers?

8. The analogous system to twos complement binary is the tens complement decimal system. Describe it.

9. By analogy with ones complement, what is the nines complement system?

10. Express -6, 17, and -23 in sign/absolute-value, ones complement, and twos complement for machine using a sign-plus-5 bits of binary information for representing integers.

11. How many bits are needed to represent an address in a memory with (*a*) 4,096 locations, (*b*) 131,072 locations, and (*c*) 32,768 locations?

12. *a.* Using the one-address instructions LOAD and STORE and the zero-address instructions ADD and MPY for a stack machine, write a code to calculate

(A * (B + C + D) * E + E * F) * (B + C + D)

using as few instructions as possible.

b. If the instruction DUP (short for *duplicate*) puts a copy of the top of the stack as a new top level (so that the sequence

```
DUP
ADD
```

doubles the top of the stack), how short can the code be made?

13. Suppose there is a machine with the three-address instruction

```
SBTST   A, B, P
```

(and no others) which first subtracts the contents of location B from the contents of location A, returns the result to location A, and then branches to location P for the next instruction if the result is 0, otherwise takes the next instruction in sequence. The arithmetic is presumed to be integer. Write a program using only this instruction to put the absolute value of the contents of location Y into location X. C(Y) may not be changed. *Hint.* Count C(Y) and $-$C(Y) until one of them reaches 0. This program can be written with nine instructions, using only three extra temporary storage locations for scratch work and one location containing a constant. *Note:* As a matter of programming practice, it must not be assumed that the contents of locations changed by the program are initialized. Rather, this must be done at the start of the program. If this rule is followed, the segment can be reused many times during one computer run.

14. If memory locations A, B, C, D, E, F, G, and Z are all different, and the contents of all except for Z may not be changed, write programs for the simple three-, two-, one-, and zero-address machines discussed above to perform the calculation $Z = (A + B + C)/(D * E * F - G)$, where the letters A, B, etc. stand for the contents of the cells of the same name. Temporary storage cells T1, T2, . . . may be used in the calculation.

15. Assume that the cost of executing each instruction in any one of the simple machines discussed above is equal to $p + m * q$, where m is the number of addresses in the instruction and p and q are constants. Thus if five two-address instructions were executed, the cost would be $5p + 10q$. Discuss the desirability of each of the four machines from the standpoint of the cost of doing the calculation in Problem 14. How does the "cheapest" machine depend on the ratio $r = q/p$? That is, divide the four costs by p so that they depend on r. (Display the results graphically.)

16. If the restriction that the contents of A through G must not be changed is removed, are the conclusions changed?

17. We have noticed that in the case of two- and one-address machines, extra instructions to move information to and from temporary storage are needed. In fact, a relation between the number of extra instructions needed in the two cases is known if the restriction that the operands on the right-hand side must not be changed is enforced. Consider an arbitrary calculation of the type in Problem 14; that is, only the four operations $+$, $-$, $*$, and $/$ are used, each involves two operands (unary minus is not allowed), all the symbolic addresses A, B, etc., are different, and their contents may not be changed (except for the left-hand side). Suppose that in the minimum cost programs (as defined by Problem 15) the two-address machine requires E MOVE orders and that there are N other orders (that means that there are N operations on the right-hand side of the "$=$" sign). Write down expressions for the cost of executing the minimal cost program for each of the machines in terms of N, E, R, and P. Noting that all of these numbers are positive, show that the two-address machine can never have the cheapest program of all four. Can it ever cost no more for the calculation than the cheapest of the other three?

18. What are the three steps taken in the fetch part of instruction execution?

19. Do you think it preferable that a conditional transfer instruction which tests the top of the stack in a stack oriented machine pop the top level of the stack after the test or leave it for reuse by future instructions? Illustrate by examples.

20. Write a program for a typical stack machine to compute the square root of the number in the top level of the stack.

21. Consider a two-address machine with the instructions

    SUB   A,B   C(A) $-$ C(B) stored as C(A).
    and   TZN   A,B   If C(A) are 0 or negative, then transfer to location B for the next instruction.

    Indicate how to perform the two-address operations ADD, MOVE, MPY, and DIV using only these two instructions. Assume that arithmetic is being performed on integers.

22. Why was it stipulated that twos complement arithmetic was used in the pro-

gram modification discussion at the start of Section 2.4? Would ones complement or sign/absolute-value arithmetic have worked?

23. Consider binary fractions (numbers less than 1) using a 12-bit word in each of the three representations discussed. (Sign/absolute-value, twos complement, and ones complement.) Discuss the rules for shifting left and right such that a single shift will correspond to doubling or halving, respectively, in the cases where its result can be represented exactly.

24. Prove the rules that were given for shifting in Problem 23 above. Start with the formula given in this chapter for the value of the various representations and show that half or double the value is the shifted representation specified.

25. How can overflow be detected during shifting operations?

26. How can the loss of accuracy be detected during right shifts?

27. Consider a machine with $32{,}768 = 2^{15}$ words of memory and a 15-bit index register holding positive integers. Assume that index arithmetic is done *modulo* 32768; that is, if the answer is greater than 32767, 32768 is subtracted from it. If the contents of index registers are added to addresses, what should be put in index register 1 so that the effective address of LOAD A,1 is A-327?

28. Show by means of truth tables that the following relations between the logical relations AND, OR, and NOT are true.

   a. (x AND y) AND z = x AND (y AND z)
   b. (x OR y) OR z = x OR (y OR z)
   c. x AND (y OR z) = (x AND y) OR (x AND z)
   d. NOT (x AND y) = (NOT x) OR (NOT y)
   e. NOT (NOT x) = x

29. Special symbols are used for the logical operations, just as the characters + and * etc. are used for the arithmetic operations. Because most computers are short of characters in their printable character set, we shall use the characters + for OR, * for AND, and − for NOT (this is a unary operation; that is, it only has one operand). This choice is partly governed by the strong resemblance between the character + and OR etc. In fact, many of the rules of logical manipulation are symbolically true for arithmetic. Thus $(X + Y) + Z = X + (Y + Z)$ is true whether + represents OR or addition and $-(-X) = X$ whether X represents subtraction or NOT. Can arithmetic relations that are not true logically and vice versa be given?

30. Design index arithmetic instructions for a typical one-address machine which will use less than three instructions inside the loop. If the increment is assumed to be 1, can it be done with one instruction in the loop?

3

system software

The system software is a fundamental part of the total computer system, providing an interface between the user needs and the capabilities of the hardware. A job that is normally done on an elaborate system can be done on a very simple computer with few or no system programs, provided only that there is sufficient memory space and time available. However, the amount of user time involved in preparing such programs as well as the difficulty of checking them can make the task prohibitively expensive. It is often pointed out that the computer can do nothing that cannot be done by hand; that it cannot, therefore, provide the human with powers that he did not previously have. It has also been pointed out that the car does not enable the human to go anywhere he could not have previously walked to, but it *does* enable him to go to many more places a lot more quickly. The car is only about 10 times faster than walking; the computer is about 10^7 times faster than hand calculation. The development of automatic programming systems over the last 15 years has increased the speed with which programs can be written by a factor of 10 to 10^2. The addition of a good software system to a hardware system enables the user not only to complete some tasks more quickly and more cheaply, but makes the computer solution of other tasks possible.

The purpose of the system software is twofold: to make it easier for the user to get his job onto the computer, and to make it easier for him to run it and test it when it is on the computer. In this chapter we are going to look briefly at the problem of getting the program onto the computer. We shall also investigate what software is needed once the program is in execution.

3.1 THE RAW MACHINE: BOOTSTRAPPING THE INITIAL PROGRAM

The basic hardware is capable of executing sequences of instructions drawn from the computer memory. It is the job of the user to get his program into the memory and begin execution at the correct point. The input/output section of the computer is capable of reading data into the memory, so this is the hardware that must be used to load the program. Internally, program, numbers, and other data are represented by "words" (or groups) of binary digits; the input instructions on a machine are capable of reading an external representation of these bits into memory. Therefore, if the program to be executed is specified in its binary form exactly as it should appear inside the memory of the computer, input instructions can be used to load it. Unfortunately this begs the question, since these input instructions must themselves be loaded into memory before they can be executed. To get around this difficulty, an *initial load sequence*, known as a *bootstrap sequence*, is usually employed.

An initial load sequence is brought into action by pressing a switch on the main computer console. This switch initiates a single short segment of code that is prewired into the computer and represents a program to start the loading process. Very few system programmers need be concerned with this process since it is built in by the manufacturer and is not usually changed. However, it represents the start of a series of more complex loading procedures, so we shall discuss it briefly. The initial load switch requires a section of code to be stored, permanently, somewhere in the computer. It is only used periodically after the computer has been stopped for some reason, and it is therefore desirable to minimize its size. On the simplest computers it can be a single instruction, although typically it consists of several. Let us suppose that the computer has input/output instructions that read single *records* of information (for example, the contents of a card) into certain memory locations. The IBM 1401, for example, can read a card into character locations 1 through 80 with a single instruction. The initial load switch can force the control unit into a *state* in which it thinks that it has just read such an instruction from the memory, and that instruction is therefore executed. The switch should also force the control counter contents to be the address of the first of the set of locations that will contain the result of the read of the single record. After the read is complete, the machine automatically fetches the next instruction to be obeyed. Since this is determined by the control counter, the next set of instructions is determined by the contents of the first record of information read in. This contains no more than a few instructions. What it can contain is enough program to read in additional program. This is the reason for the name "bootstrapping"; it is likened to the idea of pulling oneself up by one's bootstraps.

As additional items of information are read (and we shall assume for the moment that they are on cards) additional program can be read into the memory. It is necessary to decide where this program must be loaded, since both the user and the bootstrap process should agree if the results are to be of any value. It would be possible to agree that each subsequent card is to be loaded into as many locations as necessary following the last card image in memory. Since this is rather restrictive, it is more normal to agree on an input format where each card contains the address of memory locations into which the remainder of the information is to be loaded. Then the user is free to load any location in memory (except the ones containing the loading program). One additional feature is needed as a minimum. This is an indication that the end of the program has been reached and that execution is to start at a specified location. This can be included with an indication of how much (how many words) information is on each card. If the indication is that there is no information on a card, that can be taken to be the last card. The location address can then be used as the location at which execution is to commence.

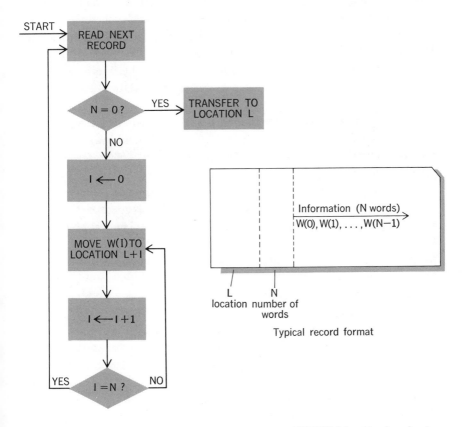

FIGURE 3.1 Absolute loader.

A program that does this form of loading into memory is called an *absolute loader*. The code that is loaded is called absolute code, since it is written with each address specified as an actual machine location. A flowchart of a typical absolute loader is shown in Figure 3.1.

3.2 THE ASSEMBLER

The absolute loader requires that the user prepare a program completely, specifying the addresses of all instructions and data words that he uses and giving the machine codes of all instructions that are used. This much detail is not only tedious but unnecessary for the specification of a program. It does not matter to the user if a given variable, which he may call X, is in location 1026 or 21734. Neither does it affect the execution of the program by the machine—provided that the correct address is available every time that the variable X is referenced. For this reason we would like to allow the user to talk about the variable X, or location X, meaning the memory cell that has been assigned for the use of X during the calculation. Thus, instead of using an absolute address, a *symbolic address* is used. If the variable X is to be added to the accumulator in a one-address machine, then an ADD X instruction is executed.

When we write ADD X, we are assuming that the system is going to understand the string of three characters A, D, D. The hardware, however, actually requires a pattern of binary digits such as 000101000000 for an ADD instruction. Since we do not want to learn, or repeatedly write, such strings of bits, we would like the machine to accept ADD instead. Terms such as SUB and MPY for the instructions subtract and multiply are called *mnemonic instructions*. A mnemonic is a device to aid the memory. These abbreviations are concise to write, yet they help the memory to recall what they do. For example, it is easier to remember that DIV, rather than 000010010001, is the division operation.

The hardware is neither capable of accepting symbols as addresses nor mnemonics as instructions. (This is not to say that a machine could not be so constructed, but most practical machines are not.) To get around this difficulty, we must expand the loading program from the simple absolute loader discussed above to a program that translates the source language of mnemonics and symbols to an object language of binary instructions and addresses. Such a translation program is called an *assembler*. Note that the loading process is becoming more complicated, but as it does, the job for the user is becoming easier. Now in order to get a program into the computer it is necessary, first, to obey the bootstrap program to bring in an absolute loader. This, in turn, brings in an assembly program which is used to translate the source program.

Throughout Chapter 2 we were using a form of assembly language. Without it, we would not have been able to describe machine instructions other than by specifying the actual binary form of the instruction. The latter form is no more necessary to the writing of programs than it is to the understanding of the principles of machine language.

3.2.1 The two-pass assembler

In order to translate the source assembly language, the assembler must replace each mnemonic instruction with its equivalent binary code and replace each symbolic address with its numerical equivalent. The former can be done by keeping a list of all mnemonic instruction names in a table. When a mnemonic is read, the table can be consulted and the equivalent binary code found. In order to do the same for the symbolic addresses, it is necessary to construct an equivalent table. The mnemonics are known ahead of time, but the relation between the symbols that a programmer uses and addresses in memory cannot be known until the program has been coded and read by the machine. Thus there are two distinct actions to be taken for symbols. The first is to set up a table of all symbols used and assign their machine addresses; the second is to take the addresses and substitute them for the symbols. These two phases are usually associated with two scans or *passes* of the source code. On the first pass, a *symbol table* is constructed in memory, giving the equivalent address for each symbol. On the second pass, the substitution is made to translate the code into binary.

The first pass has to use rules for determining what location is to be assigned to each distinct symbol. We shall discuss the most common form of assembler below, but the reader should be aware that there are as many different variations as there are machines.

3.2.2 External representation of instructions

In most assemblers, the user has to define all symbolic addresses that he uses by assigning them to specific memory locations at some point in his program. It is not uncommon to use a *fixed format* card for an assembly language program. In a fixed format, certain groups of columns, known as *fields*, are set aside for specific uses. These fields must be large enough to contain the maximum size element allowed in the field. If, for example, up to six characters are allowed in a symbolic address, columns 1 through 6 could be set aside for defining these addresses. Columns 8 through 15 could be used for the instruction mnemonic, and columns 16 upwards for the addresses. Figure 3.2 shows such a format as used for many IBM 7094 assemblers. Columns 7 and 15 are shaded because they always contain blanks, due to the size of the symbolic address and mnemonics that can be specified. Columns 73 through 80 are shown as used for identification. This is a common assembly language and Fortran language input convention that owes its origin to the fact that the IBM 704, a forerunner of the 7094, could only read columns 1 through 72 of a card. Consequently the last 8 columns could be used only for external identification.

If a symbolic address A is to refer to the memory location containing a certain instruction, say ADD B, then that instruction should be punched on a card with the symbolic address A in column 1, the instruction ADD in columns 8 through 10, and the operand address B in column 16. This then serves to define the symbol A to the assembler when it knows where the instruction is to be loaded. Since, in a one-address machine, instructions are executed from consecutive locations until a transfer is encountered, it is reasonable to load program instructions into successive locations. By assuming that the first instruction is loaded into location 0 (it is as good as any other location), it is possible to calculate, by counting, where any subsequent instruction is to be loaded. Hence, on the first pass, the assembler simply keeps track of where the next instruction is to go, so that when it recognizes a symbolic address in columns 1 through 6 (the location columns) it can enter it into the symbol table with an appropriate numerical address.

Because the symbolic addresses were limited to 6 characters, 6 columns were allocated to the location field. There is nothing magic about the number 6, the system programmer could design an assembler for names of any length.

FIGURE 3.2 Typical card format for input to assembler.

Six was used on the IBM 7090 series machines because six characters could be packed into one word, and this was convenient inside the assembly program. Other machines use a different maximum length. Usually, names are restricted to those combinations of characters which start with a letter and only contain letters and numbers (the *alphanumeric* characters). The only necessary restriction is that it be possible to recognize a name in the address field. Thus A+3 means the name A followed by + and the number 3. Hence + cannot be allowed as a character in a name. Neither can an all-numeric name such as 31 be allowed, since it cannot be distinguished from the number 31.

The address field is allowed to contain meaningful expressions involving addresses and numbers. The restrictions on the expressions depend on the assembler and loader used, so discussion will be delayed until Chapter 7, on assembler implementation.

3.2.3 Definition of data and storage locations by pseudo-orders

By placing a name in the location field, a symbolic address used to reference instructions can be defined. In addition to these addresses, which are typically used in transfer instructions, it is necessary to provide a mechanism for defining the addresses of data locations and constant locations. In some assemblers, the symbolic addresses of single-variable locations such as X need not be defined. The assembler recognizes that such symbols have been used and assigns single storage cells for their use at the end of the input code. This is similar in spirit to the action of a Fortran compiler which does not require that simple variables be declared. Dimensioned variables have to be explicitly declared in Fortran. Other languages, such as Algol, require that all variables be explicitly declared. The advantage of not declaring simple variables in Fortran or single cells in assembly language is one of a saving in writing, but its disadvantage is that there is a greater chance of error. If a symbolic address that is supposed to represent the first of a block of storage locations is not defined in assembly language, it would be assigned a single location only, so that, during execution, the program would access other locations. This problem is not as serious in Fortran because the use of the variable name may indicate to the compiler that the variable should have been dimensioned. Consequently, most assemblers demand that all symbolic addresses be defined at some point, so that omitting their definitions is illegal. In either case, it is necessary to provide for the definition of locations containing constants, to specify their contents and to be able to specify blocks of contiguous locations to be used for the storage of arrays and other multiword items. These definitions are handled by *pseudo-orders*. A pseudo-order is an instruction to the assembler rather than an instruction which is to be put in memory for eventual execution by the machine. There are two types of pseudo-orders, those that load data into the memory and those that tell the assembler certain facts about the incoming program.

Typical of those that load data into memory are the pseudo-orders which allow for the definition of decimal, octal, and hexadecimal numbers or character strings as data. Two approaches to this group of pseudo-orders exist. The first method provides several different pseudo-orders which specify the format of the data, whereas the second method provides an all-inclusive pseudo-order and uses a data format that defines its one type. The 360 assembler uses the second method. A general form of the first type of pseudo-order is:

```
    CONST   DEC  3.14159
and NUMBER OCT   173245604
```

The first pseudo DEC is supposed to convert the constant 3.14159 into binary, put it into the next available location, and define the symbolic address CONST as that location address. It is necessary for the assembler to decide whether to convert into a floating-point or a fixed-point representation (if both are available). This decision can be made in a similar manner to Fortran: if there is a decimal point present, then use floating point. Some assemblers will allow several constants to be specified on one DEC pseudo card by separating each number by a comma. In this case, subsequent numbers will load into consecutive locations. Thus if the pseudo-order

```
    ALPHA DEC  1.2,4.5,6.546,2
```

is used, then locations ALPHA, ALPHA+1, ALPHA+2, and ALPHA+3 contain the numbers floating-point 1.2, 4.5, 6.546, and fixed-point 2 respectively. The OCT pseudo operation will work similarly except that, since this is a way of specifying the contents of memory bit by bit (3 bits to each octal digit), there is no need to determine whether the fixed- or floating-point representation is intended. The octal item is not thought of as a number but as a binary—or rather octal—pattern. The octal pseudo-order is used on those machines in which the basic word size is divisible by 3, since it provides a compromise between the laboriousness of writing the bit pattern in binary and the difficulty of converting to another base. Bases that are powers of 2 are simple to convert to binary, and 8 is the largest power of 2 less than 10, so that there are enough digits in our conventional decimal system to use for the 8 possibilities in octal. Machines in which the basic length is not divisible by 3 face a problem in providing the equivalent of the octal pseudo operation. The IBM system 360, for example, uses an 8-bit byte as its basic item of information. All other items are composed of 1 or more bytes. The choice for the assembler's designer was either to use a modified octal in which the first digit was base 4 (2 bits) and the next two digits base 8, for a total of 8 bits; to use four base-4 digits; or to use two digits base 16 (*hexadecimal*, or sexadecimal, depending on how you worry about your corporate image). The first scheme is difficult to manipulate when multibyte items are being handled, the second only reduces the number of digits by a factor of 2 over binary, so the third was chosen. It has the drawback that six additional characters are needed to represent the digits from 10 to 15. Any of the characters available on the input and output media could be assigned. A common choice is to use A to F for 10 through 15 respectively, as IBM has done. Two hexadecimal digits are needed to represent one 8-bit byte. The following list gives some examples of the hexadecimal coding of an 8-bit byte, its equivalent binary pattern, and its value considered as an integer.

hexadecimal	binary	numerical equivalent (integer)
11	00010001	17 (=16+1)
0C	00001100	12
0F	00001111	15
FF	11111111	255 (=15*16+15)
A6	10100110	166 (=10*16+6)

One pseudo-order should allow for loading the binary representation of character strings. An early form of this was the pseudo-order

    CHAR 13,ABCDEFGHIJKLM

CHAR or a similar mnemonic stands for "characters." The numeric address 13 indicates that 13 characters are to be loaded, and then the 13 characters follow the comma. Since it was not always convenient to count the number of characters, an alternative form

    CHAR 'ABCDEFGHIJKLM'

is often provided. Since the ' character is used to delimit the string of characters, it cannot be used in the character string. This can be overcome by using two ' characters. Thus the single ' (apostrophe) character would be input as

    CHAR   ''''

In addition to specifying constants via pseudo-orders, many assemblers allow the programmer to express the constant required for an operand *literally*, that is, by writing it in the address field of an instruction. This is called a literal address, and is usually written by preceding the constant with an equal sign. For example, if the operand for an ADD instruction is 3.5, the instruction could be written as

    ADD   =3.5

These literals are equivalent, at the machine-language level, to putting an ordinary address in the ADD instruction and writing the constant in a data-loading pseudo-order later. The assembler translates them to the latter form.

The pseudo-orders that tell the assembler what is going on are used to place the code into locations in memory out of the normal sequence, to reserve blocks of locations for multiword items, or to tell the assembler the definition of a symbolic address. Typical of these pseudos are the following examples which are common to many assemblers.

    ORG   NUMBER

ORG (ORiGin) is used to tell the assembler that the next section of code is to be loaded into locations starting at NUMBER and continuing in sequence from there.

    BSS   NUMBER

BSS (Block Started by Symbol) tells the assembler that a block of length NUMBER locations is to be left free, so that the next instruction will be loaded NUMBER locations further on. A symbolic address in the location field of a BSS pseudo is assigned the value of the address of the first location of the block.

    A   EQU   B

EQU (EQUivalent to) tells the assembler that the symbolic address A is equivalent to B. If B is a number, then that number is entered into the table; if B is itself a symbolic address, then the value of B must be found in the table and that value used. This means that B must be defined before such an EQU statement is used. (This restriction is relaxed in some assemblers. Techniques to do this, and other restrictions, will be discussed in more detail in the chapter on assemblers.)

The ASSIGN pseudo-order is found in some assemblers. It is used to allocate a number of variables to single cells of storage. This is done by writing their names in the address field of the pseudo, each name separated from the next by a comma. For example, the following line of code

```
ASSIGN   A,B,N12345,XYZ
```

would assign one location each to A, B, N12345, and XYZ in the next four cells in memory.

It is evident that the address of an instruction or pseudo can be either a symbol or a number. It is convenient to allow arithmetic combinations of symbols and numbers, so many assemblers provide for a variety of possibilities. Addition and subtraction are nearly always allowed, multiplication frequently, while division and parenthesis are relatively infrequently allowed. However, it can be seen that the address field on a card can vary from one character to one occupying several cards, whereas the location and order fields are usually adequate if they are six to eight characters long. Rather than assign a fixed field to the address, the assembler usually allows a *variable-field-length* address. In order to tell the assembler when the address is complete, a convention, such as requiring that the first blank column terminate the address, is used.

Once the address field of a card has been terminated with a blank or by a count, the remainder of the card can usually be used for comments which help to document the action of the code. Frequently columns 73 through 80 of a card cannot be used as part of the address, but are used conventionally to punch a short identification of two to four characters followed by a sequence number so that the cards can be reordered if they are mishandled. If the initial sequencing is done by 10s or 20s, the additions can be made without frequently resequencing the deck.

3.2.4   The second pass

On the second scan through the input, the assembler produces the binary object code consisting of the machine language and binary constants defined

in the source. Where does the assembler put these binary words? One possibility is to place them directly into the memory locations indicated in the
assembly language and then to begin execution of the object program immediately after the second pass of the assembler has been completed. Such a
scheme is called a *load-and-go* scheme. It suffers from many drawbacks,
although it has the very definite advantage of speed over most other schemes
to be discussed. Among the disadvantages are the facts that:

1. A program cannot be loaded into locations which are occupied by the
   assembler code. Fancy assemblers on small machines frequently use the
   whole of the main memory, ruling out the possibility of such direct input.
2. Each time that the program is to be executed, it has to be reassembled.
   This is only serious if the assembler is slow.

The first problem can be overcome by placing the object code onto an
auxiliary storage device during the second pass of the assembler. This is not
strictly a load-and-go system, but it can still retain the speed advantages if
the intermediate storage is reasonably fast. If a copy of the intermediate
storage can also be reproduced on punched cards, for example, then the next
execution of the program does not require a reassembly as the cards can be
read back in directly. The re-input of the cards is equivalent to the job of
loading described earlier. The binary program should be output in a form
acceptable to the loader in general use at the installation.

An example of an input to a typical assembler for a one-address machine
is given below and followed by the equivalent program with all symbolic
addresses replaced with numeric addresses, as would be done by the assembler.

```
          ORG    100
START     LOAD   A
          ADD    B
          STORE  C
          TRA    D
A         DEC    13,15
B         EQU    A+1
C         BSS    2
D         ADD    =10
          STORE  C+1
          END    START
```

The address field of the last card containing the end pseudo tells the assembler
that execution is to start at that location. When this is assembled, it produces
the following code, written below with mnemonics and decimal addresses

(although it is in binary in practice):

location	instruction	addresses
100	LOAD	104
101	ADD	105
102	STORE	106
103	TRA	108
104	DEC	13
105	DEC	15
106		
107		
108	ADD	110
109	STORE	107
110	DEC	10

Note that it has placed the literal constant 10 at the end of the program and inserted its address into the instruction at location 108. This program will attempt to execute this location after it has executed location 109. This is a programming error, because data should never be executed as instructions. A transfer instruction to return control to the operating system should have been placed after the last instruction, just as a transfer instruction was placed so that control jumped around the block of data and working storage in the middle of the program. This system-return instruction will differ from one machine and one system to another. On some it takes the form CALL SYSTEM, which will be discussed at greater length in Chapters 4 and 7.

3.2.5 The 360 assembler

The assembler for the IBM system 360 machine differs in a number of ways from the design just discussed. Some of these differences are due to additional burdens imposed on the assembler by the complexity of the machine; others stem from an attempt to provide a more uniform approach to many of the pseudo-orders concerned with data loading. This section will discuss the assembler briefly in order to point out some of its features.

Input is usually from cards with three principal fields, the location, instruction, and address fields. There can also be comments and a sequence number. The rule for determining the different fields is one of blank separation. Each field must be separated from the next by a string of one or more blanks, except that columns 73 through 80 are ignored (they can contain a sequence number). This means that a one-character location symbol could appear in column 1, a blank in column 2, a one-character mnemonic such as L in column 3, a blank in column 4, and the address could start in column 5. However, if every line of code started in a different column, the coding sheet and any listings of the deck would be difficult to read. It is therefore conventional to fix the starting columns of the fields at 1, 10, and 16. A symbolic name can have up to eight characters at the most, so that there is bound to be at least one blank between the location and the instruction field. Similarly, the instruction can have up to five characters, so a blank is bound to follow that field.

The instruction mnemonics for the 360 were used in Section 2.6. They tend to use a single letter to represent each word in the instruction name such as L (Load), A (Add), S (Subtract), and so on. This cannot always be achieved. For example, *store* must be represented as ST, while L also stands for *left* (in shift instructions) and *logical*. Additional letters indicate the particular form of the instruction. Thus, by itself, the mnemonic usually means 32-bit twos complement arithmetic in fixed point. H, E, D, and P added refer to halfword fixed point, singleword floating point, doubleword floating point, and packed decimal respectively. In general, a trailing R means that the operand is fetched from another register. Thus ADR means *add double-length floating point from a register*. The simplicity of the scheme can lead the unwary into the trap of inventing nonexistent instructions. For example, from the LTR (Load and Test from Register) the user might be tempted to use an LT instruction. It does not exist!

The address field conventionally starts in column 16 and terminates at the first blank before column 73. (Character strings used as constants may contain blanks in exception to this rule.) The addresses in the multiple-address instructions are separated by commas, whereas indexing and similar modifications follow the address and are enclosed in parentheses. For example a register-to-register addition is

AR   2,4   (two register addresses, separated by a comma)

A memory-to-register addition with indexing is

A   3,B(7)   (two addresses, the second indexed from register 7)

A memory-to-memory decimal add packed is

AP   B,C   (two memory addresses)

If it is necessary to supply the length of a decimal operand, it can be stated explicitly in parentheses. Thus, we can write

```
AP   B(6), C(4)
```

meaning the 4-byte packed-decimal number starting at location C is to be added to the 6-byte number starting at location B.

Normally, it is not necessary to specify the length of variable-length operands. The assembler provides the length automatically. Obviously, it does not do this by reading the programmer's mind. It looks at the operand definition. We shall see that when operands and storage areas are defined, the amount of memory space occupied is specified. This information is used by the assembler.

The *branch on condition* instruction can be written as

```
BC   n,Addr
```

where n is the number between 0 and 15 that specifies the condition, while Addr is the branch address. n is really a part of the instruction code from the point of view that there are several different types of branches. Therefore the assembler provides a group of *extended mnemonics* to simplify the use of these instructions.

> B (Branch unconditionally) is equivalent to BC 15.
> NOP (No OPeration) is equivalent to BC 0, since the branch on condition 0 never branches.
> BP (Branch on Plus) is equivalent to BC 2, since condition 2 corresponds to testing the positive condition code.
> BH (Branch on High) is equivalent to BC 2, since condition 2 corresponds to testing the high condition code.

There are mnemonics for each of the useful condition numbers for use after compare, arithmetic, or test-under-mask instructions. Each of these instructions can set the condition register, so that its meaning depends on the type of the last instruction. The mnemonics BP and BH above are seen to be the same instruction. The former would normally be used after an arithmetic instruction and the latter after a compare, although either could be used with no ill effects.

The general pseudo-order for defining storage areas is DS (Define Storage). It appears in the instruction field. The address field determines how many bytes of storage are allocated to the area. The address of the first of these bytes can be assigned to the symbolic name punched in the location field, if any. The DS pseudo-order can use very complex address fields.† In these notes we shall content ourselves with a description of some of the simpler forms. Different types of operands in the 360 are described by single letters. We have already seen that H, E, D, and P are used to describe halfwords, single-precision fullword floating-point numbers, double-precision floating-point numbers, and packed-decimal numbers for instructions. They are also used for this in the DS pseudo-order. Suppose we wished to define a storage space for one double-precision floating-point number called B. We could write

        B   DS   D

This allocates a field of length 8 in the next group of 8 bytes that start on a double-word boundary. Thus the assembler has taken care of the restriction that double-precision words must have addresses divisible by 8. Similarly, we can reserve a block of 5 halfwords by writing

        C   DS   5H

The first of these is named C. Its address is even. Notice that the number of items is placed before the type of the item. Fullword fixed-point numbers are described by F. Thus 24 bytes of storage, starting on a multiple of 4 bytes, would be reserved by

        T   DS   6F

A packed-decimal region is specified by a P. In this case it is necessary to indicate the number of bytes required for each number. This can be done with the length modifier L. PL5 indicates a 5-byte packed number. Thus

        K   DS   4PL7

reserves 4 groups of 7 bytes. No boundary alignment is necessary since it is assumed that K will be used as an address in a variable-length instruction. If K is used as the address of an instruction such as AP, the length modifier is set to 7 unless it is specified otherwise. Thus

        AP   K,K

† For these, the reader is referred to the Assembler Language Manual, IBM document number C23-6514.

will assemble identically to

```
    AP   K(7),K
    AP   K,K(7)
or  AP   K(7),K(7)
```

and will double the number in location K. On the other hand

```
    AP   K,K+5(2)
```

will add the least significant 3 digits of K to K, since the specified length overrides the automatically specified form. (The three digits and the sign occupy the last 2 bytes of K.)

The other type descriptor that appears frequently is C for *character*. Characters occupy 8-bit bytes. C behaves identically to P in the DS pseudo, except that the maximum length of a character field in an instruction is 256 rather than the 16 of a P format. Thus

```
H   DS   5C123
```

defines 5 fields of 123 bytes each. These might be used in an instruction such as MVC (MoVe Characters).

```
MVC   H,H+123
```

would move the second group of 123 bytes into the first group.

The DS pseudo-order provides the effect of the BSS pseudo-order of many fixed-word-length machines. In addition, its sets the *length attribute* in the symbol table. This will be used to determine the length of variable-length operations as described later.

The DEC constant defining pseudo-order and its companions are replaced by the DC (Define Constant) pseudo-order. It is very similar to the DS, except that the value to be loaded into the storage area must also be specified. This is done by specifying the value of the constant inside quotes. For example, three fixed-point halfword integers equal to 5, 7, and -3 could be specified by

```
X   DC   H'5,+7,-3'
```

Note that several numbers can be separated by commas and that plus signs can be omitted, as is standard practice in both commercial and scientific

work. Decimal numbers and characters can be specified in the same way.
The length modifier can be omitted, in which case the assembler will generate it. For example

```
A   DC   2PL3'45'
B   DC   C'1234 A'
C   DC   P'13',C'AB,CD'
```

A is the first of a pair of 3-byte packed-decimal numbers. Since the length is
set to 3 bytes, they contain five digits plus sign. B is a 6-byte character string,
starting with 1, ending in A, and including a blank. C is the first of two constants. This definition introduces the use of a comma between definitions.
This is permitted. C has the length attribute of the first, namely 2 bytes,
since '13' requires 2 bytes for storage. The second constant, which begins
in storage 2 bytes after C, is a 5-byte constant AB,CD. In a character string,
the comma has no meaning to the assembler, just as a blank does not terminate the address field.

There are several other type letters that can be used in both the DS and
DC pseudo-orders. We shall not cover all of them, nor all of the combinations
that can be used. Two that will occur frequently in the DC pseudo-order are
X (heXadecimal) and A (Address). X acts like P, except that the digits are
hexadecimal, two-per-byte, and, of course, there is no special sign group. If
an odd number of hexadecimal digits is given, then a 0 is inserted on the
left to make a round number of bytes. The X is a convenient way to specify
the binary form of a word. (B for binary can also be used.)
Thus

```
A   DC   X'55555555'
```

specifies a 32-bit string of alternate 0s and 1s. But beware! It is not word-
aligned, and if it is to be used in a 32-bit fullword instruction, it must first be
aligned. This can be done by

```
    DS   0F
A   DC   X'55555555'
```

The 0F specifies zero 32-bit words, starting on a word boundary. This serves
to force the next following item to be loaded onto a word boundary. A is used
to define a 32-bit fixed-point word whose right-hand 24 bits are the address

of a variable. Thus

```
P  DC  A(T)
T  L   B
- - - - - - - - - - -
```

would set P to be on a word boundary and place in the next 32 bits the address
of the following load instruction.

LITERALS

Literals follow naturally from the above discussion. A literal is generated by
writing an = sign followed by any valid address field of a DC pseudo. Some
examples are

```
A    4,=F'23'         Add the fixed-point number 23.
AE   6,=E'13.5'       Add the floating-point number 13.5.
AH   1,=H'—9'         Add the halfword —9.
AP   A,=P'—235'       Add decimal to A the 2-byte number —235.
N    6,=X'0000FFFF'   And the Hex number 0000FFFF.
```

They have the effect of putting the constant at the end of the program and
replacing the literal by its address.

BASE REGISTER ASSIGNMENT

We have seen how the length specification will be provided by the assembler
on the basis of the length of the data at the time it is defined. The AP
instruction in

```
AP  A,B
- - - - - - - - -
A  DC  P'1234'
B  DC  PL2'1'
```

is equivalent to

```
AP  A(3),B(2)
```

We now need to discuss the base register problem. Recall from Section 2.6.4
that the address is represented by a 12-bit displacement and a base register
address. The assembler must take a memory address, such as A above, and
put it in this form, providing a base register address and calculating the dis-

placement. To do this, it must know the contents of index registers that can be used for base registers. This is done by telling the assembler, by means of the pseudo-order USING, the contents of a base register. For example

```
        BAL     15,A
        USING   A,15
    A   next instruction
```

The BAL instruction branches to location A (the next instruction), and places the address of the next location (A) into register 15. The USING pseudo-order specifies an address (A) and a register (15) to inform the assembler that, from now on, register 15 can be assumed to contain the address A. Note that the USING does not assemble into any machine instructions and therefore occupies no space in the object code. It takes effect at assembly time when it is read by the assembler. It cannot be executed, so it does not have to be in the sequence of the program's control flow.

Actually, this sequence can be specified more simply as

```
        BALR    15,0
        USING   *,15
```

The BALR instruction fetches its branch address from a register unless that register is 0 (as above), in which case no branch occurs. The USING makes use of the address *. This is used in many assemblers to mean the address of the current instruction. After such a USING pseudo-order, the assembler knows that register 15 contains a given address. Consequently, in the sequence

```
        BALR    15,0
        USING   *,15
    T   AR      5,6
    U   BC      4,T
```

the address T in the BC instruction can be assembled as a displacement of 0 relative to base register 15. Thus the BC is assembled as

```
    BC  4,0(0,15)
```

The address U is a displacement of 2 to register 15 since the AR instruction is 2 bytes long.

The programmer *must not* change the contents of registers declared as bases without telling the assembler beforehand. The assembler is told by the DROP command. Its simplest form is with a single register specified.

    DROP   15

tells the assembler that register 15 can no longer be used as a base register.

It is common to use more than one base register. Often two will be used, one for program and one for data. The only limit imposed by the assembler on the number used is 15, since only 15 registers can be used for indexing.

If the student is going to use the 360, he should refer to the manuals for the precise definitions of many of the pseudo-orders. Their usage and names differ from one type of machine to another.

3.3 RELOCATABLE LOADERS

It was stated that the assembler prepared code as though the first instruction was to be loaded into location 0, although this could be offset by use of the ORG pseudo-order. There are many circumstances in which it is necessary to be able to control the point at which loading starts. If several sections of program are to be placed in memory simultaneously, it is obviously necessary that they not overlap. This can happen when one user combines several sections of codes to form one larger program, or when several programs from different users are placed in memory simultaneously in a time-sharing environment. The assembler does not provide an adequate means for determining the place at which the code is to be loaded for two reasons: first, because it is a time-consuming process to translate from source to object, and second, because the assembler itself may occupy much more space than the object program. It is desirable to be able to load any segment of program anywhere in memory after it has been assembled. In such circumstances, sections of code can be assembled separately and loaded together into memory at execution time.

It is also desirable to leave the decision of initial load point until the last possible minute, so that the system can take account of the current environment. (In fact, programming encourages many undesirable habits. As a general rule, it is better to leave all decisions until the last possible minute so as to achieve maximum flexibility. Further, the laziest way of preparing a program is often the best, because it is usually the case that the shortest specification of a task has the most desirable properties!)

Now we are at a seeming impasse. The assembler prepares code as though it were to start at location 0 because the assembler doesn't know any better. The loader is supposed to change the assembler's mind afterwards. The solution is to require the assembler to tell the loader what would be changed if loading were to start at a different place in the main memory. Consider the assembly language code

```
        LOAD    A
        ADD     B
        TRA     C
   A    BSS     1
   B    EQU     1207
   C    STORE   A
   - - - - - - - - -
```

for a one-address machine that places one instruction in each word. If this is loaded starting at location 0, the values of addresses used are

$$A = 3$$
$$B = 1207$$
$$C = 4$$

On the other hand, if the program were to be assembled starting at location 2300, the address equivalences would be

$$A = 2302$$
$$B = 1207$$
$$C = 2304$$

The change needed is to add the starting address to some of the addresses used in the code, but not to others. The assembler can tell which addresses are to be changed. Those that are defined absolutely in pseudo-orders such as EQU do not change. The ones that *do* change if the program is moved are those that are defined in such a way that their value depends on (1) the counting mechanism used to assign successive instructions, (2) data definitions, and (3) block declarations to consecutive storage locations. The changing addresses are called *relocatable* or *relative* addresses.

In order to allow the loader to relocate code to any part of memory, the assembler must indicate which are the relocatable addresses in the object code. This can be done by allocating a bit position on the object cards for each address that can be punched on the cards. If this bit is a 1, the loader will add the relocation amount to the corresponding address. The code given in the example above would assemble as the equivalent of

```
0  LOAD   R3
1  ADD    1207
2  TRA    R4
4  STORE  R3
. . . . . . . . . . . .
```

where the R in front of the address means that it is relocatable. If this program is loaded starting at location 4108, the result will be

```
4108  LOAD   4111
4109  ADD    1207
4110  TRA    4112
4112  STORE  4111
```

as required. The way in which the example above could be punched on a card is shown in Figure 3.3.

The programmer should realize that the use of relocation-of-address fields will restrict his use of arithmetic expressions in address fields. Since only single relocation is provided in the loading method discussed, an address expression such as A+B where both A and B are relocatable would be invalid. There will be further discussion of this in the chapter on assemblers.

With this technique, a number of programs can be loaded into the main memory without overlapping each other. The loader can load each one in turn, noting where it starts and how long it is, so that it knows where it may load the next code. In order to execute these codes as parts of a single job, it

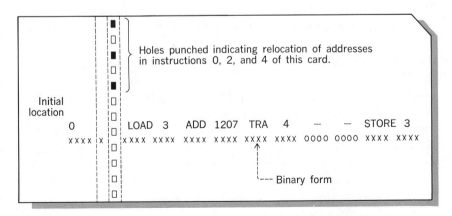

FIGURE 3.3 Relocatable loader input.

is necessary to have communication between the various sections. One of the code sections must be the *main* program that is executed initially, since execution must start at a specific place. The others must be subprograms called into play by the main program, or by programs previously called by the main program.

The user cannot be expected to know where the various code sections are going to be loaded, so a mechanism must be provided to allow him to transfer control to another section and to access data used by another section. There are a number of mechanisms used to achieve these purposes. Some of the common ones will be discussed below.

When the user is writing the assembly language code for one section and he wishes to write a transfer of control instruction to another section (which has, or will be, assembled separately), he would like to indicate the name of that section symbolically. One very common way of doing this is to use the pseudo-order CALL. This is written in the form

```
CALL  SQRT
```

if the SQRT program is to be called. The CALL assembles as a type of transfer instruction which will be discussed later. The assembler does not know what address to place in the transfer instruction, since the SQRT program will be positioned in memory by the loader after assembly has finished. There are two schemes for handling this problem.

The first is known as the *transfer vector technique*. During the first pass of the assembly, a table of all subprogram names that are used in CALL pseudos is constructed. A unique integer between 0 and $N-1$ is assigned to each entry in the table, starting at 0 and working up, where N is the number of entries in this table. The assembled program is displaced down N locations so that the first instruction is assembled as if it were to start in location N. Each time that a CALL pseudo is encountered in the second pass, the address used in the transfer instruction is the integer assigned to that subprogram name. It is indicated as a relocatable address. This means that when the program is loaded and the CALL is executed, control will be transferred to the appropriate one of the first N locations of that program segment. It is necessary for the loader to place a transfer order in each of these locations to the correct location of the subprogram required. In order that it can do this, the assembler places an internally coded representation of the symbolic name of each of the CALLed subprograms in the corresponding location at the start of the program segment. The loader is also provided with an indication of the number N of such names so that it can tell which words are to be interpreted as symbolic names, as shown in the center column of Figure 3.4. It is also necessary for the loader to find out which subprogram segments have which names, so that if the programmer writes CALL SQRT in the first segment, and means by this the third instruction of the fourth segment, the loader can generate the correct transfer instruction. To handle this, the user tells the assembler the *entry* points to each segment with a pseudo-order such as ENTRY or a similar name. For example, to indicate that a given instruction is the place to which all CALLs of SQRT should transfer, it is necessary to write in assembly language

```
           . . . . . . . . . . . . .
SQRT  LOAD  . . . . .
      ENTRY  SQRT
           . . . . . . . . . .
```

The ENTRY pseudo-order can usually be placed anywhere in the section of code that contains the definition of SQRT. When the assembler sees this, it creates an entry in a table of entry points for that section and makes a note of the address of the entry point. The second pass of the assembler uses this

Assembler inputs	Assembler outputs = relocatable loader inputs	Program in memory
1	**1**	
	2 CALLS 0 ENTRY POINTS	
	0 SQRT	0 TRA (SQRT)
	1 SIN	1 TRA 101
LOAD A	2 LOAD R17	2 LOAD 17
ADD B	3 ADD R8	3 ADD 8
CALL SQRT	4 CALL R0	4 CALL 0
CALL SIN	5 CALL R1	5 CALL 1
2	**2**	
	1 CALL 1 ENTRY POINT SIN = 1	
ENTRY SIN	0 PRINT	100 TRA (PRINT)
SIN STORE SIN1	1 STORE R13	101 STORE 113
CALL PRINT	7 CALL R0	107 CALL 100
etc.	----	----

FIGURE 3.4 Relocatable binary with transfer vectors.

table to create a list of all entry names and the corresponding addresses, which it hands onto the loader. The program that is handed onto the loader will take the general form shown in Figure 3.4.

The second method used to tie several subprograms together is known as a *linking loader*. A linking loader is essentially another assembly that accepts partially assembled programs and completes the assembly. As with the transfer vector technique, during assembly some of the symbolic addresses are undefined. A pseudo-order such as CALL causes a special table of symbols to be generated. These symbols may be left undefined in the program segment being assembled, just as in the transfer vector technique. However, in the linking technique, the number of the entry in the table is not put in as the address of the object of the CALL. Rather, the address of the location containing the CALL is placed in the special table. This means that the loader can put the correct address into the object of the CALL when it has associated the name with the correct subprogram. If there is more than one reference to the same name, then either more than one entry must be made in the table of CALLs or a chaining technique can be used. In the latter method, the address of the location containing the object of the first CALL is placed in the address field of the second, the location of the second in the address field of the third, and so on. In this way, a *chain* of addresses starting from the address given in the call table points to successive CALLs of the same name. At load time, the loader moves down this chain replacing the address field with the actual address of the program segment. The input and resulting chain-linked object are shown in Figure 3.5.

One of the advantages of the linking method is that there is one less transfer instruction to be executed in order to branch to another program segment. This reduces the execution time by a small amount in the case of very short segments. A more important advantage is that it is not limited to use for transfers of control. If it is necessary to refer to a variable in another segment by its symbolic name, then that variable name can be indicated as an external variable. The assembler can then add it to the list of symbolic names to be linked. The example in Figure 3.5 shows that the technique is independent of the fact that the variables are used in CALL pseudos. Implementation of many of these features will be discussed in the chapter on assemblers.

The system 360 loader uses a linking technique which will be discussed briefly below. In assembly language, the 360 programmer uses the pseudo-orders ENTRY and EXTRN to pass information on to the loader. Symbolic addresses are declared as external to an assembly program segment by the statement

EXTRN A,B, . . . ,X

which says the addresses A, B, . . . and X are defined in a separately assembled section of program. They must not, therefore, be defined in the section containing an external declaration for them. Their symbolic form will be passed on to the loader for linking. Each variable name declared as external in any program segment must be declared as an entry point in one

Input program		
	LOAD	A
	ADD	B
	CALL	SQRT
	CALL	SIN
	ADD	A
	CALL	SQRT
	MPY	C
	CALL	SQRT
	CALL	SYSTEM
A	DEC	10
B	DEC	12
C	EQU	107

Object code equivalent		
	SQRT	R7
	SIN	R3
	SYSTEM	R8
0	LOAD	R9
1	ADD	R10
2	CALL	–
3	CALL	–
4	ADD	R9
5	CALL	R2
6	MPY	107
7	CALL	R5
8	CALL	–
9	10	
10	12	

Loaded program

Assume program loaded starting at location 1000, SQRT at 2214, SIN at 3417, SYSTEM at 17.

1000	LOAD	1009
1001	ADD	1010
1002	CALL	2214
1003	CALL	3417
1004	ADD	1009
1005	CALL	2214
1006	MPY	107
1007	CALL	2214
1008	CALL	17
1009	10	
1010	12	

FIGURE 3.5 Linked chain method.

and only one segment. This is done with the assembler statement

    ENTRY P,Q, . . . Z

which says that P, Q, . . . , and Z are entry points to the local program segment. The symbolic addresses listed in the address field of the ENTRY pseudo-order must be defined in the same program segment. The name and associated value can then be passed on to the loader.

The 360 system uses two loaders. The first is called the *linkage editor*, and it produces a binary form of the program in which all symbolic references between different segments have been replaced with binary addresses, that is, in which the linking has been taken care of. A second program is called the *loader*. It places the binary program into core memory for execution. For the sake of simplicity, we shall not distinguish between the two but refer to them both as the loader.

The major task of the 360 loader is not relocating but linking. This is because the base register hardware addressing system provides most of the relocating necessary in the 360. At assembly time, the address field of an instruction is evaluated. Typically it will be a relocatable address. Since it must be put into a base-plus-displacement form, the assembler looks for a base register that is within 4,095 bytes of the expression and converts it to this form. Since base registers are loaded at execution time (that is, *dynamically*), they will contain an address relative to the loaded position of the program. (The most common method for loading a base register is the BALR B,0 instruction, which puts the control counter into register B.) Since the base contains the relocation factor automatically, the displacement is an absolute amount.

(Extensions of these ideas lead to the concept of *dynamically relocatable programs*. These are programs which can be moved around in memory at any time. It is very useful to have programs in this form in a time-sharing environment, where, in order to place a new program into memory, it may be necessary to move one already there to another spot. Two levels of relocatability can be sought. Complete dynamic relocatability allows for the program to be stopped at any time, moved, and restarted. A lesser level allows the program to be moved before it has actually started execution or at various check points during execution. The latter only requires that there be no location-dependent information in the loaded form of the program or at the check points. The former requires that location-dependent information never be constructed. The simplest way of achieving this with hardware is to provide a relocation register whose contents are automatically added to every memory address. Much more complex schemes have been developed in order also to tackle the problem of unnecessary program moves in time-sharing environments. † Typical 360 programs are not dynamically relocatable, although it is possible to achieve the lesser level if some of the assembler features are not used. The level of full dynamic relocatability can only be achieved by the addition of hardware, as is done in the time-sharing model 67, for example.)

The assembler input that gives rise to relocatable addresses is the A field in a DC pseudo. If B is an address in the program, then

```
DC  A(B)
```

is a 32-bit word which is relocated on loading. The 360 allows expressions to appear inside an A field, but they may only contain single relocation by each program segment. ‡

If B is an external address in a program segment, then the instruction

```
L  4,B
```

is illegal. The reason is that B must be put into a base-plus-displacement form by the assembler. Since the location of B is not yet known, no base can be assigned. Neither is it possible for the loader to apply a linking method, since 360 machine addresses are 24 bits long, whereas only 12 bits are available in the address field of an instruction. To get around this problem, the code

```
       L        4,AB
       L        4,0(4)
       -----------
AB     DC       A(B)
       EXTRN    B
```

must be used. The loader now has 32 bits in which to link the address of B at load time.

† This subject is treated at greater length in J. B. Dennis, Segmentation and the Design of Multiprogrammed Computer Systems, *Journal of the Association for Computing Machinery*, vol. 12, pp. 589–602, Oct., 1965.

‡ There is a way of assembling several sections of code together, in which case a relocation from each section can be applied. The reader is referred to the CSECT pseudo instruction in the assembler manual of the 360 for details.

3.4 THE LIBRARY

In order to avoid loading many programs from external hard-copy input such as punched card, installations usually will make the commonly used programs available in the program library. This, as the name suggests, is nothing more than a collection of programs which can be used with other programs. In order to make the collection useful and accessible, it is put on a high-speed input device so that the user can obtain a copy for the loading process without obtaining a deck of cards. The loader will first put together those subprogram segments that the user has provided and attempt to link them by one of the above methods. If some of the symbolic names requested are not indicated as entry points or external names in any of the segments, the loader attempts to find a library program of the same name. It does this by first consulting an index of library programs that is maintained for this purpose. When it finds the program required, it is copied into core by the loader in the same manner as the output from the assembler. Thus the programs in the library are kept in an assembled form ready for loading. If a search of the library index fails to find a requested program, then the job is in error. In this case execution is either inhibited or, if it does commence, it cannot be expected to continue beyond a call to one of the nonexistent programs. More advanced systems make it possible for a collection of libraries to be accessed. In such systems, the user can specify which libraries are to be used and in which order they should be searched. (It is possible that two programs in different libraries may have the same name.) These advanced systems are very useful to active programmers. A user may wish to keep a personal library of his own programs, or a group of users—as, for example, a chemistry department—may wish to keep a library of specialized subroutines. Moreover, all users find it convenient to have access to a general library for very standard programs such as SIN, SQRT, etc.

3.5 OTHER TRANSLATORS

The repertoire of the computer will usually include a number of higher-level translators. They are all faced with the same basic task—converting the input, or source program, into a binary program with meaning to the machine. Some translators will translate into assembly language code and then leave the assembler to translate to binary, others will produce binary object code, usually relocatable, directly in one or more passes.

It is highly desirable that all translators that are part of a system produce compatible object code. Thus a single loader can be used in all cases and programs written in one language can call on programs written in another. In some instances load-and-go compilers are written. In compilers, the designer is faced with a choice between fast translation or fast execution (in some cases neither may seem to be achieved). The load-and-go compiler is designed as a very fast compile method since it can be kept in memory throughout execution (the program does not load on top of it, since then load-and-go would not be possible). Therefore the compiler does not have to be reread into memory before each compilation. The loading of a compiler can account for a sizable fraction of the job time for a source deck that is only going to take a second or two to compile and execute. Therefore a load-and-go system can be very efficient for short jobs such as, for example, those that occur during program testing.

3.6 RUNNING THE PROGRAM, MONITORING

Once the program is in memory, it can be executed. The programs provided at the installation have assisted the programmer in getting his problem onto the machine. Now he must find ways to check his program during execution.

The most carefully written code will contain errors of various sorts. The programmer may have stated his program improperly so that, say, he forms $A - B$ instead of $B - A$. Those errors can only be found by the programmer checking his answers with an alternate calculation, or by checking the numerical *invariants* of the problem. (An invariant is an expression that should remain constant if the calculation is exact. For example, in a physical problem, the total energy of the system plus the incoming energy minus the outgoing energy should be constant. It may be easy to calculate this number from time to time. It should stay constant within allowable roundoff error. If it changes drastically, it is an indication that there is a numerical coding error or a machine error.)

Other errors are due to mistakes in transcribing the desired algorithm into the source language or to mistakes in the use of library programs. Frequently, these will lead the program to behave wildly. The program may, for example, try to execute a memory location that was never loaded with a program instruction or that was incorrectly overwritten by data. It may also get into an *infinite loop*, which is a repetitive cycle of instructions that will never terminate. When either of these happens, the programmer can use help. He should be told immediately if his program tries to execute an illegal instruction and, after a certain amount of time has elapsed, he must be told that he either has a program that is longer than he thought or that he is probably in an infinite loop.

To take care of these things, his program is monitored in execution by another program and the interrupt features of the hardware. We shall call this other program a *monitor* because of its function. It is frequently referred to as a *supervisor* or an *executive* program. The interrupt mechanisms cause control to be transferred to specific locations in the memory when various unusual conditions arise. When the monitor program—which occupies the locations around the area to which interrupt transfers—senses an illegal instruction interrupt, it will use programs to locate the illegal instruction and report it to the programmer, together with a printout of sections of the main memory of interest to him. A second condition can be caused by a clock or interval timer. It is set by the monitor just prior to execution. When it goes off, much as an alarm clock goes off, an interrupt transfers control to the monitor. Once again, it outputs a message to the programmer, giving him the reason for termination of his program as well as important information from the memory.

Memory protection allows sections of the memory to be declared off limits to the user's program. Any attempt to reference this area of memory can result in an interrupt to the monitor. The program can be restrained from changing or from reading the contents of locations that are protected. Some machines provide separate protection for writing and reading, some use the same signal. Some systems provide memory access keys to various sections of memory, so that a section can only be accessed by a user providing the correct key. A key, in this case, is a binary pattern, perhaps only a few bits long. It is fixed for a given user's program throughout execution.

The chief purposes of memory protection are threefold:

1. To prevent the user from changing the contents of areas of memory which will affect other users
2. To help detect potential errors in the user program
3. To facilitate the assignment of memory space to a user as he needs it

In the first instance, it is obvious that one user should not modify either the monitor or another user's program. The second aim is rather more complex. It would, for example, be reasonable to read a location in the monitor which contained data such as the current time or date—but it would almost certainly be an error to read a location containing arbitrary information (such as another user's program). If such a read were detected and reported immediately, the error could easily be located. This protection can also serve to prevent the user from accessing areas of memory currently in use for input/output. (Chapter 6 will deal with the overlap of input/output operations with computation.) Since input and output may be in progress between the memory and other devices, it is clear that errors could occur if the user read or changed the contents of memory locations involved in I/O transfers before the completion of the transfer. A protection of memory during the transfer can assist in the overlap problem.

Finally, there is the assignment of memory space. In an advanced operating environment, it is possible that other users' programs will be in memory. Although any particular user is unaware of the others, he may have less memory space than he needs. In a fully automatic system, each user would refer to memory as needed. If it was not yet allocated, it would be protected and an interrupt would return control to the monitor. The system would use this as an indication that the memory should be reassigned before the first user could continue execution.†

The monitor is stored in a protected area of memory. In order that it may reference memory anywhere, an interrupt status is defined for the machine. If the status is *interrupt allowed*, then the user is in execution and the protected area may not be used. As soon as an interrupt occurs, the status is set to *privileged user* and accesses of protected memory are enabled. While the privileged status is on, interrupts are either disallowed completely or partially inhibited, so that the monitor can complete its analysis of the problem causing the interrupt.

In many larger installations, more than one user's program may be partially on the computer at a time. As a minimum, there may be many other users' programs on an input device waiting to be read. In order to protect these from possible errors by a programmer, the input/output equipment is usually protected also. Thus one user has access to certain devices only, much as he has access only to certain parts of memory.

Many features of the monitor described above are negative—that is, they are designed to *prevent* the user from doing certain things such as, for example, using too much time. However, the monitor also provides the user with a number of positive benefits. The main facilities usually provided are for the use of input/output equipment. The problems and use of I/O devices will be discussed in a later chapter. However, they are generally complicated to use, so that the monitor will normally contain program segments which the programmer can use for accessing the I/O equipment. In many programs,

† More sophisticated techniques of memory protection are discussed in J. B. Dennis, Segmentation and the Design of Multiprogrammed Computer Systems, *Journal of the Association for Computing Machinery*, vol. 12, pp. 589–602, Oct., 1965.

for example, it is desirable to be able to find the actual time in order to control external devices. Therefore the monitor will frequently provide programs
that will read the real time clock and give the reading to the user. Programs
to take special action on overflow, machine errors, etc. are also usually provided in the monitor, since almost every user requires that such problems be
handled.

Additional aids often provided for the user include *dumps, post-mortems,
snapshots,* and *traces.* A dump is a listing of all or part of the user's area of
memory at the end of execution. It is often in octal or hexadecimal, although
it is possible to provide a more useful symbolic listing as follows:

Each translator leaves a copy of its symbol table which lists all symbolic
names used and their locations relative to the program section translated.
The loader leaves a copy of the *memory map*, which lists each program loaded
and its location in memory. (This information could be left on an auxiliary
storage device such as a disk file.) With this information it is possible for the
dump program to provide a list of the contents of all locations referenced
symbolically by each program segment. If information about the type of data
stored in each location is also retained, the dump program can convert the
binary contents to the most suitable printing format (decimal, octal, character strings, etc.).

A *post-mortem* is an analysis of the contents of memory (after execution has
been terminated) to gather as much information as possible that may be of
use to the programmer. One such analysis will be mentioned in Chapter 4,
after 360 subroutines have been discussed. Another is known as a *comparison
post-mortem*. It compares the contents of memory after execution with the
contents before. All differences are reported to the user. This enables him to
tell very quickly which data locations have been changed, and, more impor-
tantly, which program locations have been changed. Present-day programming techniques try to avoid changing the program, therefore such
changes are strong indications of error.

A *snapshot* is a dynamic dump of part or all of the memory that can be
requested by the user's program. It is essentially a library program that will
print sections of the memory conveniently. It enables the user to see when
elements of data storage areas are being changed.

A *trace* can be defined as an automatic snapshot feature. It may be possible
to request, for example, that certain registers or memory locations be printed
every time that a branch is executed. This allows the user to get a picture of
the flow of a program, since he knows that flow continues through increasing
locations between branches. It may also be possible to print the contents of
registers when certain locations are changed; for example, every time that

the contents of location AB is changed. A trace may require some hardware features for efficient implementation (an optional interrupt on every success-ful branch was provided on one of the early machines, the IBM 704). Some of its features can be implemented by arranging for the translator to produce special code when tracing is requested. Alternatively, it can be implemented by interpretation, discussed in the next section.

3.7 INTERPRETATION

The user writes programs in a source language. This is translated into a relocatable binary language which, in turn, is then further translated into absolute binary machine language by the loader. It is also possible to interpret any of these languages (source, relocatable binary, or machine language) by an interpreter, which is a program that examines—one by one—each state-ment or instruction in the language and causes the desired action to be taken immediately. Thus, if a one-address machine assembly language is to be interpreted, a statement such as LOAD A would cause the interpreter to locate the symbolic address A in a table; find out from this table where A was stored in memory; fetch the contents of A; and place them in a location within the interpreter used to represent the accumulator of the one-address machine (since the actual accumulator would be used by the interpreter). We shall discuss interpreters in Chapter 5. They are particularly useful for some forms of tracing because they can easily detect conditions such as the use of variables, for example, by placing flag bits in the name table. They can also provide symbolic error diagnostics because the program being "executed" can be stored in its source form.

3.8 MULTIPROGRAMMING AND TIME SHARING

Both of these terms refer to the use of memory for more than one piece of code which could be simultaneously executed if more than one processor were available. Some machines have more than one processor. However, if there are more such programs than there are processors, it is usual for a processor to process one program for a while, and then to switch over and process another. This switch is conveniently made when the program being processed has to wait for a slower input/output operation to be completed. Such switching allows the use of the CPU to be maximized. There is no accepted distinction between the terms *multiprogramming* and *time sharing*. In this book we shall use *multiprogramming* to refer to the presence in main memory of two or more segments of code which can be simultaneously executed but which are part of the same job. *Time sharing* will also include those cases when the pieces of code being processed simultaneously are parts of independent jobs.

3.9 TASK AND JOB SCHEDULING, CONTROL CARDS

We have seen that system programs are provided for translation, loading, and monitoring of user programs. In some of the early systems and in current systems on small machines, it is necessary for the user or operator to sequence the separate tasks which comprise a single job through the computer. For example, if a job consists of a section of Fortran code and a section of assembler code and it requires three library subroutines, the operator may have to perform the following steps:

1. Load the Fortran compiler (from cards or paper tape). This would be done with an absolute loader which is either kept in memory or is loaded by a bootstrap process.
2. Fortran compile the Fortran section of code. The output would be saved for later loading.
3. Load the assembler in a manner similar to the loading of the Fortran compiler.
4. Assemble the next section of code. The output would be kept for the loading process.
5. Load the relocatable loader via the absolute loader.
6. Feed the output from the Fortran compiler and the assembler into the machine for relocatable loading. Since three subroutines are required, the relocatable loader would type out their names to the operator. He would obtain copies of the cards or punched tape and input these to the loader.
7. Finally, the monitor must be loaded (it could have been kept in memory to monitor the other system programs). Now execution can commence.
8. When execution is stopped by the monitor, the next job can be processed.

There are two points to be noted. First, the system programs are all being loaded from hard-copy devices such as paper tape or cards, and the intermediate storage between translating and loading is also on hard copy. Second, the operator must manually sequence through the various stages of translation and execution. If backup storage devices are available (and they are in most medium-size systems) then it is not necessary for the system programs or the intermediate storage to use hard-copy devices. If the system programs are on magnetic tape, drum, or disk, then they can be loaded much more rapidly. Since the operator does not have to obtain physical copies of these programs, it is no longer necessary that he issue the instructions for the start of compiling, assembling, etc. Instead, these instructions can be fed in with the source language input and be interpreted by the system programs. This implies the existence of another system program which will perform this interpretation. We shall call this program a *supervisor* since it finds out what tasks have to be done and decides when to do them. In the simpler system, it does them immediately after they are requested. We shall examine such a simple system briefly.

In addition to the input code in Fortran and assembly language and data for the execution phase, the user must prepare a series of input cards which tell the supervisor what is required for the run. The input will normally start with one or more cards which state who the user is (for accounting purposes) and what sort of service is needed (for example, maximum time and output limits, etc.). These are usually called *identification* or *job* cards. Following this will be a series of cards called *control* cards. They are usually identified by means of one or more characters in the first few columns. Some systems use a $ sign in column 1. The 360 uses the characters // in columns 1 and 2. The character(s) will differ from system to system. In each control card will be punched one or more strings of characters which are *commands* to the supervisor. These commands may include FORTRAN, ASSEMBLE, LOAD, PUNCH OBJECT, DATA, and probably many others. Their use is as follows. Commands such as FORTRAN and ASSEMBLE tell the supervisor that the set of records following are to be compiled or assembled by the named system translator. PUNCH OBJECT tells the scheduler to pass on the word to the translator that an object deck must be punched during translation. This enables the user to avoid subsequent retranslations if the program is now correct. Alternatively, this could be supplied as a parameter to the translator. LOAD informs the supervisor that it is time to start loading the programs already translated, and DATA tells the supervisor that the set of records following is data to be made available to the program if it executes.

If the object deck is punched as a result of a translation, then that deck can normally be loaded in place of the symbolic source program and its control cards. Thus if, on the first run, the user submitted a deck with the following form

```
ID CARD
FORTRAN
(Source program in Fortran)
. . . .
ASSEMBLE
```

```
PUNCH OBJECT
(Source program in assembly language)
- - - -
LOAD
DATA
(Data for the run)
- - - -
```

he would expect, as output, some information about his programs (listings), a punched deck corresponding to the program in assembly language, and whatever output his own program generated. If now he wished to make a change to the Fortran program only, he could submit the following deck:

```
ID CARD
FORTRAN
(Source program in Fortran)
- - - -
(Object program from previous assembly)
- - - -
LOAD
DATA
(Data for the run)
- - - -
```

In a simple batch processing system, all of the user's programs and data will be in the *input stream*, which is the string of successive card images that are read on the primary input device. In some cases, some of the input may come from other devices, such as magnetic tape or disk files. In that case, it is necessary to have a method to refer to the other sources of information. Hence, in more complicated systems, commands such as FORTRAN may be followed by the names of input units or of sets of information on the disk files.

The 360 system uses an assembly-like language called *job control language* (JCL) for system control. Each JCL statement has the form

```
//name   operation   arguments
```

The two / characters must be in columns 1 and 2. No blanks may appear in the name or operation codes which are terminated by blanks. The argument string may only contain blanks under special circumstances. A few simple examples of JCL will be given and partially explained below.† A job might

† JCL, the subject of IBM manual number C28-6539, is far too complex for extensive discussion in this book.

start with

```
//PROGRAM   JOB    (299899,200,0,5),'USERNAME',MSGLEVEL=1
//FTG       EXEC   PGM=FORTRANG
//SYSPRINT  DD     SYSOUT=A
//SYSLIN    DD     DSNAME=SYS1.SYSLIN,DISP=(OLD,PASS),   X
//                 VOLUME=SER=SYSRE2,UNIT=2301,          X
//                 DCB=(RECFM=FB,LRECL=80,BLKSIZE=3200)
//FTG.SYSIN DD     *
```

This example is one which will run on at least one installation, but there will be minor differences between installations. In particular, the format and information of the first card, which contains identification and run-control information, is peculiar to the accounting system used on the machine. The names of some of the compilers may also vary locally. In this example, the name FORTRANG is used for the compiler that IBM calls IEYFORT. One of the features of the system is that it is possible for local installations to make minor changes. The first line contains a *job* card. It gives the name of the job (PROGRAM) and of the user (USERNAME). The remaining information on that card contains run-control information such as time limits and amount of output expected. The second card requests the execution of the program Fortran G, which is one of the available Fortran compilers on the 360. The name FTG is called the *step-name*, and can be used to refer to the Fortran compilation step that will follow. The compiler needs to know where certain output is to be placed. In particular, it needs to know where a listing of the program and associated diagnostics should be routed and what to do with the object of the translation. It refers to these as SYSPRINT and SYSLIN respectively. The next three lines define these sets of data. The first DD (Data set Definition) statement defines SYSPRINT by means of the argument field. SYSOUT = A indicates that it is to be placed on the output printer. The next three cards are part of a single DD statement. The first card is continued to the next by an X punch in column 72. The statement defines the set of data SYSLIN to be equivalent to a data set known as SYS1.SYSLIN, and tells the system where it is and what to do with it. In this case, the object data set is passed on to the loader at a later step. The final card defines an input file SYSIN in the step FTG by an *. This means the input card reader. The Fortran compiler is now ready to read its input from the input card reader, print a listing of the program with diagnostics, and leave the object in a data set on auxiliary storage. Consequently this group of JCL cards would be followed by a Fortran program. If this program is to be loaded, the next step would be specified by

```
//EDT        EXEC  PGM=LINKEDIT,COND=(5,LT,FTG),                         X
//                 PARM='LIST,MAP'
//SYSPRINT  DD    SYSOUT=A,                                             X
//                 DCB=(RECFM=FBA,LRECL=121,BLKSIZE=726)
//SYSUT1    DD    DSNAME=SYS1.SYSUT1,DISP=OLD
//SYSLIN    DD    DSNAME=*.FTG.SYSLIN,DISP=OLD
//          DD    DDNAME=SYSIN
//SYSLIB    DD    DSNAME=SYS1.FORTLIB,UNIT=2314,                        X
//                 VOLUME=SER=SYSLIB,DISP=OLD
//SYSLMOD   DD    UNIT=DISK,SPACE=(TRK,(99,5,1)),DISP=(,PASS),          X
//                 DSNAME=&G(G)
```

The first card requests execution of the linkage editor (loader). The remaining cards specify the locations or system names of various data sets used by the loader. SYSLIB, for example, is the name of the data set that the loader will refer to as a library. The programmer thus has the option of specifying which library should be used. After loading, it is necessary to request execution. This can be done by the cards

```
//GO         EXEC  PGM=*.EDT.SYSLMOD,COND=((5,LT,FTG),(5,LT,EDT))
//FT05F001  DD    DDNAME=SYSIN
//FT06F001  DD    SYSOUT=A,                                             X
//                 DCB=(RECFM=FBA,LRECL=133,BLKSIZE=798)
//FT07F001  DD    UNIT=(SYSCP,,DEFER)
//GO.SYSIN  DD    *
```

The final card indicates that the input data set named SYSIN in the step GO is the card reader. Since the step GO is the execution of the user's program after translation and loading, and SYSIN is the name of the principal input data set used in Fortran READ statements, this allows the programmer to specify that his data will come from the card reader. A data set stored on one of the auxiliary storage devices could have been specified.

Besides pointing out the highlights of the 360 system, this example shows how generality leads to complexity and length. On the 360, this is overcome by the provision of *cataloged procedures*. A cataloged procedure is a sequence of control-card images that have been stored in a special library of procedures on the disk file or some other storage device. The sequence is given a name so that the user can request the execution of just that procedure. The control cards given above resulted from the sequence of cards

```
//PROGRAM  JOB    (299899,200,0,5),'USERNAME',MSGLEVEL=1
//FTNMAX   EXEC   FTGCLG,PARM.FTG='LIST,ID',PARM.EDT=XREF
//FTG.SYSIN DD     *
(Fortran program)
/*
//GO.SYSIN   DD     *
(Data for execution)
/*
```

The single cataloged procedure FTGCLG contained control cards requesting Fortran G, the linkage editor, and execution of the program. The /* cards terminate an input data set in the same stream as the job control cards. The amount of work has been reduced, but the generality has been restricted. However, the user who requires generality may employ the more complex method of job control.

After a program has been executed and it terminates, whether by user error or intentionally by a transfer back to the system (a location in the monitor program), the monitor program will provide dumps of the memory and other information as requested. Then the machine is vacant until the next user's program is input. In order to minimize the loss of time in the job-to-job transition, the monitor program will immediately transfer to a supervisor program whose job is to take care of any accounting that needs to be done (computer time is normally chargeable to somebody) and then to load in the next user's program. Depending on the complexity of the machine and the sophistication of the system, the next job may be acquired from a number of places. The simplest batch processing system will allow several jobs to be stacked one behind another in the input card reader, so that they can be processed serially. In more complicated systems, there can be several input devices, and the next job can be selected from any one of them. Some jobs may have several inputs from different devices, so that the scheduler will take care of informing the operator that all of the inputs must be present when the job is being read in. The scheduler will also check, by reading labelling information at the front of each input that is read, to see that the inputs have been correctly loaded by the operator.

PROBLEMS

1. Express the following numbers in decimal, hexadecimal, and binary:

Decimal

				B	7									

							0	1	0	0	1	0	1	1

2	3	1												

2. What are the three important pieces of information that must appear on each record input to an absolute loader?

3. What would be the assembled result (using a reasonable assembler) of those of the following programs that can be assembled?

```
a.          ORG     100
            LOAD    B
      B     ADD     ONE
      ONE   STORE   B
            CALL    SYSTEM
            END

b.          ORG     200
      D     LOAD    TEN
            ADD     FOUR
            TRA     D
      TEN   DEC     10
      FOUR  DEC     4
      D     STORE   E
            CALL    SYSTEM
      E     BSS     1
            END

c.          ORG     526
            LOAD    TEN
            STORE   D
            LOAD    D
            ADD     FOUR
            STORE   E
            CALL    SYSTEM
      E     BSS     1
      TEN   DEC     4
      FOUR  DEC     10
      D     BSS     1
            END

d.          ORG     500
      B     TRA     A
            BSS     2
      A     LOAD    C
            CALL    SYSTEM
            END
```

4. Indicate which symbolic names are relocatable and which are absolute in the following section of program:

```
A   MPY   C
    ADD   100
B   EQU   A+10
E   SUB   D
    TRA   F
G   BSS   3
F   ADD   G
D   EQU   E—A
C   EQU   7
H   EQU   C+11
    MPY   H
    ADD   G+1
I   EQU   C+F
```

5. Give the locations and addresses used in the following program assuming that a transfer vector method is used, that this section of code starts loading into location 100, and that the machine has one instruction per word.

```
START  LOAD   TEN
       ADD    TEN+2
       CALL   SQRT
       STORE  A+3
       SUB    TEN+1
       CALL   SQRT
       TRA    B
A      BSS    7
TEN    DEC    17,21,33
B      STORE  A+1
       END
```

6. What is a transfer vector?
    What does the assembler produce as a transfer vector?
    To what does the loader convert the assembler transfer vector when it loads the program into memory?
7. Indicate what would be assembled as a relocatable object code for the program below if a linking method were used by the loader to handle subroutine calls.

```
LOAD   100
CALL   SQRT
CALL   SIN
ADD    30
CALL   SQRT
CALL   SIN
ADD    30
CALL   SIN
CALL   SIN
STORE  100
END
```

8. Discuss the action of a relocatable loader in assigning separately assembled sections of code to memory and linking the sections together in a system in which a transfer vector technique is used.
    Compare the assignment of memory space to code sections by the loader with the action of an assembler in assigning instructions to memory.
9. Express the following numbers in the indicated bases.

Decimal	Hexadecimal	Binary
231		
	12C	
		11110100

10. What are the differences between a linking loader and a transfer vector method as they affect the *loaded* program in regard to
    a. Memory space
    b. Execution speed

For what purpose can a linking loader be used directly that a transfer vector loader cannot?

11. Suppose that we are loading three programs into memory with a relocatable loader which uses a transfer vector technique. Assume one instruction per word. The relocatable programs have the following characteristics:

Program 1
Entry Points: 0
Called Programs: 3
            Names—#0 SQRT
                   #1 PRINT
                   #2 PUNCH
Length (including transfer vectors): 32 words

Program 2
Entry Points: 1
          Name—SQRT   Value 1
Called Programs: 1
          Name—#0 PRINT
Length (including transfer vectors): 64 words

Program 3
Entry Points: 3
            Names—PRINT   Values 17
                   PUNCH   21
                   READ   45
Called Programs: 0
Length: 100 words

If they are loaded, starting at location 0, in the order given and immediately following one another, give the locations of all transfer vectors generated by the loader, and the addresses contained in those transfer vectors. *Note:* The value of an entry point is its address relative to location 0 of that program, including its transfer vectors. Give reasons for your answers.

12. Suppose the following DC pseudo-orders are input by the IBM 360 assembler in the order shown:

```
ONE    DC  2F'2'
TWO    DC  PL2'46'
THREE  DC  X'BA'
FOUR   DC  F'1'
```

Give the contents of the following byte locations in binary: ONE+7, ONE+9, ONE+10, and THREE−2. If location ONE is byte location 24 decimal, what is the symbolic address FOUR equal to?

13. The following IBM 360 program is to test bit 1 of the 32-bit word MDR. At the start of execution, register 9 contains a 12-bit *left* justified integer which is the *position* in an array of 16-bit halfwords in memory whose *address* is to be placed in register 10 if bit 1 of MDR is a 0. The address of the first 16-bit halfword is MCODE, while its position number is 0. The second halfword has address MCODE+2 and position number 1.

12	20
Integer	Garbage

Register 9 beforehand

Fill in the blanks:

```
        L    _,MDR
        N    1,MASK          AND INSTRUCTION
        BC   4,NOBRANCH   BRANCHES IF NON-ZERO
        SRL  9,_
        SLL  9,1
        LA   10,_____(___)
NOBRANCH  - - - - - - -
          - - - - - - -
MASK      _    OF,X'_____'
```

14. The following program section is run on the IBM 360.

Location (hex)		Code	
E800		LA	10,8
E804		L	3,FIVE
E808		L	8,=F'38'
E80C		LA	12,FOUR
E810		SRDA	8,32
E814		DR	8,10
E816		SRA	8,1
E81A		MR	2,10
E81C		SLDA	2,32
E820	FIVE	DC	F'6'
E824	FOUR	DC	F'4'

What are the contents of registers 2, 3, 8, 9, 10, and 12 when the instruction in location E81C has been executed?

4

principles of programming

Modern computers contain many instructions designed to speed up common tasks. The index instructions discussed in an earlier chapter are an example of such instructions. These additional instructions are not logically necessary, since a calculation can be done using only a few different instruction types; but the resulting programs will be longer, both in numbers of instructions and in execution time. Because of the typical redundancy of the instruction code of a computer, there are many ways in which a job can be coded for any given way of programming it. If the different ways of planning the program and the different methods (algorithms) are also taken into account, then there is a confusingly large number of programs which could be written to handle a single task. One of these possibilities must be chosen—preferably the best or a close approximation to it. Since computers exist only to do a job (not to test the ingenuity of programmers), the "best" solution is always the most economical.

Programming is often spoken of as an art whose works are judged, at least in part, subjectively. Such statements are, however, made mainly because no way has yet been found to evaluate objectively all the criteria of an economical program. In the final analysis, however, the value of a program depends on its cost rather than its beauty. The system programmer may easily be carried away by the fascination of his own work, forgetting that the user, who cares nothing about programming per se, is interested only in getting correct answers as fast as possible.

The cost of a program is determined by a combination of many factors. In addition to the obvious costs of programming and running, there are the costs of documentation and future changes. Almost no large program remains constant throughout its lifetime. Errors are found long after it has been pronounced working, and additional functions must be included to cater to new needs. Many changes will be made after the original programmer has moved or left, so that it must be possible for another programmer to understand the design of the original program in order to be able to update it as necessary. The yardsticks by which a program must be measured are (in alphabetical order)

1. Clarity
2. Debugging time
3. Documentation
4. Flexibility and expandability
5. Programming and coding time
6. Space required in the memory
7. Speed of execution

The clarity of the program will reduce the programming time, reduce the need for documentation, aid in expansion, and reduce the time for debugging (the time used in removing *bugs*, which is colloquial for program errors). Debugging, which is unproductive in itself, can use up much of the programmer's time as well as that of the machine (50 percent of the total is not untypical). Documentation is the only means by which another programmer can find out in a reasonable manner what a code is supposed to do. It is usually the item most lacking in a computer installation. Well-written, well-documented programs can be expanded and modified. Programs that are obscure or poorly documented are sometimes easier to rewrite completely than to modify. Clarity and documentation are expensive in the early stages of a program, but they pay off handsomely in the later stages.

The space occupied by the program is important in the case of large programs which are executed for relatively short intervals, since the time taken to load the program into memory may exceed the actual execution time. On the other hand, the speed of execution is critically important for small, frequently used programs which are part of much larger programs. For example, a subprogram such as square root may be used very often in a large scientific code. The square root program is normally only a few instructions long (perhaps 15 to 30). It is much more important that a few microseconds be cut from its execution time than that a few instructions be removed from its length. The program is so short that it is unlikely to become too obscure. Therefore the main applicable criterion is one of speed (and of course accuracy, which we assume). Because it is difficult to relate documentation to the actual code, it is usually preferable to include the documentation as a part of the program by means of comment cards and meaningful symbolic addresses.

Because there is such a wide choice of programs available, and because the objectives are, in many cases, mutually contradictory, the programmer and coder are faced with decisions that are always open to question. In order to avoid endless argument over what should be optimized and the impossible task of picking the optimum amongst the many possibilities, programming is currently treated as an art and programs are judged subjectively, that is, after they have passed the objective tests of working correctly in a reasonable length of time. The programmer must develop a style of programming by utilizing standard methods in standard situations and by applying these conventions in a consistent manner. This chapter will discuss some of the techniques and conventions that aid in ease of programming, documentation, and modification.

4.1 PROGRAM LOOPS

If each instruction prepared by the programmer were to be executed only once, then it would be quicker, in general, to perform the calculation by means of a desk calculator than to use a computer. The savings possible in a computer are due to its ability to repeat the same or similar tasks many times, while the programmer only has to prepare it once. In order to make use of this capability, it is necessary to plan the program so that sections of the code can be repetitively executed.

Consider the following simple tasks:

1. Add the 3 numbers $X(1)$, $X(2)$ and $X(3)$.
2. Add the 10 numbers $X(1)$, $X(2)$, . . . , and $X(10)$.
3. Add the 10,000 numbers $X(1)$, $X(2)$, . . . , and $X(10,000)$.
4. Add the N numbers $X(1)$, $X(2)$, . . . , and $X(N)$.

In the first case, we would undoubtedly write

```
LOAD   X
ADD    X+1
ADD    X+2
```

where it is assumed that arrays such as X are stored in increasing memory locations, starting at the location with symbolic address X. In the second, we might write out seven more ADD operations, but we would probably use a loop with indexing as in Figure 4.1. In the third case, we would certainly use such a loop, since it is out of the question to write 9,999 ADD instructions. In the final case, we have no choice but to write a loop, since, if N is not

known until execution time (and it could change each time the set of operations is to be executed), there is no way of writing N ADD instructions.

These examples point out factors that are taken into account in planning
the use of a program loop. In some cases it is worth while not using a loop;
it is not only faster to use *straight-line program*, but it also uses less code. Some
cases are on the borderline, other cases are quite definitely candidates for
loops (although it may still be faster to use a straight-line code), while there
is no choice in still other cases. Part of the job of planning a program involves
looking for places in which a loop can be used to reduce the work and aid
the clarity and ease of debugging. A loop should always be used if there is
any chance that the number of times the basic cycle must be executed may
change at a later date. A loop should be used if the amount of code is space-
wise shorter than if straight-line code is used, otherwise straight-line code
should be used. Occasionally, a loop should be written out in straight-line
code when speed of execution is essential.

Often it is possible to form program loops when the repeated sections of

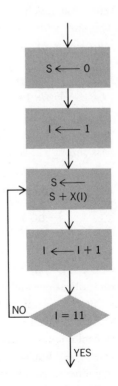

FIGURE 4.1   A program loop for summation.

code are not identical but are similar. A number of techniques can be used
to write a common program that will handle all cases. If repeated passes
through the loop require the use of different variables or constants, the numbers can be placed in an indexed array and referenced sequentially. If the
variable to be used at a point in the loop depends on a condition external to
the loop, its address can be planted in an index register prior to entry to the
loop. Alternatively, indirect addressing can be used for the same effect. If a
slightly different calculation is to be performed, depending on a condition
generated either inside the loop or external to it, then a test can be made and
followed by the appropriate piece of code. In the case of a test of an external
condition, it is more efficient to perform the test prior to entry to the loop
and set the address of the section of code in an index register at that time.
Inside the loop, an indexed transfer—requiring only one instruction to make
the decision—can be made to the appropriate section code. The latter method
is usually called a *program switch*. It is shown in Figure 4.2.

Since the code inside a loop is executed many times each time that the
code surrounding the loop is executed once, it is good coding practice to
remove as much code from the inside to the outside of the loop as possible.
This can be illustrated with the Fortran example below. Suppose the following code is written:

```
      DO 15 I = 1,100
   15 A(I) = D*E*(A(I) + S(J))/T(K)
```

One addition, one division, and two multiplications will be executed in each
pass through this loop. The program could, and should, be written as

```
      T1 = D*E/T(K)
      T2 = S(J) * T1
      DO 15 I = 1,100
   15 A(I) = T1*A(I) + T2
```

where T1 and T2 are two temporary variables. Although there are two
multiplications and a division outside the loop, the inside of the loop has been
reduced by a multiplication and a division. The saving each time that this
section is executed is 98 multiply times and 99 divide times. In fact, on a
typical computer the code will run at least twice as fast. It is possible that a
very good Fortran compiler would effectively do this reorganization. In
machine or assembly language coding, the programmer will have to do this
rearranging himself. It should be realized that the results from the two programs may differ due to differing roundoff errors.

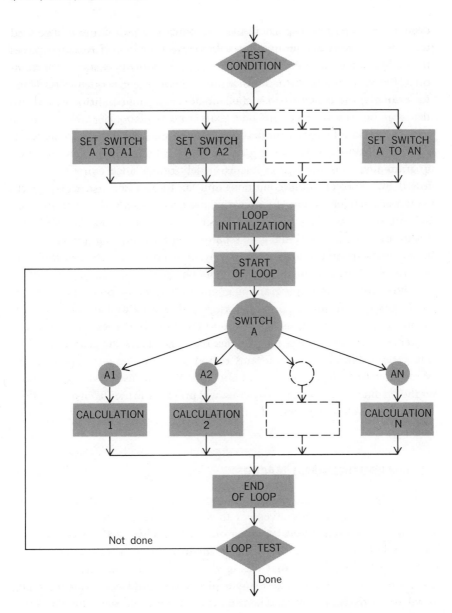

FIGURE 4.2 Use of program switch in loop.

When program loops are used, the programmer should be careful to make it clear in the program and associated documentation what the initial conditions are, where they are set, and what the end conditions are. A common coding error is a transfer to the start of the loop beyond the point where the initial conditions are set. Another is to code one too many or too few passes through the loop. This is particularly easy when the loop has to allow for 0 passes, which requires a jump around the body of the loop. Particular attention should be paid to branches out of the loop. In many instances of complex loops, the variables used in the loop are kept in more accessible registers (for example, the general registers of the 360), and must be stored back in their memory storage locations after exits from the loop.

Early machines used arithmetic operations on instructions to perform indexing of addresses and other forms of modification in loops. This form of programming causes severe problems in debugging, since many errors are caused by incorrect initial conditions and failure to reset instructions back to their original form after a modification has been made. Indirect addressing and indexing have eliminated the necessity of instruction modification, and it is therefore a good philosophy to separate the program from the variables, be they data or program switches, etc., so that no program modification is performed. Apart from making the job of debugging easier, it has a number of advantages in multiprogramming environments. A program segment which has no data or temporary storage within itself and which does not modify itself in any way is called a *pure procedure*. If it uses data, then all references must be made through index registers. It has the advantage that if it is stopped in the middle, for any reason (for example, interrupts), it can be restarted from the beginning without problems. The use of write protection on the memory containing the program will prevent the user from overwriting his program. This is a useful debug tool.

4.2 SUBROUTINES AND MACROS

Frequently the same or similar piece of code must be written in many different parts of a job. It is not convenient to make this into a loop because it is executed at random intervals among other code. There are obvious advantages to designing a system in which the identical piece of code will not have to be rewritten each time that it is used. One obvious approach is to write the code once and then make many copies of the card deck, punched tape, or whatever medium it is on. The copies can be inserted each time that they are needed. This approach is historically called using an *open subroutine*. The piece of code is called a *subroutine* since it is a subsidiary part of a larger routine, and the word *open* serves to distinguish it from *closed subroutines*, which are defined below. A *macro* is an additional facility that will enter, automatically, the section of code without messy card-duplication problems. The basic principle of either scheme is to save the programmer the job of rewriting similar pieces of code many times. Thus, if the job of raising the contents of the accumulator to the 4th power appeared many times, it would be worth while writing the section of code

```
STORE  T
MPY    T
STORE  T
MPY    T
```

once and causing it to be copied into the program each time that it is needed. In many assemblers, this could be done with the sequence

```
POWER4  MACRO
        STORE   T
        MPY     T
        STORE   T
        MPY     T
        END
```

which serves as a *macro definition* at the start of the program to be assembled. The assembler will insert the code sequence each time that the new mnemonic POWER4 is used, so that an input of

```
LOAD     A
POWER4
ADD      B
POWER4
```

would be equivalent to

```
LOAD   A
STORE  T
MPY    T
STORE  T
MPY    T
ADD    B
STORE  T
MPY    T
STORE  T
MPY    T
```

Although the programmer has been saved the job of writing the code by using an open subroutine, the sections of code still occupy space in memory.

If an open subroutine or macro is used many times, the amount of storage space used can become very large. To get around this problem, the *closed subroutine* is used. In the future, we shall refer to the closed subroutine simply as a "subroutine" and the open subroutine as a "macro." The section of code representing the subroutine only appears once in memory. Each time that it is used in the main part of the program, a transfer of control is executed to the start of the subroutine. After the subroutine has been executed, a transfer is made back to the instruction following the transfer to the subroutine. This immediately poses the problem of how the subroutine knows which location to return to, since many different parts of the main program may make transfers to the subroutine. This problem can be solved in many ways. On early computers, which tended to be one-address machines, an additional instruction had to be obeyed—prior to the transfer to the subroutine—which put its own location into a standard place, such as the accumulator. Since every transfer to a subroutine would be preceded by such an instruction, it was worth while designing a single instruction for subroutine transfer to do both jobs. By the time this was done, machines also had index registers, so it is common to find an instruction called *subroutine transfer* or *transfer and set index* in the repertoire of a computer. This instruction transfers control to the subroutine addressed and causes a location to be stored in a specified index register. This can then be used in an indexed transfer instruction to return to the initiating program. A zero-address machine will frequently put the return address into the top of the accumulator stack. It will also provide another instruction called *return* which transfers to the address in the top of the stack and then pops. If we assume that the transfer and set index instruction for a one-address machine is designated as TSX A,I where A is the address of the transfer and I is the index to be used, the example above will be entered into memory as

```
        LOAD    A
        TSX     POWER4,4
        ADD     B
        TSX     POWER4,4
        - - - - - - - - - - -
POWER4  STORE   T
        MPY     T
        STORE   T
        MPY     T
        TRA     0,4
```

The TSX instruction is assumed to put the contents of the control counter (which contains the location of the next instruction to be executed if control continues sequentially) into the designated index register (index number 4 in the example) and then to transfer to the address given in the TSX instruction by placing that address in the control counter. The TRA instruction has an address of zero modified by index register 4. Since the contents of index register 4 is the location of the instruction following the last TSX executed, the transfer instruction returns control to that instruction, as desired. The address saved in index 4 in this example is called the *link* address. It can be seen that the subroutine approach uses the least amount of storage, but that it uses more machine time because it is necessary to execute at least two additional instructions for each subroutine transfer. For this reason, subroutines should be used only under the following circumstances: (1) when the amount of work within the subroutine is such that these two or more additional instructions are not significant or (2) if the use of a subroutine substantially aids in the clarity and documentation of the program. If, for example, the subroutine were only two instructions in length plus the return transfer, then the overhead in time would be 100 percent, while the saving in space would amount to only one instruction per *call*. (A call of a subroutine or macro is a use of it in the source code, either by writing its name in the case of a macro, or by writing a subroutine transfer to it in the case of a subroutine.)

As with almost all decisions in programming, there will be many borderline cases, in which case questions of clarity, ease of debugging, etc., must be taken into account.

The next two sections will discuss subroutines and macros. As additional features are added to each facility, the reader will see that they are not interchangeable. Not all systems provide for macro assembly, whereas some form of subroutine facility is essential in any system; therefore, subroutines will be examined first.

4.3 SUBROUTINES

We have already discussed a way in which the link address can be passed to the subroutine. Naturally, each different machine organization will use a different method with the same basic principle—when the programmer writes the subroutine, he does not have to know from where it will be called. We must also examine ways in which data is passed from the calling program to the subroutine and back, and what is necessary for a subroutine to provide a well-documented, easy-to-modify program. Since subroutines will usually represent reasonably self-contained sections of code, it is quite common to want to assemble them as individual units and to retain versions of the programs in binary form suitable for a relocatable loader of the sort discussed in Chapter 3.

4.3.1 Subroutine parameters, data transfer, and common storage

It is necessary for the subroutine to have access to data in the calling program and to return results to that program. Because subroutines may be used from many different points in the program, it is wise to organize this data carefully to avoid errors and to reduce the complexity of the code. If the subroutine appears in the same section of code as the calling program, so that they are both translated at the same time, then they both have access to the same symbolic storage cells. That is, both the calling program and the subroutine could refer to the same variables such as X, TIME, COUNT, etc. However, one of the purposes of a subroutine structure is to enable sections of the code to be assembled separately and to be entered into the machine in a translated form. This is particularly true of commonly used subroutines such as square root, etc., which are coded once and made available to all users via a library. In these circumstances, it is not possible to refer to variables with the same name (except possibly via the external option in Chapter 3), since all record of the names of variables is lost after translation (the input to the loader only contains the binary program, relocation bits, entry point names and called subroutine names). It is therefore necessary to replace this lost facility with some other facility. One means, the external declaration, was mentioned in the last chapter and will be discussed later in this section.

Another method is known as *common* storage. Common storage is an area assigned by the loader at load time for storage of all variables which are used in common by more than one subroutine. Each separately assembled section of code declares the names of variables which are to be stored in common by use of a suitable pseudo-order in assembly language or a declaration statement in a higher-level language (for example, the COMMON statement in Fortran). A typical form for an assembler is the pseudo-order

S COMMON 34

which would assign the symbolic address S in the common area and allocate the next 34 words of storage, which could then be addressed as S, S+1, S+2, etc. The assembler will assign the symbolic addresses declared to be in common to consecutive locations in common. Thus if the declarations

```
A  COMMON  3
B  COMMON  1
C  COMMON  5
```

were included, and the common area began at location 1035, then the symbolic addresses A, B, and C would be equivalent to memory locations 1035, 1038, and 1039. This is handled in the loader by using additional relocation bits for common storage. The assembler will tell the loader how many common locations are required, and the loader will assign space for the maximum requested. Thus, if several different sections of code place variables in common, they occupy the same storage area at execution time. However, there is no relation between the names used, because the assignment is made by the loader. Thus, if the pseudo-orders

```
A  COMMON  1
B  COMMON  1
```

appear in one section of code, while

```
B  COMMON  1
X  COMMON  1
```

appear in another separately translated section, the variable A in the first section will correspond to B in the second, while B in the first will correspond to X in the second. Because of this, common storage has to be used with extreme care. A change in one section without a corresponding change in all other sections will cause errors that are very difficult to locate.

The 360 assembler, which produces output for a linkage editor, provides an external feature that overcomes the defects of common storage. External variables were discussed in Chapter 3. Let us recall that names can be defined in one section and referred to in a separately assembled section, provided that they are specified as ENTRY points in the former section and as EXTRN (the 360 mnemonic for external) in the latter section. Since the reference is by name, the source of confusion and error in common disappears.

Identical storage, either by means of a common area or by external names, can be used for data communication between subroutines and the calling programs, but for many needs it is not efficient. Consider, for example, a square root subroutine. This will be used to take the square root of a variety of numbers at different points in the program. If the equivalent of the Fortran statement

A= SQRT(X)

is to be executed, then a one-address code of the form

Example A

```
LOAD    X
STORE   INPUT
CALL    SQRT
LOAD    OUTPUT
STORE   A
```

would have to be written. INPUT and OUTPUT are assumed to be the locations of the input and output to and from the square root program. The movement of the data from X to INPUT and then from OUTPUT to A is unnecessary if the program can be arranged so that the data links to the subroutine are more convenient. The simplest solution for this case in a one-address machine is to use the accumulator. If the input and output from the square root program is via the accumulator, the code takes the form

Example B

```
LOAD    X
CALL    SQRT
STORE   A
```

We say that there are two *parameters* to the square root program, the input and the output. (In Fortran, we could call this a *function subroutine* because the output parameter could be represented by the name of the function.) In general, a subroutine can have many parameters, both input and output. If the method of common or external storage is used, it is necessary to copy all of the input parameters into the common area prior to calling the program and to copy the output parameters back into the desired locations after control is returned to the calling program, as was done in example A. This could be very inefficient, so methods similar to the use of the accumulator in example B are used.

The accumulator can only be used for a single input parameter and a single output parameter, so other places must be used to pass data. In order to discuss this, let us examine the various types of parameters that we may wish to pass to a subroutine or to get back from a subroutine. They include

1. A constant (for example, 2. in SQRT(2.))—input only.
2. A variable (for example, A in SQRT(A))—input or output.
3. An array (that is, a dimensioned variable in Fortran). This could be used in input or output; the subroutine would use or change any or all of the elements of the array.
4. The name of another subroutine. This is often restricted to input, but could be used for output.
5. The address of a section of code (a statement number in Fortran)—input or output.

A subroutine call will indicate a list of parameters that are to be used (in Fortran, for example, they are written in parentheses following the name of the subroutine). In machine language, each of the parameters must be in memory or in one of the accessible CPU registers. In a zero-address machine, the parameters could be put into the CPU stack, since it is arbitrarily large (at least in principle), but on other machines the parameters will have to be put in memory. They are often placed in locations following the call, which is a subroutine transfer instruction in machine language. In designing subroutine parameter lists for particular subroutines, it is tempting to try to minimize the amount of space and time by taking note of special cases, but this approach can quickly cause problems of compatibility between different translators and lead to errors in use. The parameter list should be made as uniform as possible to avoid these problems. The only item that can be used as a parameter in all cases is an address. For single variables, it must be the address of the variable in memory. This works for both input and output and takes care of constants. An array can be specified by the address of its first element, and a subroutine or section of code can also be given by its address.

   If this form of parameter transfer is used, the machine-language equivalent of the Fortran code

```
DIMENSION A(100)
- - - - - - -
CALL PROC (A,B,1.0,X—Y,SINF)
- - - - - - - - - - -
```

would be similar to

```
A  BSS     100
- - - - - - - -
   LOAD    X
   SUB     Y
```

```
        STORE  TEMP
        CALL   PROC
        PAR    A
        PAR    B
        PAR    =1.0
        PAR    TEMP
        PAR    SINF
        ---------
        TEMP  BSS  1
```

where PAR is a pseudo which simply loads the value of the address field into the next location in memory, and where some provision is made to put the function SINF into the list of subroutines needed.

When a subroutine is defined, we refer to the parameters as *formal parameters* because they are not the names of variables but place markers for variables that will be substituted when the subroutine is invoked (that is, called). When parameters are specified in a call to subroutines, they are called *actual parameters*. Thus, in the section of Fortran code

```
        CALL ABC(X)
        ----
        SUBROUTINE ABC(P)
```

P is a formal parameter, while X is an actual parameter.

The 360 conventions for subroutines require that a separate list of parameter addresses be provided and that the address of the first member of the list be placed in register 1. Thus the example above for CALL PROC (A,B,1.0, X−Y,SINF) would be implemented by the assembly code

```
            LE    0,X
            SE    0,Y
            STE   0,TEMP
            LA    1,PARLIST
            L     15,ASUB
            BALR  14,15
            -------
ASUB     DC    A(PROC)          ADDRESS OF PROCEDURE
PARLIST  DC    A(A)             LIST OF PARAMETERS
         DC    A(B)
         DC    A(CONST1)
         DC    A(TEMP)
         DC    X'80',AL3(SINF)  LAST PARAMETER
TEMP     DS    F
CONST1   DC    E'1.0'
```

The parameter list is a series of 32-bit addresses. The first 8 bits are 0 in a 32-bit address, so the first bit is used to indicate the last parameter. It is set to a 1 by the 1-byte specification in hexadecimal X'80'. This convention allows for variable-length parameter lists. The subroutine can determine how long the list is at execution time. This feature is not provided in Fortran compilers generally, except in the built-in functions similar to MAX0F(A,B, . . .), which find the maximum of a number of arguments.

The subroutine linking convention in the 360 requires that the address of the first word of the program be available in register 15 (as an initial base register) and that the link address for returns be in register 14.

CALL BY NAME

Fortran does not provide for a distinction between call-by-name and call-by-value. Let us consider the subroutine

```
SUBROUTINE EXMPL(A,B,C,D)
A = B
C = D
END
```

called by

```
CALL EXMPL(P,1.0,Q,P)
```

The effect of this program may be different on different compilers. The strictest interpretation would be to perform the two operations

```
P = 1.0
Q = P
```

which would assign a value of 1.0 to Q and P. The value of P is changed by the first statement, and this affects the result of the second statement. Now consider the call

```
CALL EXMPL(X,1.0,Q,X—Y)
```

It might be thought that this should be equivalent to

```
X = 1.0
Q = X — Y
```

so that Q would be set to $1.0 - Y$. This does not happen in Fortran compilers, since the sequence of actions is equivalent to

```
TEMP = X − Y
CALL EXMPL(X,1.0,Q,TEMP)
```

so that $X - Y$ is evaluated prior to entry and stored in a *temporary*. If actual parameters are evaluated before entry and stored in a temporary, we say that the call is *by value*. If provision is made for evaluating them each time that they are used in a subroutine, we say that they are called *by name*. Algol allows the user to state in the subroutine whether the actual parameters substituted for the formal parameters are to be called by name or by value. Those that are by value are explicitly declared as such; the remainder are by name.

(Before proceeding, the programmer should note the programming error that can be made in Fortran and that can be very difficult to locate. Consider

```
CALL EXMPL(P,1.0,4.0,P)
A = SQRT(4.0)
```

which will set A to 1.0 on most compilers, as well as have other undesirable effects. Why is this?)

The call-by-name problem introduces problems as well as flexibility into those languages that allow it. For an example of its use, consider the following taken from the Algol report.†

```
procedure   Innerproduct(a,b)Order:(k,p)Result:(y);
   value   k ; integer k,p; real y,a,b;
   begin real s;
     s := 0 ;
     for  p := 1 step 1 until k do s := s + a × b ;
     y := s ;
     end  Innerproduct
```

The parameters a, b, p, and y are used by name since they are not declared by value. Consequently, the following use of Innerproduct can be used in the inner loop of matrix multiply.

```
Innerproduct(A(I,J),B(J,K),N,J,R)
```

which will calculate the sum

$$R = \sum_{J=1}^{N} A(I,J)B(J,K)$$

† Revised Algol Report, *Communications of the Association for Computing Machinery*, vol. 6, no. 1, Jan., 1963.

This works because the parameters a and b are reevaluated each time that they are used with a new value for J, which is substituted for p.

If a formal parameter is to be used by name, it is necessary for the calling program to provide a section of code which will evaluate the actual parameter each time that it is used. This code section is best made into a subroutine. The main subroutine must know whether to treat the actual parameter as the address of data or as the address of a program that will calculate the data. The subroutine could require that all actual parameters substituted for formal parameters called by name be supplied as subroutines. In that case, it would be necessary for the calling program to know which parameters were by value and which by name. This can only be done if all subroutines in Algol are translated at the same time as their calling programs. This immediately leads to an incompatibility between Algol- and Fortran-compiled subroutines. An alternative solution is to supply all actual parameters by name. If the subroutine requires that they be used by value, then it can request an evaluation initially and save the value in a temporary. If this is done, the subroutines for the actual parameters must return the address of the data to be passed, since the parameter may be used either for output or as a subroutine. Now, in order to pass a constant as a parameter, the called subroutine would get an address from the parameter list and perform a subroutine jump to that address. This code would return an address which could then be used to access the constant. The method is inefficient, but that is the price of flexibility and generality.

An alternative solution is to use additional bits in the parameter words to indicate their type. The subroutine can examine these to determine whether they represent an address, a constant, a subroutine, etc. This provides for a lot of dynamic checking which is very useful. If, in the case of arrays, a complete description of the array (size, etc.) is provided by the parameter (it would then be called a *dope vector*), it is possible to implement languages in which the size and type of arrays are not declared in subroutines. Some of this checking can be done automatically by special hardware. Some of the larger Burroughs computers provide this, for example.

THE CHOICE OF PARAMETERS OR COMMON

In planning a subroutine, the programmer must decide which variables to assign to common storage and which to put in the parameter list. The decision should rest largely on which parameter names change from call to call and which are the same. If a given parameter is always the same variable name, then it is better to place it in common. This saves both writing time and execution time. On the other hand, if it is necessary to store information into common before each call of a subroutine, then it is better to remove the variable from common and to put it in the parameter list.

If the addresses of variables are used as parameters and they are placed in memory cells following the cell containing the subroutine call, indirect addressing can be used to access parameter values. Suppose, for example, that a subroutine is to be written to add the values of the first two parameters and to store the result in the third. (Hardly worth writing a subroutine for, but this is an example!) If the call takes the form

```
        TSX     ADD3,4
        PAR     A
        PAR     B
        PAR     C
```

the subroutine could take the form

```
ADD3    LOAD*   0,4
        ADD*    1,4
        STORE*  2,4
        TRA     3,4
```

The asterisk is assumed to indicate indirect addressing and to occur after indexing. The effect of the LOAD instruction is to first calculate the effective address by adding 0 to the contents of index register 4. This gives the address of the cell containing the instruction PAR A. Since indirect addressing is indicated, it uses the address A as the actual address of the data, so the effect is to load the contents of cell A into the accumulator.

4.3.2 Subroutine conventions

Subroutines are used as a means of making code written by one person available to another, since they are written in a form where subsequent users do not have to concern themselves with the inner workings but only with the macroscopic details. For example, if we write a subroutine for complex number multiplication, you can use it as long as you know where the parameters are to be placed. You do not have to know how it does the job.

By collecting general purpose subroutines written by many of the users of a system, a large program library can be built up which will save a user with a new job a lot of effort. Unfortunately, largeness can become a drawback if the library is not managed carefully. The information-explosion problem is inescapable, since it is bound to take longer to find the right program in a large library; the problem of inconsistent methods, however, *can* be avoided. All programs should have calling sequences which are as similar as possible in order to minimize the chance of errors in calling one program from another. Therefore it is a good idea for the programmer to use the same method in his personal subroutines as is used in the library. In addition to the questions of where the parameters are stored for transmission, there is the question of what is stored as a parameter and in what format it is stored. It is typically impossible to choose a single format that will satisfy all users, some of whom are interested in speed and others in complete generality.

In addition to the transmission of parameters, there is the problem of understanding all of these effects of a subroutine. The write-up should describe the action of the program in terms of how the output parameters are related to the input parameters and what side effects occur. Arguments can be made for the use of side effects in terms of efficiency, particularly when large arrays of data are stored in common storage, but as a general rule the use of side effects should be avoided, since it is easy to forget that variables not in the call sequence can be changed by the program. This applies at the machine- or assembly-language level to the registers on the central processing unit. It would be very difficult to check the write-up of every subroutine used to see if the program changed any registers. The index register used in the TSX instruction is expected to be changed since this is a necessary part of the calling procedure, but it would be very undesirable if information in other index registers were changed. For this reason it is usual always to use the same index register for subroutine calls and to expect every subroutine to leave the contents of all other index registers unchanged. The same attitude could be taken to the accumulator or accumulators, as the case may be, but in a one-address machine it is usual to assume that every subroutine changes the contents of the accumulator. Zero-address machines will usually expect the contents to be unchanged unless the accumulator stack is used for transmission of parameters. This is reasonable, since working space is always available on top of other data in a zero-address machine. A single-accumulator one-address code will almost always need the accumulator for calculation of answers.

When their contents have to be saved, it is certainly not convenient to avoid the use of index registers altogether (else why buy a machine that has them?). Therefore, such contents must be stored, temporarily, into cells in memory—so that they will be available during the execution of the subroutine—and then reloaded from memory at the conclusion of the subroutine, just prior to returning to the calling program. Examination of subroutines for a particular computer will usually show that the first few instructions store the index-register contents in memory and the last few reload them from memory. The memory locations used to save the contents of the index registers must not interfere with the execution of any other piece of code; hence they must be separated from the other subroutines' temporary storage. The same applies to any temporary storage used in the arithmetic performed by the subroutine. Therefore, each subroutine will have a set of temporary storage cells associated with it for use by that subroutine. The start of a subroutine might appear on a four-index machine as

```
        STX  A,1
        STX  A+1,2
        STX  A+2,3
        STX  A+3,4
        - - - - - - - - -
```

and the end as

```
        LDX  A,1
        LDX  A+1,2
        LDX  A+2,3
        LDX  A+3,4
        TRA  0,4
    A   BSS  4
```

if it has no parameters in the calling sequence. LDX and STX stand for *load index* and *store index* respectively.

Since these two sequences of instructions would be very common on a four-index machine, it might be worth the designer's while to provide two instructions, one of which performs the first set of four index stores and the other which performs the last five. This is sometimes done, but not on many machines. The other possibility is to use a macro for each of them and at least save the programmer the writing time.

Note that index register 4 was saved, although it was changed by the calling TSX instruction. If the subroutine calls on yet another subroutine, this will change index 4, so it is necessary to save and restore its contents in order to make the correct return to the outer calling program.

The IBM 360 requires that most of the general registers be saved if they are used in a subroutine. In general, registers 0, 1, and 13 through 15 will be used in the calling sequence, so they need be saved only if the called subroutine itself calls another. If registers 2 through 12 are changed by the subroutine, they should be restored prior to exit. We have seen that register

15 contains the address of the subroutine, register 14 the return link, and register 1 the address of the parameter list. Register 0 is used to return the output in the case that the subroutine is a function with an integer result. The four floating-point registers may be used by the subroutine if desired. They need not be restored, although registers 0 and 2 are used to return the result of a floating-point function. Floating-point register 0 will contain the real part and 2 the imaginary part if the variable is complex.

The 360 has a pair of multiple-register load and store instructions that are helpful in the subroutine. They are

```
        LM    R1,R2,A
and     STM   R1,R2,A
```

where the mnemonics stand for *load multiple* and *store multiple* respectively. The contents of registers R1, R1+1, . . . , R2 are moved to or from memory addresses A, A+4, ... If R1 is greater than R2, then registers R1, . . . , 15, 0, . . . , R2 are copied. The address A cannot be indexed, but it has a base register.

In the example above, the index registers were stored into an area in the subroutine. On the 360 system, the convention requires the calling program to set aside a temporary storage area for the subroutine. This is called a *savearea*, and is 18 words long. The contents of these words is shown in Figure 4.3. The first word can be ignored by the user, the next two will be discussed shortly. The remaining 15 are used for storing the contents of every register except 13. Register 13 is used to pass the address of the savearea from the calling program to the subroutine so that it can store its registers. Diagram 4.3 shows the relationship between three subroutines, $I-1$, I, and $I+1$. We are looking at the savearea associated with subroutine I, which calls subroutine $I+1$ and is called by subroutine $I-1$. The contents of the registers in the savearea are those at the time that subroutine $I+1$ is called. The second and third words of the savearea contain pointers to the saveareas of the subroutines above and below. SAVEAREA+4 contains a pointer back to the previous savearea, while SAVEAREA+8 contains a pointer to the next savearea. The former must be stored by program I, while the latter can only be done by program $I+1$. These pointers enable the system to determine which subroutines were currently invoked when a termination occurs. This provides a useful post-mortem facility. Note that register 15 contains the address of the subroutine itself. Two other conventions are needed to provide a useful diagnostic. The first is an indicator which tells that a subroutine has been completed after it has been called. The first byte of SAVEAREA+12 in

FIGURE 4.3 360 savearea usage.

the calling program should be set to 11111111 when the subroutine has completed its task. This enables the system to determine how far back up a chain of subroutines call control has returned at the time of an error. The second convention is to place the name of the subroutine as a character string at the start of the program. (The first 4 bytes contain a branch around the name, the next $n+1$ contain the length of the name n and the name as a character string.)

A typical begin and end sequence for a subroutine is shown below.

```
PROGI  CSECT
       DS     OH             Get on an even word boundary.
       USING  *,15           Use 15 as a temporary base register.
       B      *+10           Branch around program name.
       DC     X'5'           Length of name.
       DC     CL5'PROGI'     Name.
       STM    14,12,12(13)   Save registers in savearea of calling program.
       CNOP   0,4            Get on a word boundary.
       BAL    12,*+76        Branch around this program's savearea.
```

```
          DROP   15            Drop register 15 as a base.
          USING  *,12          Use register 12 as a base.
          DC     18F'0'        18 word savearea for this program.
          ST     12,8(13)      Store address of this savearea in previous
                               savearea.
          ST     13,4(12)      Store address of previous savearea in this
                               savearea.
          LR     13,12         Address of this savearea in register 13 for calls
                               to lower-level subroutines.
       . . . . . . . . . . . . . .
```

To call a lower-level subroutine, the sequence below is used:

```
          LA     1,PARLIST     Parameter list address.
          L      15,ASUB       Address of called subroutine.
          BALR   14,15
          . . . . . .          Control returns here.
   . . . . . . . . . . . . . . . . . . . . . .
```

Exit sequence:

```
          L      13,4(13)      Address of calling subroutines savearea.
          LM     1,12,24(13)   Restore registers 1 through 12.
          L      14,12(13)     Restore link address.
          MVI    12(13),X'FF'  Set completion code.
          BR     14            Return.
   ASUB   DC     A(SUBROUT)
   PARLIST DC    A(Par1)
          DC     A(Par2)
          . . . . . .
```

4.3.3 Recursion

It is possible that one subroutine may call another. We say that the second
subroutine is at a lower level in this case. An example of such a circumstance
frequently arises in library subroutines for integration and quadrature. A
library subroutine may be available to integrate a function $F(X)$ from A to B.
This requires four parameters, one to tell it what the function F is, two to
give limits A and B, and the fourth to return the answer. Numerical integration methods usually evaluate the integrand $(F(X))$ for a number of different
values of X and add these results together in some manner to get an approximation of the answer. Therefore the integration subroutine requires the
values of $F(X)$ for values of X that are determined by the integration subroutine, not by the user. For this reason, the most convenient way of telling

the integration subroutine about F is to provide it with another subroutine with one input parameter, X, and one output parameter, the value of F(X). This is illustrated in the sections of a Fortran code below.

```
Main program - - - -
CALL INTGRT(A,B,FUN,RESULT)
- - - - - -
END
SUBROUTINE INTGRT(C,D,AUX,ANS)
- - - - - -
CALL AUX(X,F)
- - - - - -
END
SUBROUTINE FUN(Y,G)
- - - - - -
G = . . . . .
END
```

(Not all Fortran compilers will accept this use of subroutine names as parameters.)

It may happen that the function to be integrated itself involves an integration of another function. The simplest example would arise when F(X) is the integral form 0 to X of another function G(X). It would be tempting to write the defining subroutine for F(X) as

```
SUBROUTINE FUN(X,F)
CALL INTGRT(C,X,FUN1,F)
END
```

and define G(X) by

```
SUBROUTINE FUN1(Y,G)
- - - - -
G = - - - - - -
- - - - -
- - - - -
END
```

The diagram in Figure 4.4 shows what is happening in terms of levels of subroutine calls, but it must be noted that the same subroutine INTGRT appears below itself, that is, it effectively calls on itself. This is not allowed in most Fortran compilers, and it is easy to see why. At the time of the first call on INTGRT, registers and the link information are saved in temporary storage cells associated with the subroutine. In the middle of executing this

FIGURE 4.4   Recursive use of a subroutine.

subroutine, a call on another subroutine is made. This eventually causes another call on INTGRT which will immediately save the current contents of the index registers, etc., in the temporary storage cells that are still being used to save information at the higher-level call. Thus the information from the higher-level call is destroyed by overwriting, and the program will not work.

It is certainly possible to design ways around this problem. We shall mention some below, but first let us examine the utility of allowing a program to call upon itself, either directly or indirectly via another subroutine. The use of a subroutine by itself is called *recursion* and a subroutine written to allow this is called recursive. We have mentioned one possible application above which could certainly arise in multidimensional integration. Another example often used is the factorial function FACT(N). A factorial can certainly be calculated by iteration, for example by

```
    FACT = 1
    DO 1 I = 1,N
  1 FACT = FACT*I
```

It could also be calculated by a recursive subroutine or function were they allowed as

```
     FUNCTION FACT(N)
     IF(N—1) 1,1,2
  1  FACT = 1
     RETURN
  2  FACT = FACT(N—1)*N
     RETURN
     END
```

It is assumed that N is a positive integer in the above program. This example shows recursion in its worst light, as the program is longer in space and speed than the corresponding iterative program. Generally speaking, recursive techniques for numerical problems will lead to slower programs than the corresponding iterative techniques, but frequently they will give shorter programs in terms of space used. (The integration example is a case in point.) The brevity of the program does lead to clarity. This is particularly true in the case of nonnumerical programs, but we shall have to wait to give meaningful examples in those cases. Since clarity and brevity are important, recursion is a very useful technique, but it should seldom be employed in short, frequently-used subroutines.

   One of the better examples of its use in numerical subroutines is given below. This is a subroutine function to integrate a function supplied as a parameter with error control. The first program INTG calculates some initial values needed and then calls the second subroutine INTG1. This subroutine calculates the integral by applying Simpson's rule to each half of the interval and compares the result with the integral found by using Simpson's rule over the whole interval. If the results agree within ERROR, this is the answer; if not, INTG1 is used separately on each half interval. The programs are written in Fortran, but are assumed to be recursive.

```
     FUNCTION INGT(A,B,F,ERROR )
     X = F(A)
     Y = F((A+B)/2.)
     Z = F(B)
     Q = (B—A)*(X + 4.0 * Y + Z)/6.
     INTG = INTG1(A,B,F,X,Y,Z,ERROR,Q)
     RETURN
     END
```

```
FUNCTION INTG1(A,B,F,X,Y,Z,ERROR,Q)
P = (A+B)/2.
P1 = .75*A + .25*B
P2 = .25*A + .75*B
Y1 = F(P1)
Y2 = F(P2)
Q1 = (B—A) * (X + 4.0*Y1 + Y)/12.
Q2 = (B—A) * (Y + 4.0*Y2 + Z)/12.
IF (ABSF(Q — Q1 — Q2) — ERROR) 1,1,2
2  INTG1 = INTG1(A,P,F,X,Y1,Y,ERROR,Q1) + INTG1(P,B,F,Y,Y2,Z,ERROR,Q2)
RETURN
1  INTG1 = Q1 + Q2
RETURN
END
```

To solve the temporary storage problem in recursive subroutines, it is necessary to make provision for different storage for each use of the program while another higher level use is still active. Since the temporary storage that must be accessed is that of the most recent call on the subroutine, a first-in–last-out queue is indicated. In other words, a stack of temporary storage is needed. The accumulator stack could be used on a zero-address machine, but this is not convenient if it is limited in length. Therefore a stack is usually created in memory. The same stack can be used by all subroutines, since the next subroutine to exit is always the last subroutine to be called. A stack can be created in memory by using a *pointer*, which is an address held either in a known memory cell or in an index register allocated for that purpose. The pointer *points* to the top word of the stack. Words can be added to the stack by increasing the pointer address and storing the words in the memory cells indicated. Words can be removed by decreasing the pointer and reading from the cells indicated. Since care must be taken not to overwrite program and other storage areas in memory, a test must be made to check that the pointer has not, in error, become too large or too small. (A desirable design for a machine includes instructions which perform all of these operations simultaneously.) It is convenient to design a set of conventions which allow for such a stack. If register 13 were used as a stack pointer in the 360, then recursion would be straightforward.

4.3.4 Reentrant programs: pure procedures

It is highly desirable to avoid instruction modification in subroutines or in any other piece of code. Therefore, parameter addresses should be used by indexing and indirect reference, rather than by planting them into instructions within the subroutine. Temporary storage access within the program should also be by indexed addresses. The index can be set by the calling program in order to take care of possible recursion; it then serves as a stack pointer for the temporary storage. If this is done, an additional desirable feature appears—the program is what is called a *pure procedure*. This means that it can be interrupted at any place during execution and restarted from the beginning. If the index register used to point to temporary storage is changed before the restart, it is possible to return it to its original value when the first execution was in progress and to continue that execution from the point at which it was interrupted. There is normally no reason for a single user to want to restart a program and later return to continue an earlier execution, but, in a multiprogramming environment where there can be several different users' programs in the main memory simultaneously, it may be desirable to switch from one user to another from time to time. If a subroutine is a pure procedure, it is possible for several different users to share the same copy of it in memory. If it is a large subroutine, for example, a Fortran translator, the saving in memory space is considerable. A program that can be executed by several different users in such a way is called *reentrant*.

4.4 MACROS

Macros were introduced in section 4.2 as open subroutines which are a halfway stage to the closed or regular subroutine. As subroutines, they are not as powerful as closed subroutines because such features as recursion are not applicable. However, we shall see that they have some features of their own that cannot be matched in closed subroutines and should therefore be considered as a tool in their own right. The principle of a macro facility is that a *definition* of an input form can be written so that each time the input form is used, it is replaced by its definition. Elaborate facilities to allow for substitution of *dummy arguments* (similar to the parameters of subroutines) are provided. Macro facilities are not used only in assemblers, although their most common implementation is as part of a system assembler. A macro processor is commonly seen simply as a translator that inputs one string of characters and outputs another in the form of assembly language for eventual input to an assembler. We shall see that the implementation may or may not take that form in practice.

In assembly language, the macro definition is usually accomplished with

the pseudo-orders MACRO and END. The first appears in front of the definition, while the latter serves to indicate the end of the definition. The macro
facility in assembly language defines a new pseudo-order, called a *macro order*,
so that future uses of this new order can be replaced by its definition. The
name of the macro order is placed in the location field of the macro pseudo.
Thus the macro order XYZ can be defined by

```
XYZ  MACRO
     LINE 1
     LINE 2
     - - - -
     LINE N
     END
```

Each time that XYZ appears in the instruction field, N instructions equal to

```
     LINE 1
     LINE 2
     - - - - -
     LINE N
```

are assembled. The replacement process essentially occurs prior to assembly,
so that it is precisely equivalent to inputting the expanded form. In the following subsections, we shall discuss some of the additional features that are
added to macros.

4.4.1 Parameters in macros

Subroutines do not use the same data cells in each call: macros are more
useful if they are similarly not restricted. Since the macro substitution is
done before execution, it is possible to change the symbolic addresses in the
instructions that make up a macro before execution time. Suppose we frequently needed a section of code to add one to the contents of a given location. The code

```
     LOAD    X
     ADD     =1
     STORE   X
```

would do it for the location X. However, each time that it is needed the
location is different. Therefore, X is made a parameter to the macro, and it

is defined as

```
INCR    MACRO   X
        LOAD    X
        ADD     =1
        STORE   X
        END
```

Because X is listed in the address field of the macro pseudo, it is defined as a dummy parameter. The macro must be called by writing

```
        INCR    TCNT
```

where TCNT is the symbolic address of the variable that is to be incremented. This macro call is *expanded* as

```
        LOAD    TCNT
        ADD     =1
        STORE   TCNT
```

so that each use of the dummy parameter is replaced by the symbolic address specified in the macro. A macro can have many parameters. For example,

```
EXMP    MACRO   A,B,ANY,C
        ADD     A
        MPY     B
        STORE   C
        ADD     ANY
        STORE   A
        END
```

It is important to remember that the parameters are dummies (that is, they are not defined outside of the macro), so that they can be used over again but cannot be referred to outside of the macro.

When an actual parameter appears in a location field as follows,

```
EX      MACRO   A,B
        ADD     A
B       ADD     A
        END
```

the use of EX by EX P,Q produces code with the address Q in the location field. This defines Q to the assembler, so that it may only be used once in this form.

Sometimes it is necessary to use a symbolic address in a location field in a macro definition so that the generated code can include a branch. For example,

```
YY      MACRO  X
        LOAD   X
        TPLUS  Y
        MPY    =—.5
Y       STORE  X
        END
```

Unfortunately, if this macro is used more than once, the address Y will be multiply defined. This can be overcome by putting Y as a second dummy parameter and giving it a new name each time that the macro is called. To save the programmer the trouble, the macro facility can be implemented so that the parameter need not be specified when it is called. Instead, some macro assemblers replace missing parameters with internally generated symbolic addresses that are all different. These can be a form that the programmer cannot use himself, and they can be generated in some sort of order. Some assemblers generate the names . . DDDD where the Ds are decimal digits generated in order. Thus, the above example would work as follows:

```
YY      MACRO  X,Y
        LOAD   X
        TPLUS  Y
        MPY    =—.5
Y       STORE  X
        END
```

which when called by

```
        YY  A
        YY  B
```

would be replaced by

```
        LOAD   A
        TPLUS  ..0000
        MPY    =—.5
..0000  STORE  A
        LOAD   B
        TPLUS  ..0001
        MPY    =—.5
..0001  STORE  B
```

This feature is not available in the 360 macro assembler. Replacements will be discussed in Chapter 7. Macro assemblers will differ as to details, but all will include a definition pseudo-order or orders, such as MACRO and END, and a means of parameter substitution. The parameters are specified in the address field of the macro call, separated by various characters. These separation characters are called *break* characters, and can either be restricted to the comma or may include others, such as the arithmetic operation characters. At definition time, each parameter is indicated by a valid symbolic name, and at expansion time, all occurrences of that symbolic name are replaced by the specified subfield of the address field. The 360 macro assembler will be discussed in Section 4.4.4.

4.4.2 Nested calls

In many cases it is convenient to define one macro in terms of previously defined macros. We refer to this as a nested call, in that one call is inside another. If the macro expansion is viewed as a character-string operation, it is easy to understand the steps involved. Consider the two macro definitions

```
COPY    MACRO   FROM,TO,COUNT,L
        AXT     COUNT,1
L       LOAD    FROM,1
        STORE   TO,1
        TIX     L,1,1
        END
SWTCH   MACRO   A,B,TEMP,N
        COPY    A,TEMP,N
        COPY    B,A,N
        COPY    TEMP,B,N
        END
```

When the macro SWTCH is used, say by

```
SWTCH   BUF1,BUF2,SPARE,LENGTH
```

it first expands to

```
COPY    BUF1,SPARE,LENGTH
COPY    BUF2,BUF1,LENGTH
COPY    SPARE,BUF2,LENGTH
```

Each of these are expanded in a similar fashion to

```
          AXT     LENGTH,1
..0000    LOAD    BUF1,1
          STORE   SPARE,1
          TIX     ..0000,1,1
          AXT     LENGTH,1
..0001    LOAD    BUF2,1
          - - - - - - -
```

etc.

It is not necessary to know anything about the instruction set for the particular machine because the macro processor deals only with character strings. Indeed, it is possible to perform macro expansion on assembly language independent of the particular machine for which the output code is intended.

It is sometimes necessary to pass parameters into macros that include commas. Since the comma is used to delimit the parameters themselves in the macro call, a scheme must be used to make the macro expander ignore commas. The simplest scheme is to surround the single parameter by parentheses and to adopt the rule that a surrounding pair of parentheses should be removed when a parameter is inserted in the expansion. Consider the definition

```
L      MACRO  A
       LOAD   A
       END
```

which serves to define L as a mnemonic for the load instruction. If we wrote

```
L      B,1
```

it would appear to be a macro with two parameters. To avoid this, we put parentheses around the parameter to get

```
L      (B,1)
```

which expands as

```
       LOAD   B,1
```

This is discussed in additional detail in Chapter 7, where the implementation of a macro assembler is examined.

4.4.3   Conditional expansion and nested definitions

Many macro assemblers provide additional features such as nested definition, conditional expansion, and recursive definition. These features make the macro into a powerful tool because with its help, code tailored to the particular situation can be generated at translation time. Such tailor-made code executes more rapidly than a subroutine that must test at execution time to distinguish between the various cases.

Conditional expansion refers to tests that can be made at translation time to decide whether or not to insert lines of code into the expanded form. The conditional mechanism is a pseudo-order that can test conditions such as the type of parameters (are they numbers, etc.) and, on the basis of the result, can inhibit the expansion of the next line of code. These mechanisms are discussed in Chapter 7 and will not be examined further at this time.

If nested definition is available, then it is possible for a macro definition to call itself. This will apparently lead to an infinite loop in the expansion process, but the conditional feature can be used to terminate the expansion.

If a macro definition occurs inside another definition, then it is possible to define macros by writing macro calls. For example,

```
DEFINE  MACRO  NAME
NAME    MACRO
        CALL    NAME
        END
        END
```

If the macro DEFINE SIN is written, then it expands to

```
SIN     MACRO
        CALL    SIN
        END
```

which serves to define a macro SIN.

4.4.4   360 macro assembler

The 360 macro assembler is the same in principle as the general form discussed except in the designation of parameters. All parameters must start with the character &. The format of the definition is slightly different. It is written as

```
        MACRO
&P  NAME    &P1,&P2, . . . ,&Pn
        LINE 1
        . . .
        LINE N
        MEND
```

The &P and &P1 are parameters which also appear in the text. Thus a macro to extract bits N through M (N < M) of register R1 and place them in R2 could be written as

```
        MACRO
&P  BITS    &N,&M,&R1,&R2
&P  SLL     &R1,&N
    SRL     &R1,31−&M+&N
    LR      &R2,&R1
    MEND
```

The parameter &P is necessary if a location field address will be used when the macro BITS is used. If BITS is used by BITS 4,7,3,5, we get

```
    SLL    3,4
    SRL    3,28
    LR     5,3
```

The 360 macro assembler allows for many special ways of handling parameters. These can be found in the assembler manual. A particularly valuable feature is the idea of a *key-word parameter*. In place of a regular parameter in the definition, the user may write &P = XXXX where XXXX is any character string. When the macro is used, the parameter is specified by writing P = YYYY, where YYYY is any character string. If the parameter is not specified, then the string XXXX is used, otherwise YYYY is used. This feature is very useful for macros with many parameters, a lot of which do not need to be specified in each use. BITS could be rewritten as

```
        MACRO
&P  BITS    &N = 0,&M = 32,&R1 = 0,&R2 = 0
        etc.
```

which defines the default conditions for the parameters as shown. If it is used
by BITS N = 7,M = 4, we get

```
SLL      0,4
SRL      0,28
LR       0,0
```

The parameters do not have to be specified in order.

4.5 ORGANIZATION OF PROGRAMS INTO SUBROUTINES

The word *segmentation* is used in two ways. One refers to an advanced method
for dynamic memory allocation which will not be discussed in this book. In
this chapter, we only refer to the process of breaking a job up into a number
of smaller jobs or segments. This is an important part of planning a large
program, since it is either going to be programmed by several people or by
one person working over a long period. In either case, it is difficult to know
the details of one section of a code while working on another section. Therefore, the interaction between different sections should be kept to the necessary
minimum. A good way to do this is to make each of the sections a separate
subroutine following all of the installation conventions. In addition to con-
tributing to the clarity of the total program when it is finished, it aids in the
debugging. Each individual subroutine should be checked separately to see
that it performs the appropriate operations on its input parameters. This
can be done by writing a program whose sole purpose is to call on the subroutine and test the results it gives. Subroutines used by the program being
tested can be provided in a form which gives known answers, so that faults
will be known to lie within the one subroutine. The hardest part of checking
a complex program is isolating an error to a given subroutine. If each subroutine is checked thoroughly first, this problem is greatly reduced. The
remaining errors are probably due to misunderstandings by one programmer
of what another subroutine does. This is usually partly due to bad
documentation.

PROBLEMS

1. A loop consists of three main parts, the initialization, the body of the loop where
    the work is done, and the incrementing and end testing. In the discussion, we
    assumed that they were written in that order. If the loop is to be executed N times

where N is a program variable, and N may take a value as small as 0, how should the loop be organized?

2. Methods suggested for a subroutine to pick up its parameter addresses included using indirect addressing or moving copies of the variable from the main program storage to storage associated with the subroutine. An example of the former was given in Section 4.3.1. The latter would give the start of a subroutine the appearance

```
LOAD*  0,4
STORE  T1
LOAD*  1,4
STORE  T2
LOAD*  2,4
STORE  T3
```

etc.

From then on, all references to the first parameter would use T1, the second T2, and so on. A copy back in the other direction is needed at the end of the subroutine.

Consider the effect of using each method in the following calls on the subroutine defined in Fortran as

```
SUBROUTINE EXAM(A,B,C,D)
A = B + C
B = A + D
RETURN
END
```

a. CALL EXAM(X,X,Y,Z)
b. CALL EXAM(1.,2.,3.,4.)
c. CALL EXAM(1.,1.,2.,1.)

3. What are the four items of information necessary to control a program loop?
4. Suppose that the following definitions have been made:

```
P  MACRO  X,Y,Z
   LEFT   2
   X      Y,Z,Z
   END
Q  MACRO  X,Y,Z
   LEFT   1
   X      Y
   END
R  MACRO  X,Y,Z
   LOAD   A
   X      Y,Z,Z
   END
```

What is the result of expanding the following:

a. R ADD,A,1
b. R Q,STORE,B
c. R P,Q,STORE
d. R P,P,P

5. What are the contents of registers 2 through 7 when the following program has been executed? (Note that JCL control cards are not indicated.)

```
        BEGIN
        L        7,D
        LA       1,LIST
        L        15,VSUB
        BALR     14,15
        L        2,LIST
        L        3,LIST + 4
        LM       4,7,A
        ABEND    16,DUMP
LIST    DC       A(A),A(B)
A       DC       F'78'
B       DC       F'13'
C       DC       F'34'
D       DC       F'17'
VSUB    DC       V(SUB)
- - - - - - - - - - - - - - - - - - - - - - -
SUB     BEGIN
        L        7,4(1)
        L        8,8(7)
        ST       8,4(7)
        L        9,0(1)
        L        4,4(9)
        ST       4,0(1)
        LEAVE
```

6. Write an IBM 360 assembler macro called MOVE which will move N words (32-bit, byte aligned) from location A to location B. N,A and B should be parameters. N may be as large as 8,192. Write a shorter macro which will work for N less than 65.

7. Draw a flowchart of the steps that the IBM post-mortem program should follow in order to give a list of the levels of subroutine calls that are active when termination occurs, assuming that standard subroutine conventions are being used. The system is assumed to have entered the main program of the job with a subroutine call; that is, the main program is treated as a subroutine of the system. Consequently, it has provided a savearea into which the main program copies the standard save information.

8. Propose a set of conventions for parameter transmittal to subroutines such that call by name or by value can be handled within the subroutine. Indicate how the following types of parameters should be handled: (a) constant, (b) variable name, (c) array name, (d) subroutine name, and (e) expression.

    Discuss the relative merits of always providing a subroutine to get the parameter versus using type codes along with the parameter address.

5

interpretation, simulation, and computer design

Interpretation was compared with translation and execution in the introduction. The basic difference is that, under interpretation, a statement is translated every time that it is executed, whereas only one translation is necessary if the result of translation is saved for repeated execution. For example, if the Fortran program

```
    DO 1 I = 1,100
  1 A(I) = B(I) — C(I)
```

is translated and executed, it is only necessary to translate statement number 1 once, whereas, if it is interpreted, it is translated 100 times. Why, one might ask, should we ever use interpretation? The answer is partly that interpreters are easier to write, and that it is sometimes possible to represent the job more compactly as an interpreter plus the source language rather than as machine language. It is also that interpretation is more useful during the diagnostic stages of program running. If a program is to be run in *production*, then efficiency is important; but during debugging, the effectiveness of error tracing is more important. This topic will be discussed briefly in Section 5.1. Interpretation is also used in preference to translation for some of the more complex languages that manipulate objects that are not particularly adapted to the computer being used. An early example of this was the interpretation of floating-point instructions on machines that only had fixed-point arithmetic. Recent examples can be found in string-manipulation languages. If the length of execution of an operation is long compared to the translation time, then the overhead of interpretation is not important.

In this chapter we shall also discuss simulation as it applies to computers.

Simulation refers to the imitation of one system by another, in this case, by a computer. Computers are frequently used to simulate, for example, aircraft in order to study their reaction to control. They are also used to simulate economic systems in order to attempt to predict the results of possible changes, such as price cuts or tax increases. They can also be used to simulate other computers. This may be desirable when a manufacturer is considering building a computer and wishes to measure its behavior without going to the expense of building a prototype. In subsequent sections of this chapter, we shall discuss the simulation of a machine and, by doing so, get an inside picture of the way in which computers work.

5.1 USES OF INTERPRETATION

Interpretation finds its chief uses in debugging programs written in other than machine language. It is also used to interpret languages for which compilers have not yet been written nor machines been built, mainly because an interpreter is shorter than the corresponding translator and less expensive than a prototype machine. When programs are being debugged, the speed of execution is not as critical as the speed of locating the bugs in the program. If a program has been translated into machine language and the symbolic information has been removed by the translator, errors that occur must be reported in terms of machine language and machine locations. Many programmers are all too familiar with the problem of reading an octal dump of memory in order to try and find out what went wrong. It is possible to add system programs that retain copies of the name tables generated by the assemblers and compilers in order to give symbolic dumps to the programmer. In such systems, the dump returned by the computer when an error is detected could list the value of each symbolic address used for data storage and an indication of those program locations that have been changed (the *comparison post-mortem* that helps detect erroneous overwriting of the code). However, this information is returned after the damage has been done. A common error in assembly language or compiler languages is to overwrite sections of program when array limits are incorrectly calculated in a loop. The damage will not be apparent until the overwritten section is executed. In the worst cases of this, the whole program has been erased when the damage is noticed and it is virtually impossible to determine the cause from a dump at termination.

Some compilers prepare codes that check all array store operations to determine that no error has been committed. In such a scheme, the attempted execution of, say, A(101) = X, if A was only dimensioned to be 100 elements, would be an error and be caught before it was executed. Such an object code can be fairly inefficient, and it would not be desirable for such a translator to be used for production programs. If two translators, an efficient one and a diagnostic one, were available, it would partly alleviate the situation, but a symbolic dump and post-mortem program would still be needed. If the source language is retained in memory without translation, then an interpreter can immediately determine when an error that attempts to access outside of the data area occurs. The diagnostic information given will indicate precisely the statement in execution at the time, and it can also indicate the value of each of the variables used, by symbolic name, because the variable must be stored by name in order for the interpreter to relate them to the names used in statements.

A trace may consist of an interpretation of machine code for a given machine by a program for that same machine, although it is usually more helpful to interpret a partially translated assembly language for the machine so that symbolic information is present for diagnostic printouts.

5.2 SIMULATION OF A COMPUTER

The next few sections will discuss the details of the simulation of a specific computer. This is done partly as an exercise and also in order to discuss computer organization in a meaningful way. Before starting the simulation, let us ask what is the difference between a computer simulator and an interpreter of the machine language for that computer. The former is certainly also the latter, since a simulator will execute the machine language of the simulated machine. A simulator, however, is a little more than an interpreter. If the only need is to interpret the language, then it is of no importance to the user how this is done. However, a simulator should mimic the machine as closely as necessary in order to derive the required measurements. When a computer manufacturer has a simulator written, he wishes to use it to determine whether some of his ideas will work. Therefore he must follow the proposed machine design as closely as possible, simulating features that are not apparent to the eventual programmers when the machine is constructed but that do affect the method of operation internally. The example to be treated below falls into the category of simulators, since it models all internal registers and data paths explicitly and generates sequences of operations that would be identical to the control signals in the machine, were it to be constructed.

5.3 AN OUTLINE OF COMPUTER DESIGN

This section will discuss some of the ways in which the central processing unit of a computer can be constructed and controlled. The building blocks which will be used consist of *registers, adders, memory units, gates,* etc. No mention will be made of the techniques used to implement these blocks from smaller logical blocks, or of the way in which these blocks are constructed out of such basic components as transistors and diodes. These topics are the subject of courses in logical design, switching theory, and switching circuit analysis.† A knowledge in these areas is not necessary for continued reading of this chapter.

The memory unit and the idea of a register were introduced in Chapter 2. A CPU contains a number of registers connected to one or more adders and one or more memory units. These connections are called data paths. Physically, they consist of wires feeding the output signal from one register to the input of another. *Gates* control the movement of data from one register to another. If two registers P and Q are connected as shown in Figure 5.1, the gate G controls the information flow. When G is turned on (*opened*), a copy of the information in register P is placed in register Q. This is necessarily a simplified account of the process, which can vary in detail from one hardware implementation to another. This process takes a finite amount of time, currently in the range 10 to 200 nanoseconds. (1 nanosecond $= 10^{-9}$ seconds.)

During the period in which the gate is open, the contents of the register supplying the information (P in the example) must not be changed. If it is necessary to move information into P after the current contents have been gated elsewhere, there must be some guarantee that the gate has closed on the output of P before an input gate is opened. This is done by performing the basic register-to-register transfers in periods of time called "cycles." One cycle is the time to open the gate, move the information from one register to an adjacent one, and to turn the gate back off again. Many machines have a *clock* which times each of these basic cycles. The machine is controlled by a sequence of gate signals, each occupying one time cycle. These signals are

† For an introduction to these topics, the reader is referred to T. C. Bartree, I. L. Lebow, and I. S. Reed, *Theory and Design of Digital Machines*, McGraw-Hill Book Company, New York, 1962.

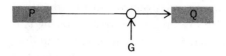

FIGURE 5.1 Gated transfer.

generated by the control section of the computer. The next two subsections will discuss possible arrangements of registers and ways in which the gate signal sequences can be generated.

5.3.1 Actual data flow

The programmer is only aware of some of the registers in a machine and of certain of the interconnecting data paths. This is because most of the registers are not accessible to the programmer but are used to implement the instructions that affect the accessible registers. For example, the IBM 7094 manual mentions the AC, MQ, and sense-indicator registers, in addition to the index registers and the control counter. In fact, there are several other registers in the CPU. We shall discuss some of them below. In some of the lower-cost machines, the registers which the programmer is told about do not exist as separate registers. For example, the IBM system 360 can have four 64-bit floating-point registers and sixteen 32-bit fixed-point registers for programmer use. The model 30 version of the 360 cannot afford the hardware to implement all of those registers in transistors, so they are stored in memory locations that are inaccessible to the programmer.

Medium- and high-speed machines employ a certain amount of parallelism in their use of gates in order to gain speed. A typical organization of a machine in the IBM 7090 speed category is shown in Figure 5.2. This is a simplified diagram and only shows some of the word-length data flow. Index registers, the control counter, and other necessary registers are not shown. In an organization of this form, the upper and lower parts of the accumulator are normally in the registers labelled AC and MQ, as in the IBM 7090. If an

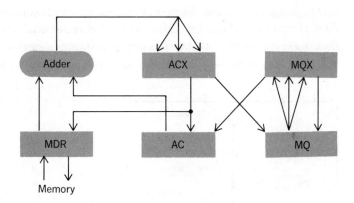

FIGURE 5.2 A simple data flow; gates are indicated by arrows.

addition is to be performed, the address is sent to memory using data flow not indicated, and a read returns the operand to the MDR. The circuitry in the adder produces the sum of the registers AC and MDR. The gate into the register labelled ACX is opened in one cycle, and then the gate back down into the AC is opened in the next cycle, returning the result. The gates shown at an angle into ACX and MQX are for shifting. The angle indicates that the gate moves bits over. Thus, if the left-shift gate from MQ to MQX is opened, bit 1 of MQ would be placed in bit 0 of MQX, bit 2 in bit 1, and so on. Repetitive use of this gate can be made for arbitrary-length shifts. In a double-length shift, the AC register would be gated, through the adder, into ACX at the same time. A similar pattern of shifts is used in multiplication and division. The reader is invited to work out the details of these operations with such a data flow. (Hints: For multiplication, put the multiplier in MQ, the multiplicand in the MDR. Shift right, testing the bottom of the MQ register. For division, shift the other way.)

In lower-cost and hence lower-speed machines, parallelism of data flow is too expensive. In this case, the concept of a *bus* is used. In electrical engineering, a bus is a piece of wire (usually thick) which distributes power to a number of devices. A *data bus* is, by analogy, a piece of wire that distributes data to various registers. Two buses are shown in Figure 5.3. They serve to route information from any one of the three registers A, B, and C to either of the registers X and Y and back again respectively. Because only one number can be on a bus at one time, the number of transfers that can be done in parallel is reduced. Also, because of additional gates (both onto and off the bus) that are used, the transfer time is increased by a small amount. However, a bus can reduce the amount of hardware needed to accomplish an instruction execution. Figure 5.4 shows the data paths for the hypothetical machine that we are going to simulate. These data paths use three buses, two for input to the logical unit, and one for output. In the future, we shall refer to this as the *simulated* or S machine. All registers are 32 bits wide except for the IR register, which is 5 bits wide. The logical unit is a group of circuits which can form a

FIGURE 5.3 Data buses.

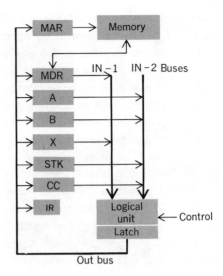

FIGURE 5.4   S-machine data paths.

number of combinations of the input buses. In particular, the twos complement sum can be formed. A 32-bit register, called *latch*, is included in the logical unit. This serves to retain the output of the logical unit when the inputs are turned off. In this way it is possible to return a result to a register which contained an input operand. For example, it will be necessary to add the content of the A register to the content of the MDR register and return the result to the A register. Although this is actually a two-step operation, consisting of first opening the gates from A and MDR onto the input buses and then opening the gate from the output bus back to A, we shall call this operation a single cycle.

The S machine will be a zero-address (stack) machine with one instruction per 32-bit word, although addresses will be *to the byte*, that is, an address will indicate one 8-bit byte in memory. Because the memory will be 32 bits wide, the bottom 2 bits of an address will be ignored in memory READ and WRITE operations. The purpose of the MAR and MDR registers was introduced in Chapter 2. The A and B registers are working registers; A usually holds the top level of the stack. X is a single-index register, CC the control counter, IR an instruction register whose use will be discussed later, and STK a register used to implement a stack scheme. The contents of the accumulator stack are actually stored in memory, starting from the maximum available address and working down. The current top level of the stack is kept in the memory location contained in the STK register. If an item is to be pushed into the

FIGURE 5.5   Stack storage.

stack, then STK is decreased by 4 and then sent to the MAR as the address
of the new top level. The bottom level is always in location $2^{32}-4$. Let us
examine the way in which a typical instruction would be executed by this
machine. A stack machine should provide an instruction ADD, which combines the top two levels of the stack by addition and stores the result back
into the second level, subsequently discarding the top level. Prior to the
execution of the ADD instruction, the STK register contains the address of
the top of the stack. The second level is in location numbered 4 larger, as
shown in Figure 5.5. In order to execute the ADD instruction, the address in
STK must be sent to the MAR register. A READ can then be used to access
the top level of the stack and place it in the MDR register. We can write this as

    STK → MAR   READ

meaning that the data paths are used to transmit the contents of the STK
register onto the IN-2 bus, that this number is passed through the logical unit
onto the OUT bus, from whence it is gated to the MAR register. A memory
READ operation is then requested, which places the top level of the stack
into the MDR. This can be followed by the sequence of steps

    MDR   → A
    4 + STK → STK
      STK → MAR   READ

which put the top of the stack into A register in order to leave it free for the second level of the stack, which is fetched by sending its address to the MAR and reading. The operation $4 + STK \to STK$ is performed by gating the contents of the STK register onto the IN-2 bus, a constant 4 onto the IN-1 bus (think of this as another register always containing this constant, although it is simpler to implement than that), performing an addition in the logical unit, and gating the result on the OUT bus into the STK. The next operation updates the contents of the STK register so that it points to the new top level of the stack.

The addition can be performed between the A and the MDR register and the result returned to the stack by the operation

    MDR + A → MDR   WRITE

Collecting these operations together, we arrive at the add sequence

    0   + STK → MAR   READ
    MDR + 0   → A
    4   + STK → MAR   READ
    4   + STK → STK
    MDR + A   → MDR   WRITE

They have been written in this way to show that each operation consists of a specification of the gate that is opened onto the IN-1 bus, a specification of the gate that is opened onto the IN-2 bus (0 means that no gate is opened), a specification of the operation of the logical unit (in the example only plus is used), a specification of the gate opened from the OUT bus, and an indication whether a READ or WRITE is to be requested of memory. The execution of an S-machine instruction such as ADD requires that a sequence of such gate signals be generated in the appropriate order. In future we shall not write the arrow, since it would appear in every line.

Let us consider two other instructions which will certainly be needed in a stack machine, the LOAD instruction and the TRANSFER instruction. These will have addresses. For the moment, let us assume that the address of the instruction has been calculated and placed in the B register. The LOAD instruction is executed with the gate sequence

    0 + B   MAR   READ
    −4 + STK MAR   WRITE
    −4 + STK STK

while the TRANSFER instruction only requires

    0 + B CC

under the assumption that the CC register contains the address of the next instruction to be executed.

    Each of the instructions in the repertoire of the S machine must be executed by such a sequence of gate operations. After we have constructed these and presumably built hardware to perform them, we still have to face the problem, "how does the machine know which sequence to execute?" The user has placed his S-machine program in the S-machine memory and wishes it to be executed starting at a given location. This location has been put in the CC register, and it is now up to the S-machine hardware to examine the instruction in that location and initiate the correct sequence of gate signals. The instruction can be fetched from memory, and the control counter CC can be incremented to point to the next instruction by sequence

    0 + CC MAR READ
    4 + CC CC

This puts the instruction to be executed into the MDR register. The hardware must look at it and determine the instruction type, place its address into the B register, and begin the necessary gate sequence. In order to follow these steps through, we need to know the form of the S instructions in detail.

5.3.2 The S-machine instruction set

Each S instruction will be assumed to occupy a 32-bit word, so that its location address is always a multiple of 4. The format of the instructions is shown in Figure 5.6. There are two types, one-address and zero-address instructions. They are distinguished by the first bit of the instruction code, that is, bit 2 of the 32-bit word. It is a 0 for one-address instructions. Instructions with addresses such as LOAD and STORE will always contain a 0 in this position so that they can be readily distinguished from the zero-address instructions.

FIGURE 5.6 S-instruction format.

(This is known as bit significance. We shall see that it will allow the control necessary to handle both type of instructions to be simplified.) In the tables below, the code for each instruction is shown, followed by its name, the amount by which the STK register is changed during its execution, and a brief description of its action. Note that the code for one-address instructions is between 0 and 31, whereas the code for zero-address instructions is greater than 32 because of the bit significance of the top bit. Zero-address instructions will not use the indirect bit, the index bit, or the 24 address bits. (This suggests that the design of the S machine is far from optimal.) For one-address instructions, the address is formed by adding the contents of the X register to the 24-bit address if the index bit is on, and performing indirect addressing with the resulting address if the indirect bit is on (that is, equal to 1). If indirect addressing occurs, then a new 32-bit word is fetched from memory, and it is also checked for indexing and indirect addressing. In this way, multiple-level indirect addressing is allowed.

ONE–ADDRESS INSTRUCTIONS

code	instruction	STK change	action
0	LOAD	−4	Load stack from memory location.
1	LDI	−4	Load immediate. Loads top of stack with address.
2	STORE	+4	Stores top of stack in memory.
3	TRA	0	Transfers control to specified location.
4	TPL	0	Transfers control if top of stack is positive or zero.
5	TMI	0	Transfers control if top of stack is negative (non-zero).
6	TZE	0	Transfers control if top of stack is zero.
7	TNZ	0	Transfers control if top of stack is non-zero.
8	ENTER	−4	Enter a subroutine by placing CC on top of the stack and transferring control.
9	LDX	0	Load index with contents of memory location.
10	LDXI	0	Load index immediate, that is, with the address of this instruction.
11	LOOP	0	Increment index register by 4 and transfer control if it is non-zero.
12	LS	0	Left shift N places, where N is the address.
13	RS	0	Right shift N places.

ZERO–ADDRESS INSTRUCTIONS

code	instruction	STK change	action
32	ADD	+4	Add top two levels of stack.
33	SUB	+4	Subtract top two levels of stack.
34	AND	+4	AND top two levels of stack.
35	OR	+4	OR top two levels of stack.
36	EOR	+4	Exclusive OR top two levels of stack.

37	NOT	0	Complement top level of stack.
38	XTS	−4	Index to stack. Puts contents of index register on top of stack.
39	STX	+4	Stack to index. Removes top of stack and places it in index register.
40	ADX	+4	Adds top of stack to index.
41	SBX	+4	Subtracts top of stack from index.
42	RET	+4	Transfers to address contained in top of stack.
43	POP	+4	Discard the top level of the stack.

5.3.3 Decoding the instruction and instruction sequencing

We have already seen how the instructions can be fetched in sequence by use of the control counter. Having fetched the next instruction from memory into the MDR, it is necessary to decode the instruction bits in order to determine its type. If it is a one-address instruction, it is also necessary to form the address in the B register for use by the gate sequence for the particular instruction. Since this is a common requirement for all one-address instructions, it should be done before the remaining 5 bits of instruction code are examined. Therefore, if the first bit of the instruction code is a 1, the next 5 bits should be used to select one of 32 gate sequences for the 32 possible zero-address instructions (not all of them are defined in this example); if it is a 0, then the effective address should first be calculated and then a 32-way test made for one-address instruction types. This means that the S-machine control needs some mechanism for testing bits 0, 1, and 2 of the MDR register in a way which can influence subsequent actions. It also needs to be able to test bits 3 through 7, but it will turn out to be more convenient to test these in the instruction register IR, so a test on the 5 bits of IR will be provided. If a one-address instruction is being treated, then the address bits in the lower 24 positions of the word must be extracted and sent to the B register. This can be done with a *partial gate*, which gates only the lower 24 bits onto the IN-1 bus from MDR, or it can be done by providing the constant, called *mask*, consisting of 24 least-significant 1s, for gating onto the IN-2 bus. We shall use the latter method. This constant can be logically ANDed with the contents of the MDR and the result sent to the B register. Bit 1 of MDR can then be tested to see if it is a 0. If not, then the contents of the X register must be added to B. Bit 0 of MDR can then be tested for 0. If it is not a 0, then the B register contents must be sent to the MAR register in order to fetch another word and to repeat the process. In order to write these steps down, we shall number all operation cycles in the gate sequence and write the testing step as

TEST BIT0 N

where N is the number of the operation cycle that is to be executed next if the test is successful. Using this notation, the instruction fetch sequence can be written as

1	0 + CC	MAR	READ	Fetch instruction.
2	4 + CC	CC		Update CC.
3	MDR	IR		Save instruction bits.
4	TEST BIT2	6		Test for one-address instruction.
5	TEST IR	32		Branch on zero-address instruc-tions.†
6	MDR AND MASK	B		24 bits of address to B.
7	TEST BIT1	9		Branch if no indexing.
8	X + B	B		Index.
9	TEST BIT0	12		Branch if no indirect addressing.
10	B	MAR	READ	Read word containing address.
11	TEST	6		Branch unconditionally to step 6.‡
12	TEST IR	64		Branch on one-address instruc-tions.†

Since, for example, the instruction code for the TRA instruction is 3, the step numbered 67 ($=64 + 3$) would be

67	TEST	125	Branch unconditionally to step 125.

while step 125 would be

125	0 +	B	CC	Change the control counter for TRA.
126	TEST	1		Execute the next instruction.

Number 125 was used as the step number for an example; it could, of course, have been any other number.

5.3.4 Micro program control

We have investigated the way in which the data flow of the S machine is used to execute the S instructions, one at a time, and to sequence from one to the next. It is done by a fixed sequence of gate signals, interspersed with tests on the top 3 bits of the MDR register and bits 3 through 7 of the IR register. Toward the end of the 1950s, the similarity between the gate sequences and the sequence of steps of any program was utilized in the construction of the

† The TEST IR step is assumed to select one of 32 steps as the next, based on the 5 bits in the IR register. These are assumed to be steps 32 through 63 in the case of zero-address instructions and 64 through 95 in the case of one-address instructions.
‡ Since no condition is given, step number 6 is always executed next.

control of computers. Prior to that time, the sequences of gate signals were generated by circuits designed for that purpose. This area of the machine was complex, because there was little similarity between the sequences used for, say, the ADD instruction, and those used for the LOAD instruction. Fast machines are still built in the same manner, but medium-speed machines are often built using the concept of *micro program control*. In this concept, the gate sequences are generated by what, in effect, is another simpler computer, called the micro computer. Referring to Figure 5.7, we see that the control unit of the S machine is a black box which can input the states of the MDR register and the 5 bits of the IR register and can output signals to each of the gates, the logical unit setting, and the READ and WRITE requests of memory. The flow of control can be thought of as sequences of program steps which consist of either outputting signals to the gates or of inputting the states of the test conditions and performing conditional branches. Each step, or cycle, in the gate sequences given above is equivalent to a program step in the micro machine. Therefore, each program step must either specify the test condition and the branch address within the micro program, or it must specify the setting of the gates onto each of the three buses, the setting of the logical unit, and whether to READ, WRITE, or just do the gating process.

An organization of a micro program control for the S machine is shown in Figure 5.8. It contains a memory in which the micro program is stored. Each step in the micro program is stored as a word in this memory which we shall call the micro memory. Since these steps are fixed if the instruction code of the S machine is fixed, it is common to use a *read-only memory* for the micro

FIGURE 5.7   Data flow and control of S machine.

FIGURE 5.8 The micro machine.

memory. This is a memory which can be read but not written. Its contents
are initially set by the manufacturer, who decides the instruction set of the
S machine. The advantage of using a read-only memory (ROM for short)
is that it is cheaper and faster than an equivalent read-write memory.

The micro organization shows a memory address register with an attached
adder for incrementing by one. This serves as a control counter for the micro
machine. Since the machine only executes control instructions and does not
read data into or out of the micro memory, the address register is only used
for accessing micro instructions, hence it can serve as a control counter without any interference. It always contains the address, in the micro memory, of
the next micro program step to be executed. Each micro instruction is
fetched from the micro memory in turn, and decoded from the memory data
register to determine which gates to open, or which conditions to test. If

conditions are tested and are true, then a new address is gated from the data register to the address register in the micro machine.

Who, we may ask, controls the micro machine? Do we need a micro-micro machine to control that, and so on, ad infinitum? At some point, hardware control must be used to sequence through the steps of one of the micro-micro . . . machines. We can see that the micro machine is already quite simple compared to the original S machine, and that its control is much simpler. Remembering that the S machine is a grossly simplified machine compared to a typical commercial machine, and noting that the micro control of a much more complex machine is not particularly more complex, we realize the micro control can effectively reduce the amount of circuitry needed in the control area. It is true that a micro memory has to be added, but the cost of this is usually offset by the savings in circuitry and the increased flexibility for implementing more complex instructions for the programmer's use.

Additional advantages accrue to the manufacturer of micro-controlled machines: they are often easier to check out during the design stage because the micro control can be easily simulated; they are easier to check out during the construction phase because checking micro programs can be plugged in (by replacing the micro memory temporarily), and these can be used to trace construction errors more readily than the regular instruction set can be used. The micro instructions are stored in the micro memory in a binary code. For the machine discussed, two different formats are needed, one for operation steps, and one for testing steps. The way in which each of these can be stored in a 16-bit-wide micro memory is illustrated in Figure 5.9. If the top bit of the word is a 0, then the word represents an operation on the gates. Each group of bits, called a *control group*, contains a coded representation of the gate action to be taken. The first 2 bits indicate whether the memory is to be accessed for a READ or a WRITE at the completion of the cycle, the

FIGURE 5.9 Micro instruction format.

next 3 bits indicate which gate is to be opened onto the IN-1 bus, the next 3 the IN-2 bus, and so on. The codes used for each of these control groups are shown in Tables 5.1 through 5.5 below. If, on the other hand, the top bit is a 1, the 16-bit word represents a test action. In this case the micro machine examines the indicated bit or bits in the S-machine data flow and performs a branch if the condition is met. This branch is effected by gating the bottom 12 bits of the micro word into the micro control counter. The conditions tested are shown in Table 5.6 for each of the eight code values of bits 1 through 3 of the micro word. Code zero always causes a branch, so it is an unconditional transfer. Codes one through three test bits 0 through 2 of the MDR respectively. If the tested bit is a 0, the branch is taken. Code four tests all bits of MDR. If they are all 0, the branch is taken. (This will be needed for conditional instructions in the S machine.) Codes five and six are not used in this example, while code seven is used to perform a test of the instruction in the IR. The 5 bits in the IR are ORed with the 5 bits in the bottom of the branch address bits in the micro word, and the result is gated to the micro control counter. An OR function is used because it is simpler to implement in hardware than, say, an addition. Since this code will only be used twice

TABLE 5.1 Memory control (2 bits)

Code value	Action
0	Nothing
1	READ†
2	WRITE†
3	Not allowed

† The READ or WRITE action is taken after the rest of the micro instruction execution occurs.

TABLE 5.2 Input bus 1

Code	Register or number gated onto bus
0	0
1	MDR
2	X
3	−4
4	Not allowed
5	Not allowed
6	Not allowed
7	+4

in the S-machine implementation, the bottom 5 bits of the branch address may be made 0 by judicious placement of the micro instructions. Under that condition, the OR is equivalent to an addition. After such a micro instruction, the next one to be executed will be one of 32, depending on the contents of IR.

TABLE 5.3 Input bus 2

Code	Register or number gated onto bus
0	0
1	1
2	77777777 octal
3	A
4	CC
5	B
6	STK
7	+4

TABLE 5.4 Output bus

Code	Output bus gated to
0	MAR
1	MDR
2	X
3	A
4	CC
5	B
6	STK
7	IR
8 to 15	Not allowed

TABLE 5.5 Function

Code	Output function
0	IN1 + IN2 (Twos complement)
1	IN1 − IN2 (Twos complement)
2	IN1 "AND" IN2
3	IN1 "OR" IN2
4	NOT (IN1 + IN2)
5	IN1 "EXCLUSIVE OR" IN2
6	Half (IN1 + IN2) (Right shift 1)
7	Double (IN1 + IN2) (Left shift 1)

TABLE 5.6 Test conditions

Code	Branch if
0	Always
1	MDR Bit 0 = 0
2	MDR Bit 1 = 0
3	MDR Bit 2 = 0
4	MDR = 0
5	
6	
7	The 5 bits in the IR register are ORed with the bottom 5 bits of the branch address and used for a branch.

5.4 MICRO PROGRAMMING THE S-INSTRUCTION SET

The instruction set, given in Section 5.3.2 for the S machine, can be implemented by means of micro programs using the micro instructions given above. This section will discuss the micro programming of the S-machine instructions by means of an annotated micro program. The micro program can be written in any way that provides a unique representation of each micro instruction. We shall write it as if each instruction were either a one-address instruction or a four-address instruction. The one-address micro instructions will be the test instructions, and will be written as follows:

```
operation
T0      J    Test MDR bit 0, branch to micro location J if 0.
T1      J    Test MDR bit 1, . . . .
T2      J    Test MDR bit 2, . . . .
TMDR    J    Test MDR for all 0s, branch if true.
TI      J    Branch on 5 bits of IR.
TRM     J    Always branch.
```

The four-address micro instructions will be written as follows:

```
operation   address field
ADDM        I1,I2,OUT,Z
SUBM        I1,I2,OUT,Z
ANDM        I1,I2,OUT,Z
ORM         I1,I2,OUT,Z
NOT         I1,I2,OUT,Z
EOR         I1,I2,OUT,Z
LS          I1,I2,OUT,Z
RS          I1,I2,OUT,Z
```

where I1 is the IN-1 bus, I2 is in the IN-2 bus, OUT is the OUT bus, and Z is either P, R, or W, meaning process only, process followed by READ, or process followed by WRITE. The address in the four-address format may take on any of the allowed values for the specified bus. Thus I1 can be one of 0, MDR, X, MFOUR, or FOUR, where MFOUR and FOUR select the constants −4 and 4 respectively. I2 can be one of 0, ONE, MASK, A, CC, B, STK, or FOUR, where ONE and MASK select the constants 1 and 77777777 octal respectively. OUT can be one of MAR, MDR, X, A, CC, B, STK, or IR. Thus, to add the contents of the MDR register and the A register and to return the result to the MDR without any memory operations, we shall write

    ADDM MDR,A,MDR,P

In writing the micro program, we shall make use of symbolic addresses for branch addresses. These will have to be translated into binary by an assembly process before the code can be used in the micro memory. In the program below, the left-hand column is the actual micro memory location of the instruction; the next column is used for a location symbolic address if it is needed. Then the operation field and the address fields of the instruction are written in the usual manner. Some absolute addresses are used, because the test of the IR register requires that the branch address contain 5 least significant 0s.

The micro code below differs from that given earlier in that the top of the stack is normally kept in the A register (rather than being returned to memory after every operation, only to be fetched back at the start of the next). This serves to shorten the micro program and increase the speed of the S machine.

location		operation	address	comments
20	FETCH	ADDM	0,CC,MAR,R	Fetch next instruction from S memory.
21		ADDM	FOUR,CC,CC,P	Increment instruction counter.
22		ADDM	MDR,0,IR,P	Move instruction bits to IR.
23		T2	ONEADR	Branch if one-address instruction.
24		TI	32	Test for 32 zero-address instructions.
25	ONEADR	ANDM	MDR,MASK,B,P	Move 24 address bits to B register.
26		T1	NOINDX	Test for no indexing.
27		ADDM	X,B,B,P	Index address in B.

location	operation		address	comments
28	NOINDX	TO	NOINDR	Test for no indirect addressing.
29		ADDM	0,B,MAR,R	Address to MAR and read next address.
30		TRM	ONEADR	Return to test for more indexing.
31	NOINDR	TI	64	Test for 32 one-address instructions.
32		TRM	SADD	Transfer to micro code for the S addition instruction.
33		TRM	SSUB	Similar for subtraction.
34		TRM	SAND	Etc. for each S instruction.
35		TRM	SOR	
36		TRM	SEOR	
37		TRM	SNOT	
38		TRM	SXTS	
39		TRM	SSTX	
40		TRM	SADX	
41		TRM	SSBX	
42		TRM	SRET	
43		TRM	SPOP	
44		TRM	ILLORD	Transfer to micro code to handle illegal instruction.
45		TRM	ILLORD	Ditto.
. . . .				
63		TRM	ILLORD	
64		TRM	SLOAD	Transfer to micro code for one-address instructions.
65		TRM	SLDI	
66		TRM	SSTORE	
67		TRM	STRA	
68		TRM	STPL	
69		TRM	STMI	
70		TRM	STZE	
71		TRM	STNZ	
72		TRM	SENTER	
73		TRM	SLDX	
74		TRM	SLDXI	
75		TRM	SLOOP	
76		TRM	SLS	
77		TRM	SRS	
78		TRM	ILLORD	More illegal instructions.
. . . .				
95		TRM	ILLORD	
96	SADD	ADDM	FOUR,STK,MAR,R	Get second level of stack.
97		ADDM	MDR,A,A,P	Perform addition.
98	DECR	ADDM	FOUR,STK,STK,P	Change stack pointer.
99		TRM	FETCH	Return to fetch of next instruction.

location		operation	address	comments
100	SUB	ADDM	FOUR,STK,MAR,R	
101		SUBM	MDR,A,A,P	
102		TRM	DECR	
103	SAND	ADDM	FOUR,STK,MAR,R	
104		ANDM	MDR,A,A,P	
105		TRM	DECR	
106	SOR	ADDM	FOUR,STK,MAR,R	
107		ORM	MDR,A,A,P	
108		TRM	DECR	
109	SEOR	ADDM	FOUR,STK ,MAR,R	
110		EOR	MDR,A,A,P	
111		TRM	DECR	
112	SNOT	NOT	0,A,A,P	Complement top of stack.
113		TRM	FETCH	
114	SXTS	ADDM	0,STK,MAR,P	
115		ADDM	0,A,MDR,W	Write top level into memory.
116		ADDM	X,0,A,P	Copy X to A as new top of stack.
117	INCR	ADDM	MFOUR,STK,STK,P	Change stack pointer.
118		TRM	FETCH	
119	SSTX	ADDM	0,A,X,P	Top of stack to index.
120	SPOP	ADDM	FOUR,STK,MAR,R	Get second level of stack.
121		ADDM	MDR,0,A,P	And copy to register.
122		TRM	DECR	Change stack pointer.
123	SADX	ADDM	X,A,X,P	Add stack to index.
124		TRM	SPOP	And pop.
125	SSBX	SUBM	X,A,X,P	Subtract stack from index.
126		TRM	SPOP	And pop.
127	SRET	ADDM	0,A,CC,P	Gate stack to CC.
128		TRM	SPOP	And pop.
129	SLOAD	ADDM	0,B,MAR,R	Get operand.
130		ADDM	MDR,0,B,P	Place in B.
131	SLDI	ADDM	0,STK,MAR,P	Stack address to memory.
132		ADDM	0,A,MDR,W	Write top of stack.
133		ADDM	0,B,A,P	New top of stack to A.
134		TRM	INCR	And change stack pointer.
135	SSTORE	ADDM	0,B,MAR,P	Address to memory.
136		ADDM	0,A,MDR,W	Write top of stack in store location.
137		TRM	SPOP	And pop.
138	STRA	ADDM	0,B,CC,P	Branch address to CC.
139		TRM	FETCH	
140	STPL	ADDM	0,A,MDR,P	A to MDR for testing.
141		TO	STRA	Transfer if positive.
142		TRM	FETCH	
143	STMI	ADDM	0,A,MDR,P	A to MDR for testing.
144		TO	FETCH	

location		operation	address	comments
145		TRM	STRA	Transfer if negative.
146	STZE	ADDM	0,A,MDR,P	A to MDR for testing.
147		TMDR	STRA	Transfer if 0.
148		TRM	FETCH	
149	STNZ	ADDM	0,A,MDR,P	
150		TMDR	FETCH	
151		TRM	STRA	Transfer if non-zero.
152	SENTER	ADDM	0,B,MDR,P	Switch B and CC.
153		ADDM	0,CC,B,P	
154		ADDM	MDR,0,CC,P	
155		TRM	SLDI	Now put B on top of stack.
156	SLDX	ADDM	0,B,MAR,R	Fetch word from memory.
157		ADDM	MDR,0,B,P	And place in B.
158	SLDXI	ADDM	0,B,X,P	Place word in index.
159		TRM	FETCH	
160	SLOOP	ADDM	X,FOUR,X,P	Increment X by 4.
161		ADDM	X,0,MDR,P	Move X to MDR for testing.
162		TMDR	FETCH	If 0, no transfer.
163		TRM	STRA	Else transfer.
164	SLS	ADDM	0,B,MDR,P	Move B to MDR for testing.
165	JLS	TO	LEFT	Left shift if B is positive.
166	REPRS	RS	0,A,A,P	Shift one place.
167		ADDM	MDR,ONE,MDR,P	Decrease count.
168		TMDR	FETCH	Finished shifting.
169		TRM	REPRS	Repeat shifting.
170	LEFT	TMDR	FETCH	Zero shifts left.
171		LS	0,A,A,P	Shift one place.
172		SUBM	MDR,ONE,MDR,P	Decrease count.
173		TRM	LEFT	
174	SRS	SUBM	0,B,MDR,P	Minus count to MDR.
175		TRM	JLS	Join left-shift program.
176	ILLORD	- - -		(This is discussed below.)

The above code handles the 26 S instructions in 156 micro instructions. The illegal instructions cause a branch to micro location ILLORD, which has not been programmed. A system decision has to be made concerning the action that should be taken on illegal instructions before it can be completed. In this example, we shall not complete it further (see the discussion on simulation in the next section). In practical machines, an interrupt should occur. This would mean adding at least 1 additional bit to the data flow that could be set and reset by micro instructions and that could be tested. Such bits would be used to indicate the interrupt status, and would be set after an illegal instruction in the S machine.

A more practical machine would have to provide a much larger instruction set, including multiply and divide operations in both fixed and floating-point forms. In order to make these operations practical, additional gates should be provided. These additional gates would make it simpler to extract sections of words, particularly the exponent part of a floating-point number. It is not the intention of this chapter to discuss all of the tricks that can be used to make micro programming an efficient means for the control of a medium-speed computer, so we won't discuss these problems further. In particular, we shall not discuss input/output, which is very device-dependent at the hardware level and the most difficult to simulate realistically. In practice, it runs concurrently with the central processor, but at its own speed. The simulation of unsynchronized operating processes is beyond the scope of this book.

In the next section, we shall discuss the simulation of the micro machine and the data flow so that the micro program given above can be used to implement a simulator of the S machine. This is the point at which a number of students become confused. So far we have described the S machine and its machine language. We then described a method of controlling it which involved writing program language used to control the gates of the S-machine data flow in a manner that caused S programs to be executed. In a sense, the micro program is interpreting the S-machine language. Now we are going to simulate the micro machine on a real machine, that is, we shall write a program in yet another language in order to make this other machine behave like the data flow and micro machine discussed. Because we are writing a simulator rather than building the machine out of hardware, we shall be able to add other features to the simulator that will make it easy for us to check out our micro program and simulator. Also, we shall see that the macro assembler on the machine being used for simulation can be used to save ourselves the work of writing any systems programs for the S machine until we are happy with its design.

5.5 SIMULATING THE S MACHINE

It is assumed that we have access to a machine that is somewhat larger than the S machine that we have been discussing, so that there is adequate space for the simulator, the micro program, and the S-memory contents to be stored. Since simulation is not efficient, it is also desirable that the available machine be fairly fast and that its word length be at least 32 bits. The available memory must be divided up into sections, so that the various pieces of the S machine can be represented. A suitable number of words, preferably a power of 2, should be allocated to the S memory. Words must be allocated to each of the registers in the data flow, and a block of memory must be allocated for storing the micro program. The remainder of the memory can be used for the simulator. Thus the allocation of memory may be as shown in Figure 5.10.

The S memory can be simulated by writing two subroutines, called READ and WRITE. When READ is called, it should take the address in the MAR register (that is, in the word in the memory being used to simulate the MAR register), AND out the bottom 2 bits and the top 30-N bits—where the number of words allocated to the S memory is 2^N—and use the remaining N bits as the address. If these N bits are added to the address of the first word of the S-memory representation in the actual memory, the result is the location in the actual memory which contains the desired word. It should be copied to the MDR register. Conversely, the WRITE subroutine should form the address in a similar manner and then copy the contents of the MDR register into the address location. Note the N-bit address should be right justified two places before performing the addition in order to remove the two least significant 0s, unless, of course, a machine such as the IBM 360 is being used, since this machine addresses to the byte and therefore requires that addresses be multiples of 4 when 32-bit words are being accessed.

The simulator program must include a cell that contains the address of the next micro instruction. This represents the micro control counter, but it is easier if the actual address of the next micro instruction in the memory of the simulating machine is stored in the simulator. A flowchart of the simulator is shown in Figure 5.11. Notice that it is essentially the same flow as that used in the micro program. The next instruction is fetched from the micro memory and the micro control counter is increased by 1.

FIGURE 5.10   Memory use in simulator of S machine.

FIGURE 5.11 Simulator.
196

A test is made to see whether it is a gating step or a testing step, and simulating code handles each case. The code can be kept very short by fetching the operands that are to be placed on the IN-1 and the IN-2 buses to fixed cells before the function bits are checked. After the function bits are checked, the operation can be performed on the fixed cells directly, and the result can then be stored back into the out register. After the gate operations have been completed, the memory bits are tested, and reads or writes are requested as necessary. The flowchart shows one addition at this point. If the unused code three is placed in the memory control group, a printout of all registers in the data flow is indicated. This is not a feasible thing to do in an actual machine, but in the simulator it only consists of suitable output requests. This can prove very handy for debugging both the simulator and the micro program because a trace of the execution of the program can be made. Part of this simulator is shown below in IBM system 360 machine language. It is not complete, but it does indicate some of the techniques that can be used. The micro control counter is kept in fixed-point register 2. The micro instruction, which is assumed to occupy a 16-bit halfword, is fetched into register 3, and the sign bit is examined to see if it is a test micro instruction. If it is not, the five control groups are extracted and placed in registers 4 through 8, each multiplied by 4 because of the addressing to the byte. The effect of indirect addressing (which does not exist in the 360) is achieved by performing a reference through a table which gives the address of the actual registers or program to be used. The contents of the IN-1 and the IN-2 registers are placed in fixed registers 4 and 5 prior to a branch to a program which handles the operation.

```
              MACRO
&A            BITS      &N,&R,&TAB
&A            SR        8,8              Clear register 8.
              SLDL      8,&N             Move N bits from 9 to 8.
              SLL       8,2              Quadruple 8.
              A         8,&TAB           Add address of table.
              L         &R,0(8)          Fetch table entry to register R.
              MEND
- - - - - - - - - -
INITIAL       L         2,AMCODE         Initialize microcontrol counter.
NEXT          LH        3,0(2)           Load next microinstruction.
              A         2,=F'2'          Increment microcontrol counter.
              LTR       9,3              Test sign bit.
              BM        TEST             Go to test types if negative.
              SLDL      8,17             Remove sign bits.
              BITS      2,6,TMEM         Next 2 bits to REG 6, indirect through
                                         MEM table.
```

	BITS	3,4,TIN1	3 bits to REG 4 indirected through IN-1 table.
	BITS	3,5,TIN2	Ditto for REG 5 and table IN-2.
	BITS	3,7,TFUN	Ditto for REG 6 and table fun.
	BITS	4,8,TOUT	4 bits to REG 8 indirected through table out.
	L	4,0(4)	IN-1 operand to R4.
	L	5,0(5)	IN-2 operand to R5.
	BR	7	Branch to function program.
TMEM	DC	A(MEM)	Addresses of tables.
TIN1	DC	A(IN1)	
TIN2	DC	A(IN2)	
TFUN	DC	A(FUN)	
TOUT	DC	A(OUT)	
MEM	DC	A(NEXT)	Table of branch addresses for control group.
	DC	A(RMEM)	
	DC	A(WMEM)	
	DC	A(DUMP)	
IN1	DC	A(ZERO)	Table of addresses of S registers or constants.
	DC	A(MDR)	
	DC	A(X)	
	DC	A(MFOUR)	
	DC	A(ERR)	
	DC	A(ERR)	
	DC	A(ERR)	
	DC	A(FOUR)	
IN2	DC	A(ZERO)	
	DC	A(ONE)	
	DC	A(MASK)	
	DC	A(A)	
	DC	A(CC)	
	DC	A(B)	
	DC	A(STK)	
	DC	A(FOUR)	
FUN	DC	A(ADDM)	Table of addresses of programs for functions.
	DC	A(SUBM)	
	DC	A(ANDM)	
	DC	A(ORM)	
	DC	A(NOT)	
	DC	A(EOR)	
	DC	A(RS)	
	DC	A(LS)	
OUT	DC	A(MAR)	Addresses of registers for output.
	DC	A(MDR)	
	DC	A(X)	

	DC	A(A)	
	DC	A(CC)	
	DC	A(B)	
	DC	A(STK)	
	DC	A(IR)	
	DC	A(ERR1)	
	DC	A(ERR1)	
	DC	A(ERR1)	
	DC	A(ERR1)	
	DC	A(ERR1)	
	DC	A(ERR1)	
	DC	A(ERR1)	
	DC	A(ERR1)	
ZERO	DC	F'0'	
ONE	DC	F'1'	
FOUR	DC	F'4'	
MFOUR	DC	F'—4'	
MASK	DC	X'00FFFFFF'	24 one bits (hexadecimal constant).
ADDM	AR	4,5	Function program for ADDM.
	ST	4,0(8)	
	BR	6	Branch to memory control group.
RMEM	L	10,MAR	Memory control group program for read.
	N	10,=X'00003FFC'	Extract 12 bit address.
	A	10,AMEMORY	Add address of start of memory.
	L	10,0(10)	Fetch word from memory.
	ST	10,MDR	Place in MDR.
	B	NEXT	Return to next micro instruction.
AMEMORY	DC	A(MEMORY)	Address of memory location 0.
AMCODE	DC	A(MCODE)	Address of micro memory location 0.
	etc.		

5.5.1 Assembling micro program and S-machine language

The simulator can be written symbolically using the assembler facilities provided by the system. If the system also provides a macro assembler, then it can be used to assemble the micro program and S-machine language programs. Macro assemblers differ in their capabilities and their formats. In this section we shall discuss typical macro assemblers and indicate how they can be used to assemble the micro program and S language. If a manufacturer were considering building machines, it would probably be worth his while to write a special assembler for this purpose. Such an assembler could provide more error diagnostics than are possible with a reasonable use of macros, although a flexible macro assembler could be used to perform almost any amount of checking at a sacrifice in assembly time.

We would like to input micro program into memory in exactly the form we wrote it earlier, that is, as an outside symbolic address (optional), an operation, and an address field. This is to be assembled into the appropriate binary patterns. There are two ways in which this can be done in many macro assemblers, by the use of conditional expansion pseudo-orders or by the use of a binary packing pseudo-order. Conditional expansion can be used to test for erroneous usage of micro instructions, but it takes longer. Many assemblers provide a pseudo-order which allows binary patterns to be assembled easily. One such pseudo, for an IBM 7094 assembler, is the VFD pseudo. The VFD is followed by an address field which can contain a string of specifications of the form N/P. Each of these assembles into N bits formed by taking the bottom N bits of the value of the address P. For example, 4/3,5/23,2/0 would assemble as three groups of 3,5, and 2 bits respectively, or as 00111011100 in binary. These bits are left justified in a word. Using this, we could define a macro

```
TO   MACRO  A
     VFD         4/9,12/A–MCODE
     END
```

This assembles as 1001NNNNNNNNNNNN where NNNNNNNNNNNN is the binary form of A–MCODE. The initial 1 indicates that it is a test step, the next 3 bits indicate that MDR bit 0 is to be tested, while the final 12 bits are the address. MCODE is the first address of the set of micro instructions. It is subtracted from A so that the address stored in the micro memory is relative to 0 in the micro memory rather than to 0 in the actual memory. Similarly, each of the test micro instructions can be implemented as macros. The process steps can be implemented with eight macros, one for each function. The ADDM, for example, can take the form

```
ADDM  MACRO  I1,I2,OUT,Z
      VFD          1/0,2/Z,3/I1,3/I2,3/0,4/OUT
      END
```

The function bits are set to 0 to indicate addition in the logical unit. The addresses provided will have to have the appropriate values from the tables of codes. This can be done by means of EQU type pseudo-orders. This means that the micro program must be assembled separately from the simulator to avoid conflict between different uses of the same symbolic names. For example, MDR stands for the location of the MDR register in the simulator.

It must represent the integer 1 in the micro code, because the MDR register has code number 1 in the IN-1 table and the OUT table.

The equivalent 360 macros can make use of the bit-length specification with an A-type field in a DC pseudo. AL.3(2), for example, generates 3 bits whose value is the binary integer 2. Using this, the two examples given above would be written as

```
        MACRO
&B  TO      &A
&B  DC      AL.4(9),AL.12((&A-MCODE)/2)
        MEND
```

and

```
        MACRO
&A  ADDM    &I1,&I2,&OUT,Z
&A  DC      AL.1(0),AL.2(Z),AL.3(I1),AL.3(I2),AL.3(0),AL.4(OUT)
        MEND
```

The S-machine language can be assembled in a similar manner by defining each S instruction as a macro. Thus the subtraction instruction will be defined in a macro assembler similar to that on the IBM 7094 by

```
SUBS  MACRO
        VFD     8/33
        END
```

while the store instruction can be defined by

```
STORE  MACRO  A,X,I
        VFD     1/I,1/X,6/2,22/A-MEMORY,2/0
        END
```

where MEMORY is the first address in the actual machine of the S memory. The one-address instructions will have to be written with fields for the index and indirect address if this method is used. This can be avoided by using conditional expansion pseudo-orders, if they are available, or by providing separate macros for each case.

The equivalent 360 macro for the STORE instruction would be

```
        MACRO
&B  STORE   &A,&X,&I
&B  DC      AL.1(&I),AL.1(&X),AL.6(2),AL3(&A-MEMORY)
        MEND
```

For the 360 system, the complete simulator could be put together in the following fashion:

Job control language for first assembly

```
      SIMULATR  CSECT
                - - - -                     Set up instructions.
                EXTRN  MEMORY,MCODE   Addresses of S memory and MCODE.
                Simulator program for executing micro instructions.
      MDR       DC     F               Definitions of S registers.
      MAR       DC     F
                etc.
                END
```

JCL for second assembly

```
                EQU definitions of S-register names as numbers.
                Macro definitions of micro instructions.
                DC     0F                   Start on full word boundary.
                ENTRY  MCODE                MCODE address for simulator.
      MCODE     ADDM   ZERO,ZERO,CC,P  First micro instruction.
                - - - -
                END
```

JCL for third assembly

```
                Macro definitions of S-machine instructions.
                ENTRY  MEMORY
      MEMORY    DC     0F              Get on fullword boundary.
                S-machine instructions
                - - - -
                END
```

5.6 EMULATION

When an installation changes from one machine to another, it frequently writes simulators for the new machine to run on the old, so that code preparation can begin well ahead of machine delivery. Code may also be written for the old machine on the new, so that existing codes can be run while they are being converted. In many installations, a large amount of machine time can be used in this mode because of the lower efficiency of a simulator. To combat this problem, the idea of writing the simulator completely, or nearly completely, in the micro language of a micro programmed machine has been used. This has been given the name emulation. Because the data paths of the host machine are designed to ease the task of micro programming its machine language, the emulator does not run as fast as the original machine were it constructed with the same technology. However, efficiencies of better than 50 percent are easy to achieve.

PROBLEMS

1. Why is interpretation useful during debugging of programs?
2. What is ROM (Read Only Memory), and why can it be used for micro programs? Could it have any use for S-machine programs?
3. How can the S-machine data paths and micro machine control be modified to allow for single-byte (8-bit) instructions in the case of zero-address instructions? Note that instructions would no longer start on word boundaries, so it would be necessary to be able to move words by multiples of 8 bits fairly easily.
4. How can an interrupt feature on the S machine be implemented? What instructions have to be added to the S-machine language, and what to the micro machine language?
5. Implement a multiply instruction using only the data flow and micro instructions given. Assume that the registers contain integers and that the result is a single-precision integer. Hint: place the multiplier, from the second level of the stack, into the MDR, and perform the multiplication a bit at a time, from the most significant bit down. Form the product in the B register, doubling it after each step in order to be able to test the next bit of the multiplier. Keep a count of the number of steps in the X register, which should have been saved initially in the memory location for the top of the stack, and, after the MDR reaches 0, complete the number of shifts needed to reach 32 total. How can the machine be modified to make this process easier?
6. Why is micro program control useful?
7. Can a micro program control system be used on a machine with the data paths shown in Figure 5.2? Why?
8. Using whatever assembler with macro features that is available, implement a macro for the S instruction LOAD such that it can be written as

```
LOAD  A     with no indexing
LOAD  A,X   with indexing
```

Design a similar notation and implement it for indirect addressing of the LOAD instruction.

6

input, output,
and backup storage

The function of a computer system is to process information. We have seen
how this is done using the memory and processor units. The computer system
must also be able to transmit information between itself and its environment.
The information to be processed must be input to the system, and the results
must be output back to the external world. The computer may be in one of
various different environments which affect the type of input/output
communication required. In the most familiar systems, the computer primarily communicates with humans who prepare the problem for solution,
provide the initial data, and wish to interpret the answers. In other applications, the input can be directly from a physical device. Complex experiments
in the physical sciences can be measured automatically by computer. In such
a case, the principal inputs to the computer are digital readings taken
directly from the various instruments used to monitor the experiment. In
other applications, both input and output may connect directly to mechanical or electrical equipment. For example, an airborne computer may be used
to calculate the position of the plane at any instant (by use of inputs from
gyroscopes and other inertial devices), to compare this position with the
desired flight path derived by computation, and then to output correction
signals to the control mechanisms of the aircraft. Computers for online
instrumentation and process control applications are usually smaller and
more specialized than the general-purpose computers that we have been discussing. In this chapter, we shall discuss the input/output that is common to
the general-purpose systems. However, the principles involved do not differ
from those in online computers.

The general-purpose computer may need to communicate either directly
with the user or with a computer-readable medium. The former will be
referred to as *input/output*, whereas the latter will be called *auxiliary storage*,

since the information is not yet "out" of its computer representation. Auxiliary storage is also called *backup storage*. Auxiliary storage can be used to transmit data to another computer either immediately or at a later time. Immediate transfer can only be accomplished by a direct data connection between two computers. With a direct data connection, each computer looks like an auxiliary storage device to the other. This sort of connection is frequently used between small special-purpose control computers and large general-purpose computers. Delayed transfers are achieved by first storing the information on a machine-readable medium, such as magnetic tape (discussed below), and then transferring the storage medium to the other machine. An important application of this storage is for transferring the information back to the machine that originally wrote it. This provides a mechanism for storing large amounts of data for a long period of time without using the expensive main memory. We shall see that some devices have the ability to store information on a medium that can be physically moved from one computer to another, while others do not. This could form one basis for classifying auxiliary storage. Input/output would always fall into the former category. Devices also differ in their speeds and capacities, and this forms another basis for classification which we shall use below. We shall refer to long-term storage devices, which are frequently used to save information over long periods of time, and to medium-term storage devices which are frequently used to save information from one short computer run to another, for additional storage during a single execution of a program, and to provide rapid access to frequently used system programs. Generally speaking, higher-speed devices have less capacity and are less likely to have removable storage media.

The next four sections will discuss the characteristics of various devices used for input/output and auxiliary storage. Section 6.5 will discuss the ways in which input/output and auxiliary storage devices are controlled by program instruction, and the remainder of the chapter will be devoted to a survey of the software systems of increasing complexity that can be provided for I/O and auxiliary storage access. When speeds and capacities of storage media are given, they are typical figures for large general-purpose installations. Lower numbers are always possible and somewhat greater numbers can be achieved, but they are expensive and technically difficult.

6.1 INPUT/OUTPUT DEVICES

Input/output devices are of two basic types: the *hard-copy* devices which are principally used in an *offline* mode such that the user does not have to be present at the computer at run time; and non-hard-copy devices, which present the output directly to the user in a nonpermanent form or read the input directly as a result of some action by the user, such as typing.

6.1.1 Punched cards

The most common form of input and output is the punched card. The card is a rectangle of heavy card stock (usually about $7\frac{1}{2}$ inches by $3\frac{1}{4}$ inches) that can be punched with a hole in any one of 960 positions on a 12 by 80 rectangular array of positions. Other sizes of cards—with 51 or 90 columns instead of the 80 columns mentioned above—are in use, but the 80-column card is the most common. Punched cards were used for machine control in the weaving industry long before they were used in data processing. The first major application of punched cards to data handling occurred during the late 1800s, when Herman Hollerith adapted them for use in the 1890 census. Because of his work, the cards are called *Hollerith cards*, and one way in which they are punched is called the Hollerith card code. This code is a means of representing alphanumeric data (that is, the alphabetic letters and the 10 decimal digits) and a few special characters such as period, comma, etc. One column is used to represent each character, so that up to 80 characters can be punched on one card. As shown in Figure 6.1, the card rows are labelled 12, 11, 0, 1, 2, 3, 4, 5, 6, 7, 8, and 9. A blank character or space is represented as no holes punched, the numerical digits 0 through 9 by a punch in the cor-

FIGURE 6.1 Hollerith punched card.

responding row, and the letters by double punches. A through I are represented by a 12-row punch together with a digit punch from 1 to 9 respectively, J through R by an 11-row punch with the digit 1 through 9 respectively, and S through Z by a 0-row punch with the digit 2 through 9 respectively. Other characters are represented by other combinations of punched holes.

When a card written in this format is read into the machine, it is converted into a string of characters in memory in a suitable code. If the standard 48-character set is used, then only 6 bits are needed to represent 48 characters. Therefore one of the 6-bit codes, such as the BCD code, can be used. This conversion is usually done by hardware, so that the programmer does not have to concern himself with the Hollerith code. In recent machines, such as the IBM 360, the EBCDIC code is used. This allows for up to 256 characters requiring 8 bits per character.

Each column of the card can contain up to 12 punches for a total of $2^{12} = 4,096$ different combinations. However, less than 64 of these are used in the usual card codes. To combat this inefficiency, the binary card is often used when the desire is to get as much information on the card as possible rather than to make it as legible as possible. The binary card can be punched in any position, so that any column can contain 12 bits of information. If a binary card is read into the computer, each column is mapped in a direct manner into 12 bits of memory, and vice versa on output punching. Since cards so punched are not readable by most printing equipment, this use of cards is solely for storage of information to be read back in at a later stage. It is very common, for example, to store programs on binary cards after they have been translated by the machine (to avoid having to retranslate them). If the EBCDIC code is used in the computer, there exists a mapping from 8-bit bytes to combinations of punches in a single column. Since 8 of the 12 bits of information are being used, the IBM 360 uses this code for storing binary information rather than provide a special set of instructions for handling binary cards. Cards can be read at speeds in the range of 1,000 to 2,000 per minute and punched at speeds of 200 to 400 per minute. Because cards are prone to error, the card reader usually reads each card twice to check for reading errors, and the punches usually also read the punched result to perform similar checking.

6.1.2 Punched paper tape

Punched paper tape is very similar to punched cards in that it consists of a heavy paper stock in which information is represented by the presence or absence of punched holes. It differs from cards in that paper tape is in continuous strips of arbitrary lengths, whereas cards are a fixed size. Tape is commonly used in three different widths containing five, seven, or eight possible information-hole positions across the tape. Each of these positions is called a *channel*. A 1-inch eight-channel tape is shown in Figure 6.2. Notice that, in addition to the eight information positions or channels, there is a ninth position that is always punched with a sprocket hole. This is to locate the position where the information should appear along the tape. Without this sprocket hole, a series of characters consisting of no punched holes would lead to a strip of completely blank tape. It would then be impossible to tell how many characters there were in such a string except by measuring the length of the tape, a procedure which would be very prone to error. The sprocket hole is also used to mesh with a sprocket gear on the slower mechanical readers. Since paper tape is prone to error, it is very common to use one of the information channels as a parity bit for the other information channels.

Systems that use paper tape as the primary input to the computer tend to differ from systems designed around cards because of the property that paper tape is continuous. Paper tape is not typically used in the higher-speed installations because it is impractical to join tapes together to make continuous input from one user to the next possible. Secondly, it is more cumbersome to change a paper tape, since the complete strip must be duplicated with the change inserted at the appropriate point. With cards, on the other hand, only the offending cards need be changed. Therefore, in a paper-tape system, the basic input programs should allow the user the ability to follow the initial input with correction tapes which modify a copy of the input internally. In

| Character with 1, 3, 6 and 8 holes punched | Character with all holes punched | Sprocket holes, 10 per inch |

FIGURE 6.2 Paper tape.

general, paper tape is cheaper (both in terms of the cost of the reading and punching equipment and in terms of the cost of the paper itself) than cards, and hence tends to be used on the small low-speed systems which are becoming very common in special-purpose control applications. Paper tape can be read at speeds of 1,000 to 2,000 characters per second and punched at 300 characters per second.

6.1.3 Printing devices

The most acceptable form of output for general-purpose use is generated by a printer. A large part of the output from a computer consists of numeric and alphabetic information which will be read by the user. Printers are devices for converting the internal character representation in the memory to the printed page. Although there is no difference in the end result, printers are classified into two basic types because of the great difference in speeds between the two. The *line printer* is a device which prints a line at a time. The computer transmits a complete line of information to the printer unit, and then it is printed. A printing mechanism exists at every print position across the line, which can vary in width from 80 characters to 150 characters in common printers. Because of the parallelism present in such a printer, it can achieve speeds of 1,000 to 2,000 lines per minute by mechanical means. Nonmechanical printing techniques (photographic, for example) can achieve even higher speeds (up to 30,000 lines per minute).

The character printer is similar to a typewriter—in fact, it is very often a modified typewriter which can be controlled by the computer. Since it only prints a character at a time across the line, it is relatively slow, of the order of 10 to 40 characters per second. (Incidentally, the reader might notice that the heavily commercial devices are usually quoted in operations per minute. The numbers are larger.)

6.1.4 Keyboard input

The other half of the typewriter mechanism used for low-speed output, the keyboard, can be used for input. Since this is at human speeds (usually about 2 characters per second and limited mechanically to about 15 characters per second) a keyboard is not an economical input for a fast computer unless its use is for rare events, and its input can be overlapped with the processing of useful work. It is frequently used for small machines as a primary input device so that the programmer types part of his program in directly, rather than typing it first on paper tape and then reading the paper tape. For example, he might make corrections to his program *online*. This type of use is now possible on larger systems by time-sharing techniques, where many keyboards are serviced in parallel to increase the data rate of input to a reasonable total level.

Two basic typewriter devices are in common use today. One is based on the IBM Selectric "golf ball" typewriter, and is marketed as the 1050 and the 2741. The other is based on the Teletype mechanisms. The Teletype Model 35 is a typewriter with numbers, special characters, and upper-case letters only, designed for easy interface to a communication system such as the telephone network. It is now available with lower-case letters as the Model 37. The Model 33 is a low-cost version of the 35. They all use the ASCII code. The IBM 1050/2741 is designed to communicate with equipment using BCD or EBCDIC codes.

6.1.5   Plotters and display devices

Although printer output is very convenient for many purposes, frequently the user needs to present the information graphically in order to be able to understand its significance. This may be in the form of a simple graph plotting one variable against another, or it may be a complex pictorial display representing a multidimensional item. For example, three-dimensional pictures are frequently represented by two-dimensional contour maps, where lines represent the paths of constancy in the third dimension (weather maps, for example, in which the contours of constant pressure are drawn to indicate the high-pressure and low-pressure regions).

If graphs have to be prepared by hand from numerical output by the computer, a large amount of output is typically needed and time-consuming drawing must be undertaken by the human. Therefore, direct graphical output devices have been developed for computer use. There are two basic types of output device, one which allows the user to put a point at any location on the output *page*, and one which allows the user to move a *pen* in any direction a given distance, with the pen either on the paper making a mark or off the paper not making a mark. The words *pen* and *paper* are not meant literally, in that the output could be on any medium which can be marked. In many devices, the two basic techniques are both available, but it is convenient to examine them separately.

The *incremental plotter* is an example of the second form of output. It is a device with a pen and a large sheet of paper. The pen can be moved a small increment in any one of several directions. In a typical plotter, it can move in any one of the eight directions separated by 45 degrees a distance of .005

inches vertically or horizontally, or .007 inches in any of the four 45-degree directions. All lines must be made up of these short, straight-line segments. The computer commands the plotter with a series of characters to make each basic plot step. The use of a plotter to draw a 45-degree triangle lying on its hypotenuse is shown in Figure 6.3. The computer subroutine library will usually contain subroutines to simplify the use of the plotter. A common package of subroutines for a plotter allows the user to move the pen from where it is currently to any given position on the page with the pen either writing or not, to draw many of the common curves such as ellipses, and to print letters and numbers on the page. The subroutines convert the demands of the user into sequences of the basic steps for the plotter. The time to plot a figure is dependent on the linear distance that the pen moves. The speed is of the order of 1 to 10 inches per second.

The cathode-ray-tube output device basically allows the user to illuminate spots on the face of the C.R.T. by specifying X and Y coordinates to the output device. With such a device, a line must be built up from many small points. Typically about 500 to 4,000 points can be displayed in each direction, and adjacent points are sufficiently close that they are joined together as far as the eye can see. Often C.R.T. displays have built-in *vector* and *character* facilities which allow them to generate straight lines and standard characters directly. This serves to decrease the computer time needed to generate a display, but not to increase the flexibility of the display from the user's point of view. The basic operations are used by subroutines to provide the same facilities as are available for the plotter. An important additional facility

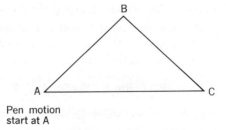

Pen motion
start at A

Pen down
Move up, right (100 steps)
Move down, right (100 steps)
Move left (200 steps)
Pen up

FIGURE 6.3 Plotting a triangle.

available with a cathode-ray tube is the *light pen*. This is a photoelectric device, shaped like an ordinary pen, which can be placed on any point on the face of the C.R.T. When the spot touched is illuminated by the program in control, a signal is generated by the photo-cell. This signal is sent to the computer, usually in the form of an interrupt. Thus the programmer can tell where the pen is positioned. By suitable programs, it is possible to follow the light pen around the screen and store inside the computer the coordinates of the various points indicated by the user. Thus the user can *draw* on the face of the C.R.T., and the light pen can be used as an input device. Its most common use is for pointing at sections of the total display on the tube.

Other devices can be used for indicating a point on the screen. One is a special tablet that is sensitive to an electronic pen held by the user. Another is a small hand-held box that the user moves over the surface of a table. Pickup devices measure the position of the hand and transmit it to the computer, which then displays a circle or a cross on the screen corresponding to the position of the hand.

Many other forms of input and output devices have been developed for special purposes. Optical scanners can *read* sets of typed characters, and some devices have achieved a limited ability to read handwritten characters. Three-dimensional pens that enable the computer to track the user's hand in three-dimensional space have been designed; and analog input and output converters can not only read information directly from experimental measuring equipment but also control experiments directly. Voice output is possible by controlling sets of audio recorders similar to tape recorders, and, experimentally, acoustic input and output has been performed by using the computer to decode the signal from microphones and to generate the signal for a loudspeaker system directly. However, most such equipment is still in a "research" status, so it will not be discussed further in this book.

6.2 LONG–TERM STORAGE AND INTERMEDIATE INPUT/OUTPUT

Problems that involve the use of very large amounts of data and that are run on many different occasions have a requirement for long-term storage devices. Problems in this class include commercial jobs such as the record keeping associated with the maintenance of customer accounts and scientific jobs such as the comparison of data gathered from a particular physics experiment with the data gathered from many previous experiments. Both of these jobs have the characteristic that very large amounts of data are involved (100 million characters should be considered typical in designing systems for this type of problem) and the characteristic that the data is to be changed in a small way (some customer accounts are changed, or some additional experimental data is added to the history file). These characteristics dictate the need for a storage device that has virtually unlimited total capacity, although it only need be accessed in a serial fashion (that is, in sequential order, one unit of information at a time). Since the electronics associated with storage devices is the expensive part of the device, a desirable form of storage is one in which the storage is on a simple medium which can be removed, kept on a shelf, and replaced. To a limited extent, punched cards are a type of long-term storage, since the card reader and punch are, in principle, capable of handling an arbitrarily large number of cards. However, cards cannot be changed (holes cannot be filled in any practical way), and cards have a non-negligible cost (approximately 0.1 cent per card). Also, card equipment is comparatively slow. However, there are a number of other devices which do not have the drawbacks of card equipment, specifically, magnetic tapes, disk files, and variations on both. These are all forms of the familiar tape recorder used for audio storage. This section will discuss the principles of a number of such devices. It is not intended to be exhaustive, since new versions are marketed almost every day. Although the manufacturer may claim a "breakthrough," the operating principles remain very similar; the speed and capacity may increase and the cost decrease.

6.2.1 Magnetic tape

Magnetic-tape storage was derived directly from audio-tape principles. The storage medium is a long strip of tape with a fixed width. Common tape systems are available with $\frac{1}{2}$-inch and 1-inch tape widths. The length of the tape is typically about 2,400 feet, and it is wound on a reel for easy handling. The tape itself is about $\frac{1}{500}$ to $\frac{1}{1000}$ of an inch thick, and it consists of a backing of flexible material, such as Mylar, with a coating of a magnetic material (an iron oxide). Information is stored on the tape by magnetizing the oxide coating in one direction or another. A *track* on the tape is a section of the width of the tape in which the magnetically coded information is stored. See Figure 6.4. Since a track is less than $\frac{1}{16}$ of an inch wide, several tracks can be placed across the tape. Half-inch tape commonly has either 7 or 9 tracks across the width, hence 7 or 9 bits can be stored in *parallel*. In order to read or write on tape, the reel of tape is mounted on a *tape drive*, which is a mechanism with two reel drives, *read heads*, *write heads*, and a *capstan* which pulls the tape across the heads at an approximately constant speed (see Figure 6.5). When the tape is written, it is pulled across the heads

FIGURE 6.4 Magnetic tape.

by the capstan, and amplifiers drive current through the write heads in order to magnetize the tape. It is read back by pulling the tape across the read heads with the capstan and sensing the voltages induced in the read heads.

In practice, the bits of information are packed very closely together along the tape; for example, 200, 556, 800, and 1,600 bits to the inch in each track are standard *densities*. Since the tape is moved at speeds around 120 inches per second, it is out of the question to start or stop the tape between characters. Therefore, the information is usually written on the tape in continuous *records* or *blocks* with gaps between for starting and stopping. These gaps are called *inter-record gaps* and are about ¾-inch long. The length of the blocks is either fixed by the computer or is allowed to vary according to the use by the programmer. It is important to understand the difference between these two possibilities, so we shall first examine the reasons for their use.

We recall that paper tape had a sprocket hole in order to allow the tape reader to know where a character was punched on the tape. In a similar manner, it is necessary for the computer to know where a set of bits (a character) is written on the magnetic tape. This is not done by a sprocket hole

FIGURE 6.5 A tape drive.

(it is difficult to punch 800 holes to the inch), but in some systems the equivalent—a *timing track*—is used. A timing track is a tape track that contains 1s in every bit position. The tape reader can use this track to indicate when a character position across the tape has been encountered, and then it can read the actual information bits. The alternative is to demand that every character written on the tape contains at least one 1 bit, so that the logical OR of all channels will contain a signal when a character is read. This is not too difficult, since it is normal to use a parity bit in every character. By using odd parity, at least one 1 bit is assured. The important difference is that if timing tracks are used, the tape must be *formatted* before use by writing a timing track all the way along the tape and leaving it there permanently. It is always possible to return to the same point on the tape by counting the timing bits. If, however, a timing track is not used, the tape drive must provide its own timing information via an electronic clock during the writing of new information. Since it is impossible to guarantee that the tape moves at exactly the same speed on two successive operations, a written block of a given number of characters may vary in length from one WRITE operation to another. The effect of this is shown in Figure 6.6. In the top diagram, the tape has been written with two blocks of information of 10,000 characters each (about 12½ inches each). In the second diagram, the first block has been

FIGURE 6.6   Effect of non-constant tape speeds.

rewritten when the tape moved 10 percent faster. Consequently, $1\frac{1}{4}$ inches of the next block has been overwritten. The bottom diagram shows the effect of rewriting the first block with the tape moving 10 percent slower. This time, about $\frac{1}{2}$ inch of the previous block remains. If the user attempted to read the second block, he would get errors in both cases.

Tape that uses timing tracks can be rewritten at any point. In general, tape without timing tracks cannot be used in this manner, but must be used sequentially. That is, before a block can be written, all blocks ahead of it on the tape must first be written. However, some manufacturers are claiming to be able to produce tape units which are sufficiently accurate that blocks can be rewritten at arbitrary points.

A comparison of formatted and unformatted tape is difficult. On the one hand, formatted tape can be changed at any point. On the other, part of the space on the tape is used for timing information that could be used for storage. (The problem of writing precisely where the bit appears in the timing track is also more difficult than writing whenever the tape-unit clock indicates.) If tape is to be rewritten at any point, then it is easier for the programmer to use *fixed-length blocks*, and, indeed, tape is often formatted in this way. However, the tendency has been to use fixed-length blocks even on unformatted tape, for system reasons. The largest computer manufacturer, IBM, uses unformatted tape, and such tape is therefore the most common.

Basic tape operations include writing and reading blocks of information. In addition, tape-handling operations are necessary to enable the program to reach the particular block needed. After a tape block has been written, it is necessary to backspace the tape to the beginning of the block in order to reread it. (Some systems allow tape to be read or written in either direction, but the majority only allow reading and writing in the forward direction.) Sometimes it is necessary to space forward over one or more blocks in order to reach something further down the tape; therefore a forward space operation is desirable.

Magnetic tape is only sequentially accessible. That is, it is more like a scroll than a book. A scroll is read by unwinding it from one end and, in order to reach a paragraph in the middle, it is necessary to roll through all previous paragraphs. In general, there are no operations to access an arbitrary block on a tape. Instead, it is necessary to skip through all the preceding blocks, one at a time.

Many of the terms introduced below are derived from business data processing. The basic unit of information in business data is the *character*, which may be part of a name, address, or numeric record. Characters are grouped together into *fields* representing the names, etc. Groups of fields are combined into one *record*, which may be the basic block written onto the tape.

Historically, the word "record" was used to mean a recorded block of information. We shall reserve the word to signify a logical group of information
typically handled as a unit by the user, and we shall use the word "block" to
mean the physically recorded group of information. A record might, for
example, contain all of the employment information relating to one employee.
Finally, all of the employee records are grouped into one *file*. In a large
organization, one file may occupy many reels of tape; whereas in a small
company, it may occupy only a small part of one reel. (A reel of tape can
contain 20 million characters.) The file concept is used in magnetic tape
recording by providing a special *end-of-file* mark which can be written by the
computer instead of a regular block. When it is read, an indicator is set
which can be sensed by the program to indicate that the end of the file has
been reached. A common analogy to draw for files, records, and characters
on tape is with a book. The paragraphs are similar to records, and the file
is the whole book. This does not take into account divisions into sections and
chapters. These the programmer must handle by careful use of multiple
end-of-file marks or other techniques. Following this analogy, fixed-length
blocks are similar to the pages of a book. Blocks do not usually correspond to
the natural division of the information into sections, paragraphs, etc., but
they *do* provide an easy way of locating a piece of information if an index is
provided. On tape, fixed blocks may not correspond to the requirements of
the information, but they can be used to advantage if the information is
indexed.

To make use of file marks, two operations are usually provided, a backspace
file and a skip-to-end-of-file operation. These make it easier to move over
multiple files with minimum program effort. The operations allowed on
typical unformatted and formatted systems are shown in tabular form below.

operation	unformatted tape	formatted tape
Write	Programmer specifies the number of words.	A multiple of a fixed number of words.
Read	Option. Either the whole block written or a number of words specified by the programmer. Restriction: cannot read downstream of a write operation.	Fixed block as written or a given number of words.
Backspace	Block or file possible.	Block only†
Forward space (skip)	Block or file possible.	Block only†
Rewind	O.K.	O.K.
Write end of file	O.K.	Not available†
Sense end of file on read	O.K.	Not available†

† It is possible to allow an extra character at the start of each block to represent a file mark,
in which case write end of file, backspace file, and sense end of file are possible.

When a file of information on magnetic tape is to be updated (that is, some of the information is to be changed), it is necessary to read the original from one tape and make updated copy on another tape on a second tape drive. The only time that this is not necessary is when fixed-block formatted tapes are used and the updated material is not longer than the original. The minimum number of unformatted tape drives for any useful operation is two, while four is a more practical minimum for most data manipulation tasks. Two tapes are needed so that one can be updated onto the other. Four are useful when a *merge*, to be discussed in Chapter 8, is to be done. An unlimited number of reels of tape can be stored on shelves and, given enough time, processed by the computer. Therefore the upper limit of storage is unbounded. The speed of operation varies between different drives and manufacturers, and the range of character rates is from a few thousand per second to 180,000 per second. Moving the tape over records and files takes about the same length of time as reading or writing, while rewinding takes from 1 to 2 minutes maximum. The time to start and stop the tape in the record gap varies from 1 to 20 milliseconds.

6.2.2 Disk files

The use of the word "files" in the name of this device should not be confused with its use to mean a group of records of information. A disk file is a device which resembles a phonograph record and its playback mechanism. Physically, a single disk platter is a circular sheet of metal about 10 to 20 inches in diameter and $\frac{1}{16}$ to $\frac{1}{4}$ inch thick. It is coated on both surfaces with a magnetic material, so that the thickness of the disk is for mechanical strength only. Information is recorded on the disk surface magnetically, just as information is recorded on magnetic tape. The difference between the recording on a phonograph record and a disk platter (in addition to the means of storing information) is that whereas a phonograph contains one continuous groove or track in a spiral, a disk surface contains many tracks arranged in concentric circles. The read and write heads (usually the same head) are mounted on movable arms which can be positioned over any one of the tracks: there may be from 100 to 1,000 tracks on a surface. A diagram of a single disk surface is shown in Figure 6.7.

A disk unit may be able to access a single surface at a time, or it may contain several platters, each with a read/write head on an arm, such that any surface can be accessed. As long as the set of disk platters can be removed, the disk file satisfies our definition of long-term, essentially unlimited storage. It has characteristics similar to magnetic tapes in that it can take a relatively

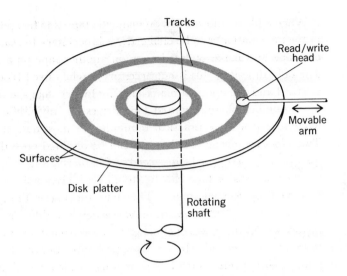

FIGURE 6.7 Disk.

long time to move from the track currently under the head to another head, just as it can take a tape reader a long time to move from one position on the tape to another relative to the transmission time for one character. However, both figures are much faster for disk files, in that a typical maximum head-movement time for a disk file is about $\frac{1}{4}$ second, whereas for a tape it is up to 4 minutes. The data rate for characters from disk is typically between 100 KC (KC = 1,000 characters) and 400 KC per second compared to 30 KC to 180 KC for tape. A large disk file will contain the same amount of information as a tape to within an order of magnitude. (Tapes contain about 1,000 characters per inch over 2,400 feet, for about 20×10^6 characters; disks typically contain from 10 to 400×10^6 characters.

The method of recording is usually a fixed-block mode rather than a variable-length block mode, since a single track is of a fixed length. A timing track is prerecorded on one surface of the file so that bits are always stored in the same physical position on repeated writes. Hence it is possible to rewrite a single block anywhere on the file without losing other blocks of previously recorded information. Additional tracks adjacent to the timing track frequently contain *format* information. This tells the controlling computer where the blocks are around the track and how long they are. Some systems allow this information to be changed, so that the length of blocks can be changed under program control. This is known as *formatting* the disk. It is not a good idea to do this frequently. Usually the installation will settle on a given format and block size.

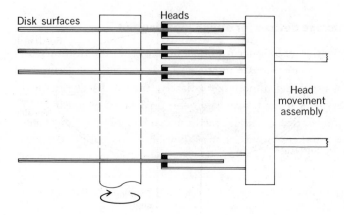

FIGURE 6.8   Multiple-surface disk file.

In order to use a disk file, the heads must first be moved to the right track (assuming that the correct disk platters are already mounted) before the read or write can be done. The former is known as the *seek* operation. More will be said about the use of input/output equipment in later sections.

While the heads are fixed in any one position, the computer has access to one track on each surface. If we visualize this set of tracks on the disk surfaces shown in Figure 6.8, we see that they lie on the surface of a cylinder. For this reason, disks are often addressed by the *cylinder address* and the *surface address*. The former refers to the position of the heads, the latter to the surface being used. When several blocks of information are to be transmitted between the disk unit and the computer, it is faster if they are on the same cylinder, so that no head movement is involved.

6.2.3 Variations of tapes and disks

Many devices have been marketed recently which are in the same class as tapes and disks: that is, they have the characteristics of removability (so that storage is virtually unlimited) and a reasonable speed and capacity for a single load. They take the form of packages of disk-like or tape-like storage media which can be mechanically accessed so that an individual piece of the medium can be placed in the read/write mechanism. In principle, they are similar to the all-too-familiar juke box, which contains array of records. Any single record can be selected mechanically and loaded into the playback mechanism. With devices of this form, capacities in the area of 10^9 characters *online* (that is, in the machine at one time) are achievable.

6.2.4 Long-term storage devices for offline input/output

An important application of long-term storage devices is in the transmission of information from one computer to another. If this transmission has to be fast in the sense of occurring almost immediately, then a direct electrical coupling is necessary; but if the transmission can be delayed as much as an hour or so, then a tape or disk or similar medium can be written by one computer and read by another—provided that they have compatible devices. Large amounts of information can be transmitted relatively inexpensively in this manner. One important specific application of this method is in the use of a second computer to perform the card reading, punching, and printing functions for a high-speed scientific type machine. Since mechanical operations on hard-copy input/output are severely limited in speed, it has been considered unwise to spend the time of a fast machine on such low-speed operations. Therefore, the information from input cards is copied onto magnetic tape or disk files by a cheaper, slower machine, and the tapes or files are loaded onto the faster machine for reading at a higher speed. The output from the faster machine is put onto tapes or disks and sent back to the low-speed machine for printing and punching. This is called *offline* conversion. The use of time sharing has made this method obsolete, since the large computer can run a time-shared program whose job is to read and print hard-copy input/output to and from disk files.

6.3 MEDIUM–TERM STORAGE DEVICES

By medium-term storage we mean the retention of information for times of a few seconds to a few days, where it is not practical to *unload* the storage medium for physical storage in a cabinet. Devices in this category are characterized by speeds ranging from those available with the long-term devices to speeds of the order of several million characters per second. The capacities of these devices range from those of long-term devices down to the order of a million characters. Applications of these devices are as extensions of the directly addressable main memory in problems in which there is inadequate main memory, and for the retention of information from one problem run to another when it is not convenient to physically reload a storage medium onto a reader. Typical situations that call for these applications are, in the former case, the sorting of large amounts of input information (probably contained on a magnetic tape) which requires many passes over the data, copying it from one storage area to another, and, in the latter case, the saving of user programs and data in a time-sharing, remote-console system, where it is necessary for the user to have almost immediate access to his information when he sits down at a console.

The needs of the examples given above can be satisfied by the use of the long-term devices mentioned above, but some problems exist for which the maximum data rate, or the average access time (to move the heads or the tape) is inadequate, so improvements must be sought. However, in a typical installation, some of the tape units available will be used mainly as *scratch* storage; that is, for the temporary storage of information during the execution of a program only. Similarly, the disk units that are used to write information for long-term storage may serve for scratch-storage purposes as well. In addition, a number of other devices can be used. These will be discussed in the remainder of this section.

6.3.1 The disk file

The disk file was discussed above as a unit with removable disk platters for long-term storage. If the platters do not have to be removable, then it is possible to put more platters in a single unit. In fact, this was the first form of disk file developed. It is physically similar to the removable-platter disk file and is used in the same manner. See Figure 6.8. However, its storage capability can be increased and, by using more than one head to read or write bits on several tracks at once, its speed can be increased considerably. The extreme form of such a disk file is one in which there is one head for every track. This is often called a *drum*, although we shall distinguish between *fixed-head disks* and drums. Since a large disk file can have 8,000 tracks, the one-head-for-one-track arrangement is only possible for the smaller disk units. This type of arrangement does, however, eliminate the positioning of the arms carrying the heads—the slowest part of a disk-file operation. The average access time then drops down to half the rotation time (about half of 35 milliseconds), since the user will have to wait—on the average—a half revolution before the desired information rotates to a position underneath the reading head so that it can be transmitted to the computer.

6.3.2 The drum

Historically, the drum was developed before the disk file, but it is convenient to think of it as a variant of the disk file with fixed heads. Instead of information being stored on a set of disk surfaces, it is stored on the surface of the drum, which may be about 10 inches in diameter and perhaps 20 inches long

FIGURE 6.9   Drum.

(although much larger drums have been developed). Because drums are more compact, they can achieve much higher revolution speeds than can disk-file mechanisms. Hence, the average access time (a half revolution) can be reduced. Typically, revolution times are in the range of 8 to 35 milliseconds. Information is usually stored in fixed-length blocks on a drum. A drum is shown pictorially in Figure 6.9. It is like a single cylinder of a disk file but, for engineering reasons, it is possible to get a higher bit density on a drum than on a disk. To achieve high data rates, several tracks may be read in parallel, so that a large number of words can be read in a single revolution. To keep the blocks to a manageable size, the tracks are divided into *sectors*. Each sector contains a block for reading and writing purposes. The computer accesses the drum by specifying a track and a sector address. After one sector has been read or written, the next-higher-numbered sector can be accessed immediately because it is possible to switch from one set of heads to another almost instantaneously.

6.3.3 Bulk-storage devices

Both CDC and IBM have recently developed bulk-storage devices which are similar to core-storage devices but of a lower speed and larger capacity than main memory. Both are in the neighborhood of 10^8 bits capacity. The IBM device functions exactly like a core store and can be addressed by the CPU in the same way. It takes 8 micro seconds per word as opposed to between 0.5 and 2 micro seconds for the main memory associated with the 360 machines. The CDC device consists of up to four groups of 3.2 micro second memory running in parallel. Whereas the regular memory contains 60 bit words, the bulk memory contains 480 bit words. Thus eight words can be read in parallel from each of four banks of bulk store simultaneously to achieve a maximum rate of 100 nanoseconds per word, which is the peak speed of the main memory, achieved by overlapping four banks of 400 nanosecond memory. Because these speeds can only be achieved if many consecutive words are moved (the first costs 3.2 micro seconds), it can only be used as a block transfer device between the main memory and the bulk store. Thus it looks rather like a drum or disk file, but it is much faster and has no delays waiting for the rotation to the start of a block. It cannot be used to provide instructions and data directly to the CPU, as the IBM device can.

6.4 SPEED AND CAPACITY COMPARISONS

The speeds and capacities of various types of storage media are shown and compared with the speed and capacity of main memories in Figure 6.10.

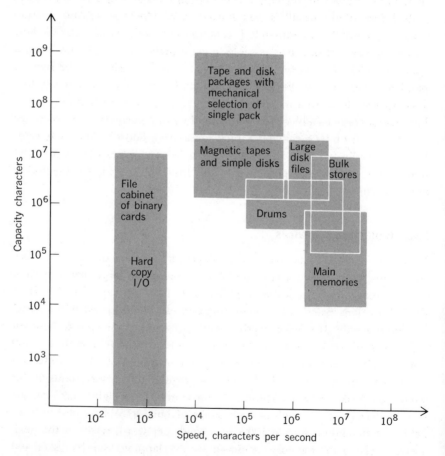

FIGURE 6.10 Current memory devices (1968).

6.5 CONNECTING INPUT/OUTPUT DEVICES TO THE COMPUTER

Each input/output unit is connected electrically to the computer so that it can send or receive characters of information from the computer. The least complex devices are the paper tape reader and punch, so we shall discuss them in more detail. Other devices are similar in principle. An eight-channel paper tape reader contains eight sensing devices for the information channels and one for the sprocket hole. When a character of 8 bits has been read, the tape must be moved. A capstan similar to that on a magnetic tape is used. A *pinch-roller* or *clutch* is used to press the tape against the revolving capstan so that it is moved. When it has moved a full character distance ($\frac{1}{10}$ inch), the sprocket hole sense device indicates that the next character can be read from the eight information sensors. It can then be transmitted to the computer. The sequence of steps taken by the paper tape reader is therefore

1. Start tape moving.
2. Wait until sprocket hole is sensed.
3. Stop tape moving and send character to computer.

Since tape reading speeds are between 10 and 1,000 characters per second, this set of three steps will take 1 to 100 milliseconds. In that time, the computer could have done 100 to 100,000 operations, so it is extremely inefficient to use the main computer to control the tape reader. To get around such inefficiencies, separate controllers are provided for input/output devices. This section will describe different ways in which these inefficiencies are overcome by features in the controller. We shall, in general, discuss only the input process. Output is essentially similar.

6.5.1 Overlap of input/output

Between 1958 and 1964, it was most common to use a separate, slower, cheaper computer to perform offline conversion of hard-copy input/output to and from magnetic tape. This avoided using high-speed equipment for control of slow-speed equipment. However—compared to the larger CPUs—disks, drums, and tapes are slow, so techniques must be used to overlap these slow operations with the much faster computational processes. All of these techniques consist of adding control equipment to the I/O unit so that it does not rely on the central processor control for all of its operational power. More recently, it has become common also to attach slower-speed hard-copy devices online, to use a small segment of the main memory, and to time share the main processor in order to copy from hard copy to disks and vice versa. This section will discuss the various levels to which the control of I/O can be taken.

Examine the set of three steps shown for reading a paper tape character in Section 6.5. The computer was kept waiting on step two, which was the slow, mechanical one. If, instead, we designed the tape reader so that it would always advance the tape to the next character after one had been read without requiring the computer to control this operation, then, provided that the tape is given time to advance between reads, the computer would only have to wait on the mechanical motion if it was not yet finished. The sequence of steps for reading a character would now be

1. Wait until next character is ready.
2. Read it into the computer.
3. Start the tape moving.
4. When next character is under reading device, stop tape.

The first step is necessary because the tape may not have had time to move to the next character after the last one was read. This will only cause a computer wait if not enough time was given between the previous read and this one. After the second step has been completed, the computer need not be concerned with the remaining two steps since a separate control in the tape reader can be used to advance the tape automatically to the next character.

All that this modification does is to eliminate the wait on mechanical motion, but it introduces an important new feature that is used in all future improvements. This feature is *parallelism*. The control of the reader can be busy moving the tape while the computer is busy processing data. Little else can be done to improve the situation until we decide how the data is actually brought into the computer from the tape. The simplest method is to provide instructions to bring the characters directly into an accumulator (if the computer has one—assume a one-address structure for the purposes of discussion). Thus a paper-tape READ instruction can be expected to put the next paper-tape character in the accumulator, and a PUNCH instruction to put the contents of the accumulator, or a set of bits from the accumulator, onto punched tape. The programmer would have to place the READ instructions uniformly in his program to make the best use of the tape reader. In some cases, he may need the character before the reader is ready, so that a wait cannot be avoided; in other cases, the character may be ready before he is, so that the tape reader waits on the computer. It is the desire to avoid these situations that leads to the next developments.

6.5.2 Interrupt controlled input/output

If the user is to achieve better overlap, it is necessary to allow a larger number of characters to be read into the computer ahead of the time that they are needed. Then the user can process them when they are needed, and the reader can be reading further characters at the same time. This is a form of load spreading. If the user needs several characters in rapid succession, they are already available in the machine, and then the reader has time to catch up while he is processing them. The computer or the tape reader will only wait when the average use of the reader is more or less, respectively, than the use of the processor over a longer period.

If the accumulator is to continue to be used for reading characters, how can the user be expected to read in characters ahead of time, and where can he put them? The only reasonable place to put them is in memory, so storage locations are set aside in memory to receive the incoming characters. The problem then is to write a program that will both perform some desired calculation and read in characters at a regular rate from the reader until the memory locations (called buffers) are full. Although this is theoretically possible, it is exceedingly tedious to program, so automatic techniques are usually provided to make it easier. The simplest is the interrupt technique. Interrupts have already been discussed. Let us recall their basic features. When an interrupt signal is received, the current computation in the CPU is temporarily stopped, the control counter is saved so that we know where execution has reached, and a branch to a known location is made. This location could contain a program to read in paper tape characters and place them in the buffers. Therefore, if an interrupt signal is available that indicates to the CPU that the next character is ready, the current process can be interrupted, the current contents of the accumulator saved, the next character read into a buffer, the contents of the accumulator restored, and processing continued in the CPU. A flowchart for this is shown in Figure 6.11. Note that there are two charts, one for the reader and one for the CPU, since they can run in parallel.

Unfortunately, this program will run into trouble when the buffers are full, since then there will be no place to put additional characters. Therefore, the program must be modified in the section for reading tape to that in Figure 6.12. Here, the buffers are tested to see if they are all full. If not, flow continues as before; otherwise a mark, indicating that no reading is occurring, is set. A character is not read, so a further interrupt will not be received by the CPU. When a character is removed from a buffer, it is necessary to start the reading process again. This can be done by testing the "not reading"

FIGURE 6.11   Basic READ flowchart.

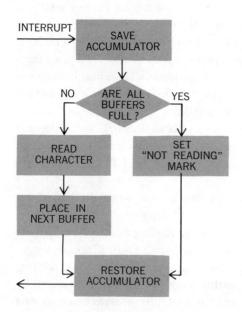

FIGURE 6.12   Modified READ flowchart.

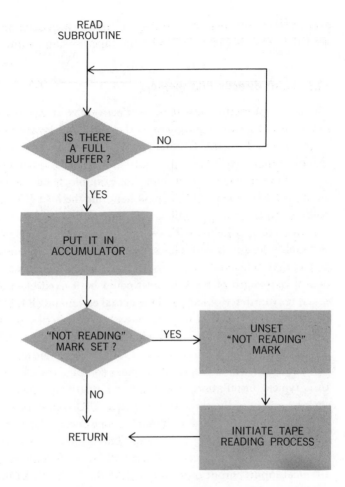

FIGURE 6.13   Reading a character to the accumulator.

mark in the subroutine used to remove a character from a buffer for use by
the program. It is illustrated by the flowchart in Figure 6.13. This particular
subroutine first tests to see if there are any full buffers. If there are none, then
it waits until there are by simply looping on the test. It appears that this loop
is infinite, but what will eventually happen is that the next character will be
ready. It will cause an interrupt which stops the program in the loop, put a
character in a buffer, and then return control to the loop. But this time, the
test gives the answer "yes," so that the computer gets the character from the
buffer. Finally, the mark for "not reading" is tested. If it is not set, then control returns to the calling program. If it is set, it is unset and the reading

process is initiated before control is returned to the calling program. This will read the next character and start the tape moving again.

6.5.3 Input directly into memory

The interrupt method was used to effectively read information into a buffer in memory. Existing equipment in the CPU and its accumulators was used to do this at a low cost. It should be noted that the amount of machine time spent per character is fairly high (order of 10 to 20 instructions are needed at least). If the character rate is high (for example, from a magnetic tape unit), all of the CPU time would be spent handling the I/O. We would have gained nothing. In this case, additional equipment can be added to the controller to communicate directly with memory. Since the result desired is to fill a set of memory locations with characters, we can design a controller which will do just that. The controller is given the starting memory address, an indication of the length of the buffer (it could be a fixed-block device, in which case it may be determined), and the actual command (READ, WRITE, etc.). It controls the I/O unit in parallel with processing by the CPU. The result is that the CPU is not interrupted after every character but only after every record. This reduces the amount of CPU time spent on I/O.

A controller which will do these more complex transfers is called a *channel*. In a typical installation, a channel is a relatively expensive device since it contains many of the same facilities as a CPU (registers and counters, etc.), so it is common to share a channel among several I/O devices. One of the devices may be operating at one time. This is shown in Figure 6.14. A channel may receive its commands from the CPU in a straightforward design. Thus a typical input/output order might take the form "Read into memory location 2564, 256 words from channel A, unit 2." Channel A is directed to connect unit 2 and is given the address and count. From then on, the CPU is free until it is interrupted by the end of the instruction. On input, the channel takes care of receiving data from a unit, possibly packing it into words (if it is received as characters), sending the address of that word and the word to memory for storage, incrementing the address to the next word, and testing for the end of transmission. Output is similar.

A channel is usually kept busy by a high-speed unit such as a disk transferring data. On the other hand, the seek operation of moving disk heads does not require any channel action once the operation has been initiated. Thus the channel itself may be overlapped with some of the mechanical operations of its units. When a channel is reading information from a low-speed unit such as a punched-card reader, the actual data transfer does not

FIGURE 6.14 Multiple units on channels.

take much channel time. If it had several registers for addresses and counters, it could handle several units simultaneously. These units would actually be staggered in their character transmission times. Several card readers and printers, for example, could each be transmitting characters to the channel. Each character might take about 4 micro seconds, and then there would be a wait of about 500 micro seconds for the next character. By staggering these, the channel can service all of them in rotation. This is called multiplexing. To multiplex means to put a group (plex) of several things into one.

A more complex design that provides more flexibility is given by a channel that can execute its own instructions from the memory. In this case, the channel has a control counter and an instruction decoder similar to the CPU. The CPU is usually given the power to set the control counter of the channel to any value. From there on, the channel executes an independent program, performing I/O transfers until it reaches a STOP instruction. The CPU can be interrupted by the channel actions if needed, so that it can initiate actions on other channels and coordinate them with the processing programs.

The control of I/O gets more complicated as it is improved for speed, and the novice programmer is likely to be appalled at the prospect of writing code for all of these simultaneously operating devices and keeping all of the interrupt signals sorted out. Never fear, the professional programmer would also be appalled if he were asked to do this. The operating system is expected to provide many subroutines that take care of the various I/O units, make their use efficient, and take care of errors which are not infrequent on I/O equipment. They are detected by parity methods and usually cause interrupts. They will be discussed in Section 6.6.1.

A sophisticated channel is nothing more than a simple computer which is directly connected to the input/output equipment. In a sense, it is like using a separate, slower computer to handle the I/O in an offline manner, but it has the important feature that it works into the same memory as the main computer (CPU) and can be controlled by the CPU. It can indirectly control the CPU by means of interrupts. Thus there is a very rapid communication between the two computers. A program for a typical channel might take the form

SELECT-UNIT	8	This causes unit number 8 to be attached to the channel.
READ-RECORD	A	If unit 8 is a tape unit, this would read the next record into locations A, A+1, A+2, . . . , etc. It would keep a selector channel busy, so the next operation must wait until the read has finished.
TEST-FOR-ERROR	B	This would cause a branch to location B if an error had occurred during the read operation.
STOP		The CPU does not have a STOP instruction, but a channel can stop. It would interrupt the CPU on most machines.

6.6 SOFTWARE FOR I/O

Because the control of input/output equipment is so complex from a programming point of view, it is necessary to adopt a set of conventions concerning the way in which it is used and to provide most of the direct control by system subroutines. This section will discuss some of the methods used to create an efficient and flexible operating system for the user. In addition to controlling the units themselves, many of the I/O subroutines are concerned with buffers. A buffer was used in the simple example of paper-tape reading given above. In machines with complex controllers, buffers are needed to hold the blocks of characters being read until they are needed by the processor.

6.6.1 Basic access and error handling

Some of the fundamental subroutines in the system area of memory perform the actual control of the I/O units. These subroutines are provided with parameters which indicate the unit and channel to be operated and the required operation. They must check that the requested operation is legal on the particular unit and then initiate the sequence of instructions to perform the operation. Depending on whether the channels execute independent programs or execute single transfer operations given by the CPU, the operation may require a number of interrupts as the various substeps are completed. These are analogous to the interrupts of the CPU in the simple paper-tape input discussed in Section 6.5.2. If the operation includes steps that transmit data between the unit and the channel, then the channel performs parity checking on the data. (Almost all I/O devices use parity bits in communication with the channel.) If an error is detected, the channel notes it in a 1-bit error register and completes the operation. At the end of processing, action must be taken. In a simple channel that does not execute its own program, an interrupt will be sent to the CPU. When it accepts it, the error bit must be tested. Now corrective steps can be initiated. These depend on the type of unit. Some typical actions are given below. A complex channel could execute the steps itself.

> Card reader   Since the card that caused the error has passed through the reader, the only thing that can be done is to send a message to the operator (on a console typewriter perhaps), asking her to re-feed the card.
>
> Printer   A note can be printed that the last line was in error, and then the line can be reprinted.
>
> Tape unit being read   The tape can be backspaced and the record reread. This process should be repeated several times (five, perhaps), because some errors are due to dust particles lifting the tape off the read heads. These can be dislodged. If it continues to fail, then the processing of that record is impossible.
>
> Tape unit being written   The tape can be backspaced and the write performed again as for read. If it continues to fail, it indicates that there is a bad spot on the tape. On unformatted tape, there is usually a SKIP operation that erases about 3 inches of tape. This can be performed after the last backspace, and then the write sequence can be recommenced. This blank piece of tape looks like an extra long record gap; it does not affect the operation of subsequent reads except to slow them down.
>
> Disk files   These can be handled by rereading or rewriting the record in error. If errors on writes continue to occur, then something is wrong with the track. Its use can be avoided automatically in more sophisticated system programs. Many disk files contain recorded information at the start of each record called the *home address*. The reading or writing program must provide a copy of this information in order to be allowed access to the record. If a match fails to occur, it can indicate either a failure by the hardware or on the part of the programmer to specify the right information. The seek can be tried a second time before the operation request is abandoned.

6.6.2 The principle of multiple buffering

In the simple example in Section 6.5.2 above, storage spaces were assigned for many characters and, in this sense, we may say that multiple buffers were being used. This had significance in that it gave a reasonable guarantee that there was always space to put incoming characters. Consider the case of blocks of characters being transferred at one time by a channel. We assume that nothing is known about the speed at which they are received, so that once a read has started into a buffer block, that block cannot be used until a signal has been received that the block is full (because until that time either the old or the new information may be present). This means that if the processor is to need characters before the read can be expected to be finished, there must be at least one other buffer of characters available. This leads to the simple scheme of *double buffering*. Initially, two buffers are filled with consecutive blocks of input from the reading unit. As the processor needs characters, it gets them (by subroutine) from the first buffer. When that buffer is empty, a read request is made to the system to refill it. In the meantime, the processor can use characters from the second buffer. The processor will have to wait if the reader does not have time to refill the first buffer before the processor has emptied the second buffer; and, similarly, the reader will be idle if the processor does not have time to empty the second buffer before the first is refilled. If the processor is using input at a more or less constant rate, then two buffers are adequate; but if the rate fluctuates, the double buffering technique can be extended in an obvious way to more buffers. The use of three buffers is shown in Figure 6.15.

Buffering such as that outlined above can be provided completely within the system area of main memory, it can be provided by the user independent of the system, or it can be provided in some combination. Many schemes are available, so in these notes we shall discuss three of the common methods. These discussions apply equally well to output buffering.

6.6.3 Serial input and output through system buffers

By serial input, we mean the sort of input that is read only once. An example of this is the primary data input to the program, probably originating on punched cards. By the time that the system is ready to read the data to the user program, it has usually been copied to a faster medium such as magnetic tape or disk. This discussion also applies to output which is not to be reread, such as the main output destined for the printer.

The user program would like the ability to read in one card image at a

CPU	Reader
WAIT	FILL BUF 1
PROCESS BUF 1	FILL BUF 2
	FILL BUF 3
PROCESS BUF 2	FILL BUF 1
PROCESS BUF 3	FILL BUF 2
	WAIT (BUF 3 IN USE)
PROCESS BUF 1	FILL BUF 3
PROCESS BUF 2	
PROCESS BUF 3	FILL BUF 1
WAIT (BUF 1 NOT FULL)	
PROCESS BUF 1	FILL BUF 2

FIGURE 6.15 The use of three buffers.

time, but it would not like to have to wait for the images to be read into memory. Therefore, the system area of main memory provides two or more buffers which it attempts to keep filled with card images from the input source. A subroutine is provided for the user to request the next card image for processing. This subroutine will copy the contents of the next image into the user area of memory and begin to refill the buffer. Functionally, it is equivalent to the simple paper-tape read program discussed above, except that card images are being discussed instead of characters. The CPU will only have to wait if the overall process time is less than the card read time, while the reader will wait if the process time is longer than the read time. Since card reading is relatively slow, it will usually be done offline, so the appropriate speeds to compare are tape speeds and process speeds.

Output functions in an analogous manner. Two or more buffers are provided in the system area. Each time that the user outputs a line to the system printer, it is placed in one of the buffers. Each time that a buffer is filled, it is written to the output device and output from the user is diverted to another buffer.

A more recent method for handling primary input/output involves putting the input and output files (that is, the set of input records and output records for a particular job) onto disk. Card readers and printers are online in such a system, and are used to continuously read new jobs onto the disk file and print completed jobs from the file. This is done by the use of buffers in the system for relaying the data between the disk and the I/O devices, in addition to buffers between the disk and the executing program. The program is "interrupt driven," that is, interrupts caused by the card reader, printer, and disk file are used to initiate further actions. In such a system, the input is read onto the disk file before a job is begun and printed from the disk file after it has been completed. This method is, therefore, similar to offline operation via magnetic tape, but it requires less operator action and is more flexible for scheduling purposes. It is sometimes called "pseudo offline"; by IBM, it is called "SPOOL" (Simultaneous Peripheral Operation Online). (A peripheral device is any I/O or auxiliary storage device.)

6.6.4 Programmer buffered I/O

When a computer system has a large number of I/O units available, it may be unreasonable to provide several buffers in the system area of memory for every unit. Also, units that can be used for both input and output are not used in a predictable way; that is, one does not know if the next block on a scratch tape will be read, since it is possible that the user may write something over it instead. It is impossible to predict which is the next record to be fetched from a disk file. Therefore, some units cannot be handled in the manner in which primary input is handled. The simplest provision to make for the programmer is to provide him with a set of subroutines that allow him to read blocks of information from any of the I/O units and routines to test to see if the transfers have been completed. If the programmer can specify which block of memory should receive the input, he is free to use any buffering scheme that he wishes. The important subroutine actions that should be available are

READ (WRITE)	into location N, M words, from channel J, unit K.
TEST	to see if channel J, unit K, is free (that is, that it has finished its previous transfer without error).

If the unit is a serial-access device, then other control operations must be provided. Tape units, for example, have to be backspaced, rewound, etc., while the heads of a disk file have to be moved from one position to another. While this could be done by the user program directly, it is usual to use system subroutines to accomplish these actions. One reason is that it is easier for a single set of subroutines to check for each of the many errors that can occur on an I/O unit. If the user program were to take an action on a unit without the knowledge of the system subroutines, they would have trouble understanding the meaning of interrupts that could occur after an action was completed. A second reason is that there is interference between units on the same channel, and it is easier to let a common subroutine handle such problems. A third and most important reason is that, at this simplest level of operation, it is usual to provide protection for some of the I/O units so that the user program cannot use them. For example, the input may be on a tape, and, in many systems, several jobs are loaded onto a single input tape, one behind another, separated by an end-of-file mark. The serial input program that buffers such input in the system area of memory will prevent one user from moving the input tape beyond the end of his input, and thus protect a user's input from an error by the previous programmer. However, this protection is for naught if the user program can access the tape unit directly and forward space over the end-of-file mark into the next user's program and data. Protection of disk files against unauthorized access allows users to leave files of data from one run to another.

This type of protection can be provided by insisting that all input/output must be done by system subroutine and by designing the hardware so that input/output instructions are protected (or privileged) instructions. This means that if the user attempts to execute them directly, an interrupt to the program monitor occurs. When the system program is called to provide the input/output operation, it first checks to see if the user is allowed the use of that particular unit.

LOGICAL UNIT NUMBERS

Since it is possible that the particular unit available for, say, scratch use may change from one run to another, it is very common to use *logical numbers* for referring to I/O units. The system area of memory contains a table relating each logical number to a physical channel and unit number. This automatically takes care of unit protection, since a disallowed unit is simply not put in the table. Thus, in a typical installation, logical units six through nine could be tape units: the first two on one channel, and the second two on a different channel. There could be more tape units physically present but not logically accessible. These could be used to advantage if a job is currently running and the next job waiting requires two tapes to be mounted. They could be mounted on the extra tape drives while the current job is running. When the current job finishes, the operator can instruct the system to change the logical assignment table so that the two tapes mounted are now, say, logical units six and eight. This leaves two spare tape drives which could be used for mounting tapes for the next user. Although better ways of handling this problem will be discussed, the above method is useful because of its simplicity, and it partially solves the important problem of loss of computer time that frequently occurs in short-job environments. If there are a number of 5- to 10-minute jobs, several with tape mounting requirements, then it is not uncommon for several minutes to be lost on a job if the tapes are not mounted ahead of time. If the operator does not start to locate the required tape until the job starts, it can easily take 2 minutes to find it and mount it. This can represent a 20- to 40-percent loss of time.

TAPE LABELING

Most software systems make use of tape labels in a way which reduces the possibility of operator error and improves the efficiency of operation. A tape label should always be used as a guard against error on any system. A tape label is one or more blocks—written on the beginning of a tape—which contain the *name* of the tape. It is always possible that the wrong tape is fetched from the storage cabinet and mounted to meet the user's request. By reading the label and checking it against its known name, such errors can be caught. For example, the CDC 3600 SCOPE system requires that all tapes have labels. These label names also appear in a printed form on the tape reel. During the input phase of the program, the user indicates, on a control card, that a given tape is required on a given logical unit. The system reads the tape labels on all tapes mounted. If the required tapes are present, the units on which they are mounted are assigned the appropriate logical unit numbers. Those that are not present are requested. The operator can mount them on any available tape drive because the system will locate them by means of the tape labels.

6.6.5 Buffer pools and symbolic addressing of files

The last section discussed transfer methods which give the user maximum flexibility, but these methods throw the burden of allocating buffer space onto the user. If he uses many different I/O devices, he will almost certainly have to use some of the buffer space for several different purposes in order to conserve memory space for program. This can create a difficult planning problem in jobs where various tapes and disk files have to be accessed almost at random, since it can be impossible to predict which units are never accessed nearly simultaneously and hence which can share buffer space.

To overcome this problem, a *buffer-pool* technique can be used. A buffer pool is a set of buffer areas in main storage that can be allocated by subroutine for use with any unit. To use a buffer pool, it is necessary to make all blocks the same length, or, less efficiently, to specify a maximum length. Each buffer is large enough to hold one block. Subroutines are written to allocate buffers from the pool when they are needed and to return them to the pool when they are free. In the simplest such system, the user would call for buffers when he needed to start a series of input or output transmissions to an I/O device. Typically, he would request two buffers in order to do double buffering. When that sequence of transfers had been completed, he would call to return the same two buffers. The pool subroutine would contain a list of all available buffer addresses. When buffers were requested, it would find them and remove them from the free list. When they were returned, it would add them to the list. It would be up to the user to write his subroutines for I/O so they could use the buffer addresses provided by the pool subroutine.

The simple buffer-pool solution does not take care of situations in which many files of data are being accessed simultaneously from many different I/O units. In that case, a request for two or more buffers for each active unit is likely to exhaust the available buffer space very quickly. At that point, the pool subroutine can do nothing except return control to the monitor indicating an error. If many files are active, in the sense that the program is in the middle of reading or writing them, then it is unlikely that all of them are being used at the same time. If there were a burst of activity on one or two files for a while, we would like to allocate buffers to those files and ignore the others. If there were an excessively large amount of activity on one file for a short period, it would be advantageous to allocate several buffers to that one file so that a backlog of input or output could be accumulated rather than having the main processor slow down. Output is easier to organize, because the actual transmission occurs after the buffer has been filled with data. If there is a sudden burst of output, then it is possible to arrange for several buffers to be filled in order and for these to be written as soon as possible thereafter. Input, however, presents problems, because the computer is unaware of the burst of activity until it actually happens. In order not to lose time, however, it is necessary to pre-fill several buffers before the first is requested. This must be handled either by means of a request from the programmer which warns the system that activity is about to commence on a particular file or by letting the system guess about future activity on the basis of previous activity. The latter is the basis of some systems, so let us take a closer look at the details.

The user will have a number of *commands*, probably in the form of subroutine calls, with which he can *open* and *close* files. The files are names of groups of records on tape, disk or similar devices which are available to the user. The OPEN command tells the system that the file specified is to be used by the programmer. It therefore makes preparations to provide it with buffer space when it is needed. At this time, it is just an entry in a table in the system area of memory. The CLOSE command is used to tell the system that the file has been completed (if it is output) or will not be needed again (if it is input). Other subroutine entries are used to request input data or to hand over output data. Because the files have fixed block lengths to simplify the buffering problem, the user works with logical records which may be of variable length. Several logical records may be packed into one physical block on the I/O device to save space. The programmer would build up an output file by calling the output programs with successive logical records of information. The system would handle them as follows:

1. If there is no buffer allocated to that device, allocate one.
2. Precede the logical record with a few characters which tell the system its length and other characteristics.
3. Copy the logical record and its heading information into the next available space in the buffer.
4. If the buffer is full, call the subroutine which handles output writing with a request to write this buffer on the specified unit. Allocate another buffer, and return to 3.
5. When the logical record has been copied, return to the calling program.

This technique will allow as many buffers as are available to be used on one output unit. In order that the buffers be returned to the pool after the output writing has been done, it is necessary for the system to process interrupts on the termination of writes and to return the buffer involved to the pool.

Input is more difficult. Unless restrictions are placed on the use of files, the system cannot tell in advance which files will be input and which will be output. The best that it can do without further information is to read one block from each file into a buffer. If all files are labelled and contain at least one block (an end-of-file mark if they are completely empty), then this procedure is feasible. Any read request can be filled by copying from the buffer. The heading information for each logical record tells how many characters to copy. When a buffer is empty, it should be returned to the pool and another filled. Operations such as backspace, forward space, etc., must be interpreted by the program, since the user is talking in terms of logical—not physical—records. If a burst of reads of a single unit is to be reasonably efficient, then several buffers should be filled in advance. This can be partly done by keeping a record of the average activity of each file over a short period and allocating more buffers to the active files. Whatever scheme is used, it is possible to fool it by performing a number of reads on a given file, to the point where it has kindly filled up several buffers, and then by rewinding the file to the beginning so that all of the buffer contents can be discarded.

Since all of the I/O reads and writes to the actual devices are done by a central system program working from system buffers in a complex pooling scheme, it is possible for the system to rearrange the order of the operations to maximize the speed. If many of the files are scattered over disks, then there will be considerable head movement from one file to another. Head movement is one of the slowest operations on a disk unit, so its time should be minimized. Since the time for movement increases with the distance of movement, the system should minimize the distance moved as much as possible. This can be done by arranging for the system to select, from all transfers waiting, the transfer with the smallest head movement. This algorithm can be dangerous in situations with two or more independent jobs being time-shared. Consider a system in which one area of core contains a user program and another contains an interrupt-driven program for reading cards to disk (SPOOL). It is possible for one program to give a series of disk references in a small region which will prevent the heads moving to service the other program, thus halting it. The access time of head movement can also be reduced by trying to place the files over different disk modules with separate head-positioning mechanisms.

The techniques discussed above have been aimed at making the I/O access mechanisms look like magnetic tape units. This is done by providing—for logical record transmission—operations equivalent to those provided for transmission of physical records. In the discussion of tapes, it was pointed out that there is an advantage to using formatted tape if the information can be indexed and accessed via a search through a much smaller index. In a sophisticated system, it is possible to provide for accessing via an index of contents. The index will contain the reference and the physical location of each logical record, so that the user can request to access a certain record, leaving it to the system to perform the index look-up, positioning of read heads, and extraction of the logical record.

The final step in relieving the user of input/output problems is to provide for symbolic access of files of information. A file of information is a group of logical records which are usually related in some sense. The only actions that interest the user are writing groups of logical records as a file, accessing files written previously in order to read the records they contain, and requesting that some files be saved permanently, that some be saved until he makes his next run, and that some be destroyed because they are of no further use. (The latter is particularly important because a constantly increasing part of the cost of computers is in saving information, a lot of which will probably never be used again.) It would be of a lot more value to the user if files were given names and the system took care of matching names against positions on physical units. In such a system, the user would create a file by telling the system that he wanted to write a file whose name was "filename" and that it was to be saved for re-use within 48 hours, for example. The system would use this information to decide, on the basis of current demands on storage space, where to put the file (on tape or disk, etc.). Future calls to the system would be used to pass logical records of information for packing into buffers and subsequent writing onto the storage unit. Each time that a file was completed, the system would index it; that is, its name would be placed in a table of file names for that user with an indication of where it was physically located. When the user returned another day and requested access to the given file, it could first be looked up in the index table. If it was indicated as being on an attached storage unit such as a disk file, the buffers would be loaded directly. If it were not immediately available, then the operator would be instructed to load the tape or other medium that contained the file. (This information is contained in the index.) When the storage medium is loaded, it should first be checked (the operator could have loaded the wrong one) by reading the label. Assuming that the operator had loaded the correct tape or other medium, a table of contents would be read from the device and consulted to find out where the file was currently located. It could then be accessed and read into the buffer area.

It is apparent that there are many inefficiencies in a completely symbolic system such as the one described above. In order to maintain some degree of efficiency, it is almost mandatory to have some form of time-sharing system in which at least two programs are in core at one time, so that, while one is waiting for I/O transfers, the other can be using the central processor. However, simple machine efficiency is not the only criterion to be applied. If the total system is easier for the user, to the point that he uses fewer machine runs to complete a job, those runs can afford to be less efficient. No more machine time would have been used and less human time would have been used—which is, after all, the purpose of a computer system.

6.7 IBM 360 INPUT/OUTPUT SYSTEMS

This section will give a summary of some of the facilities available in the IBM system 360 when Operating System 360 is being used. The purpose of this summary is not to provide complete documentation of any feature, but rather to give the reader an idea of a specific system that has been implemented to supplement the general discussions of the preceding sections. Readers who need to make use of the 360 will have to obtain details from appropriate publications. Many installations make available short write-ups which describe the most frequently used methods of input/output for their particular environment, and these are usually the easiest to start using.†

A user of the 360 must first learn a new set of names for the items that we have been discussing. This has been done by IBM partly to avoid some of the ambiguities of earlier names. (Files, for example, which refer to sets of records or to physical memory devices.) A single storage device, such as a reel of tape or a removable set of disk platters, is now called a *volume*. A group of logical records is now called a *data set* (a name unfortunately also used by communications people for a data-transmission device). In order that access to a volume be as symbolic as desired by the programmer, many volumes contain, in addition to a label, a *volume table of contents*. This contains the names of the data sets that have been stored on that volume. Operations are provided within the system for *cataloging* and *uncataloging* data sets by name.

The system provides operations, by means of subroutines, that allow the user to access specific data sets by name, to read or write records within them, to block and unblock records from longer physical blocks, to check labels

† The full details are spread across many IBM manuals. In particular, the student can refer to Operating System Data Management, form number C28-6537; Operating System Job Control Language, form number C28-6539; and Operating System Supervisor and Data Management Macro-Instructions, form number C28-6647. The first manual presents an overall picture of the system, the second can be used to find details about the DD statements, while the third can be used to find out about the various macro instructions—such as OPEN, CLOSE, DCB, READ, WRITE, GET, PUT, GETPOOL, AND FREEPOOL—available to the assembly-language programmer.

(which can appear on both volumes and data sets), to write labels on data sets for future checking, and to get control if error conditions arise. These are provided in a way which attempts to minimize the dependence of the input/ output code written by the user on the type of device actually used. In this way, a program can be run on one of many different installations with different input/output configurations. Buffers can be provided by the user, supplied on request by the system, or provided automatically by the system.

A data set may be stored on a volume in a number of ways, depending on the type of volume and the type of data. The simplest way to store records is sequentially. The *sequential* organization is the only one allowed on sequential devices such as magnetic tapes. In this organization, input or output of the next record is permitted, together with some control functions analogous to the various magnetic tape functions discussed. A *partitioned data set* is one that is broken into a number of sequentially organized members. This system provides a *directory* of each subdata set within the set at the start, and the user may access any of its members by name. The subdata sets may only be accessed sequentially. A partitioned data set is useful when groups of related data sets are to be stored. A library of programs, for example, can be stored as a partitioned data set, and each member can be accessed by symbolic name when it is needed for loading purposes. When records each have control information on which the records are to be retrieved, then an *indexed sequential organization* can be used. In this organization, the control information, called a *key*, is stored in an index for the data set. The keys are stored in order, so that access to the data set can be either in order of the keys (that is, sequentially as stored), or by reference to a particular key. This mechanism allows the programmer the flexibility of addressable storage when needed. The keys function as symbolic addresses for records. Because the system must perform searches for the keys, this method can be very slow. If addressable storage is needed for speed, then the *direct organization* can be used. This permits the user to specify a track address on a direct-access volume (a device with disk- or drum-like properties) and to write a block on the next available space on that track. Retrieval is again by means of a key, but the programmer can specify on which track the search for the key is to commence.†

6.7.1 Control of I/O

In order to gain access to a specific data set, the user issues an OPEN macro instruction, which is a call on the system. The system then locates the data set, assigns buffer space if necessary, and prepares itself so that future calls

† Details of these storage organizations can be found in IBM System/360 Operating System: Supervisor and Data Management Services, form number C28-6646-0.

on the input/output routines will be connected with the data set. The OPEN macro refers to a block of storage called a *data-control block*. This block contains all of the information that identifies the data set and the way in which it is to be accessed. In particular, it specifies the type of organization (sequential, indexed sequential, etc.), the record format (fixed-length records, variable-length records, etc.), the type of input/output operations to be used, the number and size of the buffers, and what is to happen if error or end-of-data-set (similar to end-of-file) conditions occur. The information in this block can be obtained from four different places. At assembly time, the user can specify most of the block of storage. The easiest way of doing this is by use of the DCB (Data-Control Block) macro instruction. It is desirable to leave the specification of some of the parameters until the program is loaded and run. This can be done by using the DD statement in JCL (Job-Control Language). Some information, such as the size of blocks, is specified in the data set label. If an existing data set is used, then it is not necessary for the programmer to specify this information. The OPEN macro will fill out all unspecified data in the data control block by obtaining the information first from the DD statement and then from the data-set label. Finally, it is possible for the executing program to set information into the control block.

After the OPEN has been executed, the data set can be accessed. There are various ways in which this can be done and in which buffers can be provided. In the *basic access methods*, which can be used with any of the data set organizations, buffering must be provided by the user. READ and WRITE macro instructions are used to initiate the corresponding operations. The completion of either of these macros does not mean that the actual operation has been completed; rather, it means that the information in the data-control block and system area has been set so that it will eventually be completed. To check for completion, the user issues a CHECK macro which checks for errors and waits for completion. These macros allow the user to program any buffer method that he desires. The system provides a buffer pool service for basic access methods by means of four macros. GETPOOL obtains a group of buffers for a specific data-control block. FREEPOOL returns them to the system when the user is through with them. GETBUF obtains the address of one of them for use in a READ or WRITE macro, while FREEBUF returns it to the group.

The basic methods of access force the user to consider his own buffering and his own blocking-unblocking, as the input/output operations are in terms of physical blocks. *Queued-access methods* are more automatic, in that the system performs the buffer overlap and does the blocking and unblocking. After a data set has been opened for queued access, the user can obtain logical records by means of the GET macro and write logical records by means of the PUT macro. The data-control block contains the addresses of buffers, which can either have been obtained by a GETPOOL macro or assigned automatically in the event that the user made no specification of buffers. The system keeps the buffers refilled or emptied in the case of input or output respectively. The information is copied from or to the buffers to or from the user work area when the GET or PUT is issued, so that the completion of the macro implies the completion of the I/O as far as the user is concerned.

For sequentially organized data sets, a typical set of access macro instructions would be

```
OPEN    (dcbname,(INPUT))
- - - - -
GET     dcbname,line
- - - - -
GET     dcbname,line
  etc.
- - - - -
CLOSE   (dcbname)
```

for input under queued-access methods. The *dcbname* is the address of a DCB macro discussed below, while *line* is the address of the first of a group of characters for output. For output, the word OUTPUT would be substituted for INPUT above, and the PUT macro would be used instead of GET.

Basic access would be performed in a similar manner. The data set would be opened for input, output, or both, and then READ or WRITE macros could be issued. These take the form

```
READ    decbname,type,dcbname,area-address
```

Optionally, a character length can be placed on the end of this macro. The *decbname* is the address assigned to a block of storage generated for the *data-event-control block* which contains information about the status of the transfer while it is happening. It is used in the CHECK macro which waits for termination and checks for errors. Type indicates with an SF or SB whether the information is read forward or backward. The *dcbname* is the address of the DCB macro which gives details of the data set, while the *area-address* is the memory address for the first byte into which the data is to be transmitted (that is, the buffer). Before the information is used, a CHECK macro should be issued in the form

```
CHECK   decbname
```

The data set must be closed when its use is terminated, just as for queued-access methods.

6.7.2 The DCB macro

The initial specification of the data-control block is by the DCB macro.†
The macro is written in the form

dcbname   DCB   parameter 1,parameter 2, . . . , parameter n

More than 25 different parameters can be specified. In order that each one
need not be given, all parameters are written in the form

SPEC=value

where SPEC is the name of one of the parameters and *value* is the value to be
assigned. Parameters not specified are filled out by information from other
sources or by default values, that is, by values assumed by the system. Some
of the parameters are given below

DSORG =   This parameter gives the data set organization. Its value is two
or three letters: DA for direct access, IS for indexed sequential,
PO for partitioned organization, or PS for sequential organization. U may follow any of these to indicate that the data set
cannot be moved. (This can happen if it contains the absolute
addresses of its own locations, for example.)

MACRF =   This indicates which type of access will be used, and whether
the data set will be input, output, or both. R and W indicate
READ and WRITE for basic access methods, G and P indicate
input and output for queued-access methods. An M or a T
after G or P indicates that the data is to be transmitted between
the work area and the buffer, or that the buffer is to be substituted for the work area.

RECFM =   This specifies the format and characteristics of the records in
the data set. It need only be specified if the user wishes to force
a particular format. Thus, if the data set already exists, its
characteristics can be obtained from the label. Typical letters
that can appear here include F for fixed-length records or V
for variable-length records.

LRECL =   Length, in bytes, of a record. This specifies the length of a
fixed-length record or the maximum length of a variable-
length record.

† The reader is referred to the IBM manual Operating System Supervisor and Data
Management Macro-Instructions, form number C28-6647, for full details.

BLKSIZE =	This specifies the maximum length of a block, in bytes. This is needed so that the system knows what size buffers to allocate.
BUFNO =	Number of buffers to be used. If the user is leaving the buffering to the system, he may indicate the number of buffers that he requires. For some access methods, two buffers are obtained unless specified otherwise.
EODAD =	This specifies the program address to be given control when the end of an input data set is reached. Control is transferred here when a GET or READ attempts to read beyond the end of the data set.
DDNAME =	The name of a DD statement must be specified. This is discussed below.

There are many other parameters that can be specified, and there are many restrictions on the use of these. The reader is advised not to attempt to write his own DCBs without consulting the appropriate IBM manual or instructions prepared by his own installation.

6.7.3   The DD statement

The DD statement is a JCL command which provides additional information for the data-control block. It is related to the DCB macro by means of its name, which appears in the DDNAME parameter in the DCB. The DD statement is punched as //ddname DD parameters. The blanks are the separators between the fields. The advantage of using the DD statement to specify parameters rather than specifying them in the DCB macro is that a change in the DCB requires a reassembly, whereas the DD statement is handled just prior to execution. Some of the parameters that can appear in a DD statement are listed below.

DSNAME =	This provides the name of a data set. It should be specified if a previous data set is to be referred to or if the data set being constructed will be referred to by a later process. This allows the output of one process (*job step* in 360 terminology) to be provided as input to a later step.
UNIT = VOLUME = }	These allow the user to specify the location of the data set.
DISP =	The disposition of the data set can be specified. It can be a new set or an old one. It may be cataloged or uncataloged. It can be kept for a later job step or deleted.
DCB =	Information not provided by the DCB or the data set label must be provided here. It can be obtained by using the characteristics of an existing data set or by providing a list of parameters that was not specified in the DCB.

As an alternative, the data set might be the system input or output stream. These are handled by the DD statements

      //ddname   DD   *

and

      //ddname   DD   SYSOUT=A

respectively. The attributes of the two data sets are specified, so that all unfilled parameters in the DCB statement can be completed.

PROBLEMS

1. Why do binary cards contain a seven and a nine punch in column 1 on some systems?
2. Suppose that there are six records on tape, and that some computation is to be done on each record. Two buffers, B1 and B2, each capable of holding one record, are available. Suppose the instructions available are

```
      READ      B1
      READ      B2
      COMPUTE   B1
      COMPUTE   B2
and   WAIT
```

where the READ instructions read the next record into B1 or B2 as indicated and the COMPUTE instructions perform the required computation on the buffer named. (These might be implemented as macro instructions.) Assume that the READ instruction starts the read into the buffer, but that it only waits for the previous input operation to finish. That is,

```
READ      B1
COMPUTE   B1
```

is not a usable program. The WAIT operation holds up program flow until the last input operation (into either buffer) has finished, and the COMPUTE operation completes the computation before proceeding to the next instruction. One way of performing the calculation is to repeat the sequence

```
READ      B1
WAIT
COMPUTE   B1
```

six times, but it is slow because of the waits. Write a program that will not perform any unnecessary waits, using two buffers.

   If the compute time is exactly equal to the read time, how much faster is the double-buffered program than the "bad" program given?

3. Suppose that we wish to copy blocks of information from one tape unit (U1) to another (U2) via main memory. The only instructions available are

```
READ    U1, Bi
WRITE   U2, Bi
WAIT    U1
WAIT    U2
```

where Bi, i = 1, 2, 3, . . . , are buffers in memory. READ, WRITE, and WAIT each wait until the previous operation on the specified unit has finished before control can continue to the next instruction.

   a. Write a program using two buffers, B1 and B2, to transmit six blocks from U1 to U2 as fast as possible.
   b. Write a program using three buffers, B1, B2 and B3, and a minimum of instructions to do the same.

4. Consider buffered input from the system input tape. State very briefly what happens to the information on an input card between the time that it enters the card reader on an offline computer to the point where it is read into the users' area of memory.

5. Discuss the use of buffer pools. What are they for, how are they organized, and what are their limitations?

6. Consider a process which involves reading blocks of a fixed size B from tape, processing each to produce another block of size B, and then writing each onto an output tape in blocks of size B. (Note: block = physical record.) The average calculation time for each of any 30 consecutive blocks is precisely equal to the time T to read or write each of those 30 blocks, including time for record gaps. (It is a two-channel machine.) In theory, it is possible to keep both tapes spinning and the CPU busy. If the maximum process time for one block is $2T$ and the minimum is $T/2$, how many buffers of size B are needed to keep the tapes spinning?

7. What should a system do if the user reads beyond the end of his input deck?

8. Discuss the stages of output overlap that are similar to the successively more complex stages of input overlap described in Sections 6.5.1 and 6.5.2.

7

the assembler

The assembler is a program which accepts input from the user or possibly from the output of a compiler and produces machine language, usually in a relocatable form. The input or source language is frequently in the form of card images. It has three well-defined fields containing

1. The location name (may be blank)
2. The mnemonic instruction or pseudo-order
3. The address field

Many assemblers allow comment cards to be included at any point. Such cards are distinguished by a special punch, for example, an asterisk in column 1. We shall not discuss comment cards further, assuming that the section of the assembler which reads the input will arrange to skip over such cards immediately.

The output will be presumed to be in binary card images acceptable to the loader. Normally, this output is only punched if specifically requested; the copy that the loader uses is retained on tape or disk. The decision whether to punch the output or not can be made within the scheduler by interrogating the punch option and then outputting a copy of the binary object file; or the decision can be made within the assembler by checking the option as each card image is prepared and creating a second output file if needed. In addition to the binary output, there is usually some form of printed output so that the user can check his input and have enough information to enable him to understand diagnostic results from the memory. A typical output consists of a listing of the input in 80 columns of the page and an octal or hexadecimal version of the object alongside the input. Since the object is produced in a relocatable form and the assembler does not know where the program will be loaded, the object form is given without relocation. Errors will be indicated on the listing in some form, either at the end of the listing with references

251

back to the program or by means of markers alongside the program line in error.

Most assemblers take two basic passes through the input program to produce the object. The first pass is used to produce a table of all symbolic addresses used and their address values. The second is used to substitute these values into the original symbolic form to get the binary form. If too many complications are introduced, then two passes are no longer sufficient, but it is desirable to keep the number of passes to a minimum in order to make the assembly process as fast as possible. The input for short problems can be kept in memory during the translation process, but longer programs would occupy too much space, so they must be kept on backup storage. Since such storage is typically much slower than the main memory, the time spent in each pass is largely determined by the time to fetch the information from the backup device. Thus doubling the number of passes can effectively double the translation time, although very little actual computation may be done in the extra passes.

7.1 PASS I: THE LOCATION COUNTER

The major task of the first pass is to construct a table of all names used in the program and to associate a memory address with each name. To do this, all input lines of code are read, one at a time. If a name appears in the location field, then it is put into the table (with some exceptions to be discussed later). The assembler assumes that the first instruction to be read is placed into location 0, the next into location 1, and so on. For the moment we shall ignore the problems of pseudo-orders and macros and just study the two tasks to be performed in constructing the name table. In order to know what address value to associate with a name in the location field, an account must be kept of the space used by instructions read. We call this the location counter, because it contains the address of the location into which the instruction will be loaded if no relocation is applied. This location counter is maintained during pass I and pass II in order to tell the assembler into which location the line of code currently being translated will load. After each instruction is handled in either pass I or pass II, the location counter is incremented by the length of the instruction (1 in the case of one-word instructions; 2, 4, or 6 in the case of IBM 360 instructions which can occupy 2, 4, or 6 bytes).

When a name is found in a location field, it is put into a table along with its address value. Thus each entry in the table consists of at least two parts: the name and the associated address value. Since nothing else need be done with names during pass I, this table could be constructed by simply placing

each pair of items in the next free words of an array of pairs of words. If, however, it is decided to check for double definition of names during pass I, then
it is necessary to determine if the name just read in the location field is
already present in the table. This involves some sort of table lookup procedure. We shall delay discussion of techniques for this until the next chapter
and content ourselves with some general comments at this stage. What is
actually needed is called an *associative* memory. An associative memory is a
memory device that is not addressed in the way we have discussed so far,
that is, by a numeric address which refers to a specific location in memory.
Rather, an associative memory device is addressed by means of its contents.
Initially, an associative memory is assumed to contain no information. That is,
there is a state of each word in the associative memory which represents
not used. When a word is written into an associative memory, no address is
given; the memory device stores it in any available (not used) location. When
a word is to be read from an associative memory, the contents of part of the
word are specified. The memory is expected to locate all words which match
the specified contents.

We can see that an associative memory is just what is needed for a name
table. When a name is first read from a location field, it can be entered into
the associative memory along with its address value. (We consider the pair of
items as a single word or entry.) When another name is read, it can be checked
for double definition by reading from the memory any word whose name part
agrees with the name just read. If the name is doubly defined, there will be an
entry already in the memory on the second and subsequent occurrences. If it
has not been previously used, then it can be entered (stored) into the associative memory.

In this particular use of the associative-memory principle, the same field
of the stored information is always used for matching with the name in the
READ operation. In this case, we call this field a *tag* or a *key* since it is an
identifying piece of information which serves as the address for user reference
to the memory. Associative memories have been constructed directly from
hardware, but they are not yet economical for most applications. Therefore,
we simulate the functions of an associative memory using the CPU and the
regular memory. The mechanics of the simulation will be discussed in the
next chapter. The specific operations that may have to be provided are

STORE   Place a set of information into a new location in the associative
memory or table.

READ   Locate any entries in the table that match a given tag or key.

CHANGE   Locate any entries in the table, and change them in a specified
fashion.

DELETE   Remove an entry with a given tag from the table.

In the remainder of this chapter, we shall assume that these operations are available. In practice, they are provided by suitable subroutines.

If the input lines contain only instructions, then the simple mechanism of incrementing the location counter by 1 for each line is sufficient. However, there has to be one pseudo-order in any code, the END pseudo. This tells the assembler that the complete deck has been read and that the next pass can begin. In practice, many other pseudo-orders must be interpreted because they affect the location counter in various ways. For example, a BSS 23 should increment the location counter by 23.

In order that pass I may recognize the difference between the instructions and pseudo-orders, it must examine the mnemonic coding. The mnemonic is usually a string of characters similar to a symbolic name, so that similar techniques can be used to handle mnemonics.

In this case, the table of mnemonics (in other words, the contents of the associative memory used for mnemonics) is permanent, having been set up by the assembler programmer. It contains each legal mnemonic together with identifying information. The information needed in pass I tells whether the mnemonic is an instruction (possibly what type of instruction if variable-length instructions are possible) or what pseudo-order it is. Since pass I will contain a number of sections of code for each instruction type and each pseudo-order, an easy way to handle the testing for mnemonic type is to store, with the mnemonics, a branch address which gives the address of the code used to handle the mnemonic. This is shown in Figure 7.1. The typical flow of pass I of an assembler is shown in Figure 7.2. The input line of code is read and the mnemonic extracted. The mnemonic code is looked up in the mnemonic table. If it is not present, there is an error (unless macros are allowed, as discussed later). If it is present, a branch is made to the address found in the table. Then the appropriate section of code takes care of the rest of the line. If it is a one-word instruction, the name, if any, is placed in the name table together with the contents of the location counter, and then the location counter is increased by 1. If it is an END pseudo, pass I is terminated. A BSS pseudo places a name from the location field into the name table together with the contents of the location counter, and then it increases the contents of the location counter by the appropriate amount. The code for the pseudo-orders will be discussed in detail in a later section.

Mnemonic	Branch address

FIGURE 7.1   Contents of mnemonic table for pass I.

FIGURE 7.2   Pass I flowchart outline.

7.1.1   Coding the basic assembler: pass I

The manner in which the basic code discussed above is written will depend
to a large extent on the machine being used. This section will discuss the
general problems that occur and mention typical solutions of these problems.
The first step is to read in a new line of program for translation. This is
usually a card image from magnetic tape or disk file. The operating system
will normally provide a read subroutine which will pass the image of the next
card from the input file to the program area. The call to this subroutine will

have to specify an area sufficient to store 80 characters. The operating system subroutine takes care of buffering the input file in ahead of the READ request so that there is no need for the user to worry about a multiple buffering scheme for input. However, later passes of the assembler will need to reread the input file, so additional steps depend very much on the flexibility of the system. If the input is primarily from offline loaded tape, the system probably does not allow a user program (this includes the assembler) to back up the input tape to the beginning of the assembly language input. Therefore, a copy of the input must be produced for later use. This is also a good idea if the input is relatively slow compared to other available devices, or if the number of cards per input block is low (in which case the input blocks are shorter than the record gaps). By producing a second copy on a high-speed auxiliary storage device with many cards packed in each block, the read time in the second pass can be reduced. If a copy is made, the assembler will have to produce buffers of several card images and write them out onto the auxiliary storage device. In a system in which this is necessary, it is unlikely that symbolic file handling and automatic buffering are provided, so the assembler will also have to take care of multiple buffering in order to overlap output with process time.

When a card image has been read into the program area of memory, the assembler must extract various fields from it in order to form names, mnemonics, and addresses. Some of these fields are fixed in position, so the extraction of the name is straightforward. Other fields are of variable length and position. For example, the address field of an instruction might contain ABCX+312 in one case and S-21 in another. The assembler will have to extract the name ABCX in one case and S in the other, and the numbers 312 and 21. These numbers start in different columns and are of different lengths. If the machine is character oriented or possesses instructions and addressing with these properties (such as the IBM 360 system), then it is fairly simple to work a character at a time. If the machine does not have these properties, then it is usually easier to construct a subroutine which extracts characters one at a time from the input card. The various fields are then handled as indicated below.

LOCATION FIELD

This may be a fixed-length field. Characters are extracted one at a time. If the first non-blank character is other than an alphabetic character, it is not normally an allowed name. Otherwise, subsequent characters must be alphabetic, numeric, or blank. A blank indicates the end of the name, in which case the field should contain no more non-blank characters. Two flowcharts for handling this are shown in Figure 7.3.

MNEMONIC FIELD

This may also be a fixed-length field, except that it is frequently required that it start in the first column of the field. The same program can be used as above, except that the first character must be a non-blank character. There is no logical reason to restrict mnemonics to start with an alpha character and contain only alphanumeric characters, but they frequently are so restricted, which is convenient in terms of using the same reading subroutines.

ADDRESS FIELD

This field may differ from instruction to instruction, in many cases containing a number of subfields separated by commas. Within each subfield, the address may contain expressions involving names and numbers and some of the arithmetic operators such as +, −, and * (multiply). Some assemblers allow / (divide) and parentheses as well. The first step in the process of decomposing such a subfield is to break it into separate elements such as names, operators, numbers, etc. There are many ways of doing this. In practice, it is frequently faster to perform a *lexicographic* scan of the field first. By a lexicographic scan, we mean an analysis that only concerns itself with each character one at a time, possibly taking into account the immediate neighbor of the character. The problem is to take a string of characters such as A123+123*123−B123 and to recognize that A123 and B123 are names, and that 123 is a number. In other words, we would like to break up the string into A123, +, 123, *, 123, −, and B123. This recognition can be performed very simply by scanning from left to right and noting the following:

> Names start with a letter and contain letters or digits.
> Numbers start with a digit and contain only digits.

Starting from the left, the next character is examined. If it is a letter, then a name is recognized. A sub scanner called a *name recognizer* examines consecutive characters until a non-alphanumeric character is read. This signals the end of the name. (There may have to be a check for excessive length if names are restricted to a maximum length.) After the string of characters representing the name has been scanned, control returns to the basic recognizer. The next character is examined and a branch to a basic recog-

FIGURE 7.3 Two flowcharts for location and mnemonic name READ.

nizer for numbers, names, or operators is made. The scan for a typical address field is shown as a flowchart in Figure 7.4.

The recognition process for names, numbers, etc., involves more than just

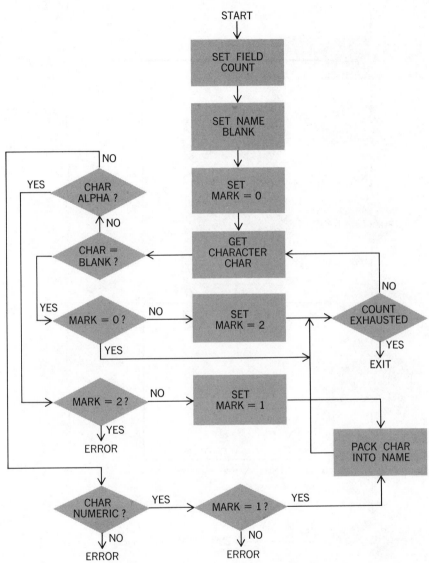

checking for the existence of the name, number, etc. Something meaningful will have to be done with the address eventually. Although the address fields of instructions need not be translated until pass II, the address fields of some pseudo-orders such as BSS, will have to be converted to numbers in pass I. This means that the characters in a name will have to be packed together in a form suitable for the table lookup process, that decimal digits will have to be converted into binary integers, and that the calculation indicated will

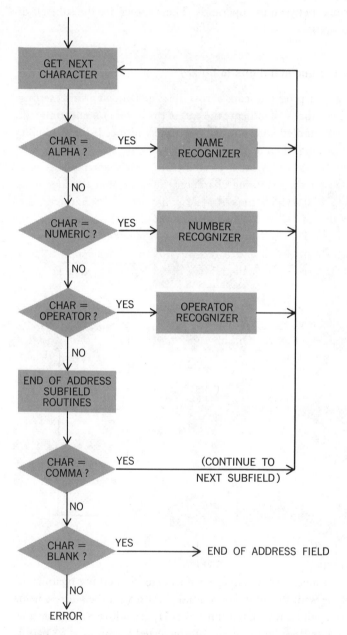

FIGURE 7.4 Branching to recognizer on basis of first character.

have to be performed between the operands. These topics are the subjects of the next three sections.

7.1.2 Converting the decimal digits to binary

The number-recognizer program scans across the digits one at a time, testing to see when a nondigit that will indicate the end of the number is encountered. This process is often handled with a table lookup technique. If the incoming characters are 8 bits long, then a 256-entry table is used ($2^8 = 256$). If they are 6 bits long, then a 64-entry table is used. Each entry corresponds to a unique binary code for the incoming character. Suppose that the incoming bit pattern is 11110010, which may represent a particular character, for example, 2. The value of 11110010 as an integer is 242, so this corresponds to entry 242 in the table. The information in the table can consist of a number of bits that can easily be tested and a recoding of the character in a form suitable for use in the recognizer. In the case of the number recognizer, we shall need to know two things: whether the character is a digit and what its numeric value is. Thus, one bit in the table can be used to indicate which characters are digits, and the recoding for digits can be a binary integer. Thus the ten digits 0 through 9 would have the "digit" bit set to a 1, and the recoding would be 00000000 through 00001001 inclusive. The recognizer can then take the following steps:

1. Set the accumulated value of the number $N = 0$ initially.
2. Table lookup the next character.
3. Test the "digit" bit.
   a. If it is 0, the end of the number has been reached.
   b. If it is a 1, go to the next step.
4. Multiply N by 10 and add the recoded form of the character.
5. Return to step 2.

7.1.3 Recognizing and converting names

The table lookup principle can be used for names also. A bit in the table can be used to indicate which are the alphabetic and numeric characters (this saves testing both the alphabetic and numeric bits separately) and then a suitable recoding of alphabetic characters can be performed. The output from the name-recognizer subprogram should be a packed name suitable for entry or lookup in the name table. The packing used will depend on the amount of time available for the operation (if the assembler is very much input/output limited, then we are not particularly concerned with packing time), the space available in the name table, and possibly on the method used for handling the lookup association in the name table. If space is not a problem, then the most straightforward technique is to pack the characters side by side in a binary representation, such as 6-bit BCD, into as many words as necessary. Thus if a 48-bit machine is used, if up to eight character names are allowed, and if a full word is to be used for a name, then all names can be made eight characters long by the addition of blanks on the right as necessary, and each character can be stored in a 6-bit representation from left to right across the 48-bit word.

In some cases, it might be desirable to use fewer bits to represent a name. Suppose, for example, that a 48-bit word was available and that names are restricted to six or less characters. If table entries are to include the name and 16 additional bits of information, then either two words will have to be used for each entry or the name will have to be represented in 32 bits or less. A six-character name with each bit represented by 6 bits unfortunately requires 36 bits. The only possibilities for characters in the name are BLANK, $0,1, \ldots 9$, and $A,B, \ldots Z$, or 37 different characters in all. These cannot be represented by less than 6 bits individually, but as a group of six character names, there are less than $37 * 37 * 37 * 37 * 37 * 37 = 2,565,726,409$ different names. Since the first character is restricted to be only a letter and blanks cannot appear in the middle of a name, there are actually fewer.

Since $2^{32} = 4,294,967,296$ is greater than $37^6 = 2,565,726,409$, 32 bits can be used to represent all possible six-character names; the only problem is how. The representation has to be such that the conversion in either direction is straightforward. One simple method is to consider a six-character name (with blanks on the right if it is shorter than six characters) as a base-37 number representation. Each character $0,1, \ldots 9,A,B, \ldots Z$, BLANK is assigned a unique value between 0 and 36, say, $0,1,2, \ldots , 36$ in the order given. The integer represented by the base-37 number is converted into binary. It will necessarily occupy less than 33 bits. For example, the name CAD31 is equivalent to $C * 37^5 + A * 37^4 + D * 37^3 + 3 * 37^2 + 1 * 37 +$ BLANK which is equal to $12 * 37^{**}5 + 10 * 37^{**}4 + 13 * 37^{**}3 + 3 * 37^{**}2 + 1 * 37 + 36 = 851,531,763$. This number, stored as a binary integer, can be used to represent the name CAD31 in the table. It can be converted back to the alphanumeric form by converting back to base 37 and then recoding the characters into the standard form used in the machine (for example, BCD). If this method is used, then the recoding performed by the character table should be into the numeric value assigned to the alphabetic characters in order to minimize the time needed for the conversion. If this representation of names is used, six characters are packed into 32 bits for an average of

5.33 bits per character, which is not too much more than the minimum possible. In fact, there are 1,617,038,380 names of six or less alphanumeric characters that start with a letter. Therefore they can be represented by a minimum of 31 bits.

7.1.4 Evaluating expressions in the address field

The final problem to be taken care of in the address field is to convert a string of names, numbers, and operators into a single number represented by the expression if it is a legal one, or to find out if it is illegal. When an expression is to be evaluated in pass I, it must normally be well defined; that is, all of the names must be previously defined in the name table. Therefore, we assume that each name has been looked up in the name table and replaced with a numeric value. The problem is to combine a string of numbers and operators. 123 + 456 can be handled from left to right, as can 123 * 456 + 789, but 12 + 34*56 + 78 can neither be handled from left to right nor from right to left, that is, its value is neither $((12 + 34)*56) + 78$ nor $12 + (34 * (56+78))$. The reason is that the *hierarchy* of the multiply is *higher* than that of the plus operator, so that the multiply must be done before either plus.

Many standard techniques for translating arbitrary expressions are used in compilers. We can use one of the simplest of these for this case. Using the concept of hierarchy of operations, note that an operation should be performed if it is flanked by operators of no greater hierarchy. In this problem, there are only two hierarchies, the lower for plus and minus and the higher for multiply. Thus in 12+34*56−78, the multiply can be done to get 12 + 1904−78, since it is flanked by the lower hierarchies of plus and minus. Now, both the plus and the minus operators are flanked by operators of no greater hierarchy (we can think of beginning and end of expressions as operators of lowest priority). In the case of equal hierarchies, the convention usually followed is *left to right*. Thus 1−2+3 is $(1−2)+3=+2$ rather than $1−(2+3)=−4$. The successive steps in reducing 12+34*56−78 are:

$$12 + 34*56−78$$
$$= 12 + 1,904−78$$
$$= 1,916−78$$
$$= 1,838$$

It is not necessary to examine the complete string at every step. It can be scanned from the left until an operator can be performed. This can be sensed by comparing an operator with the operator on either side. Initially, we know that the first operator (*beginning of expression*) is not higher than the next one, so that we know that the next one (+ in 12+34*56−78) need only be compared with the following (*). If the following does not have a higher hierarchy, the plus can be performed. In this example, the multiply has a higher priority than the plus, so we continue the scan over the multiply. The fact that the scan continued indicated that the operator (+) preceding the one currently being tested (*) has a lower hierarchy. Hence it is only necessary to compare the following one (−) with the current one. (In the case of address expressions, we know that there is no higher hierarchy than multiply, so that this test is not strictly necessary.)

In the course of this scan, we passed over one operand (12) completely, and continued over the second (34) in order to look at the multiply operator. This can best be implemented using a stack technique. The basic recognizers extract numbers and operators one at a time from left to right. At any time, we wish to compare an operator with operators on either side. If the incoming items are placed in a stack if they are to be skipped over, the last items read are the ones immediately available. Initially, a mark meaning *beginning of expression* is placed in the stack. Items are recognized in turn and compared with the top two entries in the stack. Depending on the result of the comparison, either the items in the top of the stack are manipulated and a new comparison made, or the incoming item is placed on the stack and a new item is recognized. The comparison with the top items on the stack is to determine whether the last operator has a hierarchy at least as great as the incoming operand, this being the condition for execution of the last operator which is in one of the top two levels of the stack (because of the *last-in-first-out* operation of a stack). Let us follow an example through to see what sort of comparisons we must make. Suppose the string B 3 + 4 * 5 B is to be converted, where B stands for *beginning-of-expression* or *end-of-expression*. The pairs of lines below indicate the string state as items are removed from it, followed by the state of the stack where the top of the stack is on the left.

String	3 + 4 * 5 B	
Stack	B	The first element is moved to the stack.
String	+ 4 * 5 B	
Stack	3 B	Continue scanning.
String	4 * 5 B	
Stack	+ 3 B	Continue scanning.
String	* 5 B	
Stack	4 + 3 B	The * must be compared with the + in the second stack level. * has a higher hierarchy, so continue.

String 5 B
Stack   *4 + 3 B   Continue scanning.
String B
Stack   5 * 4 + 3 B   The operator B has a lower hierarchy than the * in the
                      second stack level, so perform the multiply.
String B
Stack   20 + 3 B   The operator B has a lower hierarchy than the + in the
                      second level, so perform the add.
String B
Stack   23 B   The beginning-of-expression and the end-of-expression
                      characters are sensed together, so the evaluation is com-
                      plete. The answer is in the top of the stack.

We notice that the operations were generally in the second stack level when
they were compared with the incoming operation from the string. This
would not be true if there were errors in the expression or if other operations
such as unary minus or parentheses were allowed. Therefore the comparison
should check both the second and the top levels. When an operand (number)
is sensed as the input, it is put directly into the stack, since it is to be saved
for use in a later operation. Apparently, the rule to follow is to examine the
next item in the input and the top two levels of the stack and to perform the
step shown in Table 7.1 below.

This scheme is more complex than necessary for the simple address expressions that cannot involve parentheses, because there are only three hierarchies
in total. If, however, we introduce parentheses, the scheme can be extended
to cover the situation by adding to the second table. A pair of parentheses
indicates that the expression inside the parentheses is to be evaluated and

TABLE 7.1 Stack comparisons

Input	Top stack entry	Second stack entry	Action
Number	—	—	Move input to stack.
Operator	Number	Operator	Compare the hierarchies of the two operators.
Operator	Operator	—	If the input is higher, move the input to the stack, or else perform the operator in the stack. The action of this operator is given in Table 7.2 below.
Operator	Number	Number	Error

TABLE 7.2 Stack operations

Operation	*Action*
Beginning-of-statement	Terminate the computation, the answer is in the top of the stack.
+	If the first and third levels are numbers, add them, place the result in the third level, and discard the top two levels. If the second level is a number, discard the plus in the top level. (It is a unary plus sign.)
−	As for plus, except that a unary minus must change the sign of the number left in the top level.
*	If the first and third levels are numbers, multiply the first and third levels. Otherwise there is an error.

Note: Unary plus and minus are allowed in this table. They are sensed by also testing the third level.

then used as an operand in another operation. Therefore, when a left parenthesis "(" is sensed in the input string, it should indicate that all of the following input up to the matching right parenthesis has a higher hierarchy than anything currently in the stack. Hence, a left parenthesis should be placed into the stack immediately, as if it had a higher priority than any preceding operations. However, when another operation from the input is compared with a left parenthesis in the stack, the parenthesis must be given lowest priority so that the input operation is placed in the stack for future execution. When a right parenthesis is read from the input, it should be assigned the same hierarchal level as the left parenthesis in the stack, so that any operations in between will be performed.

The additional line needed in Table 7.2 must handle the left parenthesis which can get into the stack. Since it is given a low priority while in the stack,

TABLE 7.3 Changes in Table 7.2 for handling parenthesized expressions

Operator	*Action*
Beginning-of-statement	If the input is end-of-statement, the answer is in the top of the stack. Otherwise there are too many right parentheses.
Left parentheses	If the input is a right parenthesis, delete it from the input string and delete the left parenthesis. Otherwise there are too many left parentheses.

TABLE 7.4   Hierarchy levels

Operator	Input hierarchy	Stack hierarchy
BEGINNING	—	0
END	0	Never in stack
(	3	0
)	0	Never in stack
+	1	1
—	1	1
*	2	2

the only operations in the input string that can appear with it are right parenthesis and end-of-statement. The latter is an error caused by too many left parentheses. The beginning-of-statement may pop up to the top of the stack when too many right parentheses are present. Therefore, we must also change the first line of Table 7.2 as shown in Table 7.3.

The hierarchal level assigned to operators is shown in Table 7.4.

The greater the number, the higher the hierarchy. Consider the example $3*(4+(5+6)*7)+1$. The successive states are

```
String   3*(4+(5+6)*7)+1B
Stack    B

String   *(4+(5+6)*7)+1B
Stack    3B              * is higher than B.

String   (4+(5+6)*7)+1B
Stack    *3B             '(' is higher than *.

String   4+(5+6)*7)+1B
Stack    (*3B

String   +(5+6)*7)+1B
Stack    4(*3B           + is higher than '('.

String   (5+6)*7)+1B
Stack    +4(*3B          '(' is higher than +.

String   5+6)*7)+1B
Stack    (+4(*3B

String   +6)*7)+1B
Stack    5(+4(*3B        + is higher than '('.

String   6)*7)+1B
Stack    +5(+4(*3B

String   )*7)+1B
Stack    6+5(+4(*3B      Now perform addition.
```

String	)*7)+1B	
Stack	11(+4(*3B	Now eliminate '(' and ')'.
String	*7)+1B	
Stack	11+4(*3B	* is higher than +.
String	7)+1B	
Stack	*11+4(*3B	
String	)+1B	
Stack	7*11+4(*3B	Now perform *.
String	)+1B	
Stack	77+4(*3B	Now perform +.
String	)+1B	
Stack	81(*3B	Now eliminate '(' and ')'.
String	+1B	
Stack	81*3B	Now perform *.
String	+1B	
Stack	243B	+ is higher than B.
String	1B	
Stack	+243B	
String	B	
Stack	1+243B	Now perform +.
String	B	
Stack	244B	Here is answer.

7.2 PASS II

The purpose of pass II of the assembler is to convert the source language into binary, using the name table constructed in pass I to convert the addresses and a mnemonic table to convert the instructions. To do this, a copy of the source program must be read, a line at a time, and many of the steps of pass I repeated. The location field can be ignored because it was completely handled in pass I. The mnemonic field must be examined and a table lookup performed. In this pass, the mnemonic table must provide both a branch address or other indication of type of instruction or pseudo-order and, in the case of instructions, the binary code.

The address subfields must be converted into binary numbers for packing into the instructions or for use in pseudo-orders. The code used in the pass I handling of pseudo-order addresses can be re-used for this process. A location counter must be maintained in an identical manner to pass I. In this case, it is used to determine where to place the binary output (for load-and-go

FIGURE 7.5 Pass II.

assemblers) or what location address to put on a card image (if the output is to be used as future input to a binary loader). Pass II is also terminated when the END pseudo-order is read. In many assemblers, the END pseudo can involve an address field which is used to provide a starting address at execution time. In the case of a load-and-go assembler, the last instruction executed will be a transfer to the address evaluated from the END pseudo. If the output of the assembler is input to a loader, then this address is placed in a suitable position on a card image.

The second pass can best be coded by breaking up the job into a number of subroutines to perform the basic tasks such as *read the next line, extract the mnemonic, search for the mnemonic in the mnemonic table, convert an address subfield to binary, accept a word of output for the location specified,* etc. A flowchart of pass II is shown in Figure 7.5. The result of one pass around the instruction loop is to construct one instruction and hand it to the output subroutine.

7.3 PSEUDO-ORDERS

Pseudo-orders are contained in the mnemonic table in passes I and II and cause a branch to an appropriate program to handle each separately. This section will discuss the methods used to handle each pseudo-order, and the restrictions that these methods place on the assembler user. In principle, the addition of a pseudo-order to an assembler is straightforward, since it only requires the addition of an entry to the mnemonic table and two sections of code, one to handle it during pass I and one to handle it during pass II. In fact, some assemblers allow the user to input code at the start of the first pass for the definition of new pseudo-orders for his personal use. However this frequently requires a fairly good knowledge of the implementation of the assembler itself. The user of a system program should not have to know details of implementation in order to use the program. If a reasonable number of pseudo-orders is provided by the assembler, the use of a macro facility will frequently make it possible to construct mnemonics which have the effect of new pseudo-orders.

The most frequently provided pseudo-orders will be discussed one at a time in the sequel. However, treatment of pseudo-orders concerned with relocation will be deferred until Section 7.5.

Pseudo-orders fall into a number of classes. Pseudos are listed in Table 7.5 below for a typical assembly language of the IBM 7094 class and for the 360-class assemblers.

TABLE 7.5 Typical psuedo-orders not concerned with relocation

Class of pseudo	360 Assembler	7094 Assembler	Action
Data loading	DC $\Big\{$	DEC	Load data in decimal form.
		OCT	Load data in octal form.
		BCD	Load data in character form.
Location counter control	ORG	ORG	Set the location counter.
	DS $\Big\{$	BSS	Reserve blocks of space by incrementing the location counter.
		BTS	
		BES	
		ASSIGN	
	CSECT	—	Switch location counters.
Name table entry	EQU	EQU	Enter a name with a given definition in the table.

7.3.1 Data loading pseudo-orders

Typical data loading pseudo-orders include DEC, OCT, and character input orders for many assemblers. The IBM 360 uses DC for all cases. During pass I, any name in the location field is treated exactly as a name in the location field of an instruction, since it is to be defined as the current value of the location counter. It is necessary to determine how many words of storage will be occupied by the data given in the pseudo-order, so that the location counter can be incremented accordingly during pass I. In DEC and OCT pseudo-orders, this requires that the field be scanned to determine the number of data words provided by counting commas. A typical character-conversion pseudo is BCD, whose address field contains the number of words of BCD information to be converted (or the number of characters in some assemblers), followed by a comma, followed by the Hollerith information. The assembler need only examine the length count at the start of the address field to determine the number of words required. Other character-loading pseudos use a character as a terminating mark for the string (thus ruling it out as a character in the string). In this case, pass I must count the characters in the string until this mark is found. An example of such a pseudo is the BCI order in some IBM 7094 assemblers in which the length specification can be replaced by an asterisk, indicating that the end of the string is a blank. The user can either write BCI 2,ABCDEFGHIJ*, which inputs the character string of 12 characters (two words at six characters per word) up to the blank following the asterisk, or he can write BCI *,ABCDEFGHIJ*, which inputs the string of 11 characters up to and including the asterisk, plus a blank to fill up an exact number of words. (The final asterisk is included because the major use of this pseudo-order is to input an I/O format string which is always terminated by an asterisk.) The 360 DC instruction requires a more complicated scan. The first character determines the type of field following. It may be preceded with a repetition factor. For some characters, an L may follow with a length specification. Finally, the data will appear inside quotation marks. During pass I, the program must determine the boundary alignment and length of each field in the DC to calculate the location-counter change.

During pass II, the location field can be ignored, but the address field must be converted into binary according to the rules for the particular pseudo-order. At the same time, the location counter must be increased once for each word or byte produced. Conversion of character strings is straightforward, since the code used is either identical to the incoming code or can be converted by a character-table lookup. Octal or hexadecimal conversion can be done on the same basis, since each character supplies 3 or 4 bits, or it can be treated as an ordinary base-8 or -16 conversion problem similar to decimal. Decimal numbers must be converted a digit at a time by starting with an accumulated sum equal to 0, multiplying by 10, and adding the next digit at each step. If the number is in floating-point, a count of the number of digits after the point must be subtracted from any exponent given, and the integer answer from the conversion must be multiplied by that power of 10. Thus, if the decimal number 345.678E21 is read, the immediate result of converting 345.678 is the integer 345,678 and the count of three digits after the point. After the E has been read, the exponent of 21 is read and also converted into a binary integer. After 3 has been subtracted from this, the integer 345,678 must be multiplied by 10^{21-3} as a floating-point number. An assembly should produce the most accurate representation of the input number possible in the precision requested. The reason for converting the number initially as an integer is that there is no loss of accuracy until the scaling by a power of 10 is performed. (The arithmetic will have to have sufficient precision for this to be true.) Table lookup techniques can be used to get the required power of 10, saving both time and accuracy. It is advisable to do the arithmetic in greater precision than required and then to *round*, not truncate. Thus, double-precision should be used for E fields in the 360 and triple-precision for D fields.

7.3.2 Pseudo-orders that affect the location counter

A number of pseudo-orders affect the location counter and possibly cause names to be entered in the name table in pass I. The program used to modify the location counter in pass I and pass II can be identical, the program used to handle the entry of the names in pass I need not be used in pass II. Typical of these pseudo-orders are ORG, BSS, BTS, or DS. The first is used to set the location counter to a specific quantity. Thus ORG 345 sets the location counter to 345 in pass I and pass II, so that the next instruction read will be loaded into 345. If a name is allowed in the location field, then it should be put into the name table after the location counter has been changed and given a value equal to the new contents of the location counter. BSS and BTS both cause the address-field value to be added to the location counter. Since BSS is an abbreviation of *block started by symbol*, any name in the location field should be entered in the name table before it is incremented. BTS is an abbreviation of *block terminated by symbol*, meaning that any name in the location field should be equated to the location of the last word of the block (that is, to one less than the contents of the control counter after it has been increased). The effect of the following sequence

```
A   ORG   356
B   BSS   24
C   BTS   51
```

is first to set the location counter to 356 and enter A in the name table as 356, then to enter B in the name table as 356 and add 24 to the location counter, bringing it to 380, finally to add 51 to the location counter, bringing it to 431, and entering C in the table as 430.

As long as the addresses in the address field are purely numeric, there are no problems. However, if a symbolic address is involved, then a value has to be assigned to it in order that the numeric value of the address can be calculated. In pass I, only those names that appeared before the line currently being examined are in the name table with numeric values. Therefore, if this method is to be used, names must be defined before they are used in any pseudo-orders that affect the location counter in a manner dependent on their address field. For example, the following code could not be assembled

```
A   BSS    N
S   LOAD   A
N   EQU    10
```

because the value of the address N in the BSS pseudo is not known at the time it is read in pass I. The DS pseudo-order in the 360 is similar to the DC pseudo and can use the same piece of code in both passes, except that the DS does not actually produce object, whereas the DC must have the data specified in the address field.

7.3.3   Orders that affect the name table

It is desirable to be able to define names in the name table directly rather than by equating them to the current value of the location counter. Many names are not used as symbolic locations but as absolute integers or as symbolic names for index registers, etc. It is desirable to write a program in such a manner that if some parameters change, the program can be modified to handle the different situations. At one level, this is done by writing a program that picks up the value of parameters at execution time, as in a subroutine. At a lower level, these parameters can be given to the assembler in order to control the program assembled. Macro instructions, to be discussed later, provide a powerful technique for this type of work, but a lot can be done at a lower level to make a program flexible. For example, a program may be written to process records of information coming in from a magnetic tape with a given logical number. It could be programmed so that the record size and the tape number are fixed in the program. Blocks would be defined by BSS pseudo-orders with an absolute address. On the other hand, the program could, and should, be written so that the block size is a symbolic address, say BLKLGH, and the tape number a symbolic address, say, TAPENO. This program is assembled with these two addresses defined by use of the EQU pseudo-order. If the length of the block is 128 and the tape is number 3, then the pseudo-orders

```
BLKLGH EQU  128
TAPENO EQU  3
```

would have to appear in the deck. Since BLKLGH appears as the address field of a BSS pseudo, the EQU which defines it must appear earlier in the deck. Therefore it would be conventional to put all of the definitions at the front of the deck.

During pass I, the name in the location field of an EQU must be put into the name table together with the address calculated from the address field. It itself may contain symbolic names, so they must be defined prior to their use. That is

```
A   EQU   B+1
B   EQU   10
```

is illegal, whereas

```
B   EQU   10
A   EQU   B+1
```

is allowed.

7.3.4 Other pseudo-orders for special purposes

Particular machines often have a number of pseudo-orders intended to assist the programmer in coping with some of the unfortunate features of the machine. (Don't look for "unfortunate features" in the index of your programming manual, they will probably be listed under "advanced features.") A common example of this type of pseudo-order arises in machines which have either a subword structure (such as two instructions or more per word) or a multiple-word structure for some instructions. In machines with more than one instruction per addressable word, there are usually several versions of transfer instructions to enable the programmer to branch to any part of a word. However, there are frequently restrictions in the hardware which make it essential that some instructions appear in a special position within the word, such as at the start. In that case, a pseudo instruction is needed which guarantees that the next instruction is located in this privileged position. Similarly, if multiple-word items are involved in operations—for example, doubleword arithmetic or transfers of blocks of a given size—there may be restrictions requiring that multiple-word items have to start in special positions such as on an even-word boundary or at a multiple of 2,048 characters.

The purpose of an assembler is to save the programmer the details of specific addresses, so it must take care of such problems at the same time. Therefore, there may be pseudo-orders that force the location counter to the next even value if it is odd currently, or that do the same for block structures. In the 360, the DS and DC pseudo-orders can be used for this purpose. For example,

```
DS   0F
```

would force the location counter to a fullword boundary, while

        DS 0D

would force it to a doubleword boundary. Since these cause no data to be loaded into any locations skipped over, they must not be used in the instruction stream. The pseudo CNOP is provided for this.

        CNOP b,4

forces the location counter to the next fullword (b=0) or the next middle of a fullword (b=2). It assembles BR 0,0 instructions as necessary to fill up unused locations. This instruction branches on no conditions, hence it acts as a *no-operation* code. Similarly,

        CNOP b,8

moves the location counter to the 0, 2d, 4th, or 6th byte of a doubleword as b is 0, 2, 4, or 6. This can be done at assembly by testing the bottom bits of the location counter. However, note that the loader must not relocate program in a way that would change the alignment. In the 360, this restricts relocation to multiples of doublewords.

7.4 INTERMEDIATE LANGUAGE

In the brief discussion of pass II, it was noted that it is almost identical to pass I except for the job of outputting the binary object code and listing the translation. If the second pass is input/output limited, then this is an advantage, since pass II can be written by taking pass I, discarding the name table construction section, and adding the output section. However, if the computation time is significant, then we should consider the fact that the steps of reading, converting, and doing table lookups on the mnemonics are repeated in both sections, as is the work on the address fields of pseudo-orders. Usually the most time-consuming part of the computation time is the name table searching, followed by the mnemonic table searching. The former cannot be reduced below one search per occurrence of a name; the latter can be reduced to one search per line of code, rather than the two presently used. In order to avoid a second search in pass II, enough information must be extracted from the table in pass I and saved for pass II use. The information required by pass II included the actual binary code for the instruction and an indication of how to treat the address field. This means that a string of information must be generated by pass I and saved (on backup storage) for rereading by pass II. This string of information is a partial representation of the input code, so we call it an intermediate language—that is, intermediate between the assembly language source and the binary object language.

The use of an intermediate language is dependent on having a reasonably fast backup storage device available for saving the language from pass I to pass II. If an intermediate language is to be used, then it is worth exploring the possibility of translating everything on the card into an intermediate form in order that the speed of subsequent passes can be improved. This can prove particularly valuable if either more than two passes are used (the additional passes will not have to reread the original input which is neither densely packed nor particularly easy to read except in a character-oriented machine) or if it is not necessary to list the original input during pass II, in which case we can save rereading the original input completely.

If the input is to be translated into an intermediate language completely, then in addition to replacing the mnemonic by its binary equivalent and identifying information, it is necessary to convert the address field into a more convenient form for internal manipulation. To do this, numbers should be converted into binary and all names in the address field should be converted into a form that is more convenient to handle. If the name has already been defined, then it can be replaced by its address. In fact, there is no reason why the line should not be translated completely during pass I if the information is available. Some assemblers, typically for small paper-tape machines, allow the second pass to be skipped if all names are defined before they are used (that is, there are no forward references). In general, however, there will be forward references to names not yet defined, so the name cannot be converted to a number. To avoid re-searching the table in pass II, the name can be replaced by the address of the entry in the table corresponding to the name. (This means that names must be entered when they are first encountered, although they may not be defined until they are encountered in the location field.)

It is impossible to give general rules to determine which organization of an assembler should be used. One example will be quoted to indicate the considerations used in planning the assembler. In this particular case, the instructions of the machine were variable length, and their length could not be determined until the address type was defined. Hence, unless predefinition of symbolic names which might affect the length of an instruction was required, it was not possible to determine the value of the location counter in pass I. Hence, during pass I, all that could be done was to build a table of all names used with enough information to determine the length of any instruction which used it. Pass II performed the task of a conventional pass I by rescanning the input, now being able to compute the value of the location counter and define the values of the symbolic names in the table. A third pass was needed to do the actual translation to binary and produce an optional listing. The source program was available on magnetic tape via the system input routine, but only about three cards were packed in a block, as opposed to about 25 that could be packed into the maximum-length block allowed by the hardware. However, there was a very fast drum available for auxiliary storage.

Some estimates of the computing time indicated that all passes would be completely input/output limited, so that computational time was unimportant. However, the second pass never needed to look at the original input if an intermediate language were available, and pass III did not, provided that the listing was not required (which happens in, perhaps, 5 percent of the uses of the assembler). Therefore, the first pass was used to construct a name table containing only the BCD form, and about 6 bits of information were used to tell the second pass how to determine the length of an instruction using the name. It also translated the input into an intermediate language in which all names had been replaced by their table address. This intermediate language was stored on the drum. In addition to enabling subsequent passes to read from the faster drum, the translation also achieved a reduction of about 10 to 1 in number of words required to represent the information on one card. These steps allowed the second pass to run about 200 times faster than the first, a factor of 10 due to the reduction in number of words to be read, and a factor of 20 due to the speed of the drum over tape. This method also provided an additional benefit. The amount of main memory for the assembler was limited. The amount of information to store the length BCD names desired plus the amount of information needed to determine the address value and other important details about a name was more than the length of a word. Normally, two words would have been used for each name table entry. However, in pass I, the address information was not in the table, while in passes II and III the symbolic form of the name was not used. Hence, one section of the word was used to store both, reducing the need to one word per entry. (In order to provide a listing of all names used and their values after the translation was complete, a copy of the name table at the end of pass I was saved on the drum.)

The practical assembler will contain many features tailored to the particular environment. In many cases it is difficult to analyze the situation sufficiently to determine which of several ways are better, but typically the input/output considerations are the determining factors, so they should be examined first.

7.5 RELOCATION, COMMON AND ERASABLE

The discussion above has not taken the problems of relocation into account. We recall from Chapter 3 that the assembler is expected to produce a relocation bit with each address, a bit which tells the loader whether the relocation used for that program at load time is to be applied to that particular address. In general, numerical addresses are taken to be absolute, whereas symbolic addresses may be absolute or relocatable. An address is determined to be relocatable if it is one which "moves" with the program, that is, if it is one which is defined by the contents of the location counter. In addition to the value of the name, the name table must contain a bit which indicates whether a name is relocatable or not, as shown in Table 7.6 at the end of this chapter. When a name is put into the table, this bit must be set to a 1. Any name appearing in the location field of an instruction is relocatable, as are names in the location fields of the pseudo-orders BSS, BTS, DEC, OCT, BCD, and similar pseudo-orders. This means that we always assume that the location counter is relocatable. (This is not essential, but it would mean that information would have to be given to the loader so that it could determine whether to relocate a section of code or not. This would allow the programmer to place code absolutely in memory, a facility that can cause more problems than it solves.) If the location counter is always relocatable, then the pseudo-order ORG 100 must set the location counter to the relocatable address 100. Therefore in this instance, a numeric address is, in fact, relocatable. Following this reasoning, any name in the location field of an ORG pseudo is also relocatable. The pseudo-order that can define a non-relocatable name is the EQU pseudo. N EQU 20 should set N to be non-relocatable, since it may be used in a position where a non-relocatable address is needed, for example, as an initial count for loading into an index register.

In order to determine whether the symbol in the location field of the EQU pseudo is relocatable, it is necessary to find out if the value of the address field is relocatable. This problem must also be solved for the address field of an instruction. Therefore a set of rules is needed which can be used to determine the relocatability of an expression used as an address. When this has been determined, it can be used to determine the relocatability of the object address of an instruction, of the location field of an EQU, and to determine if the other pseudo-orders are valid. BSS and BTS should have non-relocatable addresses, otherwise the loader cannot handle the object. ORG could be allowed either relocatable or non-relocatable addresses (it is a problem, and its use should be avoided where possible since it is an anachronism in a system which is supposed to be taking care of all memory allocation).

An absolute (non-relocatable) address can be constructed from any allowable expression involving numbers and absolute-valued symbolic addresses. Thus $23*3-4*A$ is a valid absolute address if A is an absolute name. A relocatable address can certainly be formed by adding to or subtracting from a relocatable name any absolute amount. Thus, if B is a relocatable name, then B $-$ 34 is also relocatable. Some assemblers restrict constructions to just those forms: absolute expressions and relocatable names plus or minus absolute expressions. However, it is convenient to allow combinations of relocatable addresses for some purposes. A particular example occurs when a table of words is to be input through the assembler and it is necessary to know how many items there are in the table, perhaps to set an index register for counting purposes. If the address of the first entry is A and of the last B, then the expression $B-A+1$ is the number of entries. If more entries are added to the middle of the table by adding cards, it is not necessary to further modify the program, only to reassemble it. This is shown in the following example:

```
A   DEC   1
    DEC   5
    DEC   9
    - - - -
B   DEC   63
N   EQU   B—A+1
```

Repunching the first or last cards if an additional first or last entry is to be made can be avoided by the coding:

```
A   BSS   0
    DEC   1
    - - - -
    DEC   63
B   BSS   0
N   EQU   A—B
```

Thus, we would like to arrange that the difference of two relocatable-address expressions is an absolute expression. In this way, the expression $A - B + C$ would be legal unless A and C were relocatable and B was absolute. Although the address $A + C$ may be meaningful to the programmer in some situations where both A and C are relocatable, it is not possible for the loader to handle it with only one relocation bit. If, in assembly, A and C are given the values 23 and 34 respectively, then $A+C$ will assemble as 57. However, if the program is relocated so that A and C have the values 123 and 134 respectively, the address $A+C$ must be doubly relocated to achieve the correct result of 257. With only one bit, the loader can only apply either single relocation or none. It would certainly be possible to design a loader which would allow double or even multiple positive or negative relocation, but its value to the user does not usually justify the cost.

Even with only single relocation, it is theoretically feasible to allow expression such as $2*A - B$ where both A and B are relocatable, since the total relocation is still single. In practice, however, it is doubtful that it would be worth the cost of writing the assembler program to handle it.

A multiple-word structure in the machine can cause problems in relocation. If the assembler includes pseudo-orders which force the location counter to, say, an even number, then the loader must not relocate subsequent instructions by an odd amount or its purpose will have been defeated. If it is only a question of odd versus even, then it is simplest to restrict the loader to even amounts only. If, however, there is a larger block structure, perhaps involving 128 or more words, then it is unreasonable to restrict the loader to relocations which are multiples of 128 words, because each separate program would waste 64 words on the average. In this case, an alternative mechanism not involving the program area should be introduced. Usually, such blocks are needed for buffer use with input/output, so a buffer allocation scheme would be advisable.

In addition to program relocation which adjusts addresses as the program is moved around in memory, other forms of relocation are desirable. Their need arises from two sources. One is the use of common variables between subroutines that are translated into binary separately, and the other occurs because of the desire to allow separate subroutines to use the same area of storage for temporary work space rather than each using its own area, thus using much more total storage. From a logical point of view, there is no difference between these two requirements, but it is convenient to split them into the two uses. External variables can be handled by linking techniques in the loader in a similar manner to subroutine calls. In this version of common storage, the names used in different programs must be the same, and they are linked by the loader, which gets its information from the assembler. The assembler must be told that common locations are to be externally linked by a pseudo-order such as EXTERNAL. This method will be discussed in the next section. The alternative technique is to use common area assignment by the COMMON pseudo-order. In this method, the user indicates that variables are to be placed in a common area of memory at load time. At assembly time, this is thought of as a separate memory device, and common variables are assigned to this memory starting from location 0 and working up. The user defines a name by writing NAME COMMON 23, meaning that the variable NAME is to be assigned the next available location in the common area and that 23 locations are to be assigned to this use. This is programmed in pass I by using a *common location counter*. It is initialized to 0. Each time that the COMMON pseudo is read, the name in the location field is put in the name table, assigned the address value from the common location counter, and a bit is set indicating a common variable. The common location counter is then incremented by the value of the address field of the pseudo-order. It should not be a relocatable address.

At load time, the addresses which refer to common storage must be indicated to the loader. This is done with a second relocation bit. The loader chooses an area of memory to use for all common variables and adds the address of the first location in this area to all addresses with common relocation. Thus the effect of writing

```
A   COMMON   1
B   COMMON   2
C   COMMOM   1
```

in one program, and

```
X   COMMON   1
Y   COMMON   1
Z   COMMON   3
```

in another separately assembled program is that in one program location A+3, B+2, and C are identical and equal to locations X+3, Y+2, and Z+1 in the second program. A total of five locations is used in common altogether (the maximum required by either program).

In addition to the common relocation bits, the loader will need to know how many locations of common storage are needed by each program, so that it can calculate the maximum and choose an area of memory for common. Hence, when pass I is complete, the content of the common location counter is saved because it contains the number of common locations used. Common pseudo-orders can be ignored in pass II because the common location counter is not needed again. In order to pass the number of common variables used over to the loader, it must be put on the *header cards* which precede all binary program decks. These cards contain information about the number of common locations needed, the length of the program (the number of words it needs), the number of transfer vectors or links, the number of entry points, etc.

Erasable storage is identical in operation to common storage. A subroutine which does not call any other subroutines and requires temporary storage for working purposes can declare names to be erasable by the ERASE pseudo-order. There is an erasable location counter for the erase pseudo-orders in the first pass of the assembler which functions exactly as the common location counter. Another bit is used in the name table to indicate relocation, and it is also put on the binary output. The loader assigns an area of memory for this scratch working storage and relocates all erasable addresses by the address of the first location.

Suppose, for example, that P, Q, and R are to be assigned 1, 3, and 2 locations respectively, that these locations are only used for temporary storage while the containing code section is in use, and that this code section does not expect the contents of these locations to be unchanged when any other sections of code are executed. They could be placed in erasable storage by the pseudos

```
P   ERASE 1
Q   ERASE 3
R   ERASE 2
```

This method of allocation of temporary storage can be used in library subroutines such as SIN and SQRT. It achieves some saving in space, although on a larger machine the more significant benefit is that the data locations are separated from the program locations.

7.5.1 Base register assignment in the system 360 assembler

This is a problem that arises in the 360 machines because of the use of base registers. During assembly, regular 24-bit addresses can be dealt with, but these must be converted to a 12-bit displacement and a base address. This can be done by storing, in 16 locations at assembly time, the value of each general-purpose register as declared by a USING pseudo. It is also necessary to note whether each register is available as a base register or not. When a relocatable address is used in an instruction, the difference between its value and the contents of each base register value is formed. The base register which results in the smallest displacement is assembled into the instruction. If no base register gives a displacement of less than 4,096, there is an error. Note that displacements will never be relocatable. Relocatable addresses in the 360 will arise from the A type constants in the DC pseudo.

Consider the following example of a section of 360 assembly language:

```
1.      BALR  12,0
2.      USING *,12
3.      L     11,A
4.      USING X,11
5.      B     C
6. A DC       A(X)
7. C LA       4,X
        ....
8. X DS       10F
        ....
```

If we assume that the first line is assembled into location 100 and that no base registers are currently known to the assembler, the assembler will convert the first instruction into 2 bytes of object code and advance its location counter to 102. Note that the execution-time effect of the BALR is to place 102 into register 12. The next pseudo-order in line two tells the assembler that it can assume that register 12 contains the current contents of the location counter, namely 102. At this time, the 16 locations in the assembler that tell the status of the base registers indicate that all but 12 are not allowed, and that 12 contains 102. (This would be a relocatable 102.) The next instruction uses an address A which, by pass II, will have been defined as 112 relocatable. It will check this against all base registers and find that it is a displacement of 10 from register 12, so that A will be assembled as register 12, displacement 10. At execution time, the third line of code puts the address X into register 11. The next pseudo-order in line four tells the assembler that it can assume that register 11 contains X from now on. Consequently it updates its list of register contents to so indicate. Note that X is not known until pass II, but that the base-register contents are not used until pass II when the instructions are converted to binary.

7.6 ENTRIES, CALLS, AND EXTERNAL VARIABLES

When several sections of code are separately assembled or compiled but are to be loaded together, there must be some communication between them, both data and control. Common storage, discussed in the previous section, provides one mechanism for data communication, and it could conceivably be adapted to control communication. However, this would not be convenient for control usage, and it has unfortunate properties when used for data. These properties are due to the fact that it represents an absolute assignment of memory addresses by the programmer. In each separately translated section of code, variable storage must be assigned to the locations in common storage on an absolute basis so that they match between sections. Errors can easily arise in programs which contain many sections and a large amount of common storage. On the other hand, common storage is usually a more efficient mechanism for passing data to subroutines than that of using parameter techniques.

A symbolic linking technique that is efficient at execution time is needed for both data and control communication. Since the program sections are compiled separately, it is necessary that the loader be given the symbolic information and that the loader take care of linking it together. Chapter 3 discussed the transfer vector and the linking loader as two techniques that can be used for this purpose. This section will examine the implementation of these techniques in a typical two-pass assembler.

The information provided by the user to the assembler consists of source language statements such as ENTRY, CALL, and EXTERNAL (abbreviated to EXTRN in the 360). Entry statements tell the assembler that the names in the address field are to be passed on to the loader, together with information telling the loader where the corresponding address is located relative to the code being translated. For example, the statements

```
      ENTRY  A,B
  A   LOAD   =2
  B   ADD    =3
```

at the start of a program indicate to the assembler that the symbolic addresses A and B are to be given to the loader with the relocatable addresses 0 and 1 respectively. Note that the names appearing in the address field of an ENTRY pseudo-order must be defined within the program in a relocatable manner. Another program section which wishes to access the subroutines A or B may use the pseudo CALL. This tells the assembler to prepare a subroutine JUMP instruction and to indicate to the loader that the subroutine named is required. Thus the user writes CALL A to access the subroutine with the name A. The loader may either use transfer vectors or a linking technique, as discussed in Chapter 3, to relate the calls to the entry points. If several programs wish to access the same data by name, that is, to refer to it with the same name rather than by placing it in the same location with the use of COMMON, then the pseudo-order EXTERNAL can be used. If symbolic addresses are defined as EXTERNAL by the statement EXTERNAL A,B, the assembler passes the names over to the loader with an indication of where they are used. In this case, some form of linking loader must be used.

The output from the assembler must consist of lists of entry points with their respective addresses, called names, and external names, with an indication of where they are used. These are usually placed on binary card images in front of the object program and must therefore be produced prior to pass II. Hence the major processing of these statements must occur in pass I. Pass II will only have to take care of providing an appropriate address for instructions using symbolic names called or declared as external. In the case of all three pseudo-orders, the first pass has the option of either constructing separate tables of names used or of using flags in the regular name table to mark those used in this manner. The latter may lead to slightly longer tables and hence to greater lookup time, but it usually leads to a simpler organization. Hence, we shall assume that all names are placed in one table.

In the 360 assembler, the CALL pseudo is not used. The subroutine entry instruction is BALR 14,15 preceded by a L 15,SUBADDR, where SUBADDR is the address of a full word containing the address of the subroutine. If the name of the subroutine is SUB, then its address can be loaded as a constant by

```
SUBADDR   DC   A(SUB)
```

and declared as external by

```
          EXTRN   SUB
```

It need not be an externally defined subroutine. If it is, it can also be declared by

```
SUBADDR   DC   V(SUB)
```

V functions the same as A, but it can only contain a single symbol for each address, and it causes the symbol to be added to the external list. This could also be done by the sequence

```
          L      15,=V(SUB)
          BALR   14,15
```

which could be defined as a CALL by the macro facility. (Such a macro is available in the Operating System 360 Macro Assembler.)

7.6.1 Entries

During the first pass, the assembler must place any names in the address field into the name table if they are not already there. A bit must be allocated in each table entry to indicate entry names. This bit is set when the name is encountered in an ENTRY pseudo-order. Since it is preferable to allow the ENTRY pseudo-order to precede the definition of the name, the section of the assembler that enters names into the table when they are defined must allow for names to be in the table in an *undefined* state. This can be recognized by allocating a second bit which is set to a 1 when the name is defined. These bits are shown in Table 7.6 at the end of this chapter.

Between pass I and pass II processing, each name in the name table must be examined. Any names that are marked as entry points are copied onto the header cards of the object program together with their values.

7.6.2 Calls

When a CALL is recognized in pass I, the address field must be checked. It should only contain a single name, expressions not being allowed. The name must be entered into the name table—if it is not already there—and marked as called in yet another bit position. Between pass I and pass II, the scan of the name table should locate those names that are called but not defined. (It should be permissible to use the pseudo order CALL to access subroutines contained within the same section of code.) The undefined called names are placed onto the header cards of the object code as they are encountered in the scan. The way in which this is done depends on the loading method used.

If the loader is to use a transfer vector technique, then the called names must be associated with successive locations at the start of the code. A counter is initially set to 0, and as each undefined called name is found in the name table, it is marked as defined, given an address value equal to the number in the counter, and marked as relocatable. The counter is then increased by 1. This causes the called names to be equated with the first n locations of the program. Unfortunately, the first pass assumed that the code was to load into program location 0. The program must therefore be displaced by enough to leave room for the transfer vectors. This can be done by adding a displacement equal to the number n of transfer vectors to each program relocatable address in the name table during the scan of the name table between pass I and pass II, and then initializing the location counter to n instead of 0 at the beginning of pass II.

It often seems that each proposed solution to a problem introduces another problem. For example, it is necessary to know the number of transfer vectors before the name table is scanned in order to relocate the program relocatable names. Either the scan must be done twice, or this number must be calculated in pass I. As names are marked called during pass I, a count can be accumulated; but if called names are defined later, 1 must be deducted from the count. The reader can no doubt think of many other schemes.

If a linking loader is used, then it is necessary to construct a chain of addresses through each call use of a name, in addition to generating the list of called names at the beginning of the object program. Because the object code is not produced until pass II, the chain linking cannot be done until that time. Consider a set of three calls to one subroutine,

```
N1  CALL  SQRT
. . . . . .
N2  CALL  SQRT
. . . . . .
N3  CALL  SQRT
```

which are to be assembled into locations N1, N2, and N3. Because the first, in N1, is translated first, it cannot contain the address N2 of the second, which is not available. Hence, the first is put at the end of the chain, that is, it is given a 0 address field. Its location N1 can be saved in the address field of the name table entry for SQRT. When the second is encountered, the chain link N1 from the name table is put in the address field of the call and N2 is placed in the name table. In this manner the chain is built up from the end to the beginning. The effective result is

```
N1  CALL  0
N2  CALL  N1
N3  CALL  N2
```

It is necessary to place the location N3 of the last call on the header card with the symbolic name. Since this is done before pass II, this location must be constructed in pass I. Since the address of the most recently processed call on a given name was saved in the name table entry for that name, the last use will be in the name table after pass I reaches the END statement.

7.6.3 External variables

If the use of external variables is restricted to situations in which the name is used by itself rather than in expressions, then the chain-linking loader described earlier can be used. However, if expressions involving external variables are allowed, then this method will not work. (The reason is that the address field of a translated instruction may contain the remainder of the expression. Thus, if the address is $A+7$ where A is external, the address field will contain 7 and the value of A must be added to it.) In this case, the loader will have to accept a table of all uses of each external name. This provides for greater flexibility, but it slows down the loader by the increase in the size of the object deck.

External variables in 360 programs normally only appear in A or V fields of DC pseudo-orders. In V fields, they may not be used in expressions, because the V field is also used to declare the external attribute. Typically, an external variable will only appear in one DC statement because of the base-register addressing.

7.7 MACROS

Macros were introduced in Chapter 4 as a method of inserting sections of code without the tedium of repunching the same cards over again. To recapitulate on the operation of a macro, there are two important phases: the definition phase when the set of statements defining the macro are read and stored in a suitable form, and the expansion phase when the name of a macro is used and is replaced with the set of statements representing that macro. This section will examine some of the methods that can be used to process macros. It will also mention some additional features that can be added to the macro facility.

Macros are usually handled as part of the assembler, since macros are most often used in assembly language. Macro expansion schemes have been defined for higher-level languages, but their use in such environments is usually of less value. This is because a higher-level language is supposedly adapted to the type of problems being solved, and hence macros are likely to achieve less compression of the source and little additional clarity. Assembly language is difficult to follow and lengthy to write, so macros can reduce the size of the source language and increase the clarity tremendously in long programs. The clarity can be improved even if a macro is only used once.

Macros can be expanded during pass I of the assembler so as to retain a two-pass assembler, or they can be expanded prior to pass I in what is called a *prepass*. In the latter case, it can be made optional, so that non-users will not be penalized for the time of the extra pass. We shall discuss macros as though they are to be processed in pass I. This will introduce some restrictions of predefinition similar to the restrictions on the use of symbolic addresses in the EQU pseudo-orders. Finally, we shall consider ways of removing these restrictions by using prepasses.

We recall that the definition of a macro is accomplished by preceding it with the pseudo-order MACRO and following it with the pseudo END. The MACRO pseudo-order may contain parameters which are names separated by commas. When the macro is used, its name appears in the mnemonic field, and the address field contains strings of information to be substituted for the parameters. The location field may contain a name which is to be assigned the current value of the location counter. The translator must be capable of saving the set of statements comprising the definition, recognizing the use of a macro name in place of a regular instruction or pseudo-order, expanding the macro so that the expanded form is available during both pass I and pass II, and making the substitutions for the parameters during the expansion. Whereas most parts of assembly are completely input/output limited, so that we can usually use simple techniques for the computational sections and ignore speed problems, macros provide a facility for generating large amounts of code with a few input statements. Thus one card can generate many object instructions. The translator will not be input limited during these sections, and it may not be input/output limited during pass II if the listing is not too verbose. Therefore, we need to be concerned about the speed of expansion methods used. In particular, we must decide whether to perform the expansion during pass I and to pass on an expanded form to pass II, or whether to reexpand during pass II. Decisions of this type inevitably depend on many factors and are very difficult to make. For example, if we decide to use a prepass technique to avoid some restrictions, then we shall see that the expansion must be done prior to pass I, so there is no decision to make. If we decide to run pass II from the original copy of the source language, perhaps because there are no suitable auxiliary devices to make additional copies, then we have to reexpand in pass II. On the other hand, if we are producing a second copy of the input, then it could either be in an unexpanded or an expanded form. The benefits of the former are that the source is typically shorter, of the latter that pass II processing time is saved.

This decision will also be influenced by the available storage space for the macro definitions during assembly. If large amounts of main memory are available, then most programs can be expected to be such that the macro definitions will never spill over into auxiliary storage. Although a limit on the number of lines of macro definition could be set, it is better to allow any program to be assembled that can be run within the system, so eventually provisions will have to be made for the program that contains more macro definitions than can be saved in the main memory. The additional macros will have to be saved on auxiliary storage devices. Accessing them may be slow, depending on the type of device available. Magnetic tape may have to be back or forward spaced to get to the definition, disk file arms may have to be moved, while drums require an average access time of half a revolution. These all serve to increase the processing time for a macro expansion. If the available devices are too slow, then it is probably better to expand in pass I so as to avoid taking up the time in pass II.

7.7.1 Expansion methods

During the first pass, the appearance of the pseudo MACRO must cause the assembler to stop the regular assembly process and enter a mode in which a copy of the input is kept for later use. The card images must be copied, one at a time, into a storage area until an END pseudo-order is encountered. The MACRO and END pseudo-orders themselves need not be copied, but the information from the MACRO card must be saved in an index of the macro definitions. The name in the location field of the macro must be entered into this index, which is a subsidiary mnemonic table. The names of the parameters must also be saved, either in the index or at the front of the definition. After an END card has been read, the assembler returns to its normal state of examining each card for mnemonic type and handling it appropriately. In this way, an END statement will not be recognized as the end of the program section rather than as the end of a macro.

When the assembler checks the mnemonics it must also check for the presence of a macro. We must decide whether the user is allowed to redefine instructions and pseudo-orders, or whether their names are permanent. In the latter case, the mnemonic table is scanned, and if the mnemonic is found there, that definition is accepted. Otherwise, the index of macro definitions must be scanned. If it is not there, an error exists; otherwise, expansion must take place. Note that this means that macros must be defined before they are used. In the former case, the macro index must be searched first. If it is not there, the mnemonic table is scanned in the regular way. In either case, when a macro has been located in the macro index, the expansion starts. The macro index must contain a pointer to the storage location of the macro definition. Simply stated, all that has to happen is that the read section of pass I must switch over and read the definition instead of the source input until the end of the definition is reached, at which time the read section must be switched back to the original source.

Perhaps the simplest way to program this is to provide a subroutine which reads the next source language statement, and to put a switch in this program which either reads from the actual source or from the definition. In this way, the remainder of pass I is not affected in any way. This subroutine must also take care of substituting the parameters provided by the user in the use of the macro. This can be a slow operation, since it is a character-string manipulation problem. Consider the macro definition

```
COPY  MACRO  B,C
      LOAD   B+1,C
      STORE  B,C
      END
```

and the use

```
COPY  W+7,XSPEC
```

The definition contains the two statements LOAD and STORE with address fields. These address fields must be modified so that the result reads

```
LOAD   W+7+1,XSPEC
STORE  W+7,XSPEC
```

That is, the character string $W+7$ and XSPEC must be substituted for B and C respectively.

This can be done by analyzing the definition when it is first read or by reanalyzing it each time. In the former case, the definition must be scanned when it is first read, and any occurrences of the parameters must be noted by replacing them with indicators showing which parameters they are. At expansion time, these indicators must be replaced with the character string provided by the user. In the latter case, the definition must be read at expansion time, and every name (including location and mnemonic fields) must be checked against the list of parameter names. If agreement is found, then the string provided by the user must be copied in place of the parameter. Since the program is not input-limited during the expansion phase, it is preferable to do as much of the analysis as possible in the definition phase. A number of tricks can be used to speed up the processing during the latter phase. We shall examine one possible technique in more detail.

When the definition is read, the names of the parameters are placed in a table at the head of the definition. As each line of the macro is read, it is scanned to the end of the address field, starting from the location field.

Names are extracted by doing a lexicographic scan looking only for *break* characters. These are characters which cannot be legitimate parts of names (for example, plus, minus, comma, multiply, blank, etc.). Each group of characters between break characters is compared with all of the parameter names. If agreement is found, that character string is replaced with an indicator constructed by using an internal code that is not a legal character. (Since there are fewer printing characters than bit combinations in most machines, this is possible.) The indicator consists of the special code followed by the number of the parameter (in the example above, B would be 0 and C would be 1). To save processing time during the expansion phase, those statements that contain parameters can be marked in an unused bit position. At expansion time, the character strings provided by the user (delimited by commas and blanks) are placed in a parameter value table in order. As each statement is read from the definition, the bit that indicates the existence of parameter is checked. If it is off, then the image is copied directly, otherwise it is copied one character at a time. When the code indicating parameter use is sensed, the number following it is used to extract a character string from the parameter value table. This is copied in place of the parameter indicator. Then reading continues, one character at a time, from the definition statement until the end of the card is reached. This can cause problems because the length of the card image can change during expansion, so either the latter parts of the assembler must accept variable-length cards or the expansion section will have to insert or delete blanks to get the right length. As an example, the macro given above would appear in the macro definition table as

```
LOAD    /0+1,/1
STORE   /0,/1
```

where / (slash) has been used to represent the special code. When it is used by the statement

```
COPY  W+7,XSPEC
```

the two character strings W+7 and XSPEC are listed in the parameter value table as entries 0 and 1 respectively. As the definition is read, the appearance of / (slash) causes the entry corresponding to the number following to be copied in its place to get

```
LOAD    W+7+1,XSPEC
STORE   W+7,XSPEC
```

During the expansion process, the output from the READ subroutine is processed by the assembler in order to control the location counter and build up the name table. It is possible that the assembler may encounter another macro name in the mnemonic field, since the definition has not been checked to see if it contains only legal mnemonics. This is normally allowed, and it is called *nested macro use*. One macro may be defined in terms of others. The mechanism is quite straightforward. The assembler recognizes the use of a macro in the usual way, so it conditions the read section to read from the macro instead of from the input. Unfortunately, it was already reading from a macro definition, although a different one. Since it should return to reading from the first macro when the expansion of the second has been completed, it is necessary to use a push-down list for saving the state of the read section when a macro is encountered by the assembler. Each time that a macro is encountered, the address field used for the macro is copied into the parameter value table of character strings (this may involve parameter replacement if a macro is currently being expanded). Then the current state of the read section is placed in a push-down stack, and reading of a new definition commences. When the expansion of a macro is complete, the previous state of the read section is restored. This includes restoring the state of the macro-parameter value table.

An example may help to clarify the picture. Suppose the input is

```
20  A  MACRO  X,Y,Z
21     LOAD   X+4
22     Z      X,Y−1
23     STORE  X−4
24     ADD    =1
25     B      123,Y
26     STORE  R
27     END
28  B  MACRO  W,V
29     ADD    S+W,V
30     END
31     A      J,K,LOAD
       - - - - - - - - - - -
```

(The lines are numbered for reference in the text below.)

When the assembler has finished processing line 30, the macro index table contains two entries, A and B. The definitions stored for A and B are

	definition		parameter use bit
A1	LOAD	/0+4	1
A2	/2	/0,/1—1	1
A3	STORE	/0—4	1
A4	ADD	=1	0
A5	B	123,/1	1
A6	STORE	R	0
B1	ADD	S+/0,/1	1

The current entry in the push-down stack of the read section is

"Reading line 31, Source."

When the assembler reads the next card via the read section, it finds that the mnemonic field contains the macro A. Its parameters are J, K, and LOAD. It places these in a parameter value table and changes the state of the read section so that the macro A is being read. The state of the push-down stack for the read section is now

Top   "Reading line A1, macro A."
Second   "Reading line 32, source."

The parameter value table contains

entry	contents
2	LOAD
1	K
0	J

As the read section passes on card images to the main assembler, the parameters are replaced by the entries in the parameter value table. Thus the images

LOAD	J+4
LOAD	J,K—1
STORE	J—4
ADD	=1
B	123,K

are generated. When the last statement is processed by the assembler, it recognizes the use of the macro B. The parameters are placed in the parameter value table (this can be done in a push-down fashion so that the previous entries are available later) and the read section is changed to a new state. The push-down stack for the read section is now

Top   "Reading line B1, macro B."
Second   "Reading line A6, macro A."
Third   "Reading line 32, source."

while the table of parameter values is

entry	contents
1	K
0	123
- - - - - - - - - -	(separation between levels)
2	LOAD
1	K
0	J

The next use of the read section causes the image ADD S$+$/0,/1 to be replaced by ADD S$+$123,K. Since that is the end of the macro B, the stack pops up, so that it now reads

Top   "Reading line A6, macro A."
Second   "Reading line 32, source."

and the table contains

entry	contents
2	LOAD
1	K
0	J

The last line of the macro A is passed on immediately from the read section to the assembler since it contains no parameters, and then the macro A is complete. Control pops up again so that the read section is back on the source stream.

When parameters are handed from one macro to another, it is sometimes desirable to pass a sequence of addresses separated by commas across as a single parameter. Unfortunately, the use of commas indicates the separation of the various parameters. A convention of placing parentheses around single parameters was mentioned in Section 4.4.2. To process these, parentheses must be recognized in the address field of macros. When a macro use is recognized, the parameters are extracted as character strings by scanning across the address field and counting parentheses, plus 1 for left parentheses and minus 1 for right parentheses. When the count is 0, the occurrence of a comma indicates the end of a parameter. The character string should be placed in the character-string table with the leftmost and rightmost parentheses removed. This allows strings with imbedded commas to be passed down through several levels of nested macros calls. For example,

```
D    MACRO  X
     ADD    X
     ADD    X
     END
DD   MACRO  X,Y
     D      X
     D      Y
     END
D4   MACRO  X,Y
     DD     X
     DD     Y
     END
     D4         (((A,1)),((B,2))),((((C,1)),((D,2)))
. . . . . . . . . . . . . . . .
```

The first expansion of D4 results in

```
DD   ((A,1)),((B,2))
DD   ((C,1)),((D,2))
```

after one pair of parentheses has been stripped from each parameter. This provides two parameters for the macros DD. The expansion of DD results in

```
D   (A,1)
D   (B,2)
D   (C,1)
D   (D,2)
```

The expansion of the four uses of D results in

```
ADD   A,1
ADD   A,1
ADD   B,2
ADD   B,2
ADD   C,1
ADD   C,1
ADD   D,2
ADD   D,2
```

It is common to allow unnecessary commas to be omitted so that the string can be shortened and, in some cases, given more symbolic meaning. Consider the example below:

```
SIN   MACRO   OP
      OP
      CALL    SIN
      END
```

where SIN is assumed to be a subroutine which takes the SIN of the number in the accumulator of a one-address machine and returns the result there. Define a macro COS similarly, and a macro AC by

```
AC  MACRO
    END
```

which expands to nothing (this should be legitimate). Suppose we want to form SIN(SIN(COS(AC))) where AC is the number in the accumulator. This can be done with

```
SIN  (SIN  (COS  (AC)))
```

The first expansion of this results in

```
SIN    (COS  (AC))
CALL   SIN
```

The second in

```
COS    (AC)
CALL   SIN
CALL   SIN
```

The third in

```
AC
CALL   COS
CALL   SIN
CALL   SIN
```

and the fourth in

```
CALL   COS
CALL   SIN
CALL   SIN
```

which is the required result.

When the parameters are placed in the parameter value table of actual parameters, a check must be made between the number of parameters expected by the macro definition and the number provided by the user. If too many are provided, then there is an error. If there are too few, a useful facility can be provided for the user by generating new symbols. These symbols can be of a form impossible to input or of a form that is obvious, so that the user will not construct similar ones. This subject was discussed in Section 4.4.1. All macros will use the same form of created symbols. The way to implement this is to use a counter initially set to 0. At the time that macro parameters are entered into the character-string table, unspecified parameters should be provided with created symbols by generating them from the counter and incrementing the counter by 1 for each symbol generated.

The 360 macro assembler substitutes blanks for missing parameters. Instead of the above technique, the system parameter &SYSNDX can be used. This has a value of 0001 initially and is incremented by 1 for each macro expansion. It can be concatenated with other characters to form unique names. For example, a macro SUBCL to link to a subroutine could be defined by

```
           MACRO
&A         SUBCL   &NAME
           L       15,B&SYSNDX
           BALR    14,15
           B       B&SYSNDX+4
B&SYSNDX   DC      V(&NAME)
           MEND
```

Each time that the macro was expanded, the names B0001, B0002, etc., would be generated (assuming no other macro calls which would also increment

&SYSNDX). The * (asterisk) can also be used to avoid an outside name in a macro in some circumstances. However, in the above example it is not possible to predict how far the branch around the DC pseudo will jump, because the pseudo uses an A field which may skip over half a word to get on a word boundary.

An additional feature provided in the 360 macro assembler is the *keyword* parameter. This is useful in those macros which may have a very large number of parameters, many of which need not be specified each time. In the 360, they are written in the form

```
MACRO
NAME            &ALPHA=,&BETA=,&GAMMA=VALUE,&DELTA=
macro definition
MEND
```

The parameter names for the macro NAME are &ALPHA, &BETA, etc. They start with the & (ampersand) character as required by the 360 assembler. The equal sign following the parameter name indicates that the name is a keyword. The values to be substituted for the parameters must be associated with the keywords when the macro is called. They need not be specified in the order given in the macro definition, and can be omitted. If omitted, then the value to the right of the equal sign in the definition is used. Thus

```
NAME  DELTA=X, BETA=32
```

would define the parameters &BETA and &DELTA as 32 and X respectively. &ALPHA and &GAMMA would have the values null string and VALUE respectively, by default.

This feature can be implemented by adding a small name table to the front of each macro definition. At the time that the macro is used, the key words can be constructed in the correct order. Undefined parameters can then be specified by the default definition which should also be in the name table.

7.7.2 Conditional expansion

Many additional features can be incorporated into macro assemblers to add flexibility and clarity to programs. It is impossible to discuss all of the possible variations on the general theme of conditional expansion, so in this section we shall content ourselves with a discussion of the general ideas and a look at the method for handling the basic conditional expansion macro. A conditional expansion, as the name implies, is a method in which the expansion of part of a macro can be suppressed if certain conditions are met. This is useful in defining one macro to take care of several variants of basically the same program. The essential features of a conditional expansion assembler are the ability to test for given conditions on parameter names and the ability to skip over a number of lines in the definition without putting them into the expanded form. The latter can be provided by a pseudo operation such as

    SKIP D

where D is a symbolic name. The assembler skips lines until it finds a line with the symbol D in the location field. The implementation of a SKIP pseudo-order can be achieved by a simple modification to the READ subroutine which gets the next program statement from the input source or macro definition. The 360 assembler uses the pseudo-orders AGO and AGOB for skipping forward or backward, respectively, to a symbol specified in the address field.

Condition testing can be performed by a pseudo-order such as IF. Existing assemblers have many forms of this pseudo-order, so the assembler manual must be consulted for the particular assembler used. A typical IF pseudo-order takes the form

    IF A,COND,B,LOC

where A and B are address expressions, COND is a condition by which the two expressions will be compared, and LOC is either a number or a symbolic address. If the condition is met, then the assembler should skip either LOC cards if LOC is a number or to the first card containing LOC in its location field. In the 360, the equivalent pseudos are

    AIF   (A COND B)LOC
and
    AIFB (A COND B)LOC

for forward and backward conditional skipping respectively. Conditions which could be tested include string equality, inequality, numerical equality, numerically greater, etc. In the latter cases, the address expression must be purely numeric after all parameter substitution has been completed. As an example of the use of such a conditional expansion pseudo-order, suppose that we wish to construct a table of increasing powers of 2 ending at any particular value. We would like to call this macro POWER2 and give it one parameter which is the final value of the table entry. Suppose that an allowed condition in the IF pseudo is NUMEQU, standing for numerically equal. Then the macro

```
POWER2  MACRO  X
        IF      X/2,NUMEQU,0,1
        POWER2  X/2
        ADDR    X
        END
```

is an elegant if inefficient way of achieving the result. (ADDR is presumed to be a pseudo-order which simply causes the address to be loaded as an integer.) This macro works as follows. If use of it is made by

```
POWER2  8
```

the expansion starts by reading the statements of the definition one at a time. The first statement asks if 8/2 is 0, which it is not, so the skip of one statement is not obeyed. Consequently the next statement, which is another call of POWER2, is obeyed with an address field of 8/2. (This is not evaluated as 4 because macro expansion is simply a string operation except when numerical evaluation is requested, as in a conditional pseudo-order.) The second level of expansion compares 8/2/2 with 0, which it is not, so again the macro is called, this time with a parameter value of 8/2/2. This process continues, with the macro being called with parameter values of 8/2/2/2 the next time. By this time, the push-down stack which controls the read section has the entries

> "Reading line 2, macro POWER2"
> "Reading line 2, macro POWER2"
> "Reading line 2, macro POWER2"
> "Reading line 2, macro POWER2"
> "Reading line X, source PROGRAM"

while the parameter value table has the entries

entry	contents
0	8/2/2/2
-----	--------
0	8/2/2
-----	--------
0	8/2
-----	--------
0	8

During the expansion of the last call on POWER2, the comparison of $8/2/2/2/2$ with 0 shows equality numerically, since, in integer division, the result of dividing 8 by 2 four times is 0. Hence, the IF causes a skip of one statement by the assembler. Consequently the pseudo ADDR, with the parameter in the top of the parameter value table, is assembled. This gives rise to

```
ADDR   8/2/2/2
```

which after assembly is a 1. Then control pops up, which returns to the next level of use of POWER2, causing an ADDR $8/2/2$ to be generated. The complete result is the sequence

```
ADDR   8/2/2/2
ADDR   8/2/2
ADDR   8/2
ADDR   8
```

which is a table consisting of 1, 2, 4, and 8.

Conditional macros are implemented in an obvious way. When the assembler recognizes an IF, it extracts the addresses A and B, making whatever parameter substitution is called for. The condition is examined, and a branch to a section of code to handle the condition is made. This code may require the addresses to be evaluated numerically. Finally, the test is made, giving a true or false answer. If the result is true, then the section of code which implements the SKIP pseudo-order is activated. Otherwise, control continues to the next statement. In neither case does the execution of the IF pseudo-order generate assembler statements itself.

Another example of the use of conditional macros is given below. The problem is to create a macro COPY which has five parameters: the first an area of core, the second a preposition (either TO or FROM), the third the name of an auxiliary storage device, the fourth an area on it, and the fifth the length of the area. With this macro, the programmer can write instructions such as

```
COPY   A,TO,TAPE,5,B—A   WORDS
COPY   1000,FROM,DRUM,23,500   WORDS
```

The last five characters follow a blank, so they are not part of the address field and are only added to the comment field for additional clarity. The macro definition for copy will have the form

```
COPY   MACRO   U,V,W,X,Y
       IF         W,NEQU,DRUM,S1
       IF         V,NEQU,TO,S2
          (Program to call for appropriate I/O transfer
          from core to drum.)
       SKIP     END
S2     IF         V,NEQU,FROM,S3
          (Program to call for appropriate I/O transfer
          from drum to core.)
       SKIP     END
S3     WRONG
       SKIP     END
S1     IF         W,NEQU,TAPE,S4
          (Etc.)
END    END
```

The condition NEQU is presumed to be a string comparison for not equal. The result will be true (and the skip will occur) if the parameter provided is not identically equal, character by character, with the character string specified in the IF. The mnemonic WRONG need not be defined, since it will only occur in the expansion if the user does not make the second or third parameter one of the allowed words such as TO, FROM, DRUM, etc. If it does occur and it is undefined, it will cause an error to be listed by the assembler, which will indicate an error in the use of the macro.

In addition to strictly numerical addresses being used in the IF pseudo-order when numerical comparisons are to be made, there is no reason why symbolic addresses should not appear if they have already been defined, since the address-expression evaluation program is available in pass I for some of the pseudo-orders such as BSS. If this is to be done, then there is an argument for allowing arithmetic to be performed on the numerical values of entries in the name table. For example, it is quite reasonable to permit another pseudo-order which is similar to an EQU, except that it allows an existing entry to be modified if it is already defined. Let us use the mnemonic SETTO for this pseudo-order. The effect of

```
A  SETTO  A+1
```

is to increase the value of A as stored in the name table by 1. Features such as these can be combined with conditional expansion pseudo-orders to provide additional flexibility. (Note that the last feature cannot be implemented if macros are provided by a prepass that completes the expansion prior to pass I. However, a similar facility can be provided by allowing names to be given values in the prepass by the SETTO pseudo-order and using a limited name table containing only names so specified.)

The 360 Operating System assembler allows the user to declare parameter type variables (those beginning with &) as local or global variables for use in SETA, SETB, or SETC pseudo-orders. These orders assign arithmetic, Boolean, or character-string values to the parameters respectively. Global variables retain their values throughout assembly, whereas local variables are reinitialized during each new macro expansion. For example,

```
      LCLA  &E
&E    SETA  &E+1
```

appearing within a macro first defines &E as a local arithmetic variable and initializes it to 0. The SETA pseudo then increments it by 1.

7.7.3 Nested definitions

We saw that a macro definition could very usefully use nested macro calls, in which a definition calls another macro. In a *nested definition*, the definition of a macro appears inside another macro. For example,

```
A   MACRO  X,Y
    ADD    X
Y   MACRO  X
    ADD    X
    END
    STORE  X
    END
```

What can this mean? Since, when a definition is read no processing occurs, the inside macro will not be recognized but simply copied into the macro definition storage area. The program performing this copy will have to recognize that the outer END refers to the macro A rather than the inner one, so it is necessary to count the occurrences of the pseudo-orders MACRO and END. When the macro is called into use, the definition is passed to the assembler so that it will recognize the new definition at this time. It will be copied into the definition area and entered into the macro index, thus generating a new macro. This macro can be used subsequently in the outer macro. There are two schools of thought concerning what happens to the inner macro definition after the processing of the outer definition has been completed. One school deletes the inner definition from the index so that it is no longer available; the other leaves it there. In the latter case, it can be useful for defining sets of similar macros. An example of the use of this method of defining macros for SIN, etc., by using a macro DEFINE was given in Section 4.4.3.

7.7.4 Macro expansion in a prepass

If macros are expanded during pass I, we saw that it was necessary to define a macro before its use. If this restriction is to be removed, it is necessary to add at least one extra pass in order to first accumulate all of the macro definitions and then to expand them. If nested definitions were not used, it would be possible to locate all of the definitions in a prepass and then to perform the expansion during pass I as above. However, nested definitions can cause additional definitions to appear as the result of expansion, requiring yet another pass. Therefore, it is simpler to complete the expansion prior to the first pass of the assembly, and to view the macro expander as a separate translator which accepts macro language as a source language and outputs assembler language as its object. Since the checking for valid assembler language is most easily accomplished by the assembler, the macro expander will not check for validity of the object program and should be viewed as a character-string manipulation program.

The macro expander can be implemented in much the same way as a macro assembler is implemented. Statements from card images are read one at a time, and the mnemonic field is checked. Any time that a macro definition is encountered, it is copied into a definition storage area and entered in a definition macro index. Any time that the use of a macro is sensed, the definition is copied, substituting for the parameters as above. If, during one pass, no new definitions are encountered, it is known that the expansion has been completed. If new definitions are encountered, then it is possible that they were used in an earlier section of the source, so additional passes may be necessary. These passes are made over the expanded version output from the last pass, using the macro definitions that have been accumulated thus far. It is highly desirable to minimize the number of passes in a translator, since the input read time accounts for most of the translation time. The solution proposed above requires at least two passes if any macros are used, one to find the definitions and the other to expand. This is similar to the two-pass assembler, one pass is used to find the definitions of the symbols and the other is used for replacement.

We commented early in the discussion of assemblers that it was possible to have a one-pass assembler if all names were predefined, and that some assemblers for simple paper-tape machines make provision for a one-pass option. A similar technique can be used in a macro expander. If the user predefines all of his macros, he should not be penalized for the flexibility available to other users. The translator can recognize that there are no earlier uses of the defined macros and avoid the extra pass. This is accomplished by constructing a table of all different mnemonics read in a pass over the source. Initially this is empty, and as each mnemonic is placed into the output from the translator, its mnemonic field is entered into a table (unless it is already there). When a definition is encountered, it is copied into the definition storage area in the usual way, and the table is checked to see if it has been used previously. If it has, a switch is set. At the end of the pass, this switch is tested. If it is still off, then no macros were defined which had been used previously, so no additional passes are necessary. This technique would only be worth while if the processing were I/O bound.

7.8 REMOVING RESTRICTIONS ON EQU, BSS, AND ORG ADDRESS FIELDS

In the earlier discussion of these pseudo-orders, the address fields were restricted to contain only names that had been predefined, so that they could be evaluated during pass I. If this restriction is to be removed, then a problem similar to that of macro expansion arises. An arbitrarily large number of passes may be necessary to evaluate all of the name values. Consider, for example, the sequence

```
A   EQU   B
B   EQU   C
C   EQU   D
D   EQU   10
```

Four passes are needed to determine the value of A. On the first pass the value of D is found, on the second C, on the third B, and on the fourth A. It would be very expensive if the whole program were to be scanned in order to do this. Instead, during the first pass, those EQUs that cannot be evaluated can be copied into a separate storage area (there are usually few of these, so they can be kept in the main memory). At the completion of the first pass, the separate list of EQUs can be scanned as many times as necessary to complete the evaluation or to find out that no more can be evaluated, as could happen if there was a circular definition such as

```
A  EQU  B+10
B  EQU  2*A−30
```

(This does not define B as 10 and A as 20.) Since the list of EQUs is short, these scans are fast compared to a pass over the whole program.

If a BSS or an ORG uses a name that has not yet been defined in its address field, then the location counter is no longer known, so that subsequent names defined by appearance in the location fields of instructions will not be determinate. This could be solved by noting that every future name can be expressed in terms of the address appearing in the pseudo-order plus a suitable displacement. For example, the code section

```
   ORG    M+T
   LOAD   A
   ADD    B
   TRA    C
A  BSS    N
B  BSS    2
C  STORE  B
   STORE  A
D  ADD    E
- - - - - - - - - -
```

is equivalent to

```
   ORG    M+T
   LOAD   A
   ADD    B
   TRA    C
   BSS    N
A  EQU    M+T+3
   BSS    2
B  EQU    A+N
   STORE  B
C  EQU    B+2
   STORE  A
   ADD    E
D  EQU    C+2
- - - - - - - - - -
```

and could be converted to this during the first pass, so that the mechanism for handling EQUs can be used to process it. Unfortunately, there are usually large numbers of names in location fields, so this will cause a large number of EQU statements to be generated, thus slowing down the assembly. To avoid this, we can introduce the idea of a location counter "relative" to a symbolic address. When a pseudo-order—such as BSS or ORG—that has an indeterminate address field is encountered during pass I, an *internal name* can be generated. This is a symbolic address that cannot be confused with one used by a programmer and is never seen by him. The location counter is marked as being relative to this name and is set to 0. An artificial EQU is generated, which equates this name to the expression in the address field of the pseudo-order (plus the previous contents of the location counter if the pseudo was a BSS). When any future names are defined by appearance in the location field, they are entered in the name table with both the numerical value of the control counter and the address of the name to which the location counter is relative. (This requires additional space in the name table.) Let us consider the example given above. Suppose that the internal names generated by the assembler have the form $//0$, $//1$, etc., then the effect of the code is as follows:

	ORG	M+T	M+T is not yet known, so the location counter is set to 0 relative to $//0$, and the statement $//0$ EQU M+T is generated.
	LOAD	A	
	ADD	B	
	TRA	C	By this time the location counter is 3 relative to $//0$.
A	BSS	N	A is entered as 3 relative to $//0$. A new symbol $//1$ is generated, and the statement $//1$ EQU $//0+3+N$ is generated. The location counter is set to 0 relative to $//1$.
B	BSS	2	B is entered in the name table as 0 relative to $//1$. The location counter is increased to 2 relative to $//1$.
C	STORE	B	C is entered as 2 relative to $//1$.
	STORE	A	
D	ADD	E	D is entered as 4 relative to $//1$.
	....		Etc.

With this method, only one EQU will be generated for each use of an ORG or BSS with an indeterminate address field. At the end of pass I, the EQU list is repeatedly scanned in order to evaluate all entries.

7.9 THE NAME TABLE USED BY THE ASSEMBLER

In summary, the contents of the name table for a typical assembler are given in Table 7.6.

TABLE 7.6 Contents of name table for typical assembler

Contents	Use
Symbol	Coded form of the alphanumeric name used by the programmer.
Value	Binary value of the name when it has been defined.
Definition bit	Indicates that the name has been defined.
Called bit	Indicates that the name has been called.
Program relocation bit	Indicates that the name must be relocated with the program
Common relocation bit	Indicates that the name must be relocated with common storage.
Erasable relocation bit	Indicates that the name must be relocated with erasable storage.
Entry bit	Indicates that the name was used in an entry pseudo-order.
Relative bit	Used if forward references are allowed in the pseudo-orders EQU, BSS, etc. Indicates that the defined value is relative to the name given.
Relative name-table entry	

PROBLEMS

1. Suppose that multiple positive or negative relocation was to be allowed by a single relocation address, perhaps the program start address. Discuss how the expression evaluator in 7.1.4 could be extended to calculate the relocation factor. It should be able to determine that the address

    3*A − B

    is doubly relocatable if A and B are relocatable singly, for example. What restrictions could be put on expressions in order to keep the problem reasonable? Would the address

    N*A − (N − 1)*B

    be allowed where A, B, and N are relocatable? What if A and B were relocatable but N was absolute?

2. How should the CSECT pseudo-order that is available in the 360 assembler be implemented?

3. Write a flowchart for the scan of the address field of the DC pseudo-order available in the 360 assembler, ignoring problems of conversion of single numbers into internal form.

4. How could the DS pseudo in the program described in question three be included?

5. Section 7.7.2 discussed a SKIP pseudo which caused the assembler to stop generating code for a number of card images. The 360 assembler uses the mnemonic AGO for this purpose, and also has a pseudo AGOB which causes the assembler to return to an earlier card, thus assembling the code in between for another time. On the basis of assembler implementation, should a pseudo like AGOB be allowed outside of a macro definition? How should it be implemented?

6. Show that there are 1,617,038,380 names of six or less characters that start with a letter and contain only letters or digits. Suggest an algorithm for converting between such names and the integers between 0 and 1,617,038,379 such that, if the names are in alphabetical order, their numeric equivalences are in numerical order.

searching
and sorting

The need for associative memory devices is common to many applications. Some examples in the data processing field include the associating of account information for a given customer known by name (or account number), associating the address information with the symbolic address name in assemblers and compilers, and the association of employee statistics such as age, marital status, wage rate, etc., with the employee name. Outside of the computer, we meet two very common examples in the phone directory and the dictionary, both associating a set of information with a given word.

Because those associative memories that have been built are fairly expensive and relatively small, other techniques must be used in practice to simulate the associative memory. In a similar manner, the telephone numbers of all phones cannot be stored in an associative memory. The human can store a few in his head, perhaps a secretary can store a few more, but that is an expensive memory device. Instead one uses a telephone directory and performs a search for the name in order to get the number. This example is often a fruitful one to bear in mind as searching techniques are discussed, since a number of the techniques used to find a name in the telephone directory of a large city have their counterpart in computer techniques.

The basic operations needed in an associative memory are to:

Enter an item.
Remove an item.
Add to or modify an item already there.
Reference to obtain additional information when part of the item is known.

The frequency with which each of these actions is taken and the size of the total amount of information (called a file or data set) serve to determine the best way to simulate the associative memory. In some cases, such as the telephone directory, only one action is normally taken by the user—that is, to find additional information when the name is given. Hence, the alphabetic ordering technique is the best. Anybody who has tried to find the phone number of a Mr. Smith, say, in a very large city, not knowing the initials but knowing the address instead, knows that the telephone directory is not efficient for uses other than an alphabetical search.

Each item (called a record) in the file contains a set of information, such as name, address, telephone number. If one piece of information (called a field) in a record is always used to identify that record when the file is to be interrogated, that field is called a *key*. In some cases there can be more than one key for each item. Suppose we wished to find the name of a person with a given phone number, then the phone number would be the key. Obviously the phone directory, although it could be used, is not a good way of doing this operation. The phone companies usually keep an *inverse* book where the entries are sorted in order of phone number, but this requires double the space for storing the information. The phone company also needs a list of phone numbers in terms of addresses. This means three directories, or three times the space. This is a case of *multiple keys*. The amount of information can be reduced by keeping only one complete directory, sorted, say, by name. The other two can contain the phone number and name and the address and name respectively, and they can be sorted by phone number and address respectively. The amount of storage space is reduced, but it now requires two lookups if the reference is by phone number or address. The second lookup in the name directory can be simplified if the reference to it is an entry number—that is, page, column, and row—so that no search is necessary.

Sometimes each record contains a fixed number of fields or can be conveniently arranged to have this form. We then talk of fixed-length records. The alternative is variable-length records. (Example: the file of people who have books checked out from a library may be variable length. Each record could consist of the user's name—the key—followed by a variable number of fields representing the books checked out to that person.) In general, variable-length records require more careful planning for efficient handling.

Requirements such as these must be examined in planning the simulation of associative memories. This chapter will discuss some of the simple techniques for programming associative memories with specific reference to their use by the assembler name table. Some of the methods discussed will not be valuable for most assembler implementations, and the reader is invited to consider their application to other problems.

8.1 SEQUENTIAL SEARCHING

Perhaps the simplest technique that can be applied to the name table problem is the sequential method. A table is constructed sequentially in memory, using as many words as necessary per entry. For example, we may need three words for the assembler name table, the first containing the coded name, the second containing the address value (when it is defined), and the third containing flags for *defined, relocatable, called,* etc. This is shown in Figure 8.1. A table of N entries would then occupy $3N$ consecutive locations.

The four basic operations would be performed as follows:

1.	Enter a new entry	A count of the number of entries N is maintained. The incoming entry is added to the bottom of the table (the next three words in memory) and N is increased by 1.
2.	Remove an entry	This cannot be done without either leaving holes or moving other information, so in general is not allowed in this scheme. (It is not necessary in the assembler name table.)
3.	Modify an entry	The table of items is searched on the key, that is, each name (the first word of the group of three) is compared with the desired name in turn until either a match is found or until the end of the table is reached. This is the search part of the process. It yields the address of the three words of the entry or the fact that the record is not there. Using these addresses, other parts of the record can now be changed.
4.	Locate information	This is done by searching on the key as above.

If deletion is to be allowed, then the hole left should be filled by moving the last entry in the table to the space and reducing N by 1.

This technique should only be used when tables are relatively small or the

Name   Address   Called
              value   Relocatable
                               Defined

FIGURE 8.1 Name table entry.

search time will be too long. Techniques exist to make this method faster by small factors, but not by enough that one should consider searching a table the size of a phone book a record at a time. One speed-up technique often used is the following. The search loop in a one-address machine can have the form

```
A  LOAD         NAME
   SUBTRACT     ENTRY(I)
   TEST FOR 0   AND BRANCH TO FOUND IF 0
   INCREASE I   AND BRANCH TO A IF I IS LESS THAN OR = TO N
```

This loop will take four instructions on many machines. If, instead of storing the name in the name table, the difference of the ith and the $(i-1)$st name is stored (the name itself is stored as the first entry), then the code is

```
   LOAD         NAME
A  SUBTRACT     DIFFERENCE ENTRY (I)
   TEST         FOR 0 AND BRANCH TO FOUND IF 0
   INCREASE I   AND BRANCH TO A IF I LESS THAN OR = TO N
```

If the names are N(1), N(2), N(3), . . . , etc., the table entries are

```
N(1)
N(2)—N(1)
N(3)—N(2)
N(4)—N(3)
Etc.
```

After the I-th pass through the loop, the accumulator will contain NAME $-$ N(I). The (I+1)st pass will subtract N(I+1) $-$ N(I) from this to get NAME $-$ N(I+1) as desired. The loop is now three instructions long on most machines. Some machines have a compare accumulator with memory instruction which does not change the accumulator. This can also be used to reduce the size of the loop. At least one early machine (the IBM 650) had a built-in table lookup instruction which took advantage of the rotating drum memory which was its main store.

8.1.1 Expected length of search

Consider an assembly input deck with N different names and suppose that each is used M greater than 1 times. If the definitions and uses are distributed evenly but no name is used before it is defined, then, at the stage where K

names have been defined, we can expect a search to take about $K/2$ comparisons ("on the average" the search goes halfway down the table). This will be done M times before the next name is defined, or a total of $M*K/2$ comparisons will be made. Thus the total expected number of comparisons is about $M/2 + 2M/2 + 3M/2 + NM/2 = M(1+2+3+ \cdots +N)/2 = MN(N+1)/4$. We say that the length of time is *asymptotic* to $MN^2/2$ (that is, the important or fastest-growing part of the time is $MN^2/2$). Thus if we double the number of names, the search time is quadrupled.

This estimate is not exact, but it is a good approximation. It is too small because names are used before they are defined and therefore the number of entries in the table increases very rapidly as the first part of the program is read. On the other hand, many programs refer most frequently to names that are defined near to the point at which they are used (transfers for example). It is therefore a better practice to search backwards through the table, since the chances are good that the name is a recent entry and therefore near the bottom. This serves to lower the expected time of search and the two effects may cancel each other out.

8.2 BINARY SEARCHING TECHNIQUES

The length of time used in the sequential search technique is due to a lack of information about the order of the items in the table. The phone book is ordered alphabetically, which gives us this very important facility—if a name is compared against an entry in the table and it does not match, then it is possible to tell immediately if the name should appear before or after the referenced entry in the table. This means, for example, that it is possible to eliminate half the entries in one step by simply comparing the name with the middle entry. If the name is larger (alphabetically), then the name will not be found in the first half of the table, so that the first half need not be searched further.

This technique is comparable to flipping open the phone book in the center and then deciding which half to concentrate on. Most people do not use this method directly because they have some idea from the name where it might be. For example, in looking up Brown, they know that they must start about $\frac{1}{20}$th of the way through. Such considerations can be taken into account in computer methods, and they will be discussed in the next section. In this section we wish to explore the advantages and disadvantages of *binary searching techniques*, which are the extension of the idea above.

Initially we start with a large table, T, of entries—say 1,024 entries as an example. We suppose that the keys in the table are sorted into order. When

FIGURE 8.2   Binary searching.

we wish to look up name S in this table, we compare it first with the middle entry (the 512th). See Figure 8.2. If the name S happens to match the middle entry, we are lucky and have completed the process. If not, then S is either larger or smaller than entry 512. If larger, we need look only at the top half of the table; if smaller, at the bottom half. In neither case are there more than 512 entries left to examine, and in either case the half that is left is itself a sorted table T1. Therefore the same technique can be applied again. That is, name S can be compared with the middle entry of the remaining table T1 (that is with the 256th or 768th entry of the original table). Again, we can tell whether it is in the top or bottom half of table T1, so, after two comparisons, we have narrowed the possibilities down to $\frac{1}{4}$ of the original table. This process can be repeated until there is only one entry in the table to be searched, in which case a direct comparison will determine if it is name S or not. The example of a 1,024-entry table will take 10 or less steps, as can be seen from the calculation below.

number of steps	number of entries in remaining table
0	1,024
1	512
2	256
3	128
4	64
5	32
6	16
7	8
8	4
9	2
10	1

It is obvious that each additional step doubles the number of entries that can be taken care of. Thus if a total of n steps were to be taken, 2^n entries could be accommodated in the table. We need not restrict ourselves to tables which have a number of entries exactly equal to a power of 2. Other tables can be handled in two ways. The least efficient in storage space (but sometimes a faster program) is to fill up the table with "impossible" entries (for example, names that cannot be used by the programmer) until it is a power of 2 in size. When the size is a power of 2, addresses using fast shifting and logical orders can be constructed. The second method is simply to ignore the problem. The technique calls for the construction of the address of the middle of the remaining table. If the procedure saves two addresses L and M, L being the address one below the lowest entry in the remaining table and M the address one beyond the highest entry in the remaining table, the procedure is as follows:

1. If $M = L+1$, then the entry is not in the table, stop.
2. Construct $I = (L+M)/2$ (as an integer by truncation).
3. Compare entry I with the name, and
    a. if the entry is larger, set M equal to I;
    b. if the entry is smaller, set L equal to I;
    c. if the entry is equal, the name has been located, stop.
4. Repeat steps one through three.

Note that if the computer has a three-way compare for greater than, equal, and less than (as the IBM 7094 has), then one may as well do all three comparisons indicated in step three. If it has a two-way compare (greater than or equal to, for example) then it is probably worth changing the algorithm so that L is the address of the lowest entry. It then reads:

1. If $M = L+1$, compare the name with entry L for equality and stop. (Entry L is either the name or the name is not in the table.)
2. Construct $I = (L+M)/2$ as an integer by truncation.
3. Compare entry I with the name, and
    a. if the entry is larger, set M equal to I;
    b. if the entry is less than or equal, set L equal to I.
4. Repeat steps one through three.

It may appear that many more steps will be taken in the second scheme above because searching always continues until only one entry is left, but it can be shown that this only increases the average number of searches by one for large tables.

Example

Suppose that we have a table with 13 entries which, for simplicity, we shall suppose are the letters A through M. Let us consider the problem of looking up entry H in the table. (Remember that we do not know that the entries are of this simple form, so H might be anywhere.) Suppose that the table starts in location T and takes one word per entry.

location	entry
T+12	M
T+11	L
T+10	K
T+9	J
T+8	I
T+7	H
T+6	G
T+5	F
T+4	E
T+3	D
T+2	C
T+1	B
T	A

Initially, $L = T-1$ and $M = T+13$ if we use the method of three-way comparison. The steps are

$1-1$ M not equal to L+1, therefore continue.
$1-2$ $I = (M+L)/2 = T+6$.
$1-3$ $C(T+6)=G$ less than H, hence set $L=I=T+6$.
$2-1$ M not equal to L + 1.
$2-2$ $I=(L+M)/2 = T+9$.
$2-3$ $C(T+9) = J$ greater than H, hence set $M=I=T+9$.
$3-1$ M not equal to L+1.
$3-2$ $I=(L+M)/2=T+7$.
$3-3$ $C(T+7)=H=$desired name. Hence stop, we have found it.

If the letter I had been looked up, then four search steps—the maximum for this table—would have been taken.

8.2.1 Application of the binary search method to the assembler name table

The prerequisite for the use of the binary search technique is that the table be sorted into order. Keeping the table in order as it is generated is a slow process, since it is necessary to move existing information. On the average, half of the table will have to be moved for each new entry, hence the techniques discussed for the assembler are not directly applicable. What must be done is to first gather together a set of all entries to be made in the table. This can be done in pass I of the assembly. During pass I the table is unordered, so that no search of names used in address fields can be made and no check on double definition or nondefinition can be made. Between pass I and pass II, the defined names must be sorted into order. At this stage, double-definition errors will be caught when two entries with the same key are found. The names used in the address fields can be looked up by the binary search technique during pass II at the time of final translation. Because no table lookup is possible during pass I, pseudo-orders such as BSS, EQU, etc. must either have absolute addresses or be delayed until after pass I. Use of this method obviously makes it less desirable to translate into an intermediate language during the first pass. Only the instruction mnemonic can be replaced by its binary form and any location names (which have already been processed) can be omitted.

8.2.2 Comparison of the binary search technique with the sequential search technique for an assembler name table

If the number of different names is N and each is used M times, then the sort at the end of pass I will take order of $N \log_2 N$ operations if a binary

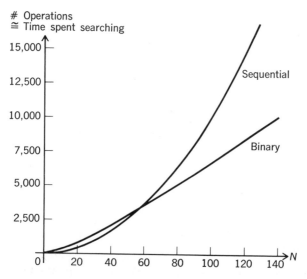

FIGURE 8.3 Comparison of sequential and binary search times.

(two-way) internal merge is used. (This will be shown in the section on sorting below.) The searching during pass II for MN names will take order of $MN \log_2 N$ operations by a binary search technique. Thus the total is $(M+1)N \log_2 N$ operations. This compares with $MN^2/4$ operations by a sequential search method. In addition, the comparison loop for the binary sort-and-search method is about twice as complex, thus we wish to compare $2(M+1)N \log_2 N$ with $MN^2/4$. Suppose that $M=4$. The result is shown graphically in Figure 8.3. We see from this figure that as N increases, the binary search method becomes preferable.

8.3 SORTING

Much work has been done to find efficient methods of sorting, since it is an important part of many large business data processing problems. It is not our intent to go over this work in detail but rather to highlight the important features. †

Two related processes that are very important in data processing are sorting and merging. By sorting we mean the process which starts with a random file and finishes with a completely ordered file. By merging we mean the process which starts with several ordered files and produces a single ordered file. In practice, both processes have to be done to do a given job. For example, a bank which is updating its ordered file (on tape) of customer accounts with the day's transactions may first sort the day's transactions into order and then merge this file with the master file to produce a new master. This will make it unnecessary to read through the master file more than once. If the master file is much larger than the daily transaction file, this approach has obvious advantages. The use of large semirandom access devices such as disk files, which make the customer records available online, will modify such techniques. Sorting itself may involve merging, particularly if the number of entries is larger than can be accommodated in high-speed store. Typically, groups of entries that can be held inside the main store are sorted by some technique and then written onto backup store. When the whole file has been processed, the result is a collection of smaller sorted files. These are now merged. The first stage of this is called *internal sorting*. It is convenient to distinguish this phase because the class of methods that can be considered is larger than the class that can be used efficiently when a backup store is used.

† The ambitious student can start with an article by C. Gotlieb, *Sorting on Computers*, in Freiberger and Prager (eds.), "Applications of Digital Computers," pp. 68–84, Ginn and Company, Boston, 1963, which summarizes many of the methods and gives a copious bibliography.

Internal sorting can be categorized in a number of ways. Three important classes of methods are those based on sequential searching, those based on merging, and those based on the radix representation of the key.

8.3.1 Sequential methods

A typical method in this category is the example invariably given in introductory Fortran texts. The first item in the file is moved to a location reserved for the smallest. It is then compared with each of the others in turn. If a smaller one is found, it is placed in the cell reserved for the smallest. When all of the keys in the file have been compared in this way, the smallest member is known. It is exchanged with the first member of the file and then attention is restricted to the remaining $N-1$ members. The smallest of the reduced file is the second smallest of the whole file, so it is exchanged with the second member and so on. After M passes, the file would contain the first M members in order. After $N-1$ passes, a file of N entries would be in order. The number of operations is proportional to $(N-1)+(N-2)+ \cdots +3+2+1 = N(N-1)/2$ which is approximately $N^2/2$ for large N. All of the sequential search methods use KN^2 operations for some value of K. (We express this by saying that they are $O(N^2)$ methods, read *order of N^2 methods*.) Thus as N increases, sequential methods increase very rapidly both for sorting and searching.

It is often convenient to sort a table *in place*, that is, without using additional storage space. This can be done sequentially by interchanging the nth entry with the nth largest, $n = 1,2, \ldots , N-1$. An alternative is to compare each entry with its neighbor in order, exchanging the two if they are in the wrong order. The largest will "float" to the top in this process. After at most $N-1$ passes, the table will be in order. If the table is already partially sorted, this method will take fewer passes. This is often called the *bubble sort*.

8.3.2 Merging methods

These are combination methods utilizing the sequential sort for smaller files and then merging techniques. One example of this is called the *quadratic selection process*. The original file of N records is broken into $\sqrt{N}$ subfiles, each with $\sqrt{N}$ records (or the nearest integer to $\sqrt{N}$). The subfiles are sorted into order by a sequential method (using approximately $(\sqrt{N})^2/2 = N/2$ comparisons each on $\sqrt{N}$ files for a total of approximately $N^{1.5}/2$ operations). The $\sqrt{N}$ subfiles are now merged by comparing the smallest of each to find the overall smallest (this takes $\sqrt{N}$ comparisons). This smallest is placed in its final position, and the process is repeated with it removed from its subfile. Since there are N records, this merging process takes $N^{1.5}$ operations for a total of $1.5\ N^{1.5}$ operations. We can therefore say that this is an $O(N^{1.5})$ method. The quadratic selection process is a special case of the *P-way merge*. In a *P*-way merge, the original file is split into *P* subfiles of N/P elements each. Each of these subfiles is sorted by some method, and then the *P*-ordered files are merged as in the quadratic selection process. This last operation takes order of $N*P$ operations. The subfiles of N/P elements could be sorted by any method. For example, another *P*-way merge could be used by breaking each subfile into sub-subfiles of $N/P/P$ elements. This process can be repeated until the sub-sub- . . . subfiles are small enough to be sorted sequentially.

An example of a *P*-way merge with *P* equal to 3 is given below. Initially, there are 18 items in the file. They are to be sorted into alphabetical order. Assume that the largest file that can be sorted rapidly by a sequential method is a 2-item file. Hence the first step is to produce 3*3 files of 2 elements each.

If the initial file contains

```
SER DOG TYU EWB EDF ZUQ WFE QWE OUT DEG CAT WEB TOO WSS
BSS TOM AAA QKX
```

the first pass produces 9 two-record sorted files equal to

```
DOG  SER
EWB  TYU
UWE  WFE
EDF  ZUG
DEG  OUT
CAT  WEB
TOO  WSS
BSS  TOM
AAA  QKX
```

The first group of these subfiles is merged as follows:

	input file		output file
	DOG	SER	
Start	EWB	TYU	
	UWE	WFE	
	. . .	SER	
Step 1	EWB	TYU	DOG
	UWE	WFE	
	. . .	SER	
Step 2	. . .	TYU	DOG EWB
	UWE	WFE	

	input file	*output file*

```
            input file      output file
            . . .   . . .
   Step 3   . . .   TYU   DOG  EWB  SER
            UWE     WFE

            . . .   . . .
   Step 4   . . .   . . .   DOG  EWB  SER  TYU
            UWE     WFE

            . . .   . . .
   Step 5   . . .   . . .   DOG  EWB  SER  TYU  UWE
            . . .   WFE

            . . .   . . .
   Step 6   . . .   . . .   DOG  EWB  SER  TYU  UWE  WFE
            . . .   . . .
```

The next two groups of three subfiles are merged in a similar way, resulting in three subfiles, each sorted and containing six elements. These three subfiles are merged together to give a single sorted file of 18 elements. How many passes of merging are needed for a file of N elements? Assume that the number of records that are to be sorted initially is fixed at Q. Then if N is less than Q, only the initial sort pass is needed. If N is between Q and PQ, then one additional pass is needed. For each factor of P, one additional pass is needed. Hence the number of passes is the smallest integer at least as large as

$$1 + \log_P \frac{N}{Q}$$

The amount of work in each pass is proportional to NP, so the total work is proportional to

$$NP\left(1 + \log_P \frac{N}{Q}\right)$$

As N increases, this increases at a rate of $N \log N$. For a given N and Q, the optimum value of P can be calculated by differentiation. It can be seen that as N/Q becomes large (which is the case of interest when merging techniques are being discussed), then the value of P for which the total merge time is minimum is $\epsilon = 2.71828 \ldots$ Since P must be an integer, 2 or 3 is optimum. In practice, merging from auxiliary storage devices is likely to be input/output limited, so that the computation time is not as significant as I/O time. As P increases, the number of passes decreases but the computation time increases. Ideally, P should be increased until the computation time is equal to the I/O time. If magnetic tapes are being used, then it is probable that the physical number of tape drives available will be the limiting factor, so the crudest rule of thumb is to use all tape drives available.

Merging techniques can be used for an internal sort by starting with files of length 1 which are necessarily sorted and performing P-way merges. Since the internal sort is not I/O limited, then a P of 2 or 3 should be chosen. In fact, a more careful analysis of the time for a given machine will usually suggest that P should be 2.

8.3.3 Radix methods

The key is usually expressed in some radix. For example, it may be expressed internally in binary, it may be a decimal number, or it may be an alphabetic name, which is radix 26. A radix method is one which takes account of the representation of the key in order to do the sorting. It can be likened to the method of alphabetizing a list of names by first sorting them into 26 piles based on the first letter, and then, treating each pile separately, alphabetizing them on the second letter, and so on. A familiar application of this technique is provided by the card sorter. A card sorter contains pockets for each row position on the card (12 pockets) plus a reject pocket which we shall ignore. It can be set to examine any particular column on the card. One pass through the sorter separates the deck according to the holes punched. Since it is easier to restack all cards together after a sort than to treat each subdeck separately, the least-significant digit of the representation of the key should be treated first. Suppose that a deck of cards contains record information to be sorted and the key is a three-digit decimal number in columns 1 through 3. The deck should be first sorted on the basis of column 3 so that all cards are in order on column 3. Then the process should be repeated on column 2. At this time, the deck is in order on column 2 but not on 3. However, those cards with identical entries in column 2 are in order on column 3. After a third pass sorting on column 1, the deck is in order. An example of such a sort is given below. The deck input to the sorter is shown on the left, while the contents of each of the 10 pockets after the sort pass is shown to its right.

Unordered file is sorted into pockets below:

input	0	1	2	3	4	5	6	7	8	9
436							436			
253			253							
856							856			
456							456			
457								457		
455						455				
364					364					
907								907		
004					004					

input	0	1	2	3	4	5	6	7	8	9
009										009
574					574					
276							276			
458									458	
473				473						
853				853						

The cards are stacked behind each other, those from pocket 0 in front, and on the second pass the reassembled file on the left below is sorted into the pockets shown:

input	0	1	2	3	4	5	6	7	8	9
253						253				
473								473		
853						853				
364							364			
004	004									
574								574		
455						455				
436				436						
856						856				
456						456				
276								276		
457						457				
907	907									
458						458				
009	009									

On the third pass, it is sorted as shown below on the first digit:

input	0	1	2	3	4	5	6	7	8	9
004	004									
907										907
009	009									
436					436					
253			253							
853									853	
455					455					
856									856	
456					456					
457					457					
458					458					
364				364						
473					473					
574						574				
276			276							

The result after reassembling into a single deck is:

```
004
009
253
276
364
436
455
456
457
458
473
574
853
856
907
```

This technique can be adapted to computer use. For internal sorting, there is no limit to the radix that could be used except that of the storage space required to provide at least one word for each pocket. It is not necessary to provide space for more than one entry in a contiguous location of memory, since subsequent entries in the same pocket could be chained together. If this technique is used for sorting files from auxiliary storage, then there must be at least as many output-file storage devices (for example, magnetic tape units) as there are pockets, so the radix used is limited. In addition, at least one input-file device is needed, and if unnecessary file-to-file copies are to be avoided, there should be as many input files as there are output files, so that on the next pass their roles can be switched.

The number of operations is proportional to the number of passes and the number of items N. The number of passes K is determined by the radix that can be used and the length of the key. To some extent, K is independent of the number of entries, except that it should be realized that the maximum number of entries is limited by the radix R and the number of passes K, because it is not possible to have more than R^K different keys consisting of K digits base R. Radix sorting is not very efficient unless the ratio of the number of keys used to the maximum possible number is large (close to 1). Roughly speaking, this is because the method is going through the motions of distinguishing between many more different keys than are actually present unless the ratio is large.

A sort using radix 2 called *radix exchange* has been developed for internal sorting. It has the property that very little temporary storage is required. Since the radix is 2, it is useful for binary machines in which the key is a fixed-point number. The unordered set of keys is scanned from the first entry, looking only at the most significant bit. When a 1 bit is found, the scan starts backward from the last entry until a key with a 0 first bit is encountered. The two entries are exchanged, and the scan continues. Two address pointers are used during this scan to remember where the forward and backward scans have reached. When the pointers meet, the file is in order on the first bit; that is, it has been divided into two subfiles based on the first bit. Each of these two subfiles can be sorted on the second bit to get four subfiles in order on the first two bits, and so on. If the key contains K bits, K address pointers will be needed for temporary storage. †

The radix exchange method described above is slow if the keys are long because the number of passes is proportional to the number of bits in the key. *Quicksort* and *quickersort* are the names of two similar methods that overcome this problem. ‡

The first step in the radix exchange is to divide the table into two by putting all keys less than 1000000 . . . 0 at the top of the table and all entries greater than or equal to this number below. This is done by scanning simultaneously from the top and bottom of the table so that keys can be exchanged when they are in the wrong relative order. Quicksort chooses one of the keys at random and uses this for the comparison instead of 100 . . . 0. Each key is examined, starting from the first, and compared with the random one chosen. When a larger one is found, the scan starts from the bottom of the table looking for a smaller one. When one is found, the larger and smaller are exchanged and the scan continues. This step is called "partition" by Hoare. It is described in Algol by

```
procedure   partition (A,M,N,I,J); value M,N;
            array A; integer M,N,I,J;
comment   I and J are output variables, and A is the array (with subscript
          bounds M:N) which is operated upon by this procedure. Partition takes the
          value X of a random element of the array A, and rearranges the values of the
          elements of the array in such a way that there exist integers I and J with the
          following properties:
```

$$M \leq J < I \leq N \text{ provided } M < N$$
$$A[R] \leq X \text{ for } M \leq R \leq J$$
$$A[R] = X \text{ for } J < R < I$$
$$A[R] \geq X \text{ for } I \leq R \leq N$$

---

† This method is described in P. Hildebrandt, and H. Isbit, Radix Exchange, *Journal of the Association for Computing Machinery*, vol. 6, no. 2, pp. 156–163, April, 1959.

‡ Described in C. A. R. Hoare and R. S. Scowen, Algorithms 64 and 271, *Communications of the Association for Computing Machinery*, vol. 4, p. 321, July, 1961.

The procedure uses an integer procedure random (M,N) which chooses equi-probably a random integer F between M and N, and also a procedure exchange, which exchanges the values of its two parameters;

```
begin    real X; integer F;
         F: = random (M,N); X: = A[F];
         I: = M; J: = N;
up:      for I: = I step 1 until N do
                    if X < A [I] then go to down;
         I: = N;
down:    for J: = J step −1 until M do
                    if A[J]<X then go to change;
         J: = M;
change:  if I < J then begin exchange (A[I], A[J]);
                          I: = I + 1; J: = J − 1;
                          go to up
                       end
else     if I < F then begin exchange (A[I], A[F]);
                          I: = I + 1
                       end
else     if F < J then begin exchange (A[F], A[J]);
                          J: = J − 1
                       end;
end      partition †
```

The result of applying "partition" to an array A is to break it into three sub-arrays of elements less than the one chosen at random, equal to it, and greater than it. This same algorithm can be applied to the subtables smaller and larger than the chosen element until they only consist of one element, at which time the table will be sorted. This is done by Hoare's Algol program

```
procedure   quicksort (A,M,N); value M,N;
            array A; integer M,N;
comment     Quicksort is a very fast and convenient method of sorting an array
in the random access store of a computer. The entire contents of the store may
be sorted, since no extra space is required. The average number of compari-
sons made is 2(M − N) ln (N − M), and the average number of exchanges is
one sixth this amount. Suitable refinements of this method will be desirable for
its implementation on any actual computer;
begin       integer I,J;
            if M < N then begin partition (A,M,N,I,J);
                          quicksort (A,M,J);
                          quicksort (A, I, N);
                       end
end         quicksort †
```

† *Ibid.*

This provides a very nice example of recursion. Quicksort sorts a table. It first checks to see that there is more than one element; if not, the table is already sorted. It then breaks the table into three subtables and sorts the first and last by use of quicksort; the middle one contains equal elements, so it is already sorted.

The comments indicated that no extra storage space is required. From a data point of view this is true, but the user should be aware that recursive procedures require storage space for each of their variables and links. This method, therefore, does use kp extra storage locations, where p is the maximum depth of recursion, proportional to $\log(N-M)$, and k is a constant dependent on the implementation of the compiler.

8.3.4 Internally sorting long records

In many business applications and in some system applications, the record is very long compared with the size of the key. Since the sorting methods discussed involve the movement of records from one part of memory to another several times, it is desirable to look for methods which avoid this movement or minimize it. We must first ask what is the desired form of the sorted file. There are three possibilities.

It might be sufficient that a chain of addresses pointing in order from one file to the next be available. This allows the file to be read in order, but it is not possible to access a particular entry such as the middle one without reading all previous ones in the chain. If this is the case, then the records need never be moved. An extra field must be allocated to each record stored. This will contain a chain address. Each file in memory is represented by a series of addresses linking one to another. As the files are changed, these address links are modified to reflect the new organization.

Suppose, for example, that the six files below were stored in the locations indicated (occupying 20 words each).

location	contents		link address
100	JONES	DATA..A	120
120	BROWN	DATA..B	140
140	SMITH	DATA..C	160
160	DAVID	DATA..D	180
180	PETER	DATA..E	200
200	BRYAN	DATA..F	—

The link address is shown as it would be set up originally. It gives the file in the order in which it was read in. A sorting process, such as a three-way merge, might start by creating three ordered files of two elements each. These files start in locations 120, 160, and 200 (this information must be saved), and the records are modified to read

```
100  JONES  DATA. .A  —
120  BROWN  DATA. .B  100
140  SMITH  DATA. .C  —
160  DAVID  DATA. .D  140
180  PETER  DATA. .E  —
200  BRYAN  DATA. .F  180
```

The three-way merge is now performed by comparing the keys in locations 120, 160, and 200. BROWN in 120 is found to be the smallest, so it is put at the start of this final chain. The first file now has a starting address of 100, since the earlier entry was removed. The next comparison shows that BRYAN is the smallest of the three keys compared. Thus the entry in 200 is placed in the output file chain by putting 200 in the address link of the record in 120. The result at the completion of the merge is

```
100  JONES  DATA. .A  180
120  BROWN  DATA. .B  200
140  SMITH  DATA. .C  —
160  DAVID  DATA. .D  100
180  PETER  DATA. .E  140
200  BRYAN  DATA. .F  160
```

which tells us that the order of the file is 120,200,160,100,180,140. It is necessary to save the starting address, 120, of the chain in the memory. This file can now be accessed sequentially starting from the first member.

A second required form for a file occurs when it must be in alphabetical order. This can occur if the file has to be written onto an output device in order. This means that the records must be moved. To avoid moving them during the sort process, a technique such as the one used above can be employed. When the file has been alphabetized, it can be physically moved. This movement need not take more than one move of each record, which is an improvement over the number of moves that would have been used if the records had been moved in the sorting process.

A third form for a file occurs when it is only necessary to calculate the address of the ith entry for any i. This is sufficient for a binary search. In this form, the records can be separated into two pieces, the key and the remainder. The remainder can be left in fixed memory locations and only the keys sorted. In order that the key be connected to the remainder, an address pointer which points to the remainder of the record can be stored with the key. In the example above, the final form of the file would be

```
100  BROWN   DATA..A  120   Brown's pointer points to his data, which is
120  BRYAN   DATA..B  200   DATA..B
140  DAVID   DATA..C  160
160  JONES   DATA..D  100
180  PETER   DATA..E  180
200  SMITH   DATA..F  140
```

The keys have been placed in order, but the remainder of the records have been left fixed. The address pointer contains the original address of the key before sorting occurred. This serves to link the key to the record.

Alternatively, a separate list of addresses pointing to the keys could be sorted on the key. The key could be accessed from this address by indirect addressing.

8.3.5 Sorting from backup storage

The need for sorting from backup storage is not likely to occur in the assembly process for any but the smallest machines, since the assembler name table can usually be kept in the main memory. Indeed, if it can't, then the assembly process must be designed very carefully so as to minimize the name table searching, for a search through a file contained on backup storage can be very slow. In this section we shall discuss some of the criteria to be evaluated when planning a sorting job which will involve multiple passes over auxiliary storage files.

The characteristics of the machine that have the greatest effect on the sort times are the size of main memory available for the internal sort process and the type and number of auxiliary storage devices available for storing the information from one pass to another. Tape units are the most commonly available devices. Since the information is only available serially from a tape unit, methods used can only access information from the current position on each tape. Usually a variant of a P-way merge will be used. If $2P$ tape units are available, then a simple P-way merge can be done as follows. On the first pass over the unsorted file, groups of records are read into the main memory and sorted internally. They are written out onto P of the tapes, each tape receiving a sorted subfile in turn. At the completion of this process, the information has been spread over P of the tapes such that each tape contains a series of sorted subfiles. A P-way merge is now performed, reading the P input streams from these P tapes and generating an output stream of sorted subfiles P times as long. The output stream is split by placing successive subfiles onto each of the remaining P tapes. Thus the result of the second pass is another set of P tapes, each with longer sorted subfiles, and P tapes that are now free. The process can be repeated, merging from the tapes that have just been prepared onto the newly available tapes.

The longer the first subfiles are made, the fewer passes will be needed in the merging process. Consequently, it is important to use a method that uses a minimum amount of temporary storage during the interval sort so that a maximum amount is available for the subfile and necessary I/O buffers. If the key is binary and short, radix exchange may be the most suitable; but if the number of bits in the key is close to N, the number of entries, it will be as slow as sequential sorting or bubble sorting, neither of which require additional storage. A second parameter that is available to the user is the choice of the physical block size of the information written on tape. We call the number of records per block the blocking factor.

If the block size is made larger, then the percentage of tape occupied by record gaps is smaller, and hence the overall tape time is reduced. On the other hand, the longer the block, the more memory space required for each buffer, and hence the fewer buffers that can be used. Since there is some chance that the input can occur from one tape for some time, it is important that there be some backup of information in the memory before it is needed. The average amount of memory space not in use is half a buffer size for each of the P input buffers. This also argues for smaller buffers.

8.4 HASH ADDRESSING

The previous section dealt with techniques that depended on the table being ordered in memory but that did not require a knowledge of where a given name appeared in the table. This contrasts with the technique that a person uses in a phone book search. He knows, for example, that the entry for Mr. Brown will appear about $\frac{1}{20}$th of the way through the book. The strategy used could be to open the book at this point and then to scan forward or backward depending on the result of a comparison of the name Brown with the entry found at the $\frac{1}{20}$th point. The corresponding computer technique would be to construct an address based on an estimate of where the name being searched is likely to appear and then to start a sequential search forward or backward from that point. Let us illustrate this by an example. Suppose that the keys are three-digit decimal numbers between 000 and 999 and that there are 100 entries in the table. If they are evenly distributed (that is, a key lies between each of 0 to 9, 10 to 19, . . . , and 990 to 999), then the address of the entry in the table would be given by the address

$A = T + K/10$ Truncated to an integer.

where the table is assumed to start in location T, require one location per entry, and where K is the key.

Unfortunately, the keys of a table will not be so evenly distributed in general, but the more that they approximate this distribution, the faster the method will be. In the worst possible case, it will not be worse than the sequential search method except that there is an additional calculation of a starting address and at some point the table has to be ordered. If it is a fixed table, such as the mnemonic table, then the sorting does not have to be done for each assembly. Therefore this is a better method than the sequential method, yet it retains most of the sequential method's simplicity.

If this method were to be used for the name table, then either the entries would have to be sorted between pass I and II (which means that no references to the table could be made in pass I unless a sequential technique were used), or else the table would have to be constructed in order. Constructing a table in order can be a time-consuming job if it has to be reordered after each new name is entered, because up to half of the entries in the table will have to be moved in order to make space for each new entry. This can be partially avoided if the table has blank spaces in it originally, so that there is a strong possibility that there will be a space for the next entry. The more spaces that are available in a given size table, the faster the entry process is likely to be. Let us return to the previous example where the keys are between 000 and 999. Suppose that there will be as many as 100 entries in the table, although initially there are none. Suppose that we allocate 200 locations for the table, so that it never becomes more than 50 percent dense. In this case, the probable address for an entry will be given by

$A = T + K/5$

When an entry is to be placed in the table, this address is calculated from the value of the key. If the addressed location is empty, the entry is placed in the table at that point. If the location is full, then the key is compared with the entry already in the table. If the table entry is larger, the next lower address $A - 1$ is examined. If this is empty, it is used to make the new entry. If its contents are larger, another step to the next lower address is taken. If it is smaller, then it is necessary to open up a space by moving everything, from this point down to the first blank space, down one position. If the original comparison showed that the table entry was smaller, then a similar process is followed in the upward (increasing address) direction. Let us examine the process when the entries 256 and 217 are added to the table after it already contains some entries. In the section of the table shown below, the left-hand column gives the memory location, the next column contains the keys already entered, and the subsequent columns show the states of the table after the next two entries are made.

In step 1, entry 256 is added to the table. The probable address of the key 256 is T + $^{256}\!/_5$ = T + 51. Unfortunately, location T + 51 is already occupied by the key 257, which is larger than 256. Therefore, the entry in the next smaller location T + 50 is checked. It contains the key 255, which is smaller than 256. Therefore, 256 is entered into T + 50 and all entries from T + 50 down are moved down one location until the next blank in T + 48 is found. In step 2, the key 217, corresponding to the probable address T + 43, is entered. The present entries in T + 43 and T + 44 are both smaller than the key 217. However the next table entry, T + 45, is empty. Therefore, 217 is entered into T + 45.

A table search process can be viewed as a means of calculating a function. The argument of the function is the key which is to be looked up, and its value is the address of the entry. If this function is known, that is, if for each key K we could calculate the address A by means of a function F such that A = F(K), then there is no need to perform a search through the table. In the technique discussed above, an approximation to F was formed by using a linear function F. It was linear because the table was to be ordered. However, if we ask what use was made of the ordering property, we shall see that

TABLE 8.1

Location	Key	After step 1	After step 2
T+40	201	201	201
T+41	203	203	203
T+42			
T+43	215	215	215
T+44	216	216	216
T+45			217
T+46	231	231	231
T+47			
T+48		246	246
T+49	246	255	255
T+50	255	256	256
T+51	257	257	257
T+52			
T+53	266	266	266

it was only to determine whether to search backwards or forwards from the probable address if the entry and the searched name did not agree. We could just as well always search in the same direction, say in the direction of increasing address, in which case the ordering would not have been necessary. This has an additional advantage. Since the table does not have to be in order, it is not necessary to move previous entries. The method for finding a name by searching is now as follows:

1. Calculate an approximate address from the key by an approximate address function F', where $A = F'(K)$.
2. Compare the name being searched for with the entry in location A.
3. If they agree, the entry has been found. Stop.
4. If the contents of the table are blank at location A, the entry is not in the table. Stop.
5. Otherwise, increase A by 1 and return to step 2.

A new entry is placed in the table as follows:

1. Construct the approximate address $A = F'(K)$.
2. Check the contents of location A.
3. If they are not blank, increase A by 1 and return to step 2.
4. If they are blank, enter the new key in location A.

This will be illustrated by repeating the earlier example, this time using the new entry method.

TABLE 8.2

Location	Key	After step 1	After step 2
T+40	201	201	201
T+41	203	203	203
T+42			
T+43	215	215	215
T+44	216	216	216
T+45			217
T+46	231	231	231
T+47			
T+48			
T+49	246	246	246
T+50	255	255	255
T+51	257	257	257
T+52		256	256
T+53	266	266	266

In step one, the entry 256 is added to the table. Since the approximate address function gives location T+51, which is not empty, the first blank location with a higher address is used, namely, T+52. Note that the table is now out of order. When the entry 217 is made in step two, the process also has to search forward two cells until a blank location is found. Note that, in this unordered technique, it is never necessary to move items already in the table; hence, the entry time is faster. However, the search time will be slower when the table becomes fairly dense, since it is necessary to search until a blank location has been found; in an ordered table, on the other hand, it was only necessary to search until either a blank location or a larger (or smaller if the search is backward) entry has been found. The unordered technique will never be slower than a sequential search.

In the above example we calculated an approximate address by means of a linear function of the key. In applications of this technique to assemblers and compilers, there is a high probability that the keys will not be distributed anywhere near uniformly over the range of possible keys. This will cause bunching in the table and slow down the search-and-entry process. Many assembly-language programs, for example, will contain names that start with the same three letters because these three letters serve to identify that section of code to the programmer. Since the ordering is not important, there is no reason why the approximate address function should be a monotonic function of the key. (A monotonic function is one which only increases—or decreases—as the value of the argument is increased.) Therefore, we should try to use an approximate address function that spreads the keys used fairly evenly over the locations used in the table. If the table is fixed, as the mnemonic table is, then various address functions can be tried until a reasonably good choice between speed of calculation and speed of search is achieved. If the table changes, as happens in the case of the name table, then an address function must be chosen without prior knowledge of the entries. The idea generally used is to mix up or *hash* the key in some way so that keys assigned in any routine fashion are unlikely to fall in the same part of the table. Such an address is called a *hash address*.

Some examples of hash addresses that could be used in an assembler name table include multiplying the name by a constant after it has been packed into an internal representation such as BCD and just using a certain number of bits from the result, or using the bottom bits of the internal representation if it has been converted as a base-37 number. In the former case, the internal form of a six character name would occupy 36 bits in BCD. If this representation is multiplied by the constant 000001000001000001000001000001000001 and bits 30 through 41 of the 72-bit binary product are used as the hash address, then a reasonable spread can be expected unless the programmer is either very unfortunate or he deliberately tries to beat the system.

8.5 CHAINING TECHNIQUES

In the previous sections, it has generally been assumed that the record positions in memory were in contiguous locations. This was necessary in methods that used address calculations such as the binary search method and the hash addressing technique. However, in sequential searching, it was only necessary that the successor of an entry be accessible directly. This was exploited in the discussion on sorting long records, where they were chained together in order to avoid moving them in memory. Chaining techniques can be exploited to advantage in a number of methods. This section will discuss various chaining techniques that can be used.

8.5.1 Sequential search with deletions

The method of sequential searching had a number of drawbacks. One was its inherent slowness, which was only offset by its simplicity. In some situations, it is desirable to replace names with the table address containing the related information. This means that deletion is not possible unless blank entries are permitted, since other entries may not be moved. Permitting blank entries slows down the entry process. If the entries are chained together in memory, the speed is not improved, but it is possible to remove entries from the chain without leaving blank entries in the table. This is shown in the following example. If the original table has the form

TABLE 8.3

Location	Key	Link to next entry
110	SAM	114
112	JOHN	120
114	BETTY	118
116		
118	PAT	112
120	BOB	

and the address 110 is indicated as being the start of the table, then the order

of the table can be seen to be SAM, BETTY, PAT, JOHN, BOB, ...
Suppose that the entry PAT is to be removed. We note that this entry is
preceded by BETTY and followed by JOHN in locations 114 and 112
respectively. In order that the successor of BETTY be JOHN, the chain link
from BETTY must be changed to the address of JOHN. That is, the chain
address in location 114 must be changed from 118 to 112. The table now has
the form

TABLE 8.4

110	SAM	114
112	JOHN	120
114	BETTY	112
116		
118	PAT	112
120	BOB	

It was not necessary to remove the key PAT in any way; it is omitted from
any search process because the chain of link addresses does not pass through
it. In this particular example, the first entry in the chain is also the first
location of the table. If this entry were to be removed from the table, the
first member of the chain would be in location 114. Therefore there must be
a cell in memory which is used to hold the address of the first entry in the
table.

If a new entry is to be added to the table, then it can be placed on the
beginning or end of the chain. In the latter case, it is necessary to save the
address of the last entry in the chain, so it is simpler to add a new entry to
the beginning of the chain unless there are reasons for preferring the end.

When an entry is added to the chain, it is necessary to find an empty place
in memory for recording the new record. Since the present records are not
in contiguous locations, there may be holes in the table. Since we did not
blank out a record when it was removed from the chain, it is not possible
(or desirable) to scan through all locations looking for an empty position.
Therefore, a method which will allow us to find empty positions must be
introduced. This method must allow the positions made free when an entry
is removed to be reallocated. A chaining principle can also be used for this
by constructing a chained list of all free positions. The starting address of this
chain must be kept in a known memory cell. When an item is to be added to
the table, the first entry in the *free chain* (sometimes called the *free list*) is
removed from that chain and used as a location for the new entry. When an
item is removed from the table, its address can be added to the beginning

of the free chain. Suppose our table is in the state

TABLE 8.5

Table start *110*
Free chain start....*118*

Location	Key	Link
110	SAM	114
112	JOHN	120
114	BETTY	112
116		0
118	PAT	116
120	BOB	0

The free chain contains locations 118 and 116. The 0 link in location 116 is used to indicate that it is the end of the chain. This only rules out location 0 as a possible table address. The table contains locations 110, 114, 112, and 120. Location 118 contains a non-blank key because it was previously used, but this key is not in the table because it is not in the table chain. If the key TOM were to be added to the table, then the procedure would be as follows. The new entry TOM is placed into the location given in the start of the free chain (118). Thus location 118 now contains TOM. The start address for the free chain is set to the link in location 118, the link in location 118 is set to the contents of the start of the table chain, and the new value of the start of the table chain is made equal to the old value of the start of the free chain. Thus the table has the form

TABLE 8.6

Table chain start...*118*
Free chain start....*116*

Location	Key	Link
110	SAM	114
112	JOHN	120
114	BETTY	112
116		0
118	TOM	110
120	BOB	0

If the entry BOB is now removed, the procedure is as follows. BOB is located in the table by a search. It is found in location 120. It is also noted that the preceding entry was in location 112. The link from location 120 (0) is copied into the link of the preceding location 112. The start of the free chain (116) is copied into the link of 120, and the address of the item being removed (120) is copied into the free-chain start storage cell. Thus the table becomes

TABLE 8.7

Table start 118
Free chain start 120

Location	Key	Link
110	SAM	114
112	JOHN	0
114	BETTY	112
116		0
118	TOM	110
120	BOB	116

8.5.2 Radix techniques with chaining: trees

Methods of searching analogous to the radix sorting techniques can be constructed. In a telephone directory lookup, the user will typically locate the first letter of the name by some combination of scanning technique and address calculation method. The second letter is frequently located in a similar manner. One could imagine this process being made easier by providing a small 26-entry index at the front of the directory indicating where each set of entries with the same first letter starts. If this were mechanized on a computer, then a memory reference would be used to find the address of, say, the words starting with an R. The second letter could be handled in a similar way by providing 26 more tables, each with 26 entries. Thus a second memory reference would tell us where all words starting with, say, RE were stored. This could be continued, but the third level would take about 17,000 memory locations, which is no longer practical. The problem that not all two-letter combinations are used arises. As more letters are handled, then the probability that all combinations will be used decreases further. Therefore, instead of storing a table of all 26 possibilities for each new combination, a table of only those letters that actually occur should be stored. This table will have to be searched sequentially, since it is impossible to predict which letter will appear where; however, it is fairly short, in no case longer than 26 entries. Since the individual table may change in size by additions and deletions, it is also wise to use a chaining method for the tables of letters. Suppose, for example, that the words LOAD, ADD, MPY, AND, NOT, NOP, and NEG were to be stored in such a manner. The table could take the form

TABLE 8.8

Table start address....1000

Location	Key	Line to next entry	Link to next table	Entry
1000	N	1001	1004	
1001	A	1002	1009	
1002	L	1003	1013	
1003	M	0	1016	
1004	O	1005	1006	
1005	E	0	1008	
1006	P	1007		NOP
1007	T	0		NOT
1008	G	0		NEG
1009	D	1010	1011	
1010	N	0	1012	
1011	D	0		ADD
1012	D	0		AND
1013	O	0	1014	
1014	A	0	1015	
1015	D	0		LOAD
1016	P	0	1017	
1017	Y	0		MPY

Note that any length names can be accommodated by this method, and that the search time will never be more than 26 times the number of characters in the word—usually very much less. It is evident that a large amount of additional storage can be used (18 locations to store seven items in this example). The percentage increase is less for larger tables. If, for example, all three letter keys are stored, 18,278 entries are used instead of the minimum of 17,576, which is only an additional 4 percent.

If this method is used for a name table, means of adding and searching must be provided. The spare locations in memory can be kept on a free chain, so that each time a new entry is made, another location can be obtained. The table is searched for the new entry, one character at a time, until a subtable is found in which the next letter is not present. This letter and subsequent letters must be added to the table. Suppose, for example, that the entry ABS is to be added to the table above. The search starts by comparing the first letter with the first table entry. The A does not match the N, so the next entry, from location 1001, is tried. This time the As match, so the search proceeds to the second character table starting in location 1009. The B is compared with the D in location 1009 and does not match. Hence it is compared with the next entry in 1010. The B does not match with the N either, and there is no next entry since the link to the next address is 0. Therefore, B must be added to this table. Suppose that the next locations available in the free chain are 1018, 1019, etc. The entry

```
1018  B  0  1019
```

is made in location 1018, while location 1010 (the last examined) is changed to

```
1010  N  1018  1012
```

by inserting the address of the new member of the subtable in the link to the next entry position. The S of ABS is entered in location 1019, and, since it is the last letter of ABS, this is the end of the chain.

```
1019  S  0  0  ABS
```

The table can accept keys in which one is an extension of another. If the entry ABST is made, the effect is to change location 1019 and add location 1020 to the table as follows:

```
1019  S  0  1020  ABS
1020  T  0  0     ABST
```

The data that has been stored in the table has a complex structure due to the chain addresses present. We refer to the structured storage arrangement as a *data structure*. The way it is stored in memory with chain addresses is just a way of representing this structure. We can visualize the structure presented above in the form of a *tree* as shown in Figure 8.4. It is drawn upside down in that the *root* of the tree is at the top of the figure. A tree consists of a set of *nodes* connected to each other by *branches*. It is such that there are no *closed circuits* in the branch connections, so that there is one and only one connection

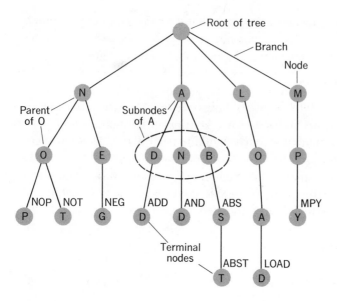

FIGURE 8.4   Tree structure.

between any pair of nodes. The nodes may be labelled, as they are in the example. One node is special, and is called the root of the tree. The branches extend from this root to each of the nodes. A node that is only connected to one other node is called a terminal node. In the example, all of the nodes connected to the root correspond to the possible first letters of names entered in the table. Thus there are four *subnodes* of the root node corresponding to the letters N, A, L, and M. The nodes are so labelled. Each of these nodes has further subnodes corresponding to the possible second letters of the keys. Thus the first letter N can be followed by the letters O or E, so there are two subnodes under the node labelled N. The nodes which also correspond to actual entries in the table are further labelled with the name of the key. This tree is represented in memory by using four elements for each node. They are the character at the node, the address of the next node to the right that is connected to the same *parent* node (the one immediately above as drawn) or 0 if there is no such node, the address of the leftmost subnode or 0 if there is none, and the actual entry if this is the last letter of an entry. (In practice, the latter would be the address of the record in storage corresponding to the key.) The data structure represented by the table above or by the tree in Figure 8.4 is an abstract entity which contains the data in a manner expressing certain relationships. A structure can be represented in many ways in a computer or on paper. We have shown just two ways for this particular structure.

8.5.3 Binary tree method

The binary search method is inflexible because it is necessary to store the information in order, so that the address of any particular entry can be calculated. However, the information is only used in a particular sequence, namely: the middle entry, then the entry $\frac{1}{4}$ or $\frac{3}{4}$ of the way up, and so on. If the table were stored so that the middle entry were in a fixed position, and if from that position it was possible to get to either of the next two entries required, and from each of those to their two successors, etc., then it need not be stored in order. This suggests storing two pointers, or chain addresses, with each entry. The search mechanism consists of comparing the desired name with the entry in the fixed position reserved for the middle entry. If the desired name matches, there is nothing further to do. Otherwise, the search continues to the entry pointed to by the appropriate one of the two pointers. Let us refer to these as the left pointer for entries that are less than the middle entry and the right pointer for those that are larger. Part of such a table is shown in Figure 8.5. Notice that it is a tree with two branches at every node and nodes labelled by a table entry. Storing the information this way for a binary search has the advantage that it is no longer necessary that

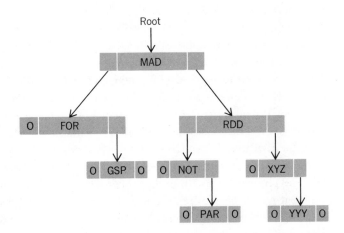

FIGURE 8.5 Binary tree.

the entry at the start (or root) of the table must be the middle entry. Whichever entry is used, it is only necessary that all other entries be to the left or right of it, depending on whether they are smaller or larger than it. Thus, in the figure, MAD is not the middle entry, but the search method would still work. If, for example, we were to look up PAR, we could check it against MAD. Since PAR is larger, we would check with the right-hand neighbor of MAD. PAR is less than ROD, so we would check it against NOT. It is larger, so the right-hand branch is taken, which leads to a match.

The search process can be handled easily with a recursive procedure. Suppose that each element is stored in an array with $N \times 3$ words, each containing a fixed-point number. Let $A[n,1]$ contain the integer representation of the key, $A[n,2]$ the index of the left or lower branch of the tree, and $A[n,3]$ the right or larger branch of the tree. An Algol form of the procedure is

```
procedure   search(A,key,pointer,result); value key,pointer;
                  array A; integer key, pointer, result;
begin if key = A [pointer,1] then result := pointer;
    else        begin  if key < A [pointer,1] then pointer : = A [pointer,2] ;
                       else pointer := A [pointer,3] ;
                       if pointer=0 then result := 0;
                       else search (A,key,pointer,result);
               end
    end  search
```

The array indices are assumed not to include 0, so that it can be returned as the result if the key is not found. The procedure is called with pointer set to the root of the tree. Although the procedure uses recursion, it could easily be rewritten to avoid it, since it calls itself once at the very end of the procedure.

This method has the advantage that names can be added to the table at any time. If a new name is to be entered, a search process is followed which will finally come to the end of a chain, indicated in the figure by a 0-link address. If the name is found in the search, then it obviously should not be reentered. When the end of a chain is reached, the new entry can be added at that point. This makes the method very suitable for assembler use, if the space for the links is available. It has the additional advantage that it is trivial to print the table in alphabetical order when the time comes. It is not simple to remove a name from the table, since—unless it is the last name in a chain—it is necessary to replace it with another for comparison purposes in searching. If the names entered are in order, then the method is very bad because the tree would be one-sided. It is then as slow as a sequential search, but takes up more space.

8.6 TABLE METHODS SUITED FOR USE IN AN ASSEMBLER

There is no easy answer to the question of what method to use in an assembler. Choice of method will depend on the type of I/O equipment available and its speed relative to the speed of arithmetic, how much main memory is available for the storage, whether it is desirable to restrict symbolic names to a maximum length that is fairly short (six to eight characters), and other factors. If the assembler will be completely input/output limited, then the simplest technique may as well be used. Since the user usually likes to get an alphabetized listing of all names that he defines, the table will have to be sorted at some point, but it can be formed sequentially during pass I and searched sequentially in passes I and II. Unless programs with many names are expected, the simplest form of sequential search for the smallest name, the next-smallest name, and so on could be made during the listing of the name table, so that the list is in alphabetic order. If fast output is available, then the sequential search is not suitable. If the names are of fixed length, a hash addressing technique may prove to be best, but if names are allowed to be arbitrarily long, or effectively so, then a radix-based search using a tree structure is probably the best. It is not difficult to alphabetize such a tree by using a sequential sort on each of the subtables (that is, the sets of subnodes of a given node). If the arithmetic time is very slow compared to the input time, then a binary search should be considered.

An interesting assembly technique that can be used if the main memory available is so small that the name table must be placed on backup storage is as follows. During the first pass, a list of all definitions and uses of names is generated. This list can be written as a file onto a backup storage device. The entries in this list take one of the two forms:

1. Definition—name—value.
2. Usage   —name—line number.

The first form is used when a name is defined by appearing in a location field. The second form is used when the name is used in an address field. The line number is the sequential number of the line of code on which the name is defined. At the completion of pass I, the list of names is sorted alphabetically. This brings the definitions and the usages of the same names together. The value of each name is placed in each usage at this time (and an alphabetical usage table giving all names, their values, and where they are used can be listed). Then the name list is re-sorted by line number (the definitions can be discarded). The result is a list of all name usages in the order in which they are used. Pass II consists of rereading the input and reading the name list at the same time. Each time that a name is used in the source, its value is available as the next entry in the name list.

The methods discussed are summarized briefly in the table below.

TABLE 8.9

Method	Handles arbitrarily large names	Speed	Memory requirements	Can names be removed	Can names be looked up in pass I
Sequential	No	Slow for large N	N spaces	Only if no pointers to the table are in use	Yes
Binary Search	No	Fast for large N	N spaces, additional at sort time	No	No (except sequentially)
Hash Address	No	Fast if a lot of memory allocated	$K*N$ where K greater than one	No	Yes
Chained Sequential	No	Slowest	Extra space for links	Yes	Yes
Radix Tree	Yes	Medium	Usually about $1.25*N$	Yes	Yes
Binary Tree	No	Close to binary	N spaces which hold names and two links	Difficult	Yes

PROBLEMS

1. Program a binary search for a table of length N.
2. Program a sequential search for a table of length N.
3. Write a program to build up a table of length N containing the integers 1 through N. Use the programs from questions one and two as subroutines to search, in turn, for each entry in the table. Use the system clock to find the total time for all references in the two cases. Run the program for various values of N (5, 10, 15, etc., stopping when too much computer time has been used) and plot the time of each method as a function of N.

4. Prove that the bubble sort (see Section 8.3.1) cannot take more than $N - 1$ passes for a table of length N.

5. Sketch a graph of the way in which the merge time for a P-way merge of a large file depends on P. Show the compute time and the I/O time separately. If I/O and compute is overlapped, indicate what P would be optimum. If I/O and compute are sequential rather than overlapped, what P is optimum based on the sketch?

6. Design a representation of a data structure similar to that in Figure 8.4 for internal computer storage. Assume that single words are to be used in the computer as elements in a table, and that each word contains a number of addresses. These addresses may be pointers to other table entries, to information to be stored, to individual letters, or they may be null. It is possible for the program to tell by the size of the address which is which. Perform the design in the three different cases where a computer word can contain (a) four addresses, (b) three addresses, or (c) two addresses.

7. Write a recursive subroutine which will make a new entry in the binary tree described in Section 8.5.3.

8. Rewrite the search program in Section 8.5.3 so that it is iterative rather than recursive.

9

an introduction to
compiling techniques

Many different compiling techniques have been described in the published literature, and there is a large body of knowledge that is passed verbally between workers in the field. At present, however, there do not exist any elementary introductions that give a background to the neophyte so that he may begin to explore the literature. The purpose of this chapter is to introduce the two basic methods of compiling, the bottom-up and the top-down methods, to indicate some of the problems that have to be tackled and to whet the student's appetite for further reading. Two languages, Fortran and Algol, will be used as examples in the discussion below because, between them, they illustrate many of the problems that are present in compilers. It is not necessary that the reader be familiar with either language in detail. The presentation will not be complete because these notes are intended as stepping-stones to more advanced work rather than as recipes for a cookbook compiler.

9.1 FORMAT OF THE INPUT STRING

In most artificial languages (that is, languages designed for communication with a machine), the input to the compiler is a string of characters, perhaps from paper tape or punched cards. We can think of punched cards as being read, a character at a time, from left to right, so that there is no essential difference between punched cards and paper tape. If we are interested in lines of information, then we can assign a particular character on paper tape to correspond to the card boundary that occurs every 80 characters. This could be the carriage return, for example. Thus, whether we wish to consider the input as a string of characters or as a sequence of lines, there is no essential difference between paper tape and punched cards. However, compilers that were historically developed for card-oriented machines, such as Fortran for the IBM machines, tend to use card boundaries and fixed fields within cards as a part of the language, whereas languages developed by groups with a bias towards paper tape tend to ignore line boundaries and to use no fixed fields. An example of the latter is Algol. In Fortran, the first five columns are given over to a statement number and cannot be used for any other purposes except comments, which, in a sense, are not part of the language. In Algol, a statement without a label can start in the first character of the line. If a statement label is used, it is typed first, followed by a colon. The following Fortran and Algol codes are similar:

fortran
```
        GO TO 17
    17  A = B
```
algol
```
    goto  L17; L17: A:= B;
```

Separate lines are not necessary for the Algol code, since the semicolon acts as a statement separator. Since L17 is also a valid variable name in Algol, it is not possible to determine whether the first three characters of the statement L17: A . . . ., belong to a label or to a variable name until the colon has been read. In the Fortran code, the existence of a label can be determined by checking the first five columns of a card. This does not present a problem in compilation, but it does point up a possible difference in approach. In Fortran compilers, a number of problems can be solved by using the format of the input. Statement numbers can be detected and the range of a statement can be found by looking at card boundaries and continuation marks only. In Algol, it is necessary to examine the surrounding structure of the input to determine the meaning of all of the input. Statement labels can only be located at the beginning of a statement by looking for a following colon, and the end of a statement can only be detected by looking for an *end* or a semi-colon in an appropriate position.

The fact that a Fortran program can easily be split into a sequence of statements whereas Algol can contain compound statements that are groups of statements has other effects on the type of compiler most suited to the job. A Fortran compiler usually contains an input section which reads one complete statement into a suitable buffer area, a section that determines the type of statement involved, a section that handles the statement number if there is one, and sections that compile object code for each possible type of statement. Consider, on the other hand, the Algol program section

```
begin real   a, real array b[1:10];
for i := 1 step 1 until 10 do
    begin real array a [1:10];
    b[i] := i;
    . . . . . . . . . . ;
    . . . . . . . . . . ;
    end
a := 3.5;
. . . . . . . . . ;
end
```

The second "statement" in this program extends down to the first **end** because the block of program between the **begin** following the **do** and its matching **end** constitutes a single compound statement as far as the **for** statement is concerned. This means that if an error which causes the first **end** to be missed occurs, then the **for** statement will be extended down to the last **end** shown. In addition to extending the range of the **for** statement beyond the intended **end,** it can cause many apparent errors to be caught by a compiler. For example, the last assignment statement "a := 3.5;" will be marked as an error because the variable "a" is used as an array name in the inner block, which was not terminated, but as a simple variable name in the outer block. This type of error will be propagated through the rest of the program because there will continue to be one **end** missing.

It is true that this type of error can occur in Fortran. A missing dimension statement, for example, could cause the statement "A(I) = I*I" to be interpreted as a function-definition statement, but the language is not as prone to such misconstructions. Because of this difference of degree rather than of kind, it is not as practical for Algol to have an input scanner to break up the string into separate statements identified as to type and then to pass control to a statement translator. A translator for Algol will be more continuous in nature. We shall see that this does not complicate the compiler particularly, but it is simpler to restrict ourselves initially to single statements under the assumption that the statement recognition has already been taken care of.

9.1.1 Key words and reserved words

The Algol example above contains two types of statements: those that start with a special word, such as **begin, end,** etc., and the arithmetic assignment statements such as "a[i] : = i;". The definition of Algol requires that words such as **begin** be special single characters. The lack of such characters on most card and paper-tape punches forces an implemented form of the language to use the usual alphabetic characters and either surround them by suitable characters to delimit the word or to *reserve* the word so that it cannot be used as an identifier by the programmer. These words are called *reserved words*. Words which determine statement type are called *key words* because they provide an immediate key to the statement type. Some Algol compilers use quotes around the key words, which are punched using the available upper case character set so that they appear as 'BEGIN,' 'END,' 'GOTO,' 'FOR,' etc., while others use reserved words and do not require the quotes. If reserved words are used, then the programmer must be careful in his naming of identifiers. The Algol statement

FOR I: = L STEP 1 UNTIL K DO GOTO M;

is a valid if stupid **for** loop. It is also an assignment statement placing the value of the variable "LSTEP1UNTILKDOGOTOM" into the variable "FORI" after blanks have been ignored. Fortran and Algol ignore blanks. A more recent language, PL/I, does not. A user should not have to know about those features of a computer or language that he does not need, so it is undesirable for a language to have reserved words that the user must know before he can write any programs.

Although Fortran uses key words to determine statement type, and these words are not distinguishable from identifier names as they stand (unless they are longer than six characters), Fortran does not use reserved words. The structure of the overall statement makes the use clear. Thus

DO 1 I = 1,2

is a DO statement, whereas

DO 1 I = 1.2

is an arithmetic assignment statement.

FORMAT(6H) = S(IH)

is a Format statement, whereas

FORMAT(IH) = S(IH)

is either an arithmetic assignment statement or a function definition, depending on its position in the program and whether a variable called FORMAT has been dimensioned.

Unfortunately, the differentiation between the different statements represented above is tedious, so a number of Fortran translators do use reserved words, preventing the programmer from dimensioning a variable named FORMAT, etc. If this is done, the recognition of different statement types is easy—as it is in Algol, where the key word can be recognized immediately.

Many statements that start with key words have a very restricted format and can be handled in a simple scan, one element at a time. An example of such a statement is the Fortran DIMENSION statement. As each variable name is read, it can be entered in a table, and the corresponding size of the array can be stored with it. It presents no greater problems than the handling of the address field of an assembly-language instruction. Other statements, such as assignment statements, have a very free format and appear to present the most complex problems to the neophyte programmer. In fact, problems concerning memory allocation and subroutine parameter handling at execution time are among the more difficult parts of a compiler. These will be discussed briefly in Section 9.4 after we have studied the two main methods for recognizing the structure of the input string of characters.

9.2 BOTTOM-UP METHODS

These form the class of methods which consist of taking the input string, saying "I have no idea what this string of characters is" and attempting to put the characters together, one at a time, to find out what each part of the string represents. This is contrasted with the top-down methods, to be discussed in the next section, which start by saying "This string is going to be a *****" and then examining each character to attempt to form a "*****". The two methods could be applied to the assignment statement "AB = CD + E" in the following way:

Bottom up:

> "A is a letter, B is a letter. A letter followed by a letter is a variable name.
> C is a letter, D is a letter. A letter followed by a letter is a variable name.
> E is a letter. A letter is a variable name.
> A variable plus a variable is an expression.
> A variable followed by an equal sign followed by an expression is an assignment statement. So we have an assignment statement."

Top down:

> "This string is going to be an assignment statement (we think).
> An assignment statement is a variable followed by an equal sign followed by an expression, therefore we need a variable.
> A variable starts with a letter, so let's look for a letter.
> A is a letter, so we are in good shape. A variable can continue with letters or digits. B is a letter, so AB is a variable. It can still continue with a letter or a digit. The next character " = " is neither, so the variable is AB. We now have the variable at the start of the assignment statement. We need an equal sign. This we have, so we now need an expression. An expression should start with a variable . . . a similar process finds that CD is a variable . . . It can contain a plus sign and another variable . . . a similar process locates the plus sign and the variable E . . . . Thus we have an assignment statement."

There are many forms of bottom-up methods. Each involves the process of scanning the input string, a character at a time, trying to combine the new character with previously scanned characters to form more complex combinations. A form of bottom-up analysis was used in Section 7.1.4 in order to compute the value of address field expressions in an assembler language. That method, known as the *operator precedence* method, will be expanded to handle assignment statements. Precedence methods rely on the fact that certain of the characters can be recognized as operators and that consequently the other elements of the input can be recognized as operands. A precedence relationship, or hierarchy, between the operators enables the program to decide which operator should be compiled first. Fortunately, most algebraic languages have the property that operator precedence methods can be used, at least for the majority of their statement types. They are often the fastest methods of compiling arithmetic assignment statements.†

The precedence methods use the ability to distinguish operands and operators. Conditions that a language must satisfy to make this possible are discussed in the Floyd paper cited above. In these notes, we are not concerned with general languages but with specific examples such as Fortran and Algol. It is evident that we can recognize operators and operands by a simple character scan of the input string, as was done in the assembler. From now on, we shall assume that a front-end subroutine will process the input and break it up into *atoms*, each atom being either an operator or

† Some of the basic ideas in this method were first presented by Samelson and Bauer, Sequential Formula Translation, *Communications of the Association for Computing Machines*, vol. 3, no. 2, February, 1960, while the idea of operator precedence methods for general languages was first explored by Floyd, Syntactic Analysis and Operator Precedence, *Journal of the Association for Computing Machines*, vol. 10, no. 3, pp. 316–333, July, 1963.

operand. If the operand is a constant, then it can be converted into binary; if it is a name, then it can be placed in an appropriate table. Name tables will require bits of information to indicate whether the name represents a simple variable, an array, or a subroutine, and whether it is real, complex, integer, etc. These entries can be made when the variable is first defined or used, and all occurrences of the name can be replaced by pointers to the table entry. Thus, by the time the detailed analysis of the statement starts, it has been converted from a character string to a more easily manageable string of atoms which can be represented in a convenient internal form.

9.2.1 Compilation of zero-address code

One of the principal reasons for our interest in zero-address code is that it can be easily compiled. Consider the problem of processing the input string of atoms, one at a time, in order to obtain a zero-address code. An expression such as A+B can compile as

```
LOAD  A
LOAD  B
ADD
```

In other words, the occurrence of operands causes a LOAD instruction to be compiled, and then the operation is compiled as the equivalent instruction. A+B*C can compile as

```
LOAD  A
LOAD  B
LOAD  C
MPY
ADD
```

The operands cause LOAD instructions to be compiled, while the operators cause arithmetic instructions to be compiled "as soon as they can be performed." This can be determined by a precedence technique similar to the one used in Chapter 7. As each operator is read from the input string, it can be compared with the last one not yet compiled. Thus, when the * (asterisk) is read, it is compared with the preceding + (plus) operator. Since * (asterisk) is "more important," that is, has a greater *precedence*, the plus is not yet compiled. The scan continues until the end of the statement, which is treated as an operator of low precedence, is recognized. This causes the multiply

TABLE 9.1

Operator	Precedence in input	Precedence in stack
Beginning of string	0	0
End of string	0	Not possible
+ or −	2	2
* or /	3	3
** (single atom)	4	4
(	5	1
)	1	Not possible

and then the add to be compiled. A precedence table can be constructed as was done in Chapter 7. We shall construct one for the common arithmetic operators and parentheses only, but any other allowed operators, such as the logical operators in Algol, can be added. In order to facilitate the testing of the operators, it is easiest to place them in a stack at compile time and to compare the top of the stack with the input operator. The rule used is similar to that used in Chapter 7. The next input atom is examined. If it is an operand, it is compiled into a LOAD instruction. If it is an operator, its value is compared with the value of the top of the stack. (Initially the stack has no value, so that the beginning of the string can be entered immediately.) If the value in the stack is at least as high, it is compiled. If the input value is higher, it is placed into the stack. (Note that the value of the "(" atom changes in this step.) When a "(" atom is compiled, no code is generated, but the corresponding ")" in the input stream is removed. If there is none, then there is an error.

Other elements in the language can be handled in a similar way, but we shall leave this as an exercise for the reader and examine problems that arise if the object code is for other than a zero-address machine. Note that there are two stacks: the execution stack, which is the accumulator stack of the machine used for operands at execution time; and the compile stack, which holds the operators not yet compiled at compile time.

9.2.2 Compilation of one-, two-, and three-address code

The simplest way to handle other machine structures is to simulate the arithmetic stack in the machine. This can be done by setting aside an area of main memory to represent the stack. The bottom of the stack can be placed in location S, the next entry in location S + 1, and so on. Unfortunately, this leads to inefficient code, as can be seen from the one-address code to calculate A * B + C * D:

```
LOAD    A
STORE   S
LOAD    B
STORE   S+1
LOAD    S+1
MPY     S
STORE   S
LOAD    C
STORE   S+1
LOAD    D
STORE   S+2
LOAD    S+2
MPY     S+1
ADD     S
STORE   S
```

In two- or three-address code, each LOAD, STORE sequence can be replaced by a move, and each LOAD, Operation, STORE sequence by an arithmetic operation. Unfortunately, this is inefficient code for a number of reasons. Some of the inefficiencies of the one-address code can be removed by avoiding redundant sequences such as STORE S+1, LOAD S+1, but there is still a lot of inefficiency compared to the shortest code

```
LOAD    A
MPY     B
STORE   S
LOAD    C
MPY     D
ADD     S
```

This object code can be achieved by returning to the method used in Chapter 7. There, the compile stack stored both the operations and the operands. In the method above, only the operations were put in the compile stack, while the operands were assumed to be available in the accumulator stack. If the operands are kept in the compile stack, then their locations in memory rather than their values must be recorded, since the latter are not available at compile time. This can be illustrated by the following example: Compile A * B + C into code which will calculate its value in the accumulator of a one-address machine.

Input   A * B + C | ("|" means beginning or end of string.)
Stack |
Code

Input   * B + C |
Stack   A |
Code

Input   B + C |
Stack   * A |
Code

Input   + C |
Stack   B * A | + has lower precedence than *, so compile the * as LOAD
Code   A, MPY B.

Input   + C |
Stack   Δ | Δ stands for the contents of the accumulator.
Code   LOAD A
        MPY B

Input   C |
Stack   + Δ |
Code   LOAD A
        MPY B

Input |
Stack   C + Δ | | has lower precedence than +, so compile + as ADD C.
Code   LOAD A
        MPY B

Input |
Stack   Δ|
Code   LOAD A
        MPY B
        Add C

The beginning and the end of string atoms now cancel each other out, and
we see that code to calculate the desired value in the accumulator has been
generated. This method will break down if more than one use is made of the
accumulator. Consider the expression A * B + (C + D) * (E + F). The
translator described above would generate

```
LOAD  A
MPY   B
LOAD  C
ADD   D
LOAD  E
ADD   F
```

and then it would not know how to handle the multiplication of the contents of the accumulator by the accumulator. The first error was committed when the LOAD C was performed without first saving the contents of the accumulator. Each time that a new LOAD instruction is generated, the current contents of the accumulator must be saved. This can be done by simulating an execution stack in a temporary storage region. Suppose it is in locations S, S + 1, etc. A count of the number of uses of the accumulator can be kept. Each time that a LOAD is to be compiled, this counter can be increased by 1 and a STORE into the appropriate location in the stack can be compiled before the LOAD. (This can be omitted for the first use of the accumulator.) When two operands are indicated as being in the accumulator, the compiler knows that the first must be in the top level of the stack. It can use it from there and reduce the count by 1. The steps in the process are shown in the example below. (Intermediate results from steps that only copy from the input to the stack have been omitted.)

Input   A * B + (C + D) * (E + F) |
Stack |
Count   0

Input   + (C + D) * (E + F) |
Stack   B * A |
Count   0   Compile LOAD A, MPY B. Add 1 to count.

Input   + (C + D) * (E + F) |
Stack   Δ |
Count   1

Input   ) * (E + F) |
Stack   D + C (+ Δ |
Count   1   Compile STORE S (= S + count − 1) since count > 0, LOAD C, ADD D. Add 1 to count.

Input   ) * (E + F) |
Stack   Δ (+ Δ |
Count   2   "Compile" (, resulting in an input) being removed.

Input   * (E + F) |
Stack   Δ + Δ |
Count   2

Input   ) |
Stack   F + E (* Δ + Δ |
Count   2   Compile STORE S+1 (= S + count − 1) LOAD E, ADD F. Add 1 to count.

Input   ) |
Stack   Δ (* Δ + Δ |
Count   3   "Compile" (.

Input |
Stack $\Delta * \Delta + \Delta$ |
Count 3   Since both operands are in the accu-
                                mulator, reduce count by 1 and com-
                                pile MPY S + 1 (= S + count − 1).

Input |
Stack $\Delta + \Delta$ |
Count 2   Since both operands are in the accu-
                                mulator, reduce count by 1 and com-
                                pile ADD S (= S + count − 1).

Input |
Stack Δ |
Count 1   Now the result is in the accumulator.

Similar techniques can be developed for two- and three-address code. These are left as exercises for the reader.

We have not discussed how more difficult aspects of the object code are handled. How, for example, indexing or subroutine calls should be compiled. The methods discussed above can be extended to recognize the use of subscripts, subroutines, etc., in a simple way. The manner in which the object code should be produced depends on the efficiency of object code desired. Should, for example, index registers in the machine be used by the object program? Some compilers, usually those that are very fast at translation, will not make much use of special registers in the machine in order to have a simple compiler. Expressions used as indices can be evaluated, using the regular arithmetic instructions, and then placed into an index register or a memory location and used to fetch the desired value from memory by indexing or indirect addressing. Other translators, typically much slower at the translation task, spend a lot of time compiling object code which will make the best use of the hardware facilities of the machine.

The resulting code is usually considerably more efficient with the latter translators than the former. The methods used depend very much on the particular hardware configuration and will not be discussed here.

9.3 TOP–DOWN METHODS

Top-down methods use an approach in which the program attempts to find strings of characters in the input that satisfy the form that it thinks the input should take. If it is unsuccessful, then it will try for some other form. Thus, in looking at the total input that is supposed to be a program, it might first try to find an assignment statement at the start of the string. If it is unsuccessful there, it could next try for a DO statement (if the language is Fortran). Eventually it will either find a recognizable statement or the input is not a Fortran program, which must begin with a valid Fortran statement. It is necessary that we be able to state clearly the types of inputs that are permitted, so we shall first examine a way of defining formally the various correct input strings and then look at a simple way of building a program that will recognize correct strings and cause code to be compiled.

9.3.1 The Backus normal-form definition of a language

It is desirable to be able to say precisely what are correct statements in an artificial language such as Fortran or Algol. Fortran is usually specified by listing each of the allowable statements in a table. Such a technique is adequate for statements such as GO TO. When arithmetic assignment statements are defined, most Fortran manuals will content themselves with the comment that they must be of the form A = E where A is a variable name and E is an expression composed of variables and constants and $+$, $-$, $*$, $/$, $**$, (, and). This definition of an expression appeals to our under-standing of the meaning and form of expressions that we use every day, which is fine for teaching purposes; but it is of no value for describing to, say, a computer what is a correct expression, or for telling a person about a new artificial language. The Backus notation was first introduced for de-scribing Algol in a formal manner. It is a notation that is suited to describing what might be called free-format languages, that is, ones in which such fixed-format ideas as card columns play no role. It is not, therefore, the best notation in which to describe Fortran, but it will be illustrated by describing familiar Fortran arithmetic assignment statements in *Backus Normal Form*, or *BNF*.

The Backus notation is a language which itself consists of statements which describe the way in which the source language (Fortran) may be written. To avoid confusion, the Backus language is called a *meta language;* it uses characters other than those used in the language being described. For example, in Fortran an arithmetic assignment statement is of the form *variable* followed by an $=$ sign followed by an *expression*. This is written as $<$arithmetic assignment statement$>$ :: $=$ $<$variable$>$ $=$ $<$expression$>$. The characters $<$ $>$ and :: $=$ are characters in the *meta language*. $<$ and $>$ are to be interpreted as a pair of parentheses surrounding a word in the meta language. The word represents a *phrase class name;* that is, it stands for a set of entities in the source language. Thus $<$variable$>$ represent the class of all variables, in this case, in Fortran, while $<$expression$>$ represents the class of all expressions. These have yet to be defined formally. Once they have, then the meta language statement above defines formally the class of all arithmetic assignment statements. It should be read as "any member of the class of 'arithmetic assignment statements' is of the form member of the class 'variable' followed by = followed by a member of the class 'expression.' " Any string of characters in the described language that satisfies this form may be an arithmetic assignment statement.

It may be necessary to express the fact that a particular phrase class can be formed in more than one way. For example, the variable above could be an identifier by itself (for example, ALPHA) or it could be an indexed variable. This is expressed either by use of the meta-language character | meaning "or" or by writing down both possibilities in separate meta statements. Thus, if the phrase classes <identifier> and <indexed variable> have been defined, variable can be defined either by

<variable> :: = <identifier> | <indexed variable>

or by

<variable> :: = <identifier>
<variable> :: = <indexed variable>

It might seem that in this way each class could be defined in terms of "smaller" classes until at some final point the classes are defined in terms of characters in the language being defined (Fortran). Consider Fortran identifiers. On many computers these can consist of six characters, the first must be a letter and the remaining may be letters or numerical digits. Thus we could write

<letter> :: = A|B|C|D|E|F|G|H|I|J|K|L|M|N|O|P|Q|R|S|T|U|V|W|X|Y|Z
<digit> :: = 0|1|2|3|4|5|6|7|8|9|
<alphanum> :: = <letter> | <digit>
<identifier> :: = <letter> | <letter> <alphanum> | <letter>
                                        <alphanum> <alphanum> |
            <letter> <alphanum> <alphanum> <alphanum> |
            <letter> <alphanum> <alphanum> <alphanum>
                                        <alphanum> |
            <letter> <alphanum> <alphanum> <alphanum>
                                        <alphanum> <alphanum>

Not a very convenient definition, and one which can certainly be expressed more concisely in English! If 8 or 10 character identifiers were allowed, it would be even less pleasant. It happens that the Backus notation is not well adapted to describing languages in which restrictions such as "a maximum of six characters can be used for an identifier" appear, just as it is not useful for handling fixed-format characters. In Algol, however, identifiers may be of any length (although some translators restrict the user to six or eight to gain efficiency). A formal description of identifiers of any length cannot be achieved by writing down all cases! To get around this problem, *recursive definition* is used. This means that the definition may define something partly in terms of itself. As long as this does not involve an infinite loop, it is satisfactory. For example, Algol identifiers must also start with a letter and can contain letters and digits subsequently. Thus, if we have formed any legitimate identifier, we can form another by adding on any letter or digit, that is, any member of the class <alphanum>. Therefore, together with the definitions of <letter>, <digit>, and <alphanum> above, an Algol identifier can be defined by

<identifier> : : = <letter> | <identifier> <alphanum>

That is to say, a letter is an identifier, and so is any identifier formed by following a shorter identifier with an alphanumeric character.

If we wish to know if A6Y is an identifier, then the steps are:

> A is a letter and a letter is an identifier;
> 6 is a digit and a digit is an alphanum, A is an identifier and an identifier followed by an alphanum is an identifier, so that A6 is an identifier;
> Y is a letter and a letter is an alphanum, A6 is an identifier and an identifier followed by an alphanum is an identifier, so A6Y is an identifier.

This can be illustrated graphically by the tree structure

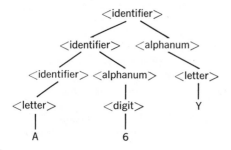

Terminal nodes of this tree are characters in the language; read from left to right they are as they appear in the source string. Nonterminal nodes are phrase class names such as letter, identifier, etc. The neighbors below them on the tree (those nodes connected by branches) correspond to one set of elements used on the right-hand side of the definition of the phrase class name. Thus, identifier appears with two subsidiary neighbors when it is defined as <identifier> <alphanum>; it also appears with one subsidiary neighbor when it is defined as <letter>.

This breakdown into the structural form is called *parsing*. It is similar to the parsing that is done in natural languages such as English. Thus in English, we say that a sentence can be constructed as subject followed by a verb followed by its object, for example:

```
<sentence>       :: =  <subject> <verb> <object>
<subject>        :: =  <definite article > <noun>
<object>         :: =  <definite article> <noun >
<verb>           :: =    throws
<noun >          :: =    boy | ball
<definite article> :: = the
```

Thus the sentence "the boy throws the ball" could be parsed in the tree form

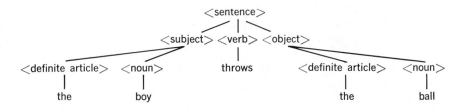

From this example, it is obvious that meaningless sentences can be constructed. For example, "the ball throws the boy" also parses. The formal description only deals with the structure of the language, not its meaning. In the same way it is possible to write quite reasonable Fortran statements that are illegal because of their meaning but are structurally sound. For example, A (15) = 34.1 is incorrect if A has not been appropriately dimensioned. We are only able to describe the structure, or *syntax*, of the language with BNF. The meaning, or *semantics*, must be described separately.

We would like to be able to define all correct statements in this formal manner. To simplify the discussion, we shall ignore indexing, subroutine calls, etc., and just concentrate on the expression on the right-hand side of an assignment statement.

An expression such as A * B − C / D should break down into a form that shows the multiplys and divides being performed before the minus. That is,

it should have the general form

Therefore, the multiplication and division operators should combine in a parse first. Let us call the items that can take part in a multiplication or division *factors* as a phrase class name. We note that a factor can certainly be an identifier or a constant, so we can write

<factor> : : = <variable> | <constant>

We shall not further define constant. A number of factors can be multiplied together to form a more complex grouping. Let us call this a *term*. We could define

<term> : : = <factor> * <factor> | <factor> / <factor>

Unfortunately, this only allows for one multiplication or division. We could have a series of several. For example, A / B * C. Again, note that the A / B should be grouped first, since the value is formed by performing operators with equal precedence from left to right. Thus we should write

<term> : : = <term> * <factor> | <term> / <factor>

This defines term in terms of itself, just as identifier was defined recursively. As long as term is also defined as a factor by itself, this is acceptable. Thus we have as a final definition of term

<term> : : = <factor> | <term> * <factor> | <term> / <factor>

This means that the parse of A * B / C * D is

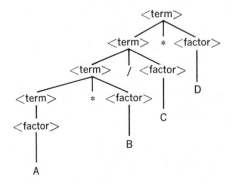

Now that we have defined the more complex group term, we can use it with the addition and subtraction operators to form expressions. By reasoning similar to that above, we write expression as

$$<expression> ::= <term> \mid <expression>+<term> \mid <expression> - <term>$$

This omits a possible form of expression. Whereas * (asterisk) and / (slash) are always binary operations with two operands, + (plus) and − (minus) can be used as unary operations. For example, −A is an expression. We therefore must modify expression to read

$$<expression> ::= <term> \mid+<term> \mid- <term> \mid <expression> + <term> \mid <expression>-<term>$$

With these definitions, the expression A * B + C + DE can be parsed as

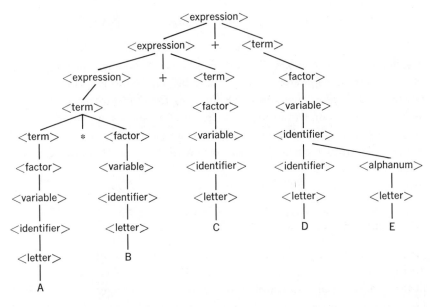

Now parentheses must be introduced. The purpose of parentheses is to override the implicit precedence of operators by an explicit statement of the order of evaluation and hence the order of parsing. Parentheses can be placed around any legitimate expression and its value can then be used as one operand at any of the binary operations. Thus we should include a parenthesized expression as one of the class factor by the definition

$$<factor> ::= <variable> \mid <constant> \mid(<expression>)$$

The expression A * (B + C) can then be parsed as

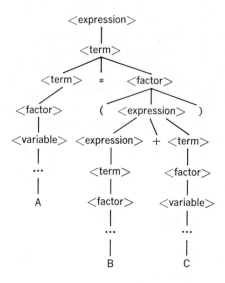

The definitions given above allow any expression containing arbitrary-length identifiers and the operators +, −, *, /, (, and) to be formed. It can readily be extended to allow the additional operators found in Fortran or Algol so as to provide a complete formal description of all strings of characters that are valid structurally, although possibly not meaningful.

The structure of Algol has been specified in just this manner in the standard description. †

9.3.2 Syntax-directed compilation

Earlier sections of this chapter discussed techniques for scanning the source language input in order to recognize the type of statement and structure of that statement and to translate it into a lower-level language. Although the ideas used are conceptually simple, there is ample room for error in coding such techniques. Further, it is often desirable to make changes in the source language that can have considerable effect on the compiler. For this reason, a number of people have written compilers that work directly from formal descriptions of the source language. Such compilers can be

† See P. Naur et al., Revised Algol Report, *Communications of the Association for Computing Machinery*, vol. 6, no. 1, January, 1963.

loosely categorized into two classes:

1. Syntax-directed compilers. Syntax-directed compilers are those that are written by the programmer but have an obvious relationship with a formal syntax description such as the Backus Normal Form. This means that changes in the description are easily integrated into the compiler.
2. Compiler-compilers. The compiler that translates the source language into the object language is "written" by a compiler-compiler; that is, it is produced automatically from a formal description of the structure or syntax and a description of the meaning or semantics. Unfortunately, there does not yet exist any good formal way of describing the latter, so a number of different compiler-compilers exist, each with their own forms of description.

This section will examine the first type of compiler, the syntax-directed compiler. The next section will give a quick review of the extension to the semantic problem.

Let us first ignore the problem of translation into object code and deal with the question of the syntactical structure. Given an input string of characters, we wish to find out if it is a legitimate string and what structure it has; that is, we wish to construct a *syntax recognizer*.

Suppose that there already exist subroutines which will recognize some of the phrase classes in the language; for example, suppose the subroutines VARIABLE, EQUAL, and EXPRESSION recognize the class <variable>, the character =, and the class <expression> respectively. It should then be possible to use these to construct another subroutine to recognize the class <assignment statement> as:

```
ASSIGNMENT STATEMENT  CALL    VARIABLE
                      CALL    EQUAL
                      CALL    EXPRESSION
                      RETURN
```

(In practice, symbolic names must be reduced to an appropriate length!) If the three subroutines are *successful*, that is, if they recognize the appropriate quantities, then the assignment statement subroutine is successful; that is, it has recognized an assignment statement.

Let us be a little more precise about what is going on. Suppose that the source input string is in some available place such as core memory and that there is a pointer, p, which is pointing at the next character to be processed. Then the subroutines should move this pointer as they recognize sections of the language. Thus, when EQUAL is called and the pointer is in fact pointing at an equal sign, it should be moved on to the next character because

EQUAL has been successful. What should happen if it is not pointing at an equal sign? Let us examine another case. In the last section, <variable> was defined as:

<variable> : : = <indexed variable> | <identifier>

In this case, <variable> should be recognized if either <indexed variable> or <identifier> is recognized. Suppose that <indexed variable> is called first and not recognized. In that case, the pointer p should be pointing to the same position as it was on entry to INDEXED VARIABLE, so that IDENTI-FIER can be used. Also, it is necessary to distinguish between the *successful* and *unsuccessful* cases on exit from the subroutine. Let us provide a parameter for the unsuccessful exit, and, to save writing, drop the CALL mnemonic and use the subroutine name as the mnemonic below. Thus the recognizer for the class <variable> could take the form:

```
VARIABLE   ENTER
           INDEXED-VARIABLE   EXIT1
           RETURN
EXIT1      IDENTIFIER         EXIT2
           RETURN
EXIT2      ERROR
```

The mnemonic ENTER stands for a piece of program that performs those functions necessary to save registers at the start of a subroutine, *including* the pointer p. RETURN restores the registers *except* for the pointer p, since it is to be moved ahead. EXIT1 is a parameter for the subroutine INDEXED-VARIABLE, such that if the subroutine is unsuccessful, a branch to EXIT1 occurs. Similarly, if IDENTIFIER is unsuccessful, a branch to EXIT2 occurs. In this case, the subroutine VARIABLE has been unsuccessful (the characters do not represent either of the possibilities allowed for <variable>), so the return should be to the parameter supplied by the call on VARIABLE with the pointer p moved back to its position on entry to VARIABLE. The mnemonic ERROR stands for a piece of program that will do just that.

<Indexed variable> was not defined in the last section, but it can be defined as

<indexed variable> : : = <identifier> (<expression sequence>)
<expression sequence> : : = <expression> | <expression sequence>,
                                                        <expression>

This raises two problems. The first arises because one possibility for

<variable> is the beginning of another. Suppose that the program had been written as:

```
VARIABLE   ENTER
           IDENTIFIER              EXIT1
           RETURN
EXIT1      INDEXED-VARIABLE  EXIT2
           RETURN
EXIT2      ERROR
```

If the string AB(I) = C is scanned by this program, AB is successfully recognized by IDENTIFIER, so VARIABLE is successful. This returns to ASSIGNMENT STATEMENT, which tests for =. The next character is (, so EQUAL fails, causing ASSIGNMENT STATEMENT to fail incorrectly and indicating that AB(I) = C is not an assignment statement. There are two ways around this problem:

1. The one used above (looking for the longer form first)
2. Combining the recognition of <identifier> by effectively writing

<variable> :: = <identifier> <index> | <identifier>
<index> :: = (<expression sequence>)

as

```
VARIABLE   ENTER
           IDENTIFIER   EXIT1
           INDEX        EXIT2
EXIT2      RETURN
EXIT1      ERROR
```

Whether or not <index> is recognized, the string has a valid identifier if IDENTIFIER is successful. (Note that this method is faster for nonindexed variables, since <identifier> only has to be recognized once.) It corresponds to a BNF form

<variable> :: = <identifier> <trailer>
<trailer> :: = <index> |

The second problem is more serious. In its simplest form it can be seen in the Backus form:

<expression sequence> = <expression> | <expression sequence>,
                                                      <expression>.

Suppose this is "recognized" by the subroutine:

```
EXPSEQ  ENTER
        EXPRESSION  EXIT1
        RETURN
EXIT1   EXPSEQ      EXIT2
        COMMA       EXIT2
        EXPRESSION  EXIT2
        RETURN
EXIT2   ERROR
```

then the problem mentioned above arises; namely, that an <expression sequence> always starts with an <expression>, hence the comma is never read in the expression sequence program. If the order is reversed to be:

```
EXPSEQ  ENTER
        EXPSEQ      EXIT1
        COMMA       EXIT2
        EXPRESSION  EXIT2
        RETURN
EXIT1   EXPRESSION  EXIT2
        RETURN
EXIT2   ERROR
```

then chaos will result. First, note that all of these subroutines will have to be recursive, so that recursive calling is not wrong per se, but it is wrong in this case since *no other element* is recognized first. Thus <expression sequence> is recognized if an <expression sequence> is recognized . . . ad infinitum. This problem arises whenever a phrase class is defined in such a way that it can start with a member of that same phrase class. This particular example can be avoided by defining:

<expression sequence> :: = <expression>, <expression sequence> |
<expression>

which can be recognized by:

```
EXPSEQ  ENTER
        EXPRESSION  EXIT1
        COMMA       EXIT2
        EXPSEQ      EXIT1
EXIT2   RETURN
EXIT1   ERROR
```

Consider the <expression sequence> A,B,C which has the syntax tree:

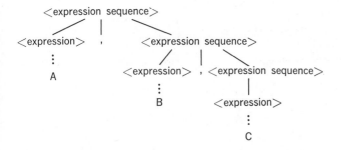

The sequence of subroutine calls for this string is given below (note the recursive use of EXPSEQ).

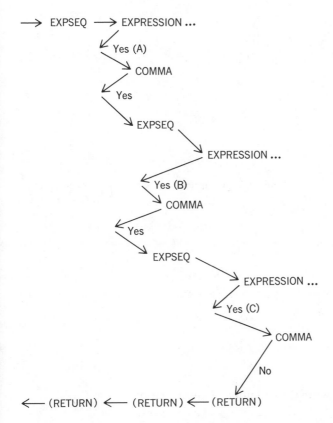

Moving to the right indicates entry to a subroutine. Returns are to the left. Unfortunately, reordering the definition is not always possible. In the exam-

ple above, it presumably did not matter whether A,B,C was parsed as above
or as

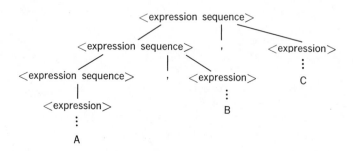

that is, as   rather than

          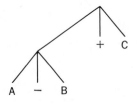

Consider, however,

<expression> :: = <term> | <expression> + <term> | <expression>
$$- <term>$$

A − B + C is parsed as

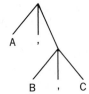

It is incorrect to rewrite the definition of an expression as

<expression> :: = <term> + <expression> | <term>
$$- <expression> | <term>$$

since $A - B + C$ would then parse as

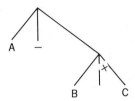

which has the incorrect value $A - B - C$. The phenomenon that is causing this problem is known as *left recursion* and will cause trouble whenever a recursive approach is used.

The recursive approach in the syntax recognition problem is called the "top-down" approach because the top of the syntax tree is checked first. The alternative is the "bottom-up" approach or iterative method. This is essentially the method that was used intuitively in the "control-stack" method in a previous section. Left recursion does not cause a problem in an iterative method when the recognition technique corresponds to the sequence of questions:

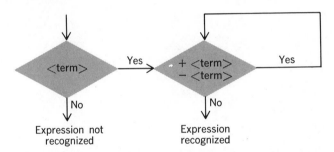

The iterative method can be continued with the top-down or recursive approach by coding

$$<expression> :: = <expression> <\pm term> \mid <term>$$
$$<\pm term> :: = + <term> \mid - <term>$$

as

```
EXPRESSION  ENTER
            TERM        ERROR
LOOP        ±TERM       RETURN
            TRANSFER    LOOP      (Regular transfer order)
```

```
±TERM        ENTER
             PLUS     M
C            TERM     ERROR
             RETURN
M            MINUS    ERROR
             TRANSFER C
```

The sequence of subroutine calls for A − B + C are now:

giving

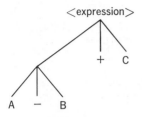

Thus to recognize the various forms of assignment statements formally described in the last section we can use the collection of programs:

```
ASSIGNMENT-STATEMENT  ENTER
                      VARIABLE             ERROR
                      EQUAL                ERROR
                      EXPRESSION           ERROR
                      RETURN
VARIABLE              ENTER
                      IDENTIFIER           ERROR
                      INDEX                RETURN
                      RETURN
INDEX                 ENTER
                      LEFT-PARENTHESIS     ERROR
                      EXPSEQ               ERROR
                      RIGHT-PARENTHESIS    ERROR
                      RETURN
EXPSEQ                ENTER
                      EXPRESSION           ERROR
                      COMMA                RETURN
                      EXPSEQ               ERROR
                      RETURN
EXPRESSION            ENTER
                      TERM                 ERROR
L1                    +TERM                E3
                      TRANSFER             L1
E3                    −TERM                RETURN
                      TRANSFER             L1
+TERM                 ENTER
                      PLUS                 ERROR
                      TERM                 ERROR
                      RETURN
−TERM                 ENTER
                      MINUS                ERROR
                      TERM                 ERROR
                      RETURN
```

TERM	ENTER	
	FACTOR	ERROR
L2	*FACTOR	E4
	TRANSFER	L2
E4	/FACTOR	RETURN
	TRANSFER	L2
*FACTOR	ENTER	
	MULTIPLY	ERROR
	FACTOR	ERROR
	RETURN	
/FACTOR	ENTER	
	DIVIDE	ERROR
	FACTOR	ERROR
	RETURN	
FACTOR	ENTER	
	VARIABLE	E5
	RETURN	
E5	LEFT-PARENTHESIS	ERROR
	EXPRESSION	ERROR
	RIGHT-PARENTHESIS	ERROR
	RETURN	
IDENTIFIER	ENTER	
	LETTER	ERROR
L3	LETTER	E6
	TRANSFER	L3
E6	DIGIT	RETURN
	TRANSFER	L3
LETTER	ENTER	
	A	E7
	RETURN	
E7	B	E8
	RETURN	
E8	C	
	- - - - -	
E32	Z	ERROR
	RETURN	
DIGIT	ENTER	
	0	E33
	RETURN	
E33	1	E34
	RETURN	
E34	2	
	- - - - -	
E42	9	ERROR
	RETURN	

(In practice, recognizers for letters, digits, and other simple characters are worth hand coding for efficiency reasons.)

Implementation of the program is straightforward. A stack for storage on entry to a subroutine is maintained. Two items are entered into this stack by the ENTRY command; namely, the return link and the input string pointer. The RETURN command discards the string pointer and branches to the return link, whereas the ERROR command restores the string pointer before branching to the return link.

Notice that syntactical definitions may be ambiguous; that is, a given character string may have two different parses. For example, if two phrase classes are defined by

$$<sentence> ::= A <clause> \mid <clause> C$$

and

$$<clause> ::= AB \mid BC$$

then the sentence ABC can be either:

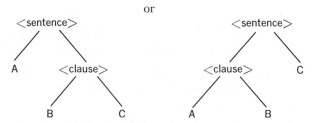

However, because the program must examine one first, the above technique will find only one of these. For example:

```
SENTENCE  ENTRY
          A        E3
          CLAUSE   ERROR
          RETURN
E3        CLAUSE   ERROR
          C
          RETURN
CLAUSE    ENTRY
          A        E4
          B        ERROR
          RETURN
E4        B        ERROR
          C        ERROR
          RETURN
```

will declare ABC to be A <clause> rather than <clause> C. Some syntax directed compilers effectively examine all cases in parallel and thus detect such ambiguities.

If the input string is illegal, then nothing is recognized. In practice, it is not helpful to be told that the program is syntactically incorrect; it is desirable to be told where the error most likely exists. It is not obvious in general how to determine this, but in a statement-oriented language such as Fortran it is possible to narrow it down to at least a single statement. This can be handled formally by defining an additional statement that is any character string followed by an end-of-statement. If this is given the bottom position in the analysis sequence, it will only be recognized when all other statements have failed. The translation (yet to be discussed) can be an error message. To perform better error analysis, it is necessary to decide at what point in a recognizer a syntactic structure has effectively been recognized. Any failures after that would be considered errors. Thus, we could determine that a string is an assignment statement after "variable =" has been recognized. Any subsequent failures would be called errors in expressions.

9.3.3 Semantics

The last section described the way in which a program could be written to take advantage of a syntactical definition of the language in order to recognize the structure of an input string. No mention was made of the way in which the input string was translated into an output string or object language. If the prescribed structure of the language bears any relation to its meaning or semantics, then we can expect to associate a meaning to each expansion or *production*, such as

<expression> :: = <expression> + <term>

which is presumably associated with the addition operation. (The Backus Normal Form syntax assigns no meaning to the character "+"; any meaning that you associate with it is due to its normal use in mathematics. We are free to define it to have any meaning, although we would be a little foolish to make it a nonstandard one!)

The meaning associated with a production can be specified by program instructions which translate or interpret the source language. Let us consider the translation of assignment statements into assembly language for a zero-address machine. (This object language has been picked because it is the easiest to derive directly from the production sequence recognized. More optimal 0 or 1 address objects require additional manipulations that tend to obscure the fundamentals.)

We are going to try to translate a statement such as

A3 = B + C1

into

```
LOAD    B
LOAD    C1
ADD
STORE   A3
```

The production tree for the statement is:

The numbers to the left of nodes are the order in which they are recognized. The obvious steps that must be taken in translation include the following:

1. Identifiers must be *packed* so that B, C1, and A3 are available for the object code.
2. By the time the variables B and C1 are absorbed into the expression, the orders LOAD B and LOAD C1 must have been compiled.
3. The ADD order must be compiled when <term> <+term> is formed.
4. A STORE order must be generated when the <assignment statement> is recognized.

An appropriate point at which to take care of step two is when a <variable> becomes a <factor>.

Suppose that, by some mechanism, the variable name recognized by <identifier> is available for use by other subroutines. In particular, define a subroutine CODE-LOAD which causes an object order LOAD variable name to be compiled. If the recognizer for <factor> is changed to

```
FACTOR   ENTER
         VARIABLE            E5
         CODE-LOAD
         RETURN
E5       LEFT-PARENTHESIS    ERROR
         EXPRESSION          ERROR
         RIGHT-PARENTHESIS   ERROR
         RETURN
```

then, when <factor> is recognized in tree positions 10 and 18, LOAD B and LOAD C1 will be compiled in that order. The variable names B and C1 are packed at the time they are recognized by <identifier>. Again, suppose that there exists a pair of subroutines SET-NAME and PACK-NAME. SET-NAME forms a new packed name consisting of the last input character processed, PACK-NAME packs the last input character processed into the existing name. We now modify the <identifier> recognizer to read

```
IDENTIFIER   ENTER
             LETTER        ERROR
             SET-NAME
L3           LETTER        E6
L3A          PACK-NAME
             TRANSFER      L3
E6           DIGIT         RETURN
             TRANSFER      L3A
```

The result is that identifier recognition causes a name to be formed for use by the CODE-LOAD subroutine.

At the start of the statement, the identifier A3 is recognized and hence is packed as a name. It is not needed until after the right-hand side has been dealt with, so it must be saved. Many ways of doing this are available. For example, in the subroutine for <assignment-statement>, code can be placed after the recognition of <variable>, which saves the variable. It can then be restored after <expression> has been recognized, immediately prior to compiling the STORE order. Another way, to be used below, is to make the cell which holds the name formed by SET- and PACK- a pushdown stack. SET-NAME adds a new level to it. CODE-LOAD removes a level. In the same way, CODE-STORE removes a level and outputs the "STORE name" object code. With the addition of routines CODE-ADD, CODE-SUBTRACT, etc. to the recognizers for $<+\text{term}>$, $<-\text{term}>$, etc., the program of the previous section will translate simple assignment statements that do not use indexed variables. $<\text{assignment statement}>$ is modified to

```
ASSIGNMENT STATEMENT    ENTER
                        VARIABLE      ERROR
                        EQUAL         ERROR
                        EXPRESSION    ERROR
                        CODE-STORE
                        RETURN
```

$<+\text{term}>$ becomes

```
    +TERM               ENTRY
                        PLUS          ERROR
                        TERM          ERROR
                        CODE-ADD
```

etc.

The reader is urged to follow the compilation of a simple statement for himself. If the example $A3 = B + C1$ is used, the following sequence of subroutine calls results:

assignment statement	output code	name stack contents
Variable		
Identifier		
Letter		
Return		
SET-NAME		A
Letter		
Error		
Digit		
Return		
PACK-NAME		A3
Letter		
Error		
Digit		
Error		
Return		
Return		
Equal		

assignment statement	output code	name stack contents
Return		
Expression		
Term		
Factor		
Identifier		
Letter		
Return		
SET-NAME		B, A3
Letter		
Error		
Digit		
Error		
Return		
CODE-LOAD	LOAD B	A3
Return		
*Factor		
Multiply		
Error		
Return		
/Factor		
Divide		
Error		
Return		
Return		
+Term		
Plus		
Return		
Term		
Factor		
Identifier		
Letter		
Return		
SET-NAME		C, A3
Letter		
Error		
Digit		
Return		
PACK-NAME		C1,A3
Letter		
Error		
Digit		
Error		
Return		
CODE-LOAD	LOAD C1	A3
Return		
*Factor		
Multiply		

assignment statement	output code	name stack contents
Error		
Return		
/Factor		
Divide		
Error		
Return		
Return		
CODE-ADD	ADD	A3
Return		
+Term		
Plus		
Error		
Return		
−Term		
Minus		
Error		
Return		
Return		
CODE-STORE	STORE A3	

(It is apparent by this time that a straightforward approach can lead to a very slow compiler! This is another case of the usual trade-off available between conceptual simplicity and speed.)

It can be seen from the above discussion that the artificial language translation program can be stated in a form that consists partly of a direct rewrite of the syntactical description and partly of subroutines executed when certain agreements are found between the input string and the syntax rules or productions. Because the first part is directly related to the syntax formalism, a number of compiler-compiler systems have been written which accept a formal description of the language and produce a working compiler or interpreter. Typically, these accept as input a set of BNF productions, that is, statements of the form

<assignment statement> :: = <variable> = <expression>

and allow any one of them to be *flagged* with the name of a program which is to be executed whenever the production or syntax rule is recognized. These programs can be written in a language suitable for compiler writing provided by the author of the compiler-compiler.†

† Examples of this are discussed in W. H. Burkhardt, Universal Programming Languages and Processors: A Brief Summary and New Concepts, *Proceedings of the Fall Joint Computer Conference*, vol. 27, part 1, pp. 1–20, 1965, and S. Rosen, A Compiler-Compiler System Developed by Brooker and Morris, *Communications of the Association for Computing Machinery*, vol. 7, no. 7, pp. 403–414, July, 1964.

9.4   MEMORY ALLOCATION

We have discussed how object code can be produced in a single pass over the source string. The code we produced above was symbolic in that we used the names of variables in the source language as the names of storage locations in the object language. We could next input the object code to an assembler and get binary machine code. To do this, we must also generate the pseudo-orders necessary for the assembler to assign storage locations to variables. As an alternative, the compiler itself could assign storage during compilation and produce machine language directly. In this section we shall discuss the process of allocating memory space to variables as though the object code were assembly language. Generally, it is fairly simple to see how the compiler could be modified to produce machine language directly.

The problems of memory allocation are greatly different between Fortran and Algol. In Fortran, there is no block structure, and arrays have a fixed size. Consequently, DIMENSION statements can be translated into block reservation pseudos (the BSS or DS pseudos in various assemblers). Simple variables are not declared specifically in Fortran, but the first time that they are used, a pseudo can be generated to reserve a space. Since these locations should not be placed between lines of code, the actual generation of the pseudos should be delayed until all of the source has been translated. This can be done by putting the variable names into a table and scanning the tables at the end of the compilation pass to generate the required pseudos. If a one-pass compiler is required, then it is necessary to assign space to the variables immediately when they are defined. This can either be done in a separate area of memory (this is facilitated by the use of base registers as available in the IBM 360), or it can be done by compiling a transfer instruction to branch around the storage area.

Algol allows for a block structure such that one part of the program can reuse storage used by an earlier part. Consider the following section of Algol code:

```
    . . . .
begin   real array a[1 : 100];
    . . . . . .
end
    . . . . .
begin   real array b[2 : n];
    . . . .
end
    . . . .
```

In the first block, 100 places must be reserved for the array "a." These locations are no longer needed after the matching **end** closes the block. In the next block shown, the array "b" requires $n-1$ locations. These can reuse the locations no longer occupied by the array "a" plus additional locations if necessary. The second block also points out another problem. Since n is not known until execution time, it is not possible to assign storage until that time. We say that the allocation must be dynamic. For the moment, we shall ignore the problems introduced by subroutines (*procedures* in the Algol terminology). Since blocks can be nested within blocks, storage can be arranged in a stack fashion in memory. Suppose we have the following block structure with the storage requirements indicated:

block 1	20 locations
block 2	25 locations
block 3	n locations
block 4	3 locations
block 5	45 locations

Block 1 contains the other blocks and requires 20 locations. These could be locations S through S+19. Block 2 requires 25 locations. These could be locations S+20 through S+44. Block 2 ends before block 3 starts, so block 3 could use locations S+20 through S+19+n. Block 4 is inside block 3, so it must use locations S+20+n through S+22+n. Block 5 can use locations S+20 through S+64 because it is only contained in block 1. These calculations must be performed at execution time, so the compiler must produce code at the beginning and ending of each block that assigns storage space. A location in memory can be assigned to each block to hold the address of the first word of storage assigned to that block. These addresses can be computed by code at the initiation of each block and can be loaded into index or base registers for use by the program.

The use of procedures complicates the problem because procedures can be called from within a block of code that does not contain the procedure. For example:

```
. . . .
procedure a
. . . . . . . . . . . .
end
begin
. . .
call a
end
```

The call activates the block of code that is contained in the procedure, although it is not nested inside the innermost current block of code. This means that it is not possible to assign storage locations for base addresses by a simple stacking principle. If the fact that procedures can be used recursively is also taken into account, it is no longer possible to assign a unique location for a base address.

One solution is to assign a unique location to each block, to save its contents each time that the block is entered, and to restore it each time that it is left. It can be saved in a word in the dynamically assigned storage area for that block. Consider a procedure that has called itself. It has two storage areas currently in use, one for its first invocation and one for its second. The base address for the second is in a location associated with the procedure.

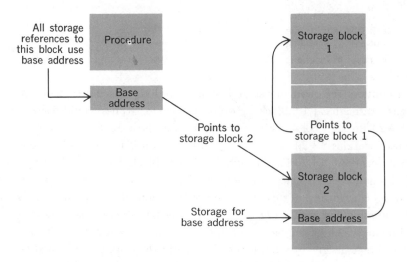

When the procedure exits from its second invocation, the base address can be restored from the copy in storage block 2 and the space in storage block 2 can be given back as free storage for future use.

9.5 ERROR DETECTION

An important part of a compiler is the code that detects errors and gives the user meaningful diagnostics. Whatever error detection is used, it is always possible for the user to give an input string that is only slightly different from a correct program but for which the compiler will give ridiculous error messages. A mission DIMENSION statement, for example, could cause a Fortran compiler to think that an indexed array is a subroutine name with parameters. Eventually there might be an error diagnostic based on that assumption. The compiler writer should try to detect many common errors, and, indeed, to correct those that are reasonably obvious, although a message should always be generated. The Fortran DO statement, for example, does not allow a comma between the statement number and the indexed variable. DO 1,I = 1,5 is incorrect: the first comma should not be present. However, the compiler should accept it as an alternative form, because it is very unlikely that the programmer meant other than DO 1 I = 1,5.

In general, bottom-up methods can be more easily changed to get sensible error messages. Top-down methods, as they stand, only give a "yes" or "no" answer. If the input is not a valid program (*well-formed string* is the technical jargon), then the method will simply say so. For a long program, that is not a very suitable diagnostic, so some other technique must be used. One method is to save the analysis that has proceeded the furthest prior to the failure to find a valid program. This could be assumed to be a correct analysis, so that the next character must either be incorrect or missing. If sensible rules to supply an alternative character can be generated, then the analysis can continue after indicating the phrase class that is being analyzed at the time of the failure.

9.6 CHOICE OF A COMPILATION TECHNIQUE

Preceding sections have only scratched the surface of the subject of compilation, so it is a little presumptuous to discuss the choice of "best" techniques. However, some general comments can be made at this stage. Top-down methods are generally more formal and consequently shorter and easier to program, debug, and document. However, error analysis tends to be more difficult. Bottom-up methods are usually faster in those cases where many levels of subroutines have to be called in order to produce a successful recognition. This is particularly the case in the recognition of an expression. Even with the simple form of expression discussed above, we saw that it was necessary for a top-down analysis to go through term, factor, variable, and identifier many times. In a practical language, there will be many more levels in an expression, and the overhead in computation time to enter each subroutine can be large.

In order to enjoy the best of both methods, it is sometimes worth employing both top-down and bottom-up methods. A bottom-up analysis subroutine with which to recognize expressions in the input string can be written. This can be used as part of a top-down syntax-oriented analysis program for the recognition of all larger constructs.

PROBLEMS

1. What precedence should be given to the equal sign if it were to be added to the operator precedence table of Section 9.2.1? How should the equal operation be handled during the compilation?
2. Suggest ways of including the Fortran IF statement in the precedence method of Section 9.2.1.
3. Add the exponentiation operator to the BNF description of expressions in Section 9.3.1. Do this by defining a new phrase class <primary> between <factor> and <variable>.
4. Write syntax descriptions of the Algol **if** and **for** statements.
5. Give a BNF description of all strings consisting of any number of "a" characters followed by the same number of "b" characters.
6. Write down all members of the phrase class list with not more than 13 characters, where list is defined by

    <list> :: = A | (<list>, <list>)

index